Power in the Balance

RECENT TITLES FROM THE HELEN KELLOGG INSTITUTE FOR INTERNATIONAL STUDIES

Scott Mainwaring, series editor

The University of Notre Dame Press gratefully thanks the Helen Kellogg Institute for International Studies for its support in the publication of titles in this series.

For a complete list of titles from the Helen Kellogg Institute for International Studies, see http://www.undpress.nd.edu

POWER

IN THE

BALANCE

Presidents, Parties, and Legislatures in Peru and Beyond

BARRY S. LEVITT

University of Notre Dame Press
Notre Dame, Indiana

Published in the United States of America

Library of Congress Cataloging-in-Publication Data

Levitt, Barry Steven.
Power in the balance : presidents, parties, and legislatures
in Peru and beyond / Barry S. Levitt.
p.   cm. — (From the Helen Kellogg Institute for International Studies)
Includes bibliographical references and index.
ISBN-13: 978-0-268-03413-9 (pbk. : alk. paper)
ISBN-10: 0-268-03413-3 (pbk. : alk. paper)
1. Peru—Politics and government—1980–   2. Executive power—Peru.
3. Legislative power—Peru.   4. Political parties—Peru.   5. Latin America—
Politics and government—1980–   6. Executive power—Latin America.
7. Legislative power—Latin America.   8. Political parties—Latin America.
I. Title.
JL3440.L48   2012
320.985—dc23

2011041941

To my mother and to the memory of my father ז"ל

Contents

Tables

Figures

Acknowledgments

The list of people who have supported this project since its journey began is extensive, and assembling these acknowledgments has been both humbling and heartwarming for me. It also reminded me that this book on institutions, and its author, found welcoming quarters in many different institutional homes along the way.

The initial impetus for this research came from a scholarly exchange run by the Duke-UNC Program in Latin American Studies, funded by the Ford Foundation. Executing my initial rounds of research was also made possible by a generous award from the Social Science and Humanities Research Council of Canada. And as the project began to evolve, the members of my doctoral dissertation committee at the University of North Carolina—my advisor, Evelyne Huber; Jonathan Hartlyn; Gary Marks; Jim Stimson; and external reader Ken Roberts—made valuable contributions to its development.

While conducting research in Peru, I first made my institutional home at the Instituto de Estudios Peruanos (IEP). Carolina Trivelli and then-director Cecilia Blondet led the way in creating a sense of community between the IEP and its visiting scholars. Chief librarian Vicky García has always been ready, willing, and incredibly able in her support of this research, then and now. I am also grateful to the social scientists at the IEP—Julio Cotler, Romeo Grompone, the late Carlos Iván Degregori, Carlos Vargas, and especially Martín Tanaka—for long-ago conversations about politics that, perhaps unbeknownst to them, left a lasting impression on me.

My next institutional home was with the National Democratic Institute for International Affairs (NDI) and the Carter Center. I am grateful to the staff at both organizations for putting their faith in a (then) relatively young man and appointing me director of political analysis of a joint election observer mission for the 2000 elections in Peru. Special thanks are due to Jennifer McCoy, Americas Program Director of the Carter Center, and to my former *compañero de trabajo,* NDI Peru Director Luis Nunes (and his assistant Cecilia Ormeño) for their ongoing support.

Other scholars in Peru were also enormously helpful over the years. Aldo Panfichi and Cynthia Sanborn generously shared their insights about politics. Rafael Roncagliolo has been an inspiring figure and a good friend too. And Fernando Tuesta has been a wellspring of thought-provoking conversation and—through his books and now his blog—an invaluable source of data on Peruvian politics. Thanks as well to Congressman Henry Pease and to Guillermo Loli of APOYO, S. A., for crucial data.

Of course, most of the research that comprises this book would have been impossible without the openhandedness and remarkable forthrightness of the more than one hundred politicians, ex-politicians, party activists, and political analysts who were interviewed for the project. Their names, too numerous to mention here, are noted in a reference list that can be found after the main bibliography. And it is, above all, *their* stories that are told in this book.

Back in the United States, I found supportive institutional homes (and great colleagues) as an assistant professor, first at Reed College and then at Emory University. Most recently, my colleagues at Florida International University have given me encouragement and good cheer, and several—including Tatiana Kostadinova and Adrian Ang—also offered extremely constructive feedback on parts of the project. Other U.S.-based scholars who have attentively commented on papers or proposals comprising parts of this project include Steven Levitsky, Kurt Weyland, and Steve Wuhs. Thank you all.

As this book neared the end of the road from conceptualization to publication, the editors and staff of the University of Notre Dame Press helped it complete its journey. Thank you to series editor Scott Mainwaring for supporting this project, to Barbara Hanrahan and Stephen Little for guiding the review and approval processes, and to Rebecca DeBoer, Wendy McMillen, Emily McKnight, and the rest of the UND Press staff for transforming a dream and a few hundred loose-leaf pages into a typeset, paperback reality. And a very special thank you to reviewers

Charles Kenney and Cynthia McClintock for the effort they put into asking the tough questions and offering genuinely helpful suggestions at the manuscript phase.

Finally, I am grateful to my daughters, Anna Clair and Alice Josephine Levitt, and my wife, Bianca Premo. Anna is, it seems, doomed to become a political junkie like her parents: at age two she could identify White House Advisor David Axelrod but not Donald Duck or Dora the Explorer. Anna, you were so patient for so long while *Papi* finished his book. (Even though *Papi* is no David Axelrod, he strives to be a pretty good *explorador* of politics.) Alice, though you didn't know it at the time, you were patient with me too—staying inside your mom's belly just long enough for your dad to gestate the copyedited version of this book. And Bianca: You gave me essential feedback on multiple drafts of this project over the many years it took to complete, and you proofread chapters of this manuscript too. But far more important was what you were able to show me about the grammar of life itself. Books do not "get written"; writers write books. The same simple truth holds for everything worthwhile that we do. Thank you for your love, your sense of humor, and your wisdom about the metaphysics of the active voice—in writing, in marriage, in living.

1

Introduction
On Power

Politics is defined as both the science and the art of balancing power.

—Maurice Hariou, 1916[1]

Institutions and Politics in Peru

Only four blocks separate the main buildings of Peru's national legislature, the Congreso de la República, from the seat of presidential power, the Palacio de Pizarro. If it were not for the noise and bustle of downtown Lima, these institutions would be almost within shouting distance of one another. This is not only a matter of urban geography but also a metaphor of institutional design, since these two elected branches of national government are indeed constitutionally tasked with conducting an ongoing conversation of sorts, over matters of law and governance. The language of this exchange consists of votes and vetoes, appointments and dismissals, investigations and reports. Its syntax is highly structured by formal rules meant to maintain some semblance of balance, or at least the potential for balance, between the two sides of the conversation. Yet despite these rules, interbranch dialogue has escalated into wars of words (and more than words), or been drowned out by executive monologue, on numerous occasions throughout Peru's political history.

At times, however, a rather more equitable institutional rapport has been sustained. In the transition from military to civilian rule in the late 1970s, Peru's political institutions underwent a process of democratization that was flawed and erratic yet nonetheless very real. By the mid-1980s the legislature had become an arena for meaningful debate and consequential political action. But this fledgling democracy was battered by civil war and economic chaos in the late 1980s. An "outsider" president was elected in 1990 and then seized power in a 1992 self-coup. Notwithstanding the restoration of nominally democratic institutions within a few months, the president governed virtually unconstrained for the remainder of the decade. Power tilted sharply away from Congress, as it was transformed from a legislative chamber to a mere echo chamber for the political will of the executive. Then, in late 2000 and 2001, Peru experienced another process of democratic renewal. In the first years of the twenty-first century, Congress could once again hold up its end of the interbranch conversation, giving voice to preferences beyond those of the presidential palace.

The central argument of this book is that political party disintegration, combined with weak constitutional adherence among political elites, produced a dramatic increase in executive power and the concomitant deterioration of the legislature's power in 1990s Peru. The decline of constitutional norms among political elites and the rise of what I call "electoral movements" fundamentally altered the way that power was sought and wielded by those political elites. As rule of law returned in 2001 and political parties made a modest but decisive comeback, presidential power was reduced, and the legislature grew stronger.

Thinking about politics in Peru in this way also led me to consider what the absence of effective rules and organized parties might mean for politics elsewhere, in democracies "old" and "new." My ideas were inspired by a critical reading of institutionalist theory, particularly the scholarship that this approach has produced on presidentialism and legislative-executive relations.[2] Though the term actually encompasses several different approaches, at its core the "new institutionalism" in political science holds that rules—everything from constitutional design to traffic laws—are socially constructed and have an autonomous impact on political, social, and economic outcomes (Peters 1999; Przeworski 2004). This school of thought focuses on the design and creation of, as well as the behaviors induced by, the "rules of the game." In this view, institutions have an explanatory power of their own, independent of individual traits of actors or of collective histories, economic realities, and social contexts (Olsen 2009, 8–9).

Institutionalist analysis has become increasingly prevalent in comparative politics over the past generation, with aspirations toward a general theory of politics.[3] Students of presidentialism in particular owe a debt to Matthew Shugart and John Carey and their 1992 work, *Presidents and Assemblies,* for moving beyond the realm of the "old" democracies and dissecting the institutional arrangements that allocate power in a broad range of separation-of-powers systems.

I first read *Presidents and Assemblies* in Lima, Peru, in the late 1990s. On days I was not gathering data or cold-calling politicians, I would spend my time reading about how the formal rules of the game, enshrined in constitutions and electoral laws, were supposed to define legislative-executive relations and shape the powers of Peru's president. When I would pause from my reading to rest my eyes, look out the window onto Lima's streets, and think about what I was observing "in the field," however, the game of politics looked very different. Elections were being rigged with the thinnest veneer of legality; political parties were mere shells of organizations; then-President Alberto Fujimori (1990–2000) and his intelligence advisor, Vladimiro Montesinos, participated in the formal institutions of governance but also governed through mafia-like networks of corruption; and the legislature served as little more than a mouthpiece for the executive branch. I could not help but feel that focusing on constitutions and electoral laws would not fully explain what I was observing in Peru. More field research and a six-month stint as codirector of an election observation mission in Peru only further confirmed this feeling. The formal rules of the game had a reasonably predictable impact on politics during the 1980s and again in the first decade of the twenty-first century, but in the 1990s the rules simply did not matter much, as they did not as strongly condition the behavior of Peru's politicians and political elites.

Institutionalist theory does not, of course, mechanically equate the formal rules of the game with the allocation of real power. It does, however, presume that formal rules play a strong role in configuring actual political outcomes. Pioneering studies of presidentialism in Latin America showed that the region's political systems tend to be designed so that the institutional sources of executive power—electoral laws and constitutions—offset one another (Mainwaring and Shugart 1997; Shugart 1998). Presidential systems either grant leaders strong control over parties (and thus, presumably, control over copartisans in the legislature), confer extensive constitutional powers that allow the president to make laws without (or against) the support of the legislature, or feature a moderate balance of partisan and lawmaking powers. Under very few circumstances are formal institutions intentionally designed to foster hyper-presidentialism.

Yet there is a gap between what the formal rules suggest presidential powers should be and the empirical evidence of how powerful presidents actually are in some new democracies. In 1980s Peru, critics of presidents Fernando Belaúnde Terry (1980–1985) and Alan García (1985–1990) justifiably complained about these leaders' propensities for unilateral decision making, but on the whole these executives were still constrained by formal rules and institutions. By the 1990s, the partisan powers that electoral rules gave to Peru's governing leaders seemed irrelevant in the face of what I learned about President Fujimori's political organization: that it was fluid, noninstitutionalized by design, held together by extra-institutional means and wholly dedicated to supporting the president. This support seemed to have less to do with the timing of elections, the rules for candidate selection, or other institutions of partisan control and more to do with the utterly personalistic nature of the organization and the way its leader wielded power. Similarly, the president's lawmaking powers—and restrictions on these powers—as allocated by Peru's constitution seemed to be a poor approximation of the country's real political structures. Fujimori and Montesinos's flagrant capture and domination of an entire political system belied the written word of the constitution.

As Fujimori stepped down, as Montesinos was arrested, and as Alejandro Toledo was elected freely and fairly, relatively few of the formal rules governing legislative-executive relations were altered in the process. Yet presidential power fundamentally changed in a period of just a few weeks in late 2000 and was markedly curtailed during the Toledo presidency (2001–2006). Something other than the formal rules of the game must be responsible for reviving, in the first decade of the twenty-first century, the nascent checks and balances that Peru had last displayed in the 1980s.

I ultimately concluded that the factors that have shaped the strengths of Peru's executive and legislature over the two decades from 1985 to 2006 are not the rules of the game per se, but rather two much more elemental facets of political order and organization in that country. The first of these is constitutionalism, specifically the extent to which the rules that

govern executive power and legislative-executive relations actually chan-
nel and constrain the political behavior of flesh-and-blood politicians. The
second is the organizational form of the executive's party (or lack thereof)
and, more broadly, the ways in which the presence or absence of organized
parties—in and out of government—constrains or empowers executive
leadership.

It could be argued that entities other than legislatures—such as
courts, ombudspersons, comptrollers and regulatory agencies, and regional and local governments—can and do serve to constrain the power
of the executive. Nevertheless, in presidential systems the power of these
other government branches and agencies often derives from the executive's
or (more often) the legislature's powers to create such bodies, to appoint
and dismiss their members, and to fund their activities (Moreno, Crisp,
and Shugart 2003).[4] If the legislature has some modicum of autonomy
from the executive, and some capacity to make and enact decisions, then
political checks and balances—as well as "horizontal accountability"
(O'Donnell 1999a; Kenney 2003b), or "horizontal exchange" (Moreno,
Crisp, and Shugart 2003)—can work quite well in a separation-of-powers
system. My research on Peru's legislature revealed significantly more institutional autonomy and capacity in 1985–1990 and 2001–2006 than
in the 1990s. Legislative autonomy and capacity were particularly weak
after Fujimori shut down Congress, the judiciary, and other state entities
in a 1992 presidential self-coup (*autogolpe*) and then reshaped—many
would say deformed—the assembly, the courts, and other state agencies
for the remainder of the decade. Some formal rules were changed along
the way, but these changes were endogenous to executive power: they reflected hyper-presidentialism more than they caused it, and they could
and would be changed again by a reinvigorated legislature after Fujimori's
November 2000 resignation.

It could also be argued that the explanation for changes in executive
power lies in the simple distinction between minority and majority presidents. The size of the president's legislative caucus does indeed play a role
in shaping legislative-executive relations in Peru. As we will see, President
Fujimori was much less constrained by Congress after 1992, not only because of his system-shattering *autogolpe* but because of the legislative
majority that he manufactured in its wake and maintained until 2000.
Likewise, President Toledo's often pitched battles with the legislature in

2001–2006 cannot be properly understood without acknowledging that his group was a minority caucus that legislated through a very tenuous coalition. And yet my research also revealed that the size of the president's legislative caucus can only explain so much. In President García's first term (1985–1990), for example, his *own* copartisans in the legislature acted to curtail some of his most unilateralist tendencies. What is more, legislative election results are themselves conditioned by factors such as elite constitutional adherence and party-system institutionalization, or lack thereof, particularly in newer democracies.

All of these observations led me to rethink some elements of the new institutionalist scholarship on Latin America. At the same time, they also pointed me back to an older, albeit less well-defined, body of literature about Latin American politics. As a way of explaining configurations of political power, scholars writing in this tradition emphasized not the rules themselves but the absence of rule of law, or the weakness of representative institutions and political parties, or both.[5] Dieter Nohlen (2003; 2006) has revived this approach, synthesizing it with the new institutionalism through the practice of what he calls "contextualized institutionalism." Other scholars, too, have called into question the centrality of formal institutional rules for stability and consolidation in newer democracies (Alexander 2001; Weyland 2002).

Taken to its extreme, though, skepticism about formal institutions would lead to a different set of pitfalls: a too easy reliance on stereotypes of political dysfunction in Latin America and on deterministic or tautological claims. One could dismiss questions about democratic crises with the explanation that political power in postcolonial Peru has "always" been somewhat informal and that national institutions—indeed, the state itself—have been perennially weak. But taking history and context seriously is not the same as assuming historical stasis, in political institutions or anywhere else. Saying that parties and constitutions have "always" been weak does not mean that they were always *equally* weak and does not explain why they were stronger in some historical moments than in others.

In fact, from the late 1970s to the late 1980s, Peruvian politics became markedly more institutionalized. And in the first decade of the twenty-first century, democratic processes in general, and horizontal accountability in particular, were revitalized in remarkable if also untidy ways. Thus, the scope of this book—the decline and partial rebirth of constitutional norms and political party organizations and, consequently, the fall and rise of the legislature's ability to constrain the executive from 1985 to 2006—encompasses critical moments of change.

Larger historical patterns do matter, and in the next section I present a brief sketch of the development of Peru's national political institutions. Yet, as I go on to illustrate in the rest of this book, the past three decades alone have witnessed remarkable processes of political institutionalization, deinstitutionalization, and reinstitutionalization. Past is not always prologue.

Constitutionalism, Political Parties, and the State in Peru's History

A panoramic view of Peru's history—colonial, nineteenth-century, and twentieth-century—underscores the significance of the institutional changes that took place in the late 1970s and early 1980s. It introduces some key political actors and organizations (especially APRA) and traces the origins of several major features of Peru's 1979 and 1993 constitutions back to the 1933 Constitution. It also highlights the fitful and uneven development of constitutional norms and organized political parties, as Peru oscillated between dictatorship and democracy.

In the colonial era, Lima was an important political, religious, and cultural center, the administrative capital of a viceroyalty that once encompassed most of Spanish South America. Economic elites reaped the rewards of mercantile commerce and agricultural and mining operations. These, in turn, relied on the indigenous population of the Andes, who had been caught, since conquest, in a web of forced, coerced, and poorly paid labor systems. Administratively, the Spanish Empire in the New World forged a legal and political distinction between a "republic of Spaniards" and a "republic of Indians," an imagined division that was nonetheless reinforced by both geographic and social distance. A rift divided the Pacific coast region, where Lima is located, from the highlands and jungle lowlands of Peru, where the majority of the population was (and is) of Indian ancestry (Thurner 1997). Indeed, fear of the Indians and of the large coastal population of slaves of African descent prevented many in elite and middle sectors of society from embracing independence, until the armies of the two great South American "liberators," Simón Bolívar coming from the north and José de San Martín coming from the south, had nearly converged (Klaren 2000).

The immediate postindependence period of the 1820s and '30s saw Peru's "founding fathers" draft no fewer than six successive constitutions in a period of fifteen years. In many fledgling Latin American republics, the most conflictive issues among constitutional framers were the role of the Catholic Church in society and the power balance between centralized and regional authorities. While some of these were important in Peru too—the country was wracked by internal conflicts among regional caudillos, or military chieftains—the issue of executive power has also loomed large in its constitutional debates (Chirinos Soto 1986; McClintock 1994; Werlich 1978).

Between 1821 and 1845, the presidency changed hands forty-three times, mostly among military strongmen of varying strengths and support bases. Ramón Castilla, a caudillo, rose to the presidency in 1845, served until 1851, and then returned (via a coup) for 1854–1862. During these periods, he attempted to broaden participation and shore up a central state. With Peru's financial situation improving as a result of revenues from the export of guano, Castilla abolished slavery and repealed the head tax on Indians; he also attempted to professionalize and unify the military and build a public school system. But the guano boom was short-lived, and subsequent economic decline was compounded by Peru's loss to Chile in the 1879–1884 War of the Pacific, further weakening the central state.

Small, caucus-style political parties began to emerge in the late nineteenth century, but national institutions were still hobbled by the power of local caudillos. Compared to Mexico, an ethnically and historically comparable case, Peru's nineteenth- and early twentieth-century national institutions had less durable linkages with regional and local politics, and public associational life—civil society—was less developed (Mallon 1995; Forment 2003). Suffrage was largely restricted by wealth and literacy requirements. The exercise of political rights was also limited by elite pressure and occasionally violent repression, particularly in rural areas (Cotler 1995). In the "Aristocratic Republic" ushered in by Nicolas de Piérola in 1895, the central state became more institutionalized and the size of the electorate grew, yet voter coercion was still commonplace and the rules of the political game were manipulated by Piérola's successors.

Twentieth-century Peru thus inherited a distinct postcolonial legacy from the nineteenth century. Politics was dominated by a heterogeneous array of regionally based groups of oligarchs, represented in national politics by loosely organized elite caucus parties. Constitutionalist norms among civilian political elites were weak. Piérola, the so-called democratic caudillo, had twice seized power by means of a coup. Reformer Guillermo Billinghurst rose to the presidency in 1912 after widespread civic unrest convinced Congress to appoint him and then was ousted by the military in 1914 as he tried to dissolve Congress to avoid impeachment.

In 1919 strikes, popular protests, and an opposition ploy to keep presidential election winner Augusto Leguía from taking office provoked a civil-military coup, initiating an eleven-year period of authoritarian "modernization from above" under Leguía. During this era, as urban middle- and working-class sectors of Peru grew and became more involved in formal politics, two groups emerged that would continue to play a prominent role in Peruvian politics throughout the twentieth century. One, led by José Carlos Mariátegui, would become the Socialist (later Communist) Party of Peru. The other, led by Víctor Raúl Haya de la Torre, would coalesce into the populist Alianza Popular Revolucionaria Americana, or APRA (Collier and Collier 1991).

Haya founded the APRA movement in 1924 while in exile in Mexico and envisioned it as a pan–Latin American organization. APRA was officially established as a political party in Peru in 1930. Its ideology would swing both left and right over the next seven decades, but at its inception it was anti-feudal and anti-imperialist, and it sought to foment a revolution of sorts, based on autonomous state capitalism as a precursor to socialism (Cotler 1995). The party was not deeply committed to constitutionalism, viewing procedural democracy as a tool of oppression and an obstacle to the achievement of a more genuine "functional democracy" (Werlich 1978, 204).

APRA grew in strength and numbers in the 1930s, though its efforts at political mobilization focused more on the coastal regions than on the interior, with its large rural peasantry. It did not press for expanded suffrage as other Latin American populist parties did. Nonetheless, the movement was repressed. The antipathy of the military toward the party created a decades-long schism in Peruvian politics, and the collective experience of repression became central to the identity of *apristas* (Hilliker

1971). At the grassroots level, individuals and families identified with APRA in a sectarian, almost religious manner (Vega Centeno 1986; Otero interview 1999). The party also forged linkages with organized civil society, especially labor unions. In the early 1930s, the focal point of organized labor was the General Confederation of Workers of Peru (Confederación General de Trabajadores del Perú, or CGTP), dominated by the Communists but with some APRA participation. The CGTP was banned in the 1930s, and a new Confederation of Workers of Peru (Confederación de Trabajadores del Perú, or CTP), founded in the 1940s, was ultimately taken over by APRA. At its peak, CTP represented approximately 75 percent of Peru's organized workers (Collier and Collier 1991; Payne 1965).[6]

Leguía was overthrown in 1930 by Luis Miguel Sánchez Cerro, an army officer. Sánchez Cerro went on to win the presidency in a national election the following year, defeating the APRA's founder-leader Haya de la Torre. *Apristas* (and non-*apristas*) suspected vote fraud, and for the next two years Peru was wracked by political violence and repression. Amidst this conflict, on April 18, 1933, Peru adopted a new constitution, institutionalizing many of the formal rules that would endure in subsequent charters.

The 1933 Constitution gave form to Peru's bicameral legislative structure, consisting of a Chamber of Deputies (lower house) and a Senate (upper house). The president was to be elected by popular vote, with the power to appoint and dismiss cabinet members. In a deviation from a purely presidential model, cabinet ministers were also subject to parliamentary confidence; both the executive and the legislature had the authority to dismiss cabinet members (Shugart and Carey 1992; Kenney 2004). There was "separation of powers" but not a strict "separation of survival" between the assembly and the president.

Just twelve days after Peru's constitution was promulgated, President Sánchez Cerro was assassinated by a young APRA militant. In lieu of a vice president, the chain of presidential succession required that Congress elect a successor to serve out the duration of the deceased president's term. The assembly voted overwhelmingly for General Oscar Benavides — despite the fact that the just-adopted constitution explicitly barred active-service military officers from holding the office of president (Werlich 1978).[7] Though the ink on the constitution had not yet dried, the immediate desire for stability prevailed over the rule of law. General Benavides then illegally kept himself in office. He barred the candidacy of Haya de la Torre in 1936 elections and disqualified the results when Haya's surrogate appeared to be leading the vote count; he forced Congress to extend his term by another three years; and finally he disbanded Congress and governed as a military dictator until 1939.

Other parts of the 1933 Constitution were either never put into practice (e.g., a senate organized along corporatist principles) or delayed for decades (e.g., elected municipal and departmental councils). What is more, Benavides bequeathed to his successors extra-constitutional executive powers. On paper, Peru's 1933 Constitution had greatly empowered the legislature. Only a one-fifth majority was required to interpellate (i.e., question) a minister, and a simple plurality of legislators' votes could censure a minister—including the premier—and force his resignation. Presidents, by contrast, could neither dissolve the legislature nor even veto legislation.[8] Moreover, the "power of the purse," the ability to control taxing and spending, lay squarely in the hands of the legislative branch (McClintock 1994). But Benavides would ensure that the firm hand of executive power was not so easily stayed. According to the 1933 charter, constitutional amendments required the approval of a majority of both houses of the legislature in two successive sessions of parliament. However, since Benavides had dissolved the legislature, in 1939 he decided to submit a list of ten constitutional "reforms" to a national plebiscite—unforeseen in the constitution itself—the results of which were, in reality, a fait accompli. These "reforms" weakened the legislature and strengthened the executive; parliament was shorn of its fiscal powers, and its capacity to investigate the executive branch and hold it accountable was sharply reduced.[9] The presidency, by contrast, gained expanded decree authority and veto power.[10]

From 1939 to 1945, the elected president, Manuel Prado y Ugarteche, wielded these executive powers moderately. He by and large respected the rules of the game. He also gradually incorporated the APRA party into politics (though he did not formally legalize it until just before his term ended). Then from 1945 to 1948, APRA, the Communists, and a regionally based party participated in a coalition government that for a time backed President José Luis Bustamante. The 1939 "reforms" enacted by General Benavides were reversed by Congress in 1945, notwithstanding attempts by President Bustamante to veto this return to the original spirit of the 1933 Constitution. With a veto override by the legislature, even the presidential veto itself was (re)abolished. But in response, President Bustamante pioneered two techniques, one quasi-constitutional and one extra-constitutional, for expanding executive control under the rehabilitated 1933 charter. First, he interpreted a transitory provision of the constitution as allowing him to return a bill to the legislature with "*observaciones*" (i.e., exercise a partial veto). Second, and far more potent, the executive branch and the administrative bodies it controlled simply refused to implement many of the laws and statutes passed by Congress (Werlich 1978, 237).

Simmering tensions between President Bustamante and the APRA were brought to a boil by an *aprista*-linked naval mutiny in 1948. General Manuel Odría was installed in a conservative military coup, and for the next eight years the Peruvian state again repressed Communists and *apristas*. Odría assumed the presidency "provisionally," suspended constitutional guarantees for nearly two years, and then won the presidential election of 1950 by barring all three of his main challengers from running for office. Though some political opposition was tolerated during his 1950–1956 term, Odría continued to repress APRA and the Communist Party and impede the development of autonomous civil society organizations, especially labor unions.

APRA returned to electoral politics with the 1956 Pact of Monterrico, which its secretary general, Ramiro Prialé, signed with Prado and Odriá. APRA threw its support behind Prado with the promise that— once reelected—he would again legalize the *partido del pueblo* (Klaren 2000). Prado kept his word, and his second term, 1956–1962, was again a period of political opening. In this Faustian bargain, however, APRA limited its popular-sector mobilization, turning away from its more radical roots (Graham 1992).

In the 1950s and '60s, a wave of new parties emerged (Collier and Collier 1991). Among them were the centrist Popular Action (Acción Popular, AP) and the Christian Democrats (Partido Demócrata-Cristiano, PDC). Led by Fernando Belaúnde, AP became a national political organization but remained a cadre-based rather than a mass-based party; its leadership was personalistic and its program centrist and nonideological. The nucleus of the PDC never developed into a major national party: its left wing was siphoned off into more radical parties, and its right wing splintered in 1967 to form the Partido Popular Cristiano, or Popular Christian Party (PPC). APRA remained Peru's largest and best organized political group. Though it was strongest in *"el norte sólido"*—Peru's north coast and parts of the northern highlands—it was now indeed a national party organization. An adage from the mid-twentieth century held that there are three things found in every town in Peru: a church, a police station, and an APRA party headquarters. Nevertheless, the party remained a polarizing force.

Presidential elections in 1962 yielded no immediate winner by plurality, as none of the candidates surpassed the threshold of 33.3 percent of votes cast. The coalition that was poised to emerge in the legislature to indirectly elect the president was an unlikely alliance between APRA and supporters of the ex-dictator Odría. But the military would countenance neither the APRA in government nor an unstable coalition of erstwhile political enemies backing a second term for Odría. A coup nullified the vote results, and new elections were called for 1963. With the boundaries of what the military would consider acceptable now drawn, Fernando Belaúnde of the centrist AP won the 1963 contest (with new support coming from the Christian Democrats).

In the five years that followed, a congressional coalition of UNO (National Odriísta Union, Odría's personalistic party) and APRA stymied Belaúnde's moderate reformist program. The stalemated president would not finish his term. On the reasons for this breakdown, analysts are of several minds (see McClintock 1994). Some emphasize the timidity of Belaúnde's reformism, which developed Peru's physical infrastructure but did not address fundamental social and economic tensions. Others point to divided government and the intransigence of the right-wing APRA-UNO coalition, which used Congress to harass the president and render the country ungovernable—also stoking the long-standing anti-APRA sentiment of the military.

In 1968, a self-styled "officers' revolution" led by General Juan Velasco broke the gridlock of divided government. Constitutionalism again disintegrated as the military stepped in to rule. This time, though, it framed its role as a "progressive" force in Peru's political development, seeking to avoid full-blown social upheaval by implementing economic and social modernization from above.[11] Velasco's Revolutionary Government of the Armed Forces fundamentally changed the structure of the state. It also organized and mobilized large swaths of the Peruvian populace—especially peasants and indigenous peoples—previously excluded from formal politics.

Influenced by leftist political and economic ideas, the military government carried out an ambitious if poorly implemented agrarian reform (García 2005). It carved out an increased economic role for the Peruvian state, which had not shifted to statism and import-substitution industrialization in the 1940s and '50s, as Argentina, Mexico, Brazil, and many other Latin American countries had done (Stokes 1995; Cotler 1986). Yet now it nationalized much of the banking, insurance, telecommunications, and other industries, and gave workers a voice in the productive activities of firms through the establishment of Industrial Communities. The revolutionary generals also organized the political representation of a variety of social sectors in the National System of Support to Social Mobilization (SINAMOS)—which had the effect of legitimizing mass political mobilization, albeit in a top-down fashion (Huber Stephens 1983).

As a consequence of these policies, the APRA party was weakened, and left parties were indirectly strengthened. The military government broke the APRA-led CTP by creating its own government-sponsored labor federation[12] and, more importantly, legalizing the Communist-led CGTP. In the 1970s, the CGTP again became Peru's preeminent labor federation; by the 1980s, only dockworkers and a shrinking number of sugar industry workers remained under APRA control (Graham 1992; Santander Estrada interview 1999; Vílchez Cruza interview 1999; Negreiros Criado interview 1999).[13] APRA also failed to attract the interest of the growing number of university-educated Peruvians, many of whom were dismayed at the party's opportunistic right turn. By the 1970s young intellectuals enjoyed new opportunities for political activism and leadership in the government-sponsored social movements of SINAMOS, in the fledgling parties of Peru's "New Left" (which gained prominence in the late 1970s and 80s), and in think tanks and nongovernmental organizations backed by foreign donors (Franco Ballester interview 1999; Negreiros Criado interview 1999; Grompone interview 1999). Yet although Peru under Velasco was politically dynamic, it was also undeniably authoritarian.

Thus, throughout most of its history as a republic, Peru experienced brief periods of democratic deadlock alternating with lengthy dictatorships of varying ideological stripes.[14] The democratic institutional development of Peru prior to the 1980s was erratic. Military interventions were frequent. In the forty-six-year period between the 1933 and 1979 constitutions, the election of 1945 was the only rule-bound transition from one elected president to another. In these four and a half decades, the country experienced only twenty years of democracy—semi-democracy, really, as suffrage was limited by literacy restrictions, and the participation of the APRA or the Communist Party (or both) was frequently blocked. These parties endured, but their development was stifled by long periods of exclusion and repression. Authoritarian rule and weak civilian control over the military thus contributed to the weakness of the party system. Pendular swings between constitutional and extra-constitutional rule also weakened the capacity of constitutional norms to constrain elite political behavior and created deep disjunctures between formal rules and actual political practices. In sum, neither constitutionalism nor political party organizations were very robust in mid-1970s Peru.

Continuity and Change: Peru's Democratic Transition

Still, this book is not a story of continuity, of a "permanent crisis" or the inherent debility of Peru's political institutions. The 1968–1975 phase of the military regime had radically increased the mobilization and integration of highland and Amazonian Peruvians, fundamentally altering the political arena for all elected regimes that followed it. A conservative countercoup led by General Francisco Morales Bermúdez ousted the ailing Velasco in 1975. But the mobilization of civil society under Velasco made possible the mass demonstrations faced by Morales Bermúdez in 1976–1977. A 1977 general strike was the largest and most comprehensive in Peru's history, and its success was due in large part to left party organizing. In the face of rising social unrest and decreasing legitimacy, the military accelerated plans to withdraw from governing.

The 1978–1980 transition to democracy, one of the first of the so-called Third Wave of democratization in Latin America, brought with it not just free and fair elections but universal suffrage with no literacy restrictions, giving millions of people the right to vote unhindered for the first time. To illustrate the magnitude of this change: in the 1963 presidential elections 2,070,718 citizens were eligible to vote (and 1,954,284 voted) out of a total population of roughly 11,000,000; in the 1980 elections, the number of registered voters increased to 6,471,105 (and 5,174,920 voted) out of a total population of roughly 17,000,000.[15] What is more, political elites demonstrated increased fealty to the rules of the political game, and political parties both old and new developed and grew.

A consensus emerged among political elites in the late 1970s that a return to constitutional rule was a vital priority. General Morales Bermúdez negotiated the terms of regime transition with centrist and right-wing political parties, the APRA and the PPC, though left parties and the deposed AP were still excluded at this stage.[16] In 1978, after ten years of military rule, Morales Bermúdez called elections for a constituent assembly, to be charged with writing a new charter. The hundred-member assembly was elected by proportional representation in a single national district, and twelve political parties won seats. The most active contributors to the drafting of the constitution were, again, the APRA, with thirty-seven members, and the PPC with twenty-five members. But the assembly also included a large contingent of leftist politicians, including the formerly jailed and several-times exiled Hugo Blanco, elected in absentia. The constitutional framers were politically diverse and brought serious intellectual heft to the task of reconstructing the rules of the game in Peru. Constituent Assembly members interviewed for this book unfailingly spoke in glowing terms of the good-faith contributions of their fellow *asambleístas,* even those from rival parties with whom they vehemently disagreed about policy and ideology. Shared norms of constitutionalism trumped even long-standing political enmities: the assembly, generated by the military, was presided over by none other than APRA's founder-leader, Haya de la Torre.

Then the 1980 elections brought deposed President Fernando Belaúnde back to power. Belaúnde faced serious economic and political challenges: problems with military impunity and executive overreach tested the durability of constitutional norms almost from the start of the new regime (Cotler 1995; Kenney 2004). On the other hand, the rules enshrined in the 1979 Constitution guided governance processes and constrained the behavior of political elites in the first half of the 1980s to an extent seldom seen before in Peru.

Political parties were changing too. Haya had always maintained a strong personal grip on the APRA party organization, which contributed to its uneven development, ideological incoherence, and difficulty adapting (Duff 1985). And since the party had never been allowed to govern, few *apristas* had any experience in elected office or public administration. Anticipating a democratic transition, Haya recognized these shortcomings in the mid-1970s and created training programs, under his personal auspices and sheltered from the party's conservative "old guard," for the future politicians of Peru. The Buró de Conjunciones (Bureau of Linkages) was a group of approximately fifty youths who studied with Haya to prepare them for political leadership. A smaller and more elite group, including a young Alan García, was inducted into an Escuela de Dirigentes (School of Leaders), which served as a shadow organization to the mainstream APRA structure, with each trainee apprenticed to one of the party's leadership positions (Graham 1992).

Haya's long-standing aspirations to become president of the republic ended, frustrated, with his death just three weeks after signing the 1979 Constitution. And the political disorganization of APRA after Haya's death benefited the rival Acción Popular. Not only did Belaúnde win the presidency (for the second time) in 1980; his AP combined with the PPC to form a right-leaning majority coalition in the legislature. Within a few years, though, it was the left that was making the greatest political strides. In the Constituent Assembly, the impact of left-wing parties was diluted not only by their legislative inexperience and minority status in the assembly but by their fragmentation as well. A coalition was briefly formed to run a unified slate of leftist candidates for the 1980 general elections, but this coalition, ARI (Alianza Revolutionaria de Izquierda, or Revolutionary Alliance of the Left), was short-lived, and it ultimately presented five different slates. Their electoral failure led most of these leftist parties to form a more durable alliance after the 1980 general elections, called the United Left or Izquierda Unida (IU).

In the 1983 municipal elections, AP lost ground both to APRA and to the IU, which won 33 percent and 29 percent, respectively, of the vote nationwide. The IU unified behind the candidacy of Alfonso Barrantes to win the mayoralty of Lima. Barrantes and the left soon set their sights on the presidency in the 1985 general elections. AP was flagging after several years of lackluster governance in the face of a sluggish economy, but the IU faced stiff competition from an APRA party that had overcome the internecine squabbling that followed Haya's death and found a new leader: Alan García Pérez.

The year 1985 was a watershed for constitutionalism and party de-velopment in Peru. Institutions of governance and political representa-tion appeared sturdier than ever. Power peacefully changed hands from one elected government to another. After decades of exclusion and perse-cution, a president from the APRA party was elected. Conservative groups like PPC and left parties unified in the IU, all playing by the same politi-cal rules of the game, were harbingers of democratic development. A party system with relatively stable groups representing left, center, and right looked to be emerging. And although contemporary analysts in the 1980s lamented the dominance of the executive over the legislature under both Belaúnde and, especially, García, the political "conversation" between the two branches was, by the standards of the region and of Peru's own his-tory, relatively balanced and constructive. But not for long.

Political Violence and Economic Crisis in the 1980s

Why, after a decade of apparent democratic consolidation, did both con-stitutionalism and organized political parties begin to wither in Peru in the late 1980s? Analysts of that era have thoroughly chronicled the mul-tiple causes of institutional decay, and I review them here only in pass-ing (Cameron 1994; 1997; Cameron, Blanaru, and Burns 2006; Carrión 1998; Cotler 1995; Dietz and Meyers 2007; Kenney 2003a; 2004; Levit-sky and Cameron 2003; Lynch 1999; Roberts 1996; Tanaka 1998). They point to a confluence of exogenous shocks to Peru's political system so se-vere that neither weak rule of law nor the disintegration of political parties seems particularly surprising. The two most powerful blows to politics-as-usual were an increasingly violent and extensive guerilla insurgency (and state counterinsurgency) war and a dramatic economic downturn marked by hyperinflation, a decline in real wages, and a scarcity of basic consumer goods.

The most fearsome of the armed guerilla organizations was the Mao-ist group Sendero Luminoso, or Shining Path (see Degregori 1987; 1989; McClintock 1989; 1998; Palmer 1994). It began its activities in the im-poverished highland areas around the city of Ayacucho in 1980. The Shin-ing Path was notorious for the zeal of its militants and the sheer violence it perpetrated against civilian persons and property, many of them the very *campesinos* (peasants) on whose behalf they purported to be warring. It directed its violence not only against the state—attacking Peru's infrastructure and assassinating police and military officers, local and national politicians—but against organized civil society too. Trade unionists, peasant activists, and community organizers of all political stripes, but particularly those on the democratic left, were targeted. In 1984, a second armed movement emerged: the Movimiento Revolucionario Túpac Amaru (Túpac Amaru Revolutionary Movement or MRTA), a more traditional (Communist, pro-Cuba) guerilla group that grew to control part of Peru's jungle territory and levy "taxes" on the area's drug traffic.

The economic cost of the insurgency and counterinsurgency has been estimated at $21 billion—roughly the size of Peru's foreign debt by the mid-1990s (Teivainen 2000, 151). The cost in terms of human life from violence perpetrated by the two insurrections and the military and paramilitary responses was initially estimated to be roughly 25,000 people, with hundreds of thousands more displaced (Webb and Fernández Baca 1994). The figures ultimately calculated by Peru's Truth and Reconciliation Commission (CVR, Comisión de la Verdad y Reconciliación) were even more shocking: an estimated 69,280 killed or disappeared, and between 600,000 and 1,000,000—mostly poor, rural, and indigenous people—displaced (CVR 2003). Though the peak year for political violence across the nation was 1984, the four next-worst years were 1989, 1990, 1991, and 1992 (CVR 2003; Webb and Fernandez Baca 1994; 1999). The cumulative effects of this violence, coupled with a late-1980s shift to attacks on the capital city in particular, meant that the damage to political institutionality in Peru only grew more severe over the years.

In the late 1980s, a major economic crisis also befell Peru.[17] Deficit spending increased under President Alan García. Already-strained relations with international financial institutions worsened, and Peru was declared ineligible to receive new loans. The attempted nationalization of the banking system in 1987, which I describe in chapter 3, further reduced investor confidence. Inflation exploded in September 1988: monthly inflation rates were consistently above 30 percent and as high as 114 percent. Peru's currency was overvalued, and multiple exchange rates were simultaneously set by the government, which led to a rise in black-market transactions in goods and currency and a contraction of the formal economy. Price controls on utilities, fuel, and foodstuffs led to hoarding and created a scarcity of privately produced goods. This also bankrupted the state-owned enterprises that produced or marketed goods such as food and fuel; the combined losses of state-owned enterprises in 1988 alone was $1.2 billion. Stabilization packages in 1988 and 1989 induced economic stagnation but did not halt the inflationary spiral (Graham 1992; Velarde 1994). GDP contracted by 8.8 percent in 1988 and by 14 percent in 1989. The purchasing power of the minimum wage dropped 49 percent between 1985 and 1990, and full-time, formal-sector employment declined to just 18 percent of the economically active population (Rudolph 1992).

What was the impact of these twin crises — insurgency and economic chaos — on constitutionalism? Conflict between the state and insurgents over the control of populations and territory in many of Peru's highland and jungle regions eroded the rule of law in those areas. By 1990 almost half of Peru's population lived in emergency zones, in which many basic human rights were suspended and military, not civil, authority was supreme. The heavy-handed counterinsurgency strategies of three successive governments in the 1980s and 90s further reduced human rights and the quality of life in rural areas. The ongoing threat also prompted the state to organize and sponsor local militias. Sectors of the APRA party quietly revived its tradition of paramilitary activity. In the past, the party had maintained strong-arm gangs called *búfalos;* 1988 saw the emergence of the Comando Rodrigo Franco, a clandestine "death squad" named after an assassinated APRA party bureaucrat. The severe economic crisis and the civil war thus created an overall climate of lawlessness among political elites. A sense of desperation sharply contracted political time horizons and opened the door for the implementation of drastic, unconstitutional solutions. The constitution itself was decreasingly viewed by political actors as a "coordination point," a self-binding set of rules for politics (Linz and Stepan 1996; Weingast 1997).

Pervasive anxiety over economic survival and over the expanding reach of Sendero and MRTA violence weakened "diffuse support" for the existing political system among the public at large too (Easton 1965; Muller, Jukam, and Seligson 1982; Seligson and Carrión 2002). Kurt Weyland (1996b) has argued that as the economic crisis worsened, the fear of further losses led a majority of Peruvians to take a risk and support new, neoliberal policy ideas. A similar argument could be made for constitutionalism and the rule of law. As the economy tanked and the guerilla war spread, Peruvians of various classes and regions were increasingly willing to let their leaders suspend the normal rules of the game. (The support that 80 percent of Peruvians gave to President Fujimori's self-coup suggests that by 1992 the mass public was at best ambivalent about constitutionalism.)

These twin crises had a deleterious impact on political party organizations as well. The economic crisis (and subsequent neoliberal reforms) further weakened an already-struggling organized labor sector and likewise dealt a severe blow to neighborhood associations and other civil society organizations that comprised the social bases of the political parties of the left (Roberts 1999). It reduced the time and resources that individuals and groups could bring to the political parties themselves; politics was an activity that Peruvians struggling to survive economically could ill afford. Party militancy also became dangerous. Sendero attacks had a chilling effect on overall political participation, and parties on the left faced the additional threat of being targeted by counterinsurgency forces. And for the IU, the insurgencies laid bare a fundamental tension within the coalition (Roberts 1998). A few of the more radical parties in the IU were only nominally committed to electoral democracy and tacitly supported the MRTA and affiliated organizations, though generally not Sendero.

Perhaps most importantly, the leaders of Peru's traditional parties were themselves blamed for these crises, and the parties were punished by voters at the polls. Voters in countries with stable party systems (in which new groups face high barriers to entry) tend to punish only the incumbent party in bad economic times. But voters in more volatile systems like Peru's tend instead to punish *all* major parties in moments of crisis, especially those that have previously held power. They opt instead for minor parties or entirely new contenders (Benton 2005). This tendency was exacerbated by the inability of the so-called traditional parties, AP and APRA, to renovate their top leaders, which in the 1990s meant that they could not escape association with the troubled 1980s presidencies of Belaúnde and García respectively. Personalistic leadership within the leftist IU coalition also contributed to the disintegration of that coalition in 1989, as I explain in chapter 4.

The irony here is that the electoral movement organizations that came to displace political parties in Peru's electoral arena were even *more* personalistic. And in the 1990s, the Fujimori government acted strategically to ensure that conditions would continue to be unfavorable for the rebirth of organized political parties. Unfair electoral competition, state intelligence surveillance, and the occasional use of targeted repression dissuaded the organic development of political parties worthy of the name. Instead, a new form of populism emerged "in which a leader attempts to build personalistic ties to the impoverished masses while pursuing neoliberal economic policies" (Barr 2003, 1161). These neopopulist political strategies linked poor citizens directly to the state—and to the executive branch in particular—without the intermediation of mass political parties (Weyland 1996a; Sanborn and Panfichi 1997).

By the beginning of the twenty-first century, the crises that gutted rule of law and drove organized parties out of Peru's political arena had long abated. Guerilla activity was minimal, and the economy was booming, growing on average nearly 5 percent per year under President Alejandro Toledo. From 2001 on, political competition was much freer and fairer than it had been in the 1990s. More to the point, there was a dramatic improvement in constitutionalism and rule of law among political actors. That first decade of the century also saw the remarkable resurrection of a few of Peru's traditional parties, the APRA in particular.

But as the story of this book begins in 1985 Peru, constitutionalism (the extent to which political elites obey rules that effectively constrain their behavior) and party organizational strength (their stability, organizational complexity and linkages with citizens) are at their peak. More precisely, they are at a precipice, teetering, on the verge of falling into the abyss.

Theoretical Framework

I argue in this book that those two processes of decline—the weakening of elite constitutional norms and the disintegration of political party organizations—contributed to the vertiginous rise of executive power in Peru. Presidential power then abated again in the early years of the twenty-first century, the result of a dramatic revitalization of constitutional norms and a modest, partial revival of organized political parties. That is the main story told here: the centrality of constitutionalism and party organizations for explaining change over time in the legislative-executive balance of power in Peru—and, as we shall see in chapter 6, elsewhere in the region as well.

But there is more at stake than just tweaking the existing institution-alist models of executive-legislative relations in Latin America. Analyzing change over time in the case of Peru brings to light the underlying assumptions and the limits of a purely institutionalist approach to presidential strength. Working inductively from a case study of Peru, we can construct a more empirically grounded theoretical approach and in doing so seek out empirically richer responses to the important questions posed by the institutionalist literature. What are the factors that shape the legislative-executive balance of power in new democracies? The answers, I argue, lie beyond the details of the formal "rules of the game" per se.

Let us begin with the deceptively straightforward premise that rules and institutional structures are good predictors of political outcomes only when those rules and structures are adhered to, or at least when they elicit some consistent responses among political actors. I argue in this book that—under largely the same formal rules—constitutional separation of powers and limitations on executive action in Peru were strengthening in the 1980s but then declined precipitously in the 1990s. The power of the president became so much greater than the rules of the game would have suggested, ultimately altering the nature of the regime itself. And though the formal rules changed only modestly in 2000–2001, there was a re-markable return to constitutionality and to elite adherence to the rules, which constrained the executive anew.

In similar fashion, the organizational development of political par-ties and the coherence of the party system declined in the late 1980s, bot-tomed out in the 1990s, and made a modest recovery in the first decade of the twenty-first century. True, many political party organizations in the 1980s tended toward personalistic forms of leadership and were resistant to change and renovation at the highest levels. Yet, as I demonstrate in this book, the parties of the 1980s served to curb executive power in a va-riety of ways. By the 1990s, Peru's traditional parties gave way to a much more fluid, ad hoc form of organizing to contest elections, which greatly exacerbated the imbalance of legislative-executive power in favor of the executive. And in 2000–2006, some traditional party organizations re-covered, but ad hoc electoral movements continued to capture a sizeable portion of votes. The result was an executive with a volatile coalition in a legislature that was unruly, to be sure, but also increasingly able to make laws, represent constituents, and rein in the power of the president.

Looking Ahead

The organization of this book proceeds from a theoretical discussion about institutions to an in-depth case study of change over time in Peru to a broader comparative analysis of Latin America. In chapter 2, I outline current institutionalist theories of presidential power and contrast them with a more inductive, "meta-institutionalist" approach. I argue that the impact of formal constitutional and electoral rules as independent variables is far less important than the larger issue of elite norms of constitutional adherence: the "rule of law" as it applies to intrastate relations. I also introduce the concept of the "electoral movement," an ad hoc and personalistic organization created by a presidential hopeful for the purpose of contesting an election. Within electoral movements, the effects of formal rules that structure intraparty relations—electoral systems and candidate selection processes, for example—can differ appreciably from the impacts of these same rules on more institutionalized political parties. These two variables, constitutionalism and party organizational form, help explain the rise and fall of hyper-presidentialism in Peru.

The content of Peru's constitutions, and the impact of constitutional rules on presidential power, are thus explored in chapter 3. Peru's constitutions and, in particular, the formal lawmaking powers that they granted to the executive branch changed relatively little between 1985 and 2006. What did change, however, was *adherence* to the rules, and expectations of adherence to the rules, among Peru's political elites. Battered by twin crises of economic chaos and escalating political violence, the force of constitutional norms deteriorated from the 1980s to the 1990s and then rapidly recovered after 2000.

This same crisis period brought about dramatic changes in Peru's party system. Political parties had appeared to be growing increasingly strong in the 1980s. The demise of traditional party organizations and the rise of electoral movements in the 1990s reshaped Peru's political arena. In 2001–2006, organized parties made a modest comeback and competed with electoral movements old and new. Change over time within and among these parties and movements is the subject of chapter 4.

Changes in adherence to constitutional norms and in the nature of political party organization in Peru—more than changes to the formal rules of the game—fundamentally altered relations between president and assembly. There was more of a balance of power between legislatures and executives in the 1980s, and again in 2001–2006, than there was in the 1990s. Constitutional limits on executive power were far more effective. Legislative strength was bolstered by the organizational strength of political parties—not just parties of the opposition holding the executive in check, but the governing party itself constraining its president within certain limits of power. Thus, the decline of constitutional norms and organized political parties in the late 1980s and early 1990s led to a vertiginous rise in the power of the president and a reduction in the power of the legislative branch vis-à-vis the executive. Then, after the fall of Fujimori, constitutionalism was revitalized, and organized political parties—especially, but not exclusively, the APRA—returned to compete, somewhat successfully, against electoral movements. Concomitantly, the legislature regained power after 2000, as the executive lost its dominance of institutional politics in Peru. In chapter 5 I more closely examine change over time in this dependent variable for the case of Peru, documenting enormous variations in the legislature's aptitude for representation, lawmaking, and holding government accountable from 1985 to 2006.

In chapter 6 I test the hypotheses I derived from studying the case of Peru by analyzing a larger time-series data set that I constructed for eighteen Latin American countries. Using a variety of statistical techniques, I model the effects of the institutional rules of the game as well as the two "meta-institutional" variables that I drew inductively from my study of Peru—constitutionalism and party organizational form—on the dependent variable, presidential power. While the data do offer some support for institutionalist theory, I find that the "meta-institutional" approach offers more powerful explanations and more robust predictions of executive strength.

Chapter 7 briefly presents my overall conclusions. Institutional power is grounded not only in the formal rules of the political game but, above all, in the propensity of players to follow rules in the first place and in the ways that teams of players organize themselves for the competition. These explanatory variables prove to be powerful tools for understanding presidentialism and the legislative-executive balance of power in Peru and across Latin America.

## 2

Beyond Formal Rules and Institutions
Theorizing Executive and Legislative Powers

Hecha la ley, hecha la trampa.

(When a law is made, a trap is set.)

—Spanish adage

"Hecha la ley, hecha la trampa." This maxim is ubiquitous throughout the Ibero-American world, and its meaning goes beyond literal translation. At its most benign, it suggests that "every rule has a loophole." It also insinuates a profound distrust of laws and institutions, which, in this view, are not tools for promoting the public good but rather traps for ensnaring unsuspecting subjects. What is more, it implies a tension between formal rules and political outcomes, one that has been altered—but not alleviated—by the waves of democratization that have spread across contemporary Latin America.

I begin this chapter by examining the concept of democracy as it relates to questions of power and accountability in legislative-executive relations. I then look at the advances made by institutionalist theory in analyzing new democracies such as those found in Latin America. Finally, I develop an alternate explanation for presidential power in general and the rise and fall of presidential power in Peru in particular. In this alternative model, two other factors—elite norms of constitutional adherence and party organizational forms—mediate the effects of exogenous forces and themselves help shape the legislative-executive balance of power. Consequently, these factors also have an impact on the quality and durability of democracy itself.

Democracy, Delegative Democracy, and Competitive Authoritarianism

What exactly do we mean by democracy? As countless social scientists from Gallie (1956) to Collier, Hidalgo, and Maciuceanu (2006) have told us, the concept of democracy is an essentially contested one. Scholars of newer democracies created typologies of democracies, "democracy with adjectives," that highlight one or more ideal-typical features of the advanced industrialized democracies that are absent or deficient in the systems they examine (Collier and Levitsky 1997). Though many of these typologies were purely descriptive, a few were built on important theoretical and empirical arguments.

In a series of seminal articles, Guillermo O'Donnell provided a particularly useful point of departure for discussing regimes that, while not authoritarian, are not consolidated democracies either (1994a; 1994b; 1996). These regimes do embody the major elements of polyarchy (Dahl 1971). They periodically hold reasonably free and open elections with relatively low barriers to participation and with some genuine political competition. But for O'Donnell, many are "delegative democracies," in which executive officeholders, once elected, are relatively unconstrained by other institutions of government. Rules are not necessarily well established or universally followed by political actors and agents of the state; democratically elected politicians may employ undemocratic practices.[1] The regime also has a plebiscitary quality. Although opposition groups, legislators, and the press may be free to voice criticisms, elections—especially for the executive branch—are virtually the only effective mechanisms for accountability.[2]

A more extreme version of this phenomenon would cross into the category of competitive authoritarianism. In such regimes, "formal democratic institutions are viewed as the principal means of obtaining and exercising political authority," but "incumbents violate the rules so often and to such an extent . . . that the regime fails to meet minimum standards for democracy" (Levitsky and Way 2002, 52). Peru in the 1990s might indeed be considered a competitive authoritarian regime (see McClintock 2006; Carrión 2006). One could argue that such systems, by definition, exclude themselves from the theoretical domain of institutionalism, as we would not expect authoritarian leaders to follow formal rules. Yet even in competitive authoritarian regimes, incumbents "may routinely manipulate formal democratic rules, [but] they are unable to eliminate them or reduce them to a mere façade" (Levitsky and Way 2002, 53). *Some* rules still matter, at least some of the time. By problematizing constitutionalism and examining which rules are followed, when, and by whom, we can address urgent questions about political power across a variety of regime types, democratic and hybrid.

In both delegative democracies and, especially, competitive authoritarian regimes, there tends to be a preponderance of executive power and an absence of countervailing "horizontal accountability" from (O'Donnell 1999a), or "horizontal exchange" with (Moreno, Crisp, and Shugart 2003), other branches of government—particularly the legislature. Kenney (2003b) has convincingly argued for conceptually distinguishing horizontal accountability, separation of powers, and checks and balances. Yet all three may be in short supply in these sorts of hybrid regimes, and all three touch on (though not all are limited to) relations between presidents and assemblies.

My inquiry into concentrations of power in these regimes thus begins with the executive branch and its legislative counterpart. And one of the most basic concepts that political scientists use to analyze the legislative-executive relationship is the distinction between presidential and parliamentary systems of government.

The Presidentialism Debate

Presidential or separation-of-powers systems are those in which voters directly or indirectly choose among candidates for the executive branch by means of popular election. This process is separate from the election of representatives to a legislative assembly, even if the different votes are cast on the same day (and even if selections are made using two separate parts of the same ballot). In parliamentary systems, by contrast, voters elect the

legislature, and that assembly in turn chooses—and may also remove—
the executive.

Some scholars have argued that presidentialism tends to endanger
the quality and stability of democracy while parliamentarism tends to enhance them (Linz 1990; Linz and Valenzuela 1994; Stepan and Skach
1994). Their critiques of presidentialism cluster into three sets of arguments (Shugart and Carey 1992). First, the set length of the president's
term makes it difficult to constitutionally remove an unpopular or ineffective president, which in turn tempts opponents to take extra-constitutional
action. Second, presidentialism is, they argue, majoritarian rather than
consensual or broadly representative.[3] Winners might have received the
support of just a fraction of all voters, but elections still create a "false
sense of popular mandate" for presidents (Blondel and Suárez, 1981).
Winning executive power becomes a zero-sum, high-stakes, winner-take-
all game. Third, presidentialism is characterized by a potentially fractious
dual democratic legitimacy. Both presidents and assemblies are popularly elected and can lay claim to representing "the will of the people."
Since the survival of executives and the survival of legislatures are not mu-
tually dependent, incentives for compromise among these dually legitimate branches are not strong, and a political deadlock may ensue.[4] Direct
presidential election also privileges candidates that have broad popular
appeal, regardless of their level of experience in government.

Yet even critics of presidentialism can agree that popular election
of presidents is highly democratic. It is, arguably, a more efficient and
accountable way of translating voter preferences into the composition
of government (see Horowitz 1990; Strom 1990; Samuels and Shugart
2003). More recent scholarship has also called into question the supposed
downsides of presidentialism, refuted parliamentary systems' record of
stability, and pointed to traits beyond presidentialism versus parliamentarism that better explain regime stability in new democracies (Shugart
and Carey 1992; Mainwaring and Shugart 1997; Power and Gasiorowski
1997; Cheibub 2002a; 2002b; 2007). And aside from a single referendum
in Brazil, no Latin American polity has seriously considered a shift from
presidential to parliamentary government.

Since presidentialism seems to be here to stay in Latin America, understanding this institution better is imperative. The pioneers of institutionalist analysis in the region tended to focus on two sets of formal rules:

the constitutional division of lawmaking power between the legislature and the executive, and the institutional rules and electoral laws that enhance or detract from leaders' control over legislators from their party (Mainwaring and Shugart 1997). I consider each of these sets of variables in turn and preview why the case of Peru might demonstrate the potential pitfalls of viewing legislative-executive relations primarily through the lens of formal institutions.

Rethinking Constitutional Powers

One set of rules that institutionalist scholars point to is the constitutionally delineated lawmaking powers allocated to presidents and legislatures and the way they affect executive strength. These powers are, first, the type and strength of the president's veto powers; second, the availability of different modes of presidential decree authority; and third, the executive's exclusive right to introduce legislation in certain policy areas (Shugart and Carey 1992).[5] Based on the nature of these powers, some authors (e.g., Shugart and Mainwaring 1997) categorize presidents' lawmaking powers as potentially dominant, proactive, reactive, or potentially marginal. Thus, for example, the constitutional prerogatives of Peru's presidency—a weak veto, some authority to rule by executive decree, and exclusive rights to introduce budget legislation and, in some periods, tax legislation—have been labeled "proactive." Yet observing the power wielded by President Fujimori after April 1992, we might say that even "dominant" seems too mild a judgment.

Why the discrepancy between formal rules and actual political practices? Although it may seem obvious, it bears mentioning that even the most thoughtfully crafted constitution will not produce the expected outcomes if that constitution is not generally heeded by political actors and is not treated as a meta-institutional framework, altered only occasionally and according to preestablished rules. Institutionalist metrics can thus fail to capture the real-world force of a president's lawmaking powers. Countries like Peru have lengthy track records of extra-constitutional governance, and taking its constitutions at face value can of course be misleading (Jones 1995a). Yet so can disregarding the impact of rules altogether.

Norms of constitutionalism—adherence to the rules of the political game among political elites—must thus be examined and need to be distinguished from any specific constitutional structures and from the political culture of the society at large. Weber saw the legitimacy of modern states as resting on "the belief in legality, the readiness to conform with rules which are formally correct and have been imposed by accepted procedure" (1947, 131). Constitutionalism, as I deploy it here, is the degree of Weberian "legality" among state actors in particular: the presumption among politicians and bureaucrats that they must follow the rules, and the expectation that others will do likewise, at least most of the time. It is the rule of law in its narrowest sense. As Cameron, Blanaru, and Burns (2006, 4) put it, one of the ways that "constitutions can contribute to the rule of law . . . [is] by requiring that [even] the executive abide by the law."

A norm of any kind is, admittedly, an elusive target for empirical research, revealing itself through behaviors that must be contrasted with some alternate or even counterfactual behavior (Peters 1999, 164). Gauging the strength or weakness of a norm of constitutionalism involves measuring key political actors' adherence to the concrete rules and more abstract precepts laid out in constitutions and other laws that shape how governing is to be done. Examining a country case study over time, as I did for this book, allowed me to use thick description of events, close reading of texts, participant-observation research, and personal access to the actors themselves—particularly useful tools for assessing something as intangible as a norm.

Where do constitutional norms come from? What gives a constitution the power to shape the behavior of elite political actors in particular? Constitutional theorists like Dennis Mueller (1996) and Stephen Holmes (1999) dismiss the notion that constitutions are "only words." As Holmes wrote, "Admittedly, a constitution is merely a piece of paper—but so is a cashier's check for ten million dollars. Pieces of paper do matter—do make grown men [sic] jump—to some extent and under specified conditions. The questions facing the comparative constitutionalist are: when, how, and why?" (ix–x).

Recent developments in rational choice scholarship suggest that making and preserving a constitution is similar in structure to a coordination game (Hardin 1989; 1999). In this view, a constitution is neither an expressions of inherent rights, as theorists of "natural law" hold (Mc-Ilwain 1947; Blaustein and Sigler 1988), nor a meta-contract for society, as theorists of positive law believe (e.g., Wormuth 1949), nor a framework imposed and enforced by a Hobbesian Leviathan. Instead, an effective constitution is better thought of as a coordination point reinforced by the consent of powerful individuals and groups and by widespread societal agreement on the benefits of having rules in general and a specific set of rules in particular (Weingast 1997). In successful constitutional democracies, a social consensus about the rules of the game supports a Pareto-optimal, rule-bound equilibrium. Political elites follow the rules, fearing reprisals from one another (and sometimes the disapproval of the mass public too). But where constitutionalism is less effective, the sovereign authority can operate with impunity or make alliances with some groups in society to oppress other groups.

Historical sequencing reinforces these patterns. In many "old," advanced industrialized democracies, the development of the norms and institutions associated with the rule of law historically preceded the emergence of representative democracy (Zakaria 1997). Conversely, in all but a few of the newer democracies, representative government predated, or developed alongside, the rule of law. As a result, constitutionalism can be weak or inconsistent (Linz and Stepan 1996; O'Donnell 1996). A less optimal, asymmetric equilibrium can emerge instead. Indeed, most of the early constitutions of the fledgling Latin American republics facilitated state collusion with, or capture by, elite sectors of society. These charters were blueprints not for a limited, liberal state but rather for a state that was infrastructurally weak yet afforded elites powerful mechanisms for social control (Mann 1984; Sajó 1999; Pereira 2000). Anxious about high levels of inequality and large lower classes, framers emulated the presidentialism, but not the liberalism, of the U.S. Constitution, allocating significant powers to the state in general and to the executive in particular (Schor n.d., 10).

In the years that followed, elite political actors in most of Latin America did not necessarily view constitutions as long-term frameworks for politics. Constitutions were readily altered by those in power when a change in the rules of the game seemed to be advantageous, if only in the short term. This in itself undermines a constitution's potency as a coordination point for political actors. One of the conditions that make con-

stitutional adherence possible is a concern for the future: the belief that societal groups and political actors are in a long-term systemic relationship,
with many "repeated plays of the game" (Weingast 1997). If the players
believe that they are in a single-shot game, or that some other political
actors or groups may not be around tomorrow, then the Pareto-optimal
equilibrium is unlikely to prevail.[6]

I do not mean to dismiss contemporary constitutionalism in Latin
America as a façade or an outright failure. Far from it. However unevenly
constitutionalism may be developing, it is plain to see that the formal rules
of the game have become more central to Latin American politics than
ever before (Hartlyn and Valenzuela 1998, 7). The constitutions that
accompanied Third Wave democratic transitions effectively expanded
suffrage, promoted political participation, and broadened the language
of rights and freedoms.[7]

Nevertheless, adherence to constitutions cannot be taken for granted,
especially in newer democracies. We must look beyond the details of laws
and constitutions and see the political game as it is understood by the players themselves. Useful theories of presidential strength in Latin America
must be supported by evidence of the actual practices of presidents, legislators, and other state actors. Having strong constitutional norms means
that the document (or its unwritten precepts), and the laws made in accordance with it, comprise the only legitimate framework for political action.
Where constitutionalism is weak or absent, extra-constitutional strategies
are available to political elites (with or without the support of the public
at large).

This, in turn, empowers those actors who command greater material and coercive resources. By contrast, stronger constitutional norms can
constrain even those actors who would otherwise enjoy de facto power.
In presidential systems, de facto power has tended to reside in the executive branch (see Cameron, Blanaru, and Burns 2006, 2). Though this has,
historically, been the case in much of Latin America, it is not bound to
always be so. Weak constitutional norms could (and sometimes do) empower legislatures or courts, armed forces or social movements, as we see
in some of the comparative data analyzed in chapter 6. This is precisely
why the question of constitutionalism is so interesting.

So if we wish to understand the constitutional separation of powers
in newer presidential democracies, we must look more broadly at norms

of constitutionalism and adherence to the formal rules of the political game among actual and aspiring political elites—not just the details of any specific constitutional arrangement. In chapter 3, I assess the decline and subsequent rise of rule-abiding behavior among Peru's political elites. In other words, I study changes not only to constitutions but to constitutional*ism*.

Rethinking Partisan Powers

Constitutional powers are not the only institutional factors shaping executive strength. Another frequently studied set of rules is comprised of "partisan" powers: the president's institutional power relationship with her own party in the legislature (Shugart and Carey 1992; Mainwaring and Shugart 1997). These refer to presidents' and other party leaders' control over legislators—that is, party discipline—which stems in turn from control over legislative candidate selection, control over the order in which candidates are elected off party lists, and whether voters' personal votes for a legislative candidate accrue to the party at large (i.e., whether or not votes are "pooled"). Scholars also point to whether the president's party enjoys a congressional majority and to the institutional factors that shape the odds of achieving such legislative majorities: for example, electoral laws that govern the timing of elections or affect the number of different parties a legislature is likely to have.[8]

The assumption implicit here is that party organizations function according to a certain ideal type, largely based on the historical experiences of parties in Western democracies. There is a growing body of empirical research questioning whether the link between electoral rules and the power that a president or presidential candidate wields vis-à-vis legislators from his party also holds true in newer democracies. A comparative analysis of eleven Latin American systems raised doubts about a linear causal relationship between formal partisan powers and party discipline (Coppedge 2001b). Individual case studies also illustrate alternate causal mechanisms for party discipline. In Costa Rica, both legislators and executives are barred from seeking immediate reelection, but the incoming president controls patronage appointments and future career options for outgoing legislators; party loyalty can still be rewarded (Carey 1997b).

In Mexico, at least during the era of PRI dominance, the "carrot" of future political appointments for term-limited politicians was complemented by another extra-constitutional "stick": the informal yet overwhelming power that presidents exerted as heads of a hegemonic party organization (Weldon 1997). A similar argument could be made about the Colorado party in Paraguay (see Abente 1995) or strong "party machines" in other political systems.

More common in contemporary Latin America are seemingly weak, ad hoc political groups that diverge even further from the ideal-typical parties of the older, Western democracies. If legislators' support for the president is personalistic rather than programmatic, if groups that contest elections have such short time horizons that nomination to a future list of candidates is of secondary importance, if legislators cannot bargain well with presidents from their own parties because they have no autonomy or no political career independent of the president, and if party discipline can take extra-institutional forms, then electoral laws may not be a good indicator of a president's partisan powers. In other words, some political parties are not really parties in the sense presumed by institutionalist theory.

Scholars of comparative party institutionalization have generated a debate in which contributors tend to speak past, rather than to, one another.[9] Some focus on internal party politics, others on a party's relationship to voters or groups in society; some use structural or organizational criteria to assess parties, while others emphasize attitudes, values, and beliefs (Randall and Svåsand 2001). Among Latin Americanists, Dix (1992) borrows Huntington's (1968) criteria for institutionalization—adaptability and longevity, organizational complexity, autonomy, and internal coherence of functions and procedures—to assess the region's parties.[10] Levitsky (1998) differentiates between the institutionalization and routinization of party rules and procedures, on the one hand, and the "infusion of value"—members feeling that the party is something meaningful in its own right—on the other. And in their influential treatment of this question, Mainwaring and Scully (1995) gauge the level of institutionalization in Latin American parties and party systems by looking at four factors: stability in the patterns of party competition, strength and longevity of party-society linkages, degree of legitimacy accorded to parties and elections, and organizational strength of parties.[11]

My analysis incorporates insights from all of these scholars but ultimately centers on this last indicator—organizational strength—and on perspectives that see parties primarily as organizations of politicians. Specifically, I propose that not every group competing for elections should be considered a political party. This of course flies in the face of what is perhaps the most frequently quoted definition of a political party: in Giovanni Sartori's famously minimalist definition, "a party is any political group that presents at elections, and is capable of placing through elections, candidates for public office" (1976, 64). I instead maintain that some forms of organizing for elections are so ad hoc and so personalistic that no subtype of political party, however diminished, captures its key features.

And the scholarly literature does not suffer from a shortage of typologies of political parties. As summarized by Gunther and Diamond (2001), these may be categorized into elite parties, mass-based parties, ethnicity-based parties, electoralist parties, and movement parties—with many different subtypes of each. As an overall trend, electoralist parties are gaining ground lost by mass parties, and parties of *all* types now decreasingly monopolize the channels of access to the state (Schmitter 2001).

Even the oldest parties in the oldest democracies have decreased their focus on organization-building, and candidates and politicians have become more powerful than party bureaucracy insiders (Katz and Mair 1994; 2002; Panebianco 1988). But this same trend has particularly strong implications for new democracies, which are forging party systems under conditions that seem less propitious than past eras for the formation of stable party organizations (Perkins 1996; Van Biezen 2000; Webb and White 2007). In the absence of a dense network of intermediary organizations, and in the presence of new mass-media and polling technologies, the most efficient way for political elites to compete for votes may be to eschew party organizations in favor of more direct, media-intensive ways of connecting with voters.[12]

This tendency is further exaggerated in political systems with direct election of the executive, as is the case in virtually all of Latin America. Parties that run presidential as well as legislative candidates are more engaged in vote-seeking rather than policy-seeking behavior, and tend to develop campaign organizations that are far more focused on presidential elections than on legislative races (Samuels 2002a).

Nevertheless, some groups are so singularly dedicated to the election of a particular executive candidate that they are no longer recognizable as parties. This distinction is more than semantic. In some groups, candidates for the executive in a "presidentialized" party may play the starring role in the show, but in the future the show might go on with another actor in the lead. In others, however, one figure is—and may continue to be—the only actor that really matters. These differences are, I believe, so consequential as to merit their own subtype of political organization.

Gunther and Diamond use the term "personalistic party" (a subtype of electoralist parties) to refer to a loosely organized group whose main goal is the "acquisition or retention of power by party leader" (2001, 11). I prefer the term "electoral movement": an ad hoc group formed to launch the candidacy of a particular individual for a particular election. I use the term "movement" not, as Gunther and Diamond do, to imply a social base of activists or grassroots support for the group, but rather to connote such a group's temporary status and fluid organizational form. Though I develop this concept in detail for the first time here, the term has been previously used in passing by a number of scholars of new democracies (Remington and Smith 1996; Ellner and Hellinger 2003; Tanaka 2006).[13]

Electoral movements differ from modern political parties—not just mass parties, but also, for example, elite-centered cadre parties or electoralist catch-all parties—based on three criteria, in the spirit of V. O. Key (1964).[14] First, parties and electoral movements differ in terms of organizational complexity. Parties will have more layers of bureaucracy, a more sophisticated power structure, more internal rules, and larger paid staffs than electoral movements. Catch-all or even cadre parties will develop enough of an organizational presence to ensure the group's continuity, support its leaders, and manage its candidates. Most importantly, parties will also have some autonomy from the group's top leader, some existence outside of the career of any single aspiring or actual office holder.

Second, party politicians are likely to remain active in politics beyond any one particular electoral period. Electoral movements tend to be organized for a particular set of elections and can rapidly disintegrate afterwards, especially if they do not win the "all-or-nothing" spoils of a given electoral cycle (i.e., the presidency and/or a legislative majority). Because time horizons are short and the group label less valuable, politicians elected from an electoral movement are more prone to abandon their grouping—by party switching or opting for "independent" status—than are those elected from a political party. Likewise, since electoral movements are organized primarily to launch the candidacy of one particular aspirant (often to executive office), if that candidate is successful, he or she may detach from the movement or dominate it completely but will seldom be outlasted by it. In a new twist on Sartori's definition, Patricio Navia has astutely noted that real political parties are more than just solutions to short-term coordination problems. They are, in his words, "groups of office-seeking politicians *who stay together after they lose an election*" (Navia and Saiegh 2001; italics mine). Electoral movements are not.

Third, parties—at least mass parties—will have roots within society in the form of active local party chapters, affiliation with social movements (labor unions, religious groups, etc.), or lasting ties to civil society organizations. Catch-all parties have weaker linkages with the electorate and mobilize almost exclusively around election campaigns. Cadre parties, as their name suggests, consist of a small group of politicians and their backers, with few if any societal linkages and little emphasis on membership rolls as a resource. Electoral movements, while perhaps drawing consistent support from certain demographic sectors, are similarly unmoored from organized social groups, partisan or otherwise. In other words, electoral movements and cadre parties both lack "participatory linkages" (Lawson 1980; Lawson and Merkl 1988).

Do electoral movements, by definition, always empower executives? Not necessarily. It would be just as reasonable to predict that this organizational form would be a source of weakness, not strength. And in fact, in some cases it is, as the comparative data analyzed in chapter 6 indicates. For example, Ecuadorean president Lucio Gutiérrez's electoral movement (the January 21 Patriotic Society Party) was not much help in governing or in keeping him from being run out of office by the legislature. Here I am merely hypothesizing that, on balance, weak parties are more likely to empower the executive. Even in Peru, President Alejandro Toledo's electoral movement was less a source of strength than were President Alberto Fujimori's movements. And as we shall see, this was in part because organized parties returned to the legislative *opposition* and hemmed in Toledo as Fujimori had not been, at least not since 1992.

I tell that story in chapter 4, where I assess the political groups that contested elections in Peru between 1985 and 2006. The main political or-

Table 2.1.   Electoral Movements and Political Parties Compared

	Electoral Movements	Cadre Parties	Catch-All Parties	Mass Parties
Organizational Complexity	Low	Moderate	Moderate/High	High
Stability/Time Horizons	Low	High	High	High
Linkages with Voters and Citizens	Low	Low	Moderate	High

ganizations with which Peru emerged from the authoritarianism of the 1970s were indeed political parties—some cadre, some catch-all, some mass. By the early 1990s they were supplanted by a plethora of groups that were *not* exactly political parties. These were electoral movements aimed at launching the careers of particular personalities, and their organizational dynamics were unlike parties of any kind—cadre, catch-all, or mass. And in 2001–2006, a few of the so-called traditional parties from the 1980s returned to prominence on the opposition benches of the legislature, though they now shared the political arena with electoral movements.

The Dependent Variable: Presidential Power and Legislative-Executive Relations

The goal of this book is to train the light of empirical investigation on particular facets of institutional theory and to test the impact of formal rules on actual presidential power and legislative-executive relations. The meta-institutionalist approach I introduce here also points to two other independent variables—elite-level constitutionalism and party organizational forms—that might help to explain legislative and executive power, illuminating the gaps between constitutional provisions and actual political practices and between ideal-typical political parties and ad hoc electoral movements.

But in order to assess these different approaches, we must first consider how to measure and interpret the balance of power between legislative and executive branches. In methodological terms, we must operationalize our dependent variable. Thinking about what a legislature does or does not do—whether it is strong or weak vis-à-vis the executive—in turn requires us to consider our assumptions and expectations of what the functions of a legislature *should* be.

Legislatures are multipurpose entities, and perspectives on their proper role(s) in the governing process have long fascinated political thinkers.[15] If we aggregate the various views, historical and contemporary, we might conclude that legislatures should perform at least some measure of each of three different functions: lawmaking, accountability, and representation.[16]

With a few exceptions, legislatures in Western Europe and North America have historically been more active in performing these functions than their counterparts in newer democracies.[17] Among presidential systems in particular, the lawmaking prowess of the U.S. Congress is the exception rather than the rule, even as the power of this legislative body has itself waxed and waned over the last two centuries.[18] In Latin America, national legislatures were, through most of the region's republican-era history, stereotyped as feckless façades for executive-dominated systems, regardless of what powers were assigned to them by constitutions (Scott 1966; Mezey 1979).

The "Third Wave" of democratic transitions led scholars to set the bar higher. From the 1980s on, legislatures came to be perceived as sites of more consequential political action, and with this change came new expectations. Scholars of "new" democracies in Latin America and elsewhere placed much of their hope for improved quality of democratic governance squarely on the shoulders of the legislative branch (Close 1995; Needler 1995). They expected Latin American legislatures in newly (re)-established democracies to take an active role in representation, lawmaking, and accountability. Indeed, the health of a democracy has proven to be strongly contingent on the presence of a legislature with the autonomy and capacity to properly exercise these functions (Fish 2006; Fish and Kroenig 2009), while an overly dominant executive branch is thought to imperil the quality of democracy (O'Donnell 1999b).

Yet the rigorous analysis of checks and balances in Latin America is complicated by several factors. First, legislatures may voluntarily delegate away authority to the executive as part of a strategic calculation of interest.[19] Second, legislative and executive branches in much of the region are integrated in ways that do not easily fit our definitions of either a parliamentary or a pure presidential system (Cox and Morgenstern 2002). And in recent years, the Latin American presidency has also become parliamentarized in another way: executives are increasingly subject to impeachment or removal by legislatures (Pérez-Liñan 2005; 2007).

What is more, intragovernmental checks and balances on the executive need not come exclusively from the legislature. In Latin America in recent years, at politically crucial moments, this function has been served by courts, by human rights ombudsmen, and by other bureaucratic actors.[20] However, none of these enjoys the same democratic legitimacy as an elected legislature. The "dual legitimacy" problem that so concerned presidentialism's critics (e.g., Linz 1990) emerges as a potential strength: a popularly elected branch of government that can check the power of a popularly elected executive. Moreover, those other "agencies of restraint" often rely on legislatures to legally empower them, appoint or dismiss their members, and fund their activities (Collier 1999; Moreno, Crisp, and Shugart 2003).

Mindful of the above caveats and complications, the focus of this book remains trained on legislatures as the chief institutional counterweights to executives in Latin America's separation-of-powers systems. Latin American cases vary widely in terms of the strength of legislatures and the nature of legislative-executive relations (Morgenstern and Nacif 2002; Payne, Zovatto, Carrillo Flórez, and Allamand Zavala 2002; Alemán 2004). In Latin America, it is usually the executive who is the "first mover," designing policy and initiating laws and policy. Legislatures have a variety of ways of responding to these initiatives, but even at their most effective they tend to be reactive rather than proactive. What is more, there is a broad range of reactive modes: legislatures can be anywhere from "subservient" to "venal" to "workable" to "recalcitrant" in their relations with the executive (Cox and Morgenstern 2002; Morgenstern 2002, 442). In some countries at some moments, legislatures have real bargaining power over national policy (Morgenstern 2002). In others, legislators at least maintain the capacity to exact side payments or pork-barrel spending from executives in exchange for their support (see Samuels 2002b on Brazil). But many Latin American assemblies have been less able to consistently serve as a check on presidential power.

Less institutionalized legislatures have not tended to attract much attention from scholars of legislative institutions, perhaps because of a scarcity of data or the opacity of political processes. In chapter 5 I help fill this gap in the scholarly literature for one such case. I conduct a comprehensive assessment of change over time in the power of Peru's legislature, as observed in three key functional areas: lawmaking, accountability, and representation.

But before returning to this dependent variable, I first analyze change over time in politicians' adherence to the rules of the game (chapter 3) and in their political party organizations (chapter 4), two factors that were crucial in shaping legislative-executive power relations—in addition to, and often despite, the powers allocated by Peru's constitutions, electoral systems, and formal laws.

3

Constitutions and Constitutionalism in Peru, 1985–2006

In Peru, we have very good laws, but one is missing: a law that

says that all the other laws should be complied with.

—Nicolás de Pierola, President of Peru, 1895–1899[1]

Not the rules themselves, but rather adherence to the rules: that is what Nicolás de Pierola seemed to be lamenting. And ironically, the president's quip rings true precisely for the commanding heights of state power. Since the promulgation of Peru's 1933 Constitution (which set the mold for two subsequent charters), constitutional rule has broken down completely on five separate occasions. Even during ostensibly democratic periods, constitutional norms have been episodically weak or uneven. Constitutions matter—sometimes.

In this chapter, I first consider Peru's twentieth-century historical experience with constitutionalism. I then compare the constitutions of 1979 and 1993, the two constitutions that were in effect in Peru during the period under study, highlighting the extensive similarities between the two documents as well as their limited differences. But the main focus of this chapter is not the constitution itself; it is, instead, *adherence* to the constitution, and to the rules of the game more broadly, among political elites. I demonstrate that practices of constitutionalism changed dramatically at several points in the twenty-one years from 1985 to 2006.

The content of Peru's constitutions changed modestly during this period. In moving from the 1979 charter to the 1993 charter, framers made only minor changes to institutions shaping the balance of lawmaking powers between the legislature and the executive: rules on presidential decree authority, veto power, and the right to exclusive introduction of legislation (Shugart and Carey 1992; Mainwaring and Shugart 1997). Presidential decree authority (at least on paper) *weakened* slightly after 1993, while veto power and exclusive introduction of legislation remained largely unchanged. And another important feature of legislative-executive relations in Peru—making cabinet ministers subject to censure and parliamentary confidence votes—has been in effect since the 1930s.

Other legal and institutional shifts in the 1990s, such as restructuring the judiciary and lifting the prohibition on immediate presidential re-election, did indirectly bolster executive power. However, these "reforms" were initiated by an already-powerful executive and implemented by an already-docile legislature.

What changed most drastically was not so much the content of the constitution but rather constitutional*ism*—constitutionally prescribed and proscribed behavior on the part of politicians, and the norms and expectations surrounding that behavior. These rose, fell, and rose again over the past three decades. If political actors regularly bend or break the rules, then the formal rules of the game will not strongly condition (or predict) the strength or weakness of legislatures and executives. Under such circumstances, disparities emerge between the de jure powers granted by constitutions and the de facto exercise of power.

Norms of constitutionalism have historically not been strong in Latin America in general and have a particularly tumultuous track record in Peru. Yet rule adherence among competing political elites did increase with the 1978 transition to democracy and reached a peak in the mid-1980s. The rule of law—especially among Peru's rulers themselves—then began a phase of decline. As I suggested in chapter 1, the reasons for this decline are several. The late 1980s and early 1990s was a period of unprecedented economic crisis and violent social conflict in Peru. The guerilla wars that had been raging mainly in the rural highlands descended on the capital city with force. Political analysts voiced concerns over the possibility of a military coup as early as 1987. Hyperinflation raged, reaching an annual peak of over 7,000 percent in 1990 (Kenney 2004, 23). Shortages of consumer goods were endemic. These multiple crises contributed directly to a decline in constitutionalism.

Though this downward trend began in the second half of the 1980s, its most egregious manifestations were seen in the 1990s, with devastating effects on the configuration of power between the elected branches of national government. A president's seizing power in a 1992 "self-coup," the widespread use of military and intelligence services for political ends, the evisceration of judicial autonomy, and the strategic plying of massive corruption in order to secure presidential reelection, to name just a few examples — these all greatly strengthened the executive and weakened the legislative branch. After Peru fully emerged from its crises of guerilla insurgency and economic meltdown, regime change in 2000–2001 brought with it the rapid revitalization of constitutional norms. And this return of the rule of law among political elites was indisputably a constraint on the new president, Alejandro Toledo.

Peru's Constitutions

Peru's 1978–1979 Constituent Assembly designed a new constitution very similar to the preceding 1933 charter. The system adopted was presidential, though, again, legislators could censure ministers, forcing their resignation, and also had the power to vote no confidence against the entire cabinet. Moreover, the 1979 Constitution, like its predecessor, provided for a bicameral legislature.

There were, however, some important departures from the 1933 Constitution, spurred on by Peru's more recent historical experiences. The 1979 document decreased the power of the legislature and concomitantly increased the power of the presidency, to avert the paralysis that contributed to the demise of the previous democratic regime. During the 1963–1968 period, seven or eight ministers were censured by the legislature, and three more resigned in anticipation of such a motion (see Kenney 2004, 336–37). Under the new constitution, the threshold for parliamentary censure of ministers was raised substantially, and the president could dissolve Congress and call for new legislative elections in the face of repeated censures.[2] The executive was also granted the exclusive power to introduce budget bills and was given increased decree authority, a veto (albeit a weak one, as I explain below), and other tools with which to break or deter gridlock. Under the 1933 Constitution, legislators could allocate state funds independently of the executive; in the 1979 document, the legislature could not increase expenditures in the budgeting process, and if the legislature refused to approve the budget, it nonetheless automatically passed by decree. The 1979 Constitution also stipulated that the executive may decree "extraordinary economic measures" if it is in the "national interest."

The 1979 charter ultimately met its demise in the *autogolpe* of 1992, an event I detail later in this chapter. It was replaced by a new constitution approved in 1993. As we compare the rule of law in the 1980s, the 1990s, and the first years of the twenty-first century, however, it is critical to understand that the 1979 and 1993 constitutions actually included striking similarities. In particular, the two charters converged around many of the issues that institutionalists point to as indicators of presidential strength. The formal rules directly governing legislative-executive relations differed only slightly. Institutional traits that *did* change included: the size and the number of chambers in the legislature, the design of the constitutional court and oversight agencies, and the rules for presidential reelection. But as we shall see, the impact these changes had on presidential power was due as much to extra-constitutional machinations as to formal constitutional rules.

Comparing the 1979 and 1993 Constitutions

As Table 3.1 indicates, both the 1979 and the 1993 charters created systems with presidents (on a slate with two vice presidents) elected by majority runoff to a five-year term concurrent with the term of the legislature. The rules for the majority runoff in both constitutions stated that, if no presidential candidate wins a majority on the day of the general elections, a second round is held within thirty days after the final results from the first round are officially tallied.[3]

Both constitutions gave a range of political actors the power to introduce legislation (aside from budget bills). Under the 1979 charter, legislation to be voted on in the parliament could be introduced by the president, individual senators and deputies, the Supreme Court, and ministries and state agencies germane to the policy area in question. Under the 1993 charter, legislation could be introduced by the president; by individual

Table 3.1. Comparing Peru's 1979 and 1993 Constitutions
Changes and differences between documents are indicated in boldface.

	1979	1993
Presidency	President and 2 VPs	President and 2 VPs
	Majority runoff	Majority runoff
	5-year term	5-year term
	No immediate reelection	**Max. 2 consecutive terms (to 2000)**
		No immediate reelection (as of Nov. 2000)
Assembly	Concurrent elections;	Concurrent elections;
	bicameral	**unicameral**
	60 Senators, PR, single national district; 180 Deputies, PR, 26 multimember districts	**120-seat Congress, PR, single national district (to 2000), 25 multimember districts (as of 2001)**
		(25% gender quota for each party list instituted in 1997; raised to 30% as of 2001 elections)
Subnational Government	**Elected regional governments;** elected municipal governments	Elected municipal governments; **specifies date of next municipal election and alludes to future elected regional government in transitory dispositions only**
Introduction and Passing of Legislation	President, individual senators and deputies, Supreme Court, and relevant **regional state entities**	President, individual congresspersons, **other branches of the state, autonomous public institutions, municipal governments, professional associations; also, by citizen initiative**
	Passed by simple majority of congresspersons **in each chamber**	Passed by simple majority of congresspersons
	"Organic laws" that structure the state require absolute majority **of both houses.**	"Organic laws" that structure the state require absolute majority.
Legislating Between Chambers	**If legislation is rejected in chamber of origin it cannot be reintroduced in either chamber; if chamber rejects legislation proposed by other chamber, a 2/3 majority by initiating chamber can override veto, but 2/3 majority in opposing chamber can override the veto override.**	N/A

Table 3.1. (cont.)

	1979	1993
Presidential Veto	Full and partial vetoes (*observaciones*); returns all or part of legislation to Congress; override by absolute majority **of both houses**	Full and partial vetoes (*observaciones*); returns all or part of legislation to Congress; override by absolute majority; **as interpreted, president can promulgate non-vetoed parts of law while *observaciones* are considered by Congress**
Exclusive Introduction of Budget Legislation by President	President introduces annual budget. Assembly may neither increase budget nor create items, except for within its own internal budget.	President introduces annual budget. Assembly may neither increase budget nor create items, except for within its own internal budget. **All supplementary credits and transfers of entries initiated by executive, after budget approved, require 2/3 majority.**
Tax Legislation	Tax laws must be passed independent of and prior to budget bill.	Taxes cannot be passed within budget bill itself. **No taxes with specific ends. Assembly can pass special, temporary region-specific taxes by 2/3 majority.**
	Local and regional governments may levy taxes.	Local and regional governments may levy taxes.
Presidential Decree Legislation	Economic and financial decrees (CDA)	Economic and financial decrees (CDA)
	Congress may delegate decree powers (DDA), but decrees are subject to majority approval in Council of Ministers.	Congress may delegate decree powers (DDA), but decrees are subject to majority approval in Council of Ministers.
	Annual budget decreed, if not approved by Congress **by Dec. 15**	Annual budget decreed, if not approved by Congress **by Nov. 30**
Ministerial Appointment	President appoints prime minister and appoints individual ministers proposed and approved by prime minister.	President appoints prime minister and appoints individual ministers proposed and approved by prime minister.
	Congress does not vote on cabinet investiture.	**Prime minister must present cabinet to Congress, within 30 days of appointment, for vote of confidence.**

Table 3.1. (cont.)

	1979	1993
Interpellation of Ministers	15% of **deputies** may introduce motion; 1/3 majority to pass motion.	15% of **Congress** may introduce motion; 1/3 majority to pass motion.
Dismissal of Ministers by Assembly	**Chamber of Deputies** can censure entire Council or individual ministers; censure vote initiated by 25% of **deputies** and approved by absolute majority of **deputies; in final year of term, requires 2/3 majority.**	**Congress** can censure entire Council or individual ministers; censure vote initiated by 25% of **Congress** and approved by absolute majority of **Congress.**
Votes of Confidence	Initiated by individual ministers or by Council of Ministers; confidence or no confidence approved by absolute majority of **deputies** No confidence or censure of president of Council of Ministers is tantamount to censuring entire Council of Ministers, and cabinet is dissolved.	Initiated by individual ministers or by Council of Ministers; confidence or no confidence approved by absolute majority of **Congress** No confidence or censure of president of Council of Ministers is tantamount to censuring entire Council of Ministers, and cabinet is dissolved.
Presidential Dissolution of Assembly	President can dissolve **Chamber of Deputies** if **three or more** Councils of Ministers are censured in their entirety or receive no-confidence votes; new **deputies elected, per current electoral law (within 30 days)**, under same electoral rules; **no more than one dissolution per presidential term**, and not within final year of term or during a state of siege **or state of emergency. Senate cannot be dissolved.**	President can dissolve **Congress** if **two or more** Councils of Ministers are censured in their entirety or receive no-confidence votes; new **Congress elected within four months,** under same electoral rules; **president rules by decree in the interim, but Permanent Commission of Congress maintains its oversight functions;** no dissolution within final year of term or during a state of siege.
Impeachment of President	**Deputies may impeach president; Senate passes judgment, suspends president, refers case to judiciary.** President can only be charged with treason, impeding elections, improperly dissolving Congress, or impeding the functions of Congress, the Electoral Tribunal, or the **Constitutional Tribunal.** President may also be vacated by Congress if physically or morally incapacitated, or for leaving country without legislature's permission.	**Permanent Commission of Congress may impeach president; rest of Congress passes judgment.** President can only be charged with treason, impeding elections, improperly dissolving Congress, or impeding the functions of Congress, the Electoral Tribunal, or **other electoral institutions.** President may also be vacated by Congress if physically or morally incapacitated, or for leaving country without legislature's permission.

Table 3.1. (cont.)

	1979	1993
Emergency Powers	With approval of Council of Ministers, president may declare all or part of nation in state of emergency for up to 60 days (renewable by decree), with some constitutional guarantees suspended; may declare state of siege for 45 days, but renewal requires approval of Congress, and constitutional guarantees not to be suspended may be listed in decree.	With approval of Council of Ministers, president may declare all or part of nation in state of emergency for up to 60 days (renewable by decree), with some constitutional guarantees suspended; may declare state of siege for 45 days, but renewal requires approval of Congress, and constitutional guarantees not to be suspended may be listed in decree.
Constitutional Amendments	May be proposed by president with approval of Council of Ministers, by senators and deputies, **by Supreme Court (on judicial matters)**, or by petition of **50,000 citizens**; must be passed and then ratified, in consecutive **legislative years**, by absolute majorities of both **deputies and senators.**	May be proposed by president with approval of Council of Ministers, by Congress members, or by petition of **0.3% of voting population**; passed by absolute majority in Congress; **ratified by referendum** or by **2/3 of Congress** in two consecutive **legislative sessions.**
Constitutional Courts	**9-member Tribunal chosen (3 each) by Executive, Congress, and Supreme Court** (Ruling of unconstitutionality requires **6/9 majority** of Tribunal) Can be accused by **deputies** and removed by **Senate**, for prosecution by judiciary	7-member Tribunal elected by 2/3 majority of Congress (Ruling of unconstitutionality requires **6/7 majority** of Tribunal) Can be accused by **Permanent Commission** and removed by **Congress**, for prosecution by judiciary
Ombudsman's Office		**Defensoría del Pueblo defends citizens' constitutional rights and supervises public functions and services of state.** **5-year term** **Appointed and dismissed by 2/3 majority of Congress**

Sources: Original texts; Chirinos Soto 1997; Mainwaring and Shugart 1997; Tuesta Soldevilla 1994.

members of Congress; by ministries, state agencies, and autonomous units of government; by state-sanctioned professional associations (the *colegios profesionales*); and—in a wholly new development—by citizen initiative.

In the 1979 document, legislation was passed by a simple majority in each of the two assembly chambers, the Senate and the Chamber of Deputies. ("Organic laws," those that structure state institutions, delineate fundamental rights, or are otherwise mandated by the constitution, required an absolute majority—more than half of all legislators in each of the two chambers.) If legislation was rejected in the chamber in which it originated, the bill could not be reintroduced in either chamber. If one chamber rejected legislation proposed by other chamber, a two-thirds majority by the initiating chamber could override it, but a two-thirds majority in the opposing chamber could override the override and successfully block the legislation. In the 1993 version, legislation still passed by simple majority, with an absolute majority again required to pass organic laws. Since the legislature was now unicameral (see below), the issue of one chamber blocking legislation proposed by the other chamber was no longer relevant.

On the issue of the president's own lawmaking prerogatives, both constitutions seem, on the face of it, to grant the executive relatively modest powers. Shugart (1998) theorizes that constitutions designed by political insiders during fairly rapid regime transitions tend to keep the legislative powers of presidents weak. Peru's recent charters were designed in this sort of strategic environment, with a few crucial differences. The 1979 charter was designed by a diverse group under a "veil of ignorance" (Rawls 1971); framers did not know who would be in power next. As we shall see, in 1993 the identity of the executive was known, and his supporters dominated the constitution-making process. Nonetheless, both constitutions created similar presidential lawmaking powers.

Presidents in Peru had (and have) veto power, including the powerful partial veto: executives could accept part of a proposed piece of legislation while sending other parts back to the assembly for review.[4] However, in both the 1979 and the 1993 constitutions, the assembly could override this veto with just an absolute majority. Therefore, presidential veto in Peru might be considered weak.

This is somewhat counterbalanced by other forms of lawmaking powers. In both documents the power of the president is strong on budgetary matters, for example. The executive is granted exclusive authority to introduce budget legislation. Budgets must be balanced. The legislature may neither increase the budget nor add line items to it, except within the legislature's own budget for operating expenses.[5] If the legislature does not approve the annual budget by a certain date, the president may pass it by decree. In both documents, the president (with the approval of the Council of Ministers) may decree a state of emergency in all or part of the national territory, under which constitutional rights and liberties are suspended. The president also has the power to declare a "state of siege."

In addition to budget bills and emergency powers, the president was also granted a more general capacity to rule by decree. Decree authority can take one of three forms: executive and administrative rule making, delegated decree authority (DDA), or constitutional decree authority (CDA) (Carey and Shugart 1998). Both the 1979 and the 1993 constitutions granted Peru's president all three forms of authority. Executive and administrative rules are those decrees passed by the president, by ministers, or by a state agency for the purpose of implementing an existing law. DDA allows the assembly to grant the executive the power to issue decrees on matters that normally would require legislation passed by that assembly; the scope of the decree authority may be broad or alternatively may be delimited to specific policy issues and/or time periods. CDA grants executives the capacity to issue decrees under certain conditions without explicit delegation on the part of the legislature. Under the 1979 charter the most commonly used—and controversial—CDA stems from Article 211(20), which permitted the executive "to dictate extraordinary measures on economic and financial matters, when so required by the national interest and with the duty to give notice to the Congress" (translated in Schmidt 1998).[6] These decrees stayed in force for up to six months. The Law of Parliamentary Control, passed by Congress in 1992 and derided by Fujimori as one of the "illegal" acts that "forced" him to close Congress, attempted to curtail CDA by requiring cabinet approval of decrees and, most importantly, allowing a joint session of the legislature to suspend these presidential decrees. It is ironic, then, that on paper the 1993 Constitution spawned by that *autogolpe* placed nearly identical limitations on the president's constitutional decree authority.[7] As we shall see in chapter 5, these new limits on decree authority did not prove very effective during the rest of the 1990s, but they gained new life in the 2001–2006 period.

The 1979 and 1993 charters shared other important features of institutional design, such as those covering relations among the cabinet, the president, and the legislature. Both documents set up systems that, while not quite "president-parliamentary" (Shugart and Carey 1992), were not purely presidential either. The president appoints a prime minister of her own choosing and appoints other ministers who must be "proposed and approved" by that prime minister. The president can also dismiss these ministers, with no obligation to consult the legislature. However, the legislature can compel a minister to come to Congress to be questioned. The legislature can also censure ministers—individually or as a cabinet—and force their resignation. In both charters, individual ministers or the entire Council of Ministers can initiate a vote of confidence on their performance, and in both charters the parliamentary censure or vote of no confidence of the prime minister or the entire Council of Ministers results in the dissolution of that cabinet. The president is also given similar powers in both constitutions to dissolve the legislature if cabinets are censured repeatedly (see Table 3.1 for details and vote thresholds).

Presidents accused of a limited number of serious infractions can, on the other hand, be impeached by a majority of the legislature—though the 1979 Constitution more stringently required the additional step of a formal trial by the judicial branch. More controversially, under both constitutions the presidency may be "vacated" if the president is deemed by Congress to be physically or morally incapacitated or if he leaves the country without the legislature's permission.

There are a few minor differences between the two frameworks for presidentialism. But on most counts, the constitutional blueprint for executive power did not change from the 1979 document to the 1993 document. Key provisions such as executive lawmaking powers and cabinet authority were strikingly consistent across the two constitutions.

What *did* differ? There were a few constitutional changes (or subsequent institutional reforms) with the potential to affect presidential power and the relationship between the legislature and the executive. These include adopting provisions for national plebiscites; shifting to a unicameral congress (first with a single national electoral district, later with multiple districts); restructuring the Constitutional Tribunal and state oversight agencies; and allowing immediate presidential reelection. I examine each of these changes in turn.

First, Article 32 of the new constitution opened the door to citizen-led referenda to pass national laws and municipal ordinances or even to reform the constitution itself. In terms of its effect on presidential power, at first blush it would seem to empower the public at large and weaken politicians. However, as we will see, the sort of neopopulist, plebiscitary leadership that Fujimori deployed appealed directly to the public, without the intermediation of political parties or legislative representatives. The executive also had extensive resources that could be (mis)used to influence the voting public on referendum issues. Perhaps Fujimori was more confident in his ability to manipulate public opinion than in his capacity to maintain control over the legislature. Yet on the one occasion that Fujimori was faced with a hostile referendum (on the legality of his third term of office), he used Congress to block it. Thus, the net impact of this rule change on presidential power is not obvious.

Second, in the 1993 Constitution the legislative branch was transformed from a bicameral to a unicameral entity and was significantly reduced in size. Under the 1979 Constitution, the assembly had consisted of a Senate and a Chamber of Deputies. The Senate had sixty seats elected by proportional representation in a single national district, and the Chamber of Deputies had a hundred eighty seats elected by proportional representation in twenty-six (mostly) multimember districts with district magnitudes ranging from 1 to 40 (mean = 6.9). The 1993 Constitution instead created a unicameral hundred-twenty-seat congress elected by proportional representation in what was, according to a vaguely worded transitory provision of the document, to remain a single national district "as long as the decentralization process continues." This shattered a form of linkage between legislators and their constituents, albeit one that was never very strong (see chapter 5). It also eliminated a legislative veto point and obviated bargaining between houses. Finally, reducing the total number of legislators also enabled the Fujimori government to more effectively control the legislature—and, in 2000, attempt to illicitly "purchase" a crucial legislative majority—by means of payoffs to individual members of Congress (see below).

Third, the structure of the judiciary and of constitutional and administrative oversight changed. After Fujimori's 1992 self-coup, a judicial overhaul was implemented in the name of rooting out corruption, but its real effect was to create a judiciary utterly lacking in independence from the government of the day. In similar fashion, Peru's constitutional court appeared, on paper, to be strengthened by the 1993 Constitution — but would be completely neutralized by the late 1990s, as I explain later in this chapter. Previously, the nine-member Tribunal of Constitutional Guarantees created by the 1979 Constitution was appointed by the executive, parliament, and Supreme Court (three members each) and could be removed by Congress for criminal or constitutional infractions. It was able to review the constitutionality of laws and delegated decrees but could not review constitutionally delineated (CDA) decrees.[8] Under the 1993 Constitution, the revamped seven-member Constitutional Tribunal was elected by a two-thirds majority of Congress. Its powers were expanded to include all laws, decrees, rules, and treaties. The 1993 document also recognized new rights and expanded the legal bases on which a law could be judged unconstitutional. However, the formal rules later developed for the tribunal reduced its effectiveness: for a law to be found unconstitutional, a six-sevenths majority of magistrates was required (and magistrates could still be removed by Congress).[9]

The 1993 Constitution also created an ombudsman's office, the Defensoría del Pueblo. Article 162 charges this office with both defending constitutional rights and liberties and supervising the "fulfillment of the duties of state administration and public services to the citizenry." The head of this agency, the *defensor del pueblo,* serves for five years. He or she is elected by, and can only be removed by, a two-thirds majority of Congress. As we shall see, this agency was in fact unique in maintaining the integrity of its oversight functions even in the 1990s — a success that was due not only to the institutional rules that created the post but to extra-institutional factors as well.

Fourth, and perhaps most importantly, the 1993 Constitution allowed immediate presidential reelection. Reelection was a highly controversial issue in Peru (and in much of Latin America) throughout the twentieth century. Previously, not only did Peru's 1933 Constitution prohibit presidents from seeking a second consecutive term of office, but its Article 142 stipulated that the prohibition on reelection could not be subsequently modified or repealed by constitutional amendment or a change in organic law, and that any politician who advocated for such a change could be fired and banned from politics for life.[10] The 1979 Constitution drew on the 1933 Constitution and banned the immediate reelection of the president, though it omitted the harsh second-order sanctions of the 1933 charter. Under the 1979 rules, an elected president had to sit out one presidential term before being eligible to run again for this office; ex-presidents could also enjoy the position of senator-for-life (along with the parliamentary immunity to prosecution that this conferred). As we shall see, in the 1980s Alan García vetted the idea of a constitutional amendment that would have allowed him to run for reelection. But his plan was stymied by opposition in Congress—including some members of his own party.

President Fujimori took a different approach in 1992–1993, shutting down Congress and closely supervising the rewriting of a charter by a new Democratic Constituent Congress (CCD). In fact, some constitutionalists (e.g., Ferrero Costa 1993; García Belaunde 1996) who have analyzed the relatively small number of changes to the 1979 Constitution concluded that the principal reasons for promulgating the 1993 Constitution were to attempt to justify the self-coup ex post facto and, more importantly, to allow the president to run for immediate reelection. While this "reform" put Peru in the company of other Latin American countries (e.g., Argentina, Brazil, Venezuela) that lifted reelection bans in the 1990s, the benefits and risks to democracy continued to be hotly debated among scholars and politicians alike.[11] (In the case of Peru, the eventual verdict was clear: President Fujimori's manifest abuses of power compelled Congress to reinstate the prohibition on immediate presidential election after his departure from politics.)

What most of these changes in formal rules share is a crucial complementarity with informal or illegal tactics. Such tactics were deployed by politicians in the 1980s too, though violations in that era were less brazen and did less damage to the system as a whole. Plebiscites and presidential reelection are powerful tools in the hands of leaders who play fast and loose with the rules and misappropriate state resources to win public support. Judicial safeguards against such abuses are ineffective when buffeted by extra-institutional power.

Overall, comparing just the content of the 1979 and 1993 constitutions, the constraints on the executive should have been roughly the same in the 1980s, the 1990s, and the first decade of the twenty-first century. Yet they were not. The executive was, in fact, far more constrained in the 1980s and the years 2001–2006 than the 1990s. If the 1980s were a decade during which the rules were frequently bent by incumbents, the 1990s were a decade in which these rules were "conveniently" rein-terpreted, rewritten at will, or broken with impunity. The 2001–2006 period, in sharp contrast to the preceding decade, was remarkable for the rapid, if uneven, renewal of rule-abiding behavior at the highest levels of Peruvian politics. The damage done to elite norms of constitutionalism apparently was not permanent. Notwithstanding the challenges posed by the authoritarian legacy of the 1990s and by a cascade of scandals in the Toledo administration, the rule of law during 2001–2006 was rela-tively strong, and the president's power was subject to sharp constraints. As we shall see, these constraints are only partly explained by Toledo's lack of a legislative majority.

Over the twenty-one-year period examined here, fluctuations in presi-dential power were more the result of changes in elite adherence to the rule of law—in the abilities and propensities of politicians and other state actors to follow and enforce the rules of the game—than the minor shifts in the formal rules from the 1979 Constitution to the 1993 Constitution (and its reform in the early twenty-first century). It is to that decline and subsequent revival of constitutionalism in Peru that I now turn.

Norms of Constitutionalism, 1985–1992

The 1985 election of Alan García to the presidency—and the APRA party to a majority in the legislature—was a historic event in Peru. Dur-ing his first term, President García was rightly pilloried by critics as a heavy-handed, overly personalistic leader; some even called him authori-tarian. And the party that backed him had historically had a polarizing effect on Peruvian politics. Yet García's inclinations to flout the rule of the game were also *constrained* by that very same party and were reined in as well by shared expectations of constitutional adherence across party lines. Numerous scholars and politicians have noted, with the benefit of hindsight, that constitutional norms were stronger among political elites in the 1980s than in previous periods—and were far more effective in that decade than in the one that followed (Tanaka 1998; Cameron interview 1998; Pease García interview 1999).

The rule of law among state actors was, to be sure, imperiled in a va-riety of ways during the first García presidency. The judiciary was increas-ingly politicized, state resources were misused for clientelistic purposes, and high-level corruption was endemic (Crabtree 1992; Kenney 2004; Quiroz 2008). In putting down an outbreak of prison riots among incarcerated *senderistas* in three different prisons in 1986, security forces killed more than two hundred prisoners, including at least one hundred who were simply executed in cold blood (Crabtree 1992; CVR 2003). More generally, human rights abuses and targeted assassinations by state security forces and paramilitaries were on the rise again by 1988, after falling in the first few years of the García government (CVR 2003). Civil-military relations were strained, and multiple coup plots imperiled constitutional rule, though none succeeded. The head of the air force is reported to have attempted a coup in 1987 in response to the president's decision to unify the various branches of the military into a single Defense Ministry (Kenney 2004). Another civil-military standoff in 1988, possibly related to a coup or self-coup plot, led to the resignation of pro-APRA general Victor Raúl Silva Tuesta (Kenney 2004; Jara Ladrón interview 1999). And according to one insider, Luis Bedoya of the Popular Christian Party (PPC) was offered the presidency via a "civil-military pact" in 1988–1989, as Peru fell into deep economic and social crisis (Power Manchego interview 2000).

Thus, the period 1985–1990 had its share of intrastate conflict and infractions of the rule of law at the highest levels of government. Nevertheless, while the rules were sometimes broken, constitutionalism still held: the rules were still the rules, and while corruption and abuse tainted the political system, they did not completely subsume it. As we shall see in chapter 5, the legislature took an active role in investigating some of the most egregious abuses by the government, including the prison massacres. What is more, on several potentially game-changing issues the executive was effectively deterred or constrained by the legislature and by other political elites. And in one crucial area of constitutional adherence—the formation of regional governments—the executive took significant (if also opportunistic) measures to make good on the 1979 charter.

What follows is a brief recounting of three key episodes from the 1985–1990 period: García's flirtation with a constitutional reform allowing him to seek immediate reelection, his failed attempt to nationalize Peru's banking system, and his hasty implementation of the regional governments promised by the 1979 Constitution. In each of these episodes, García demonstrated a tendency to try to bend the rules of the game to his advantage and "go it alone" in his decision making. As a leader he had a reputation for impulsivity, and as with any political actor, the temptation to trespass a rather new and fragile set of rules must have been strong. Yet in each case, García's impulses were moderated in favor of upholding the constitutional rules of the game.

The Thwarted Reelection Bid

In the first year after García was swept into power in 1985, his approval ratings as president hovered above 80 percent for almost twelve straight months (Reyna 2000, 55). García's heterodox economic policy initiatives—such as freezing prices and wages, promoting domestic investment, and limiting payments on Peru's foreign debt—enjoyed widespread public support among the masses of lower-class Peruvians and had not yet led to the economic chaos that would characterize the latter half of this term. He also forged close cooperative relations with industrial elites and professional organizations.

During this extended presidential honeymoon, García's closest allies among the APRA legislators initiated congressional debate on a constitutional reform that would have allowed him to run for immediate reelection in 1990. This debate began in March 1986 and continued on and off until July 1988 (Graham 1992). At the time the reelection proposal was first vetted, a poll in the capital city demonstrated that 64.4 percent of *limeños* were in favor of it (Reyna 2000, 84). Among political elites, at first only members of the president's closest circle within the APRA, men like Alfonso Ramos Alva, supported the idea. Later the proposal gained some traction among APRA congressmen such as septuagenarian party stalwart Armando Villanueva, Education Minister Grover Pango, radical faction leader Carlos Roca, and even Prime Minister and Minister of Economy and Finance Luis Alva Castro (who would himself be the APRA presidential candidate in 1990). The initiative also won the support of a small number of independents, including Deputy Héctor Marisca, who sponsored legislation proposing this election "reform." Although García seldom spoke publicly of his reelection, he encouraged these efforts to change the rules (Graham 1992; Reyna 2000).

In the end, however, the scheme was undone by the misgivings of the National Executive Council of his own party. Concerned about García's policy missteps and his heavy-handed style of governing, and thinking of the long-term electoral fate of the party—and their own electoral aspirations, in some cases—the APRA's top political committee repeatedly refused to endorse this constitutional reform (Reyna 2000, 84). The president's approval ratings eventually fell so low—down to 9 percent by January 1989—as to make this ploy much less appealing to fellow *apristas*. But even at the height of García's popularity the idea never gained the broad support of the APRA congressional caucus either. Constitutional strictures and long-term party strategy still had the force to deter presidential power grabs like this one.

The Attempt at Banking System Nationalization

In 1987, as the government's heterodox program of economic reactivation was faltering and the president's poll ratings were beginning to drop, Alan García and a handful of advisers embarked on a radical new economic policy track: to nationalize all domestically owned private banks and financial institutions in Peru. According to some accounts, this initiative was cobbled together in fewer than two weeks, and it involved neither the cabinet (which was notified less than twenty-four hours prior to the public announcement) nor the legislature, nor the APRA party head office—not even the economists of Peru's Central Bank (Graham 1992). In fact, most of the politicians and bureaucrats from García's own party first heard word of the plan in the president's address to Congress on July 28, Peru's independence day. In that speech, he pronounced: "Today, the financial system in Peru is the most powerful instrument of the concentration of economic power, and thus of political power, and is the greatest obstacle to the democratization of production and of surplus accumulation. Therefore, at this moment, I propose to Congress its nationalization, reserving credit, financial and insurance activity for the state" (quoted in Reyna 2000, 121; translation mine).

Because of policies implemented during the Velasco years of the military regime (1968–1975), Peru's banking system was already 80 percent state-owned. Moreover, up until the very moment of the presidential address, the García government had been actively pursuing a corporatist policy-making style, working hand in hand with the same banking and finance groups whose holdings he now planned to expropriate.

Reactions within the APRA party and the government were mixed. Several ministers privately expressed disapproval, while at least two cabinet members (Industry Minister Romero Caro and Fisheries Minister José Labarthe) and two dozen vice ministers and other top bureaucrats resigned in protest. Within the legislature, the Solidarity and Democracy (SODE) group, allied with the APRA, broke their coalition and opposed the measure. Among APRA deputies and senators, only a handful initially broke with party discipline and completely opposed the proposal.[12] Yet many more *aprista*s in Congress, particularly in the Senate, had serious, if quieter, reservations. While the proposal passed easily in the Chamber of Deputies, it was held up in the Senate, where the APRA majority was slimmer and its senators tended to hail from the more conservative wing of the party. Lengthy debates within the upper house pitted a coalition of the APRA and the center-right parties, who argued for moderating the proposal, against the more radical parties of the left, who thought the nationalization did not go far enough.[13] At this stage the Senate modified the measure so that banking conglomerates could protect many of their nonlending institutions from expropriation.

The bank nationalization initiative progressed in fits and starts, alternately lurching forward at the president's insistence only to be restrained by the legislature, by the courts, and by mounting public disapproval of the measure.[14] The heavy-handed tactics of the government also led to the birth and rapid growth of a neoliberal movement in Lima, called Movimiento Libertad, which would launch the presidential campaign of novelist Mario Vargas Llosa in 1989–1990.

In August and September 1987, García allowed the measure to be debated in the legislature while awaiting the results of several judicial proceedings launched by banks in an effort to halt the nationalizations. As the president waited, he stated publicly that he would respect the courts' findings. The government also tacitly allowed the banks to begin selling off a bare majority of shares to their employees as a way of avoiding expropriation. But in October the president and his interior minister launched a physical assault, using the military and the national police to take over central branches of several of Peru's largest banks.[15] A judge ruled that it was unconstitutional to take over these banks while court cases related to the expropriation initiative were still pending. In retaliation, that judge was removed and replaced by a pro-APRA magistrate who reversed the ruling. An emboldened García endorsed another militarized takeover of a bank in early 1988.

Yet by mid-1988, the bank nationalization had been further modified several times within the legislature. Subsequent court rulings on the unconstitutionality of the initiative were respected, and no more independent-minded judges were removed from office. President García's unilateral tactics and his personalistic style of governing pushed the rule of law in Peru to the edge, but constitutionalism prevailed. There were limits that even the president nicknamed Caballo Loco (Crazy Horse) would not or could not trespass.

Regional Governments, Hastily Assembled

The 1979 Constitution created — on paper, at least — an entirely new level of formal politics: elected regional governments. However, the post-transition government of Fernando Belaúnde, 1980–1985, simply shelved the idea. The APRA platform on which Alan García ran in 1985 promised to fix this egregious breach of constitutionality and make regional government a reality.

After the APRA victory, the government's National Planning Institute (INP) was put to work on the technical details of regionalization. Yet the complex political and legislative initiatives that regionalization required were not set into motion until late 1988. Rushing regionalization through Congress in fact required numerous special legislative sessions in the first half of 1989.

With the economy in a tailspin, and political violence increasing dramatically, APRA leaders calculated that it was likely to lose control of the presidency and legislature in 1990 but could dominate some of the new regional governments. This strategy was facilitated by the design of the regions, both geographically and institutionally. Rather than grant each of Peru's departments (the existing subnational divisions) its own regional government, García pushed through a plan that created eleven regions plus the "special zones" of Lima (the capital city) and Callao (the main port that serves the capital). Some regions combined part or all of two or three different departments; several joined a populous, pro-APRA department together with a less populous and less *aprista* area.[16] But local consultations were held to air grievances and incorporate local preferences, and eventually the number of regions grew to seventeen, though internecine fighting over jurisdiction completely paralyzed several.

Like their geographic boundaries, the electoral systems of regional assemblies were also designed at least in part with political gains in mind. There were great incongruities in the ways each region chose the members of its assembly, but almost all combined a minority of directly elected delegates with a majority designated by corporatist representation from different social and economic sectors. The executive branches of each region would then be indirectly elected by these regional assemblies. The APRA had hoped that its local notables in labor, business, agriculture, and professional associations would do well in winning the designated corporatist seats in regional assemblies, giving the party control over many of the newly formed governments and the resources they were to be allocated.

But although this process of endogenous institutional design was (not surprisingly) shaped by the political motivations of the party in power, creating these regional governments nonetheless represented a significant attempt at ameliorating an enormous gap in Peru's adherence to its 1979 Constitution. The measures that made regionalization possible were approved by the legislature according to the rules of the game. The García government consulted local populations on issues of institutional design. The baroque electoral system and gerrymandered boundaries of the regions may have raised suspicions, but when elections were held for those assembly positions chosen directly by voters, the rule of law prevailed, and the vote counts were tallied fairly.[17] In both direct elections and the corporatist selection of delegates, APRA candidates did in fact lose many regional contests to opposition groups in 1989 and 1990.

Overall, then, while critics had plenty of fodder with which to accuse the García government of violating the rule of law, at several key political junctures it was indeed upheld or even enhanced. In attempting to implement, however haphazardly, a democratic regionalization plan, García fulfilled an unkept promise from the 1979 Constitution. And on issues such as presidential reelection and bank nationalization, the president was held in check by constitutional norms and by other political actors.

Not only did the parties of the opposition play a more active role in governing (as we shall see in chapter 5), but García's own APRA party also enforced constitutional norms and served as a check on presidential power.

Even as the lame-duck president tried to free himself from these partisan restraints (as we shall see in chapter 4), other party politicians had longer time horizons—and career aspirations of their own—that led them to rein in García and uphold constitutionalism. Whether political elites upheld the rules of the game out of normative considerations or sheer political survivalism, the end result was clear, at least in those three episodes. The rules of the game, enforced in part by other party politicians, constrained the executive and strengthened the legislature. (I further explore the role of parties—and the president's partisan powers—in chapter 4.) The above analysis indicates that, in the late 1980s, constitutionalism was sorely tested but endured.

Constitutionalism in a Time of Cholera: Divided Government, 1990–1992

Peru's traditional parties and coalitions, as they were, performed poorly in the 1990 elections. APRA had presided over the worst economic crisis and bloodiest internal conflicts of Peru's modern history; and as I explain in chapter 4, the leftist Izquierda Unida (United Left) bloc was torn apart by internal divisions. A runoff for the presidency pitted the famed novelist Mario Vargas Llosa, representing a new center-right, neoliberal coalition (Frente Democrático, or FREDEMO) against Alberto Fujimori, a politically unknown former university rector who, in the months preceding the election, created a makeshift political organization called Cambio-90 (Change '90). Vargas Llosa was a staunch and vocal advocate of neoliberal "shock therapy" for Peru's ailing economy. Fujimori, on the other hand, campaigned on a promise of "no shock," without any clear ideological program or package of economic reforms. Fujimori won the election in the second round of balloting, and the ad hoc group that served as his party was soon severed from an effective role in governing. Moreover, Fujimori's first policy initiative was to rapidly attempt to pull Peru's economy out of its tailspin with a neoliberal economic reform package. This was just the first of many surprises.

The victory of Alberto Fujimori in the 1990 presidential elections—a meteoric rise from the administration building of an agricultural university to the Palace of Pizarro—was, in several ways, a foray into new political territory. To begin with, Peru was experiencing truly divided government for the first time since the 1960s.[18] Fujimori's shaky Cambio-90 electoral movement won just 17.8 percent of seats in the lower house and 22.6 percent of Senate seats. APRA won less than a third of each house of the legislature: 29.4 percent of deputies and 27.4 percent of senators, including outgoing president Alan García (a senator-for life, per the 1979 Constitution). The parties of the FREDEMO coalition together held 34.4 percent of the lower house and 33.9 percent of the upper house. And fractured left coalitions combined to win just 11.1 percent of deputies and 14.5 percent of the Senate (Tuesta Soldevilla 2001; Kenney 2004).

In his first months in office, Fujimori made a deal with the APRA party: he agreed not to investigate any cases of corruption from the García era in exchange for APRA's legislative votes on some key issues. But this mutual support was rather limited, as APRA still opposed many of Fujimori's economic plans. Even if Fujimori could shore up APRA legislative support by suffering the increasingly bad publicity generated by press reports of García-era scandals, the APRA did not control enough seats to give the president a dependable legislative majority. A coalition with left parties was unlikely, given Fujimori's rapid rightward shift. The president's conversion to neoliberalism did gain him the backing of the center-right and right-wing parties, at least for his initial wave of economic reforms. But FREDEMO had dissolved back into its three separate member groups (see chapter 4) and was not a reliable source of disciplined congressional voting. Neither was Cambio-90 itself: some of Fujimori's own members of Congress opposed neoliberal shock therapy. And by 1991, a majority of legislators, cutting across all parties and both legislative chambers, began to oppose the increasingly draconian internal security measures being proposed (Kenney 2004, 174). For the president, coalition-building was thus "fraught with serious, possibly insurmountable obstacles" (Kenney 2004, 106).

Instability in legislative-executive relations was exacerbated by the second breach that the 1990 elections represented: the demise of Peru's traditional parties, which I further explore in chapter 4. Fujimori both capitalized on this trend and contributed to it, building on the growing distrust that Peruvians of all social strata felt for the "political class." He railed against Peru's political system: bureaucrats and judges, party organizations, legislators, and indeed the institutions of modern representative democracy itself (Conaghan 2005). Thus the president denigrated constitutional norms from the bully pulpit of executive office.

A decline in constitutionalism was reflected in other areas too. Over the first fifteen months of his presidency Fujimori passed major counter-insurgency and economic stabilization measures by decree. In November 1991 alone, Fujimori attempted to push through a comprehensive package of 117 new laws that accelerated the privatization of state-owned enterprises, deepened other structural economic reforms, and expanded military powers to combat insurgents. While the decree authority was itself constitutional, the counterinsurgency laws virtually eliminated the rights of persons and property in emergency conflict zones. Congress pushed back against both the economic measures and, in particular, the security-related decrees. By February 1992, sixteen of these decrees had been reversed, and an additional twelve had been modified by congressional legislation. The 1992 Law of Parliamentary Control, which limited the president's constitutional decree authority, was itself of dubious constitutionality, having no concrete basis in the 1979 charter (Kenney 2004; but see also Abad Yupanqui and Peralta 1993). Additionally, in December 1991 the Senate passed a motion stating that the president's recent actions "morally disqualif[ied]" him, which some legislators interpreted as grounds for vacating the presidency per Article 206 of the 1979 Constitution. The motion generated confusion about its meaning and consternation about its consequences among legislators and constitutionalists, and it was narrowly defeated in the Chamber of Deputies. Such questionable use of Article 206 would have been tantamount to a fast-track impeachment (Kenney 2004).

Upbraiding politicians and judges as "corrupt," "venal," and "obstructionist" for failing to take "urgent" measures—and citing the Law of Parliamentary Control as an unconstitutional limitation on presidential power—on April 5, 1992, Fujimori dissolved the Congress, shuttered regional governments, "reorganized" the Supreme Court along with the Constitutional Tribunal and much of the judiciary, and suspended the 1979 Constitution (see Fujimori 1992). The military was called in to control protesting crowds. Numerous notables, including prominent politicians and journalists, were arrested in sweeping attempts to neutralize opposition to this *autogolpe,* or self-coup.

Scholars disagree about the proximate causes of the self-coup of 1992. Many foreign analysts and most Peruvian scholars believe that the *autogolpe* was part of Fujimori's—and the military's—agenda from 1989 or 1990 onwards (see, for example, Planas 1997; Cameron 1997; Lynch 1999).[19] These analysts contend that Fujimori did not genuinely seek to reduce the level of conflict between the executive and the legislature (McClintock 1994). This argument is supported by the fact that negotiations between Prime Minister Alfonso de los Heroes and the parties of the former FREDEMO coalition had reached a successful conclusion by late March 1992, giving Fujimori some medium-term support for his reform programs. The coalition was to be formalized in Congress on April 7 but was preempted by the April 5 *autogolpe*.

Other analysts point instead to the tensions between Fujimori and the legislature (Kenney 1997; 2004; see also Delgado-Guembes 1992; Murakami 2007; inter alia). Fujimori supporters denounced rule-altering tactics on the part of the Congress (e.g., the Law of Parliamentary Control) as the real breach of constitutionalism, an illegal usurpation of the president's constitutional powers. Even if one does not accept this interpretation, Fujimori may still have viewed closing Congress as a matter of political survival. As noted above, even in the absence of an impeachable crime, he could have been ousted by the legislature for "moral incapacity." He could not unilaterally force the constitutional dissolution of the Chamber of Deputies (which required that the deputies first pass three no-confidence motions or censures of entire cabinets).[20] And since Fujimori did not have much of a party organization, running congressional candidates in new elections within thirty days of shutting down the Chamber of Deputies was no guarantee of a larger or more disciplined legislative contingent.

The final straw for Fujimori may have truly been a matter of "domestic politics" in both senses of the phrase. On April 2, 1992, a Senate commission convened in order to investigate allegations of executive corruption in handling foreign aid donations of clothing from Japan — allegations leveled by none other than Fujimori's own wife, First Lady Susana Higuchi de Fujimori. This looked to Fujimori like the beginning of a process that might well end in his removal. Three days later, the nation would be on lockdown (and the First Lady herself, in an acrimonious divorce process, would likewise soon be a virtual prisoner in the presidential palace).

Fujimori would pay no political price for coveting expedient policy-making or political survival over the formal rules of the game. To the contrary: there were few defenders of the constitutional order among political elites willing and able to punish the leader for transgressing the rules as per Weingast's model (1997). The political parties and civil society groups that might have channeled opposition were already weakened. And to the extent that public opinion mattered, polls taken soon after the coup demonstrated widespread support for Fujimori: in Lima, his presidential approval ratings soared to over 80 percent (Palmer 1996). Nationwide support for the *autogolpe* itself proved to be durable as well, with 70 percent backing the coup right after it happened and 59 percent still approving of the "rupture of constitutional rule" one and even two years afterwards (Lynch 1999, 251).

All of these reasons might help explain the coup, but none of them—not even the Law of Parliamentary Control—justifies it in constitutional terms. The 1992 *autogolpe* was the most flagrant breach of constitutionalism in Peru since the end of the military regime in 1978–1980. A two-year period of divided government ended in a manner not unlike the 1963–1968 Belaúnde presidency. Interbranch conflict—acrimonious, but mostly within the boundaries of the constitution—was followed by a breakdown of constitutionalism itself.

Weak Constitutionalism in Peru, 1992–2000

Faced with international disapproval, President Fujimori moved to return to constitutional rule, albeit in a tightly controlled form. New elections for a Democratic Constituent Congress (CCD) were held in November 1992 but were boycotted by most of what used to comprise Peru's political party system. The CCD—dominated by its pro-Fujimori majority—drafted a new constitution that was then narrowly approved in a 1993 national plebiscite. As emphasized above, the new charter did not significantly alter the formal rules for legislative-executive relations. Both constitutions had similar provisions for executive lawmaking powers and partisan control, provisions that, in theory at least, should have fostered only moderate executive strength. Yet the 1992–2000 period was marked by utterly unconstrained presidential power. What most changed was not the constitutional architecture per se, but rather constitutional*ism*.

If the government of President Alan García and the first two years of minority government under President Alberto Fujimori tested the limits of constitutionalism in Peru's fledgling democracy, beginning with the coup the Fujimori regime flagrantly trespassed these limits, rewriting some of the rules of the game to the advantage of the incumbent government and breaking other rules that proved inconvenient. Rule of law among political elites declined precipitously as the executive was strengthened and other branches and levels of government were weakened or destroyed.

Congress was shut down entirely, and when it reopened as a constituent assembly in January 1993, it had been refashioned to better suit President Fujimori's needs (see chapter 5). But this was not the only elected body to be dismantled. Peru's regional governments were replaced with appointed Provisional Councils of Regional Administration (singly, a Consejo Transitorio de Administración Regional, CTAR). Although these administrative entities had the Orwellian title of "provisional," Fujimori never planned to phase them out, and they ran a host of state programs from 1992 until a year after he left office. The CTARs were invariably headed by close Fujimori allies, many of them former military officers, and with little administrative transparency they could not be effectively held accountable by the legislature (see chapter 5; Alvarado Contreras interview 1999; *Caretas,* Sept. 23, 1999).

The *autogolpe* also marked the initiation of a series of highly politicized and frequently unconstitutional judicial "reforms." Jurisdiction over wide swaths of criminal law—anything related to terrorism, broadly defined—was transferred from civilian to military courts. What is more, the coup itself involved the temporary closure of all of the nation's courts and the firing of hundreds of judges, including those of the Supreme Court and Superior Courts. In replacing these judges, the Fujimori government attended to narrowly political considerations rather than the genuine reform of a much-criticized judicial system (Landa 2001; McFarland Sánchez Moreno 2001). Replacements tended to be chosen from among the minority of lawyers who were sympathetic to the self-coup. New judges were also denied the job security that might have made possible a more autonomous judiciary. As late as 1997, only 403 (26 percent) of the country's 1,473 judges had tenure. The rest were granted less secure statuses such as "substitute" (59 percent) and "provisional" (15 percent), both of which required annual renewal of contracts. This ensured that legions of judges across numerous levels and jurisdictions were pliant and easily pressured by the government. Moreover, politically sensitive cases often "coincidentally" landed in the courtrooms of pro-government or untenured judges. Even in the Supreme Court only 16 of 32 justices had job security (Landa 2001).

The 1993 Constitution, on paper, held great promise for increasing the autonomy of Peru's judiciary relative to the 1979 Constitution and the practices of the 1980s (Schmidt 1998). The new charter gave control over the appointment and sanctioning of judges to the National Magistrates' Council (Consejo Nacional de la Magistratura, CNM), an autonomous collegial body of lawyers, judges, prosecutors, and legal educators set up by the state. Yet this promise went unrealized, largely as a result of political machinations. Responsibility for the overall judicial reform process was put in the hands of a former navy officer closely allied with Fujimori, rather than a retired judge or prominent legal scholar. At the same time, less autonomous entities, such as an ad hoc Magistrates' Court of Honor and the Judicial Coordination Council, both handpicked by the government, took over the work of the CNM. The power of the CNM was further curtailed by the fact that it was effectively prevented from appointing any more full-time judges. This was because the National Magistrates' Academy, responsible for training and certifying judges, remained under the control of the Executive Commission of the Judiciary, another proxy for the executive branch. Finally, in 1998, what little power the CNM wielded was eliminated by congressional legislation, precipitating the resignation of all seven of its members (McFarland Sánchez Moreno 2001; Landa 2001). One consequence of this unconstitutional political maneuvering: the World Bank suspended a $22.5 million loan for promoting judicial reform (*Caretas,* March 26, 1998).

After the approval of the 1993 Constitution by plebiscite, Peruvians went to the polls in 1995 and reelected President Fujimori along with a solid legislative majority. Election day was not entirely free of fraud.[21] The weeks and months leading up to the election were even more emblematic of the weak hold that the rule of law had on the regime. The president distributed campaign items paid for with state funds (Conaghan 2005). He also inaugurated a record number of public works—schools, water filtration plants, bridges, and other projects—in the months leading up to the elections. When the National Elections Tribunal attempted to curb these activities during the campaign period, the president ignored the tribunal and invoked his role as provider of order and progress in Peru, stating that "the country cannot be held back by an electoral conjuncture" (*Caretas,* Dec. 7, 1994). In January 1995 the CCD passed a set of rules that allowed the president to continue to tour the country, essentially campaigning with state funds and relying on the military and regional bureaucracies for the logistics of his campaign organization. A clause forbidding the president from engaging in explicit "political proselytizing" during these events went largely unenforced.[22]

Notwithstanding these flaws, independent election observers and even critics of the government agreed that the results showed a victory for Fujimori and a majority for *fujimoristas* in Congress. The problem for constitutionalism was not so much the 1995 elections as the fact that the resulting congressional majority was willing to rubber-stamp executive initiatives of dubious legality.

During Fujimori's second term in office, such initiatives were increasingly directed at ensuring a constitutionally questionable third term in office. In August 1996, the pro-Fujimori majority in Congress passed Law 26657, the "Law of Authentic Interpretation." This piece of legislation essentially stated that the article concerning presidential reelection in the 1993 Constitution was not to be applied retroactively. Thus, the president's first term would not count toward the two consecutive term limit stipulated by that constitution, since he was initially elected under the 1979 Constitution. The Lima Bar Association petitioned the Constitutional Tribunal to declare the law unconstitutional. As the tribunal considered the case, several of the more independent-minded magistrates were subjected to intimidation and scare tactics.[23] When the tribunal did issue its final decision, three members, with the other four abstaining, ruled not that the reelection law was unconstitutional (which would have required a six-sevenths majority) but that it was "inapplicable" to the case of this particular president.[24] Though the concept of inapplicability is well developed in Peruvian and other Latin American jurisprudence, it was not clear that this ruling was in accordance with the organic law that governs the tribunal's workings. And so, accusing the three justices of presenting a mere position paper as a judgment of the full court, Fujimori's allies in Congress voted to impeach them (Inter-American Court of Human Rights 1999). The impeachment process caused a fourth judge, the tribunal's president, Ricardo Nugent, to resign—though Congress could not or would not name a replacement, effectively forcing Nugent to continue to serve.[25] Congress then changed the organic law so that, with four members, the tribunal would continue to function but could no longer issue rulings on the constitutionality of laws (Conaghan 2005).

The National Elections Tribunal, the judicial arm of Peru's electoral agencies, was also the target of manipulation. In December 1997, Congress voted to allow all magistrates and prosecutors—whose respective associations elect two of the five members of the tribunal—to vote in elections for that electoral agency, regardless of whether they had tenure or were merely appointed provisionally (and were thus more susceptible to political pressure). This law was complemented in May 1998 by another dubious change in the rules of the game, requiring a four-fifths majority of the National Elections Tribunal to issue legal challenges on electoral issues.

In exerting their influence over the Constitutional Tribunal and the National Elections Tribunal, Fujimori and his legislative majority were operating in a gray area of legality. Changes to rules and personnel were always in the service of the incumbent president, and cumulatively they had a deleterious effect on the culture of constitutionalism among political actors. These changes were usually undertaken according to the letter of the law, at least as the presidents' supporters interpreted it. Nevertheless, they may still have violated higher-order principles such as those spelled out in Article 3 of the 1993 Constitution: "sovereignty of the people, the democratic rule of law and the republican form of government."

A somewhat clearer violation of the rules of the game can be found in the government's response to civil society groups' attempts to hold a referendum on Fujimori's reelection. The 1993 Constitution afforded citizens a mechanism for weighing in directly on this issue: a plebiscite initiated by citizen petition. But as signatures for this ballot measure were being collected in late 1996, Congress passed a law requiring that proposed referenda additionally be approved by at least two-fifths of the legislature.[26] This law—which, like the "Law of Authentic Interpretation" itself, seemingly altered the constitution—was passed by a simple majority in just one legislative session, contrary to the prescribed procedure for constitutional reform. The result was that the referendum initiative, which had the support of over 70 percent of all Peruvians and was endorsed with the signatures of almost 1.5 million citizens,[27] died an unnatural death at the hands of the legislature in August 1998.

In addition to these quasi-legal maneuverings, the Fujimori government deployed the National Intelligence Service (SIN) as an instrument of political "dirty tricks." The government and the SIN heightened their efforts to control the media from 1997 to 2000. By means of bribery and blackmail, the SIN increasingly dictated the content of nearly all broadcast television stations as well as numerous radio stations, newspapers, and magazines, including both "serious" publications and the ubiquitous tabloid press. In one prominent case, Baruch Ivcher, an Israel-born entrepreneur, was smeared in the press and then actually stripped of his Peruvian citizenship after the television station he co-owned broadcast investigative reports critical of the president. As a noncitizen, Ivcher could no longer keep his ownership stake in Canal 2, one of Lima's most-watched channels.

In addition to high-profile cases like this one, hundreds of lesser known journalists as well as opposition politicians and leaders of civil society groups were spied on, verbally harassed, physically assaulted, or threatened with death. When some of their cases were taken to the Inter-American Court of Justice in San José, Costa Rica, Fujimori unilaterally withdrew his country from this international body, citing as a pretext the court's ruling on an unrelated case involving Chilean citizens convicted of terrorism in Peru. The absence of a functioning Constitutional Tribunal, the general weakness and dependence of the judiciary, and the abrupt (and legally dubious[28]) self-extrication of Peru from the jurisdiction of the Inter-American Court system: all of these yawning gaps in the rule of law left little legal recourse for opponents of the regime.

While specific violations may have been covert, the government's general flouting of constitutionalism was not. To the contrary: the inability of the rule of law to constrain the president and his government was broadly acknowledged in late-1990s Peru, not only by critics but by supporters as well. In an April 1998 survey in Lima, a majority (82.5 percent) of respondents—and even a majority (68.4 percent) of those who approved of President Fujimori—said that laws were not respected but rather were remade to suit the government of the day (IMASEN 1998).

In this context of disregard for constitutional norms by the ruling political actors, the 2000 elections were born under a bad sign. They also attracted the attention of international organizations and foreign election observers, including an observer mission from the Organization of American States with unprecedented autonomy and a mandate to inform the public of its findings on an ongoing basis. Two U.S.-based NGOs, the National Democratic Institute and the Carter Center, also established a long-term observer presence.[29]

As the election date drew near, the rule of law among Peru's political elites declined further. Most of the country's mass media outlets increasingly displayed a striking bias in favor of the incumbent and engaged in slander and disinformation about opposition candidates and domestic and international observers. This media support for Fujimori was achieved through an elaborate network of corruption run by the National Intelligence Service, engaging in bribery, blackmail, trumped-up legal charges, and hostile corporate takeovers. Opposition politicians and civil society groups were targeted for harassment, intimidation, and sabotage. The courts and electoral authorities were indifferent or hostile to complaints about these tactics and were, without fail, extremely accommodating to Fujimori and his new Peru 2000 electoral movement.

As the campaign wore on, the military and intelligence services' involvement in organizing campaign events on behalf of President Fujimori's reelection became ever more obvious. Civilian bureaucrats manipulated government aid programs and used funds from state coffers in a concerted effort to sway the election results. The national tax service was used punitively against political opponents and public figures who questioned the reelection bid, auditing the personal accounts and businesses of those who dared to oppose the president. And *fujimorista* politicians coordinated a massive signature fraud, illegally using thousands of official documents from the state electoral authorities in order to fabricate a registration petition for Peru 2000.

The only state entity that had any success at constraining the executive without facing retribution was the Ombudsman's Office, the Defensoría del Pueblo. The *defensor*, Jorge Santistevan de Noriega, survived in part because of the high vote threshold required to remove him (two-thirds of Congress), in part because of the high level of public support he enjoyed in Peru (despite smear campaigns in the media), and in part because of his dense network of contacts with powerful diplomats, international organizations, and foreign aid donors in North America and Western Europe.

When the first round of the elections took place in April 2000, the vote tabulation was fraught with delays and (in the congressional contest at least) mathematically impossible changes in candidates' vote totals. Subsequent analysis has downplayed the degree of outright fraud in the presidential contest itself (Schmidt 2005). But the months and years of illegal maneuverings leading up to the elections had made even the most neutral observers highly suspicious.[30] On election day, independent parallel vote tabulations by the OAS observer mission and by the highly professional Peruvian NGO Transparencia predicted that no presidential candidate would win a first-round majority.[31] And when the official results came in, they indeed gave Fujimori's coalition fifty-two of a hundred twenty legislative seats and just under 50 percent in the presidential contest, necessitating a runoff election between Fujimori and opposition presidential candidate Alejandro Toledo.

But holding a second round under the same unfair conditions as the first did not satisfy opposition candidates and pro-democracy groups. Alejandro Toledo withdrew from the second-round race, protesting the grossly uneven playing field. Domestic and international observer groups declined to continue monitoring the contest. The presidential runoff elections held on May 28, 2000, thus had fewer than two candidates and no neutral observers.

Within weeks of the elections, before the new term had even begun, a sufficient mass of incoming members of Congress had been "convinced"—by means of cash payments—to switch to Fujimori's coalition. The president was thus assured of a legislative majority. The Organization of American States, highly critical of the elections, would impose (and itself coordinate) a political reform process for Peru but could not reverse the results of the illegitimate election itself. Fujimori in this way maintained his grip on the presidency of this increasingly polarized country—or so he thought.

The Rule of Law Returns to the Heights of Power, 2000–2006

The Fujimori government did not make it far into its ill-gotten third term. In late August 2000, Peru's intelligence service claimed to have uncovered an arms trafficking operation that shipped weapons from Jordan to Colombia's FARC guerillas. Based on the Jordanians' reaction, however, it became clear that the upper echelons of Peru's military and intelligence services had themselves been involved in the transactions (Conaghan 2005). Then, on September 14, 2000, a cable news network aired the first in what would be a long series of videos that confirmed critics' worst fears about the regime and put its mafia-like tactics on display for all to see. The videos showed intelligence advisor Vladimiro Montesinos engaged in bribery and corruption with members of Congress, other politicians and candidates, top-level military officers, and media moguls, among others.[32]

Buffeted by these scandals, and with its legitimacy already weakened in the wake of the 2000 elections, the regime imploded. On September 16, 2000, President Fujimori announced that the intelligence services would be dismantled and called for new elections in April 2001, elections in which Fujimori would not run. This pledge proved unnecessary. In the next two months, both Fujimori and his shadowy intelligence chief, Vladimiro Montesinos, would flee Peru. Montesinos, in fact, fled twice; after his first exit on September 23, he spent a month trying to finagle political exile status in Panama but was denied and returned to Peru. Fujimori put on an elaborately staged "manhunt" for his erstwhile right-hand man. Then the president and several ministers issued a secret decree to fund a non-existent military operation targeting FARC guerillas allegedly on Peruvian soil and siphoned off $15 million to pay Montesinos to leave for good on October 29 (Paéz 2009). That same day, Colonel Ollanta Humala led a brief military uprising in the southern highlands mining town of Toque-pala. The rebellion was ostensibly launched against Fujimori, but Monte-sinos later claimed that it was in fact a plot to help *him* escape from Peru (*New York Times,* May 21, 2006).

And, finally, Fujimori himself fled. As scandal cascaded into scandal several Peru 2000 legislators left the group, internal divisions flared up, and the president's legislative caucus began to disintegrate. Fearing his imminent removal from power once opposition groups gained control of Congress, Fujimori traveled to Japan following an economic summit in Brunei and faxed his letter of resignation from a Tokyo hotel on November 20, 2000. Congress, with its new balance of forces, refused to accept the letter and instead "vacated" the office based on the president's "moral incapacity." Fujimori's first vice president, Francisco Tudela, had already resigned, but his resignation had not yet been ratified by Congress, which was now led by the opposition. The second vice president, Ricardo Már-quez, was initially ready to step in but decided instead to resign in the face of clear opposition from the legislature—which could have imme-diately removed *him* from office too, had he ascended to the presidency. This left the new president of Congress selected just days earlier, Valentín Paniagua, a long-standing member of the Acción Popular party, next in line for the presidency. On November 22, 2000, Paniagua was sworn in as interim president of the republic.

The final months of the Fujimori regime had severely battered constitutionalism. With the election debacle and the ensuing scandals, resignations, and flights from justice, state authority itself seemed to be sinking. But from the depths of corruption and illegality to which Peru had plummeted by 2000, Paniagua's interim presidency reached a high-water mark of good governance in just five months. The new national unity government made decisions by consensus votes of most major political groups. Even before Paniagua took over the executive branch, Congress had begun repairing some of the most egregious breaches of the previous decade. The Constitutional Tribunal was rendered functional once again, as the resolutions that deposed its three dissident members were repealed.[33] Congress changed Article 112 of the 1993 Constitution to once again ban immediate presidential reelection. It also modified the Organic Law of Elections not only to strengthen Peru's electoral authorities and safeguard the political neutrality of the state in electoral processes but also to create new state-funded television spots for presidential and legislative candidates (the *franja electoral*) and to set up a new legal framework and administrative rules (who could compete, how early parties had to register, etc.) for presidential and legislative elections to be held in April 2001.

This extraordinary electoral process took Peru into uncharted political territory, but it was guided by existing constitutional procedures. New presidential elections were appropriate under the succession clauses of Article 115 of the 1993 Constitution. Banning presidential reelection anew and shortening the president's and legislators' terms of office to just one year were passed as a constitutional reform package (Law 27365) by two successive, if artfully scheduled, legislatures, in accordance with Article 206.[34]

Once Paniagua was at the helm, other changes were instituted. Congress remained a single chamber, per the 1993 Constitution, but was divided into twenty-five electoral districts.[35] (The system of proportional representation with an optional double preferential vote was maintained.[36]) Perhaps most boldly, the new government also began weeding out *fujimontesinista* elements—allies of Fujimori and Montesinos—from the military, the intelligence service, and the national bureaucracy as a whole.

The president and Congress worked together to ensure that the 2001 elections would be run "by the book," despite the pressing timetable and the political shambles they had inherited. The elections were not perfect, of course. There were problems distributing ballots in a few parts of the country. Some sectors of the popular press remained financially beholden to corrupting interests. And notwithstanding the fact that seven major parties had signed a "Civic Pact" to promote clean elections, the campaigns brought out a fair amount of mudslinging and scandalmongering. Nonetheless, the 2001 elections were as clean as the 2000 elections were tainted—which is to say, substantially.

The winner of the 2001 presidential elections, after a June 3 runoff, was none other than Fujimori's chief challenger from the year before, Alejandro Toledo. His Perú Posible electoral movement won forty-seven of a hundred twenty seats in congressional elections (see chapters 4 and 5). In terms of constitutionalism and the rule of law, the five years during which he served as president were notable both for their contrast to the totalizing corruption and mafia-like power structure among political elites under Fujimori and, ironically, for the perennial embroilment of President Toledo in middling personal and political scandals. Overall, with many fits and starts, the rebound of constitutionalism that began during the transitional government continued to consolidate under Toledo.

As in previous eras examined in this chapter, such changes (this time positive) had less to do with the rules themselves and more to do with the propensity for rule-abiding behavior among political elites. Taylor (2007, 21) attributes this in part to the cooperation and coordination practiced by anti-Fujimori politicians as they abruptly found themselves in charge in late 2000 and steered the ship of state toward new elections in 2001. Another explanation would be that public opinion had shifted in reaction to the flagrant violations depicted in the *vladivideos* that were aired day after day. Leadership may have mattered too: Paniagua set the tone with a leadership style that emphasized transparency and adherence to democratic rules. And for Toledo, opposing the practices of the Fujimori regime was his political "brand," the signature issue on which he ran in 2000 and won in 2001. Overall, a change in elite political culture was palpable and cannot be attributed solely or even primarily to formal rules, though some rules were indeed modified in the early years of the twenty-first century. (Most significant of these was the renewed ban on immediate presidential reelection.)

Under Toledo, a comprehensive constitutional reform process was initiated in 2002. The process itself reflected a new decentralization and democratic openness in Peruvian politics; for example, public forums on constitutional reform were held in various regions of the country. An immense amount of effort on the part of members of Congress went into crafting this reform package, at the cost of ignoring other pressing legislative issues (*El Comercio,* July 16, 2006). The vast majority of the articles proposed by the Constitutional Committee of Congress were approved— nearly unanimously—by the full Congress as of January 2003.[37] However, as the cooperative spirit of the interim government faded and Toledo grew more unpopular, support from opposition groups flagged, and the omnibus reform package was shelved in favor of piecemeal reforms to organic laws and other rules.[38]

While the formal rules of the political game changed only modestly, adherence to the rules improved dramatically. The regeneration of constitutionalism under Paniagua and Toledo took many forms, but one that grabbed the lion's share of media attention was their attempts to undo the damage and punish the misdeeds of the prior regime. After months of collaborative police work across international boundaries, Montesinos was captured in Caracas, Venezuela, in June 2001 and deported back to Peru in the final weeks of the Paniagua government. President Toledo and the legislature then set up five "mega-commissions" with a combined budget of almost 7 million soles (roughly $2 million) to investigate the network of corruption created by Fujimori and Montesinos. Special prosecutor José Ugaz and anticorruption judge Saul Peña Farfán, tasked with bringing Montesinos and others to justice, became minor celebrities in Peru and beyond. Ugaz ferreted out multimillion-dollar foreign bank accounts and links with a rogues' gallery of international arms dealers and drug traffickers.

Ultimately, much of the *fujimontesinista* mafia would be unraveled and hundreds of accomplices—including members of Congress, former ministers, and many other high-level politicians and bureaucrats—would be charged with corruption and abuse of power. Right-wing groups in Congress sought leniency in the sentencing of some convicted military officers, but the courts generally opted for by-the-book sentencing (Alvarado Dodero interview 2007). Bringing the former president himself to justice would take longer: diplomatic efforts to have Japan extradite Fujimori were unsuccessful, and authorities of Peru's Foreign Ministry missed an opportunity to nab him themselves when he brazenly strolled into their consular offices in Tokyo in May 2005 to renew his national identity card (agenciaperu.com, May 18, 2005).

While many prominent political players from the 1990s were brought to justice, it took more time to weed out lower-level corruption and less prominent vestiges of the *fujimontesinista* mafia. The authoritarian values and the politicized use of state resources that flourished under Fujimori were stubbornly rooted in government bureaucracies. Nevertheless, transparency improved markedly in 2001–2006, so while public perceptions of corruption increased, the actual amount of corruption, especially high-level corruption, was likely decreasing (Ausland and Tolmos 2005; Solari de la Fuente interview 2007).[39]

Opacity and suspicion lingered in other areas too. The widespread use of electronic surveillance in the late 1990s created a culture of justifiable paranoia within Peru's political class. In 2001 the APRA party complained that it was being spied on by the executive ("La Oreja," *Caretas,* Dec. 20, 2001). In 2003 President Toledo himself had his phone tapped and his recorded conversation broadcast on television ("Del Chupón," *Caretas,* Aug. 29, 2003).

One of the most high-profile steps that Peru took toward transparency and transitional justice was the creation of, and support for, a Truth and Reconciliation Commission (Comisión de la Verdad y Reconciliación, CVR). First proposed by Paniagua and then immediately implemented by Toledo in September 2001, the CVR spent nearly two years interviewing more than fifteen thousand Peruvians in more than five hundred locations around the country, in an effort to uncover the origins, events, and consequences of Peru's armed conflict in the 1980s and '90s. The commissioners found that the Shining Path had the most blood on its hands, having caused 54 percent of violent deaths. But the Peruvian state did not escape scrutiny. Military and police forces were held responsible for 32 percent of fatalities; the Belaúnde, García, and especially Fujimori governments were each excoriated for a variety of crimes and abuses (CVR 2003). For this the CVR itself came in for some harsh criticism, mainly from the political right.[40] Nonetheless, the commission had the full support of the state, and its work won the approval of a majority of Peruvians (Apoyo Opinion y Mercado 2003). Though this entity was not contemplated by the constitution, by giving citizens a voice and holding the state accountable for its past actions—even during a violent insurgency—the CVR contributed to rebuilding a culture of constitutionalism among political elites.

The Toledo government also attempted to reform the police, military, and intelligence services. In November 2001 the president created two special commissions to restructure the military and the national police in ways more amenable to democratic governance. The SIN was immediately replaced by the Consejo Nacional de Inteligencia, or CNI, a much smaller entity with more oversight and less bureaucratic and financial autonomy than its nefarious predecessor (LAN-RA, Nov. 6, 2001). But success in reorganizing the intelligence services proved elusive for Toledo. The job of heading the CNI was a revolving door: eight different people (one appointed twice) served in the three years of the agency's existence (Serrano Torres 2006).[41] Then Toledo surprised Congress (and many ministers too) by deciding to close the CNI and start anew with another institutional template (BBC News, March 23, 2004).

For several months thereafter it was unclear that Peru even had a functioning intelligence agency (LAN-RA, Jan. 11, 2005). One of Toledo's more reputable former CNI chiefs (and twice-appointed former interior minister), Fernando Rospigliosi, noted in an interview that the CNI had been utterly useless since it was created (*Cosas,* March 2005). The government indeed seemed caught by surprise when Sendero Luminoso guerillas briefly took seventy-one workers from the Camisea gas project hostage in June 2003. After the incident ended, areas of suspected Sendero activity remained under emergency rule, reminiscent of the 1980s and '90s (BBC News, June 26, 2003). Though he curbed the powers of an intelligence service run amok, Toledo struggled to balance pressing concerns about security and governance with respect for constitutional rights and freedoms.

Rebuilding other institutions crucial for justice and democracy was also challenging. After the recomposed Constitutional Tribunal (TC) voted in March 2002 to release Luis Bedoya de Vivanco, an imprisoned former mayor who had been in the pay of Montesinos, an angered Congress turned what should have been a vote to replace (on schedule) four members of the TC into a full renovation of the entire tribunal. Two months later, however, they rehired the three justices whose terms were still in question (those who had been previously impeached by the *fujimorista* legislature in 1998) and appointed four new justices (LAN-RA, March 2002; Alva Orlandini interview 2005; *El Peruano,* May 31, 2002).[42]

Notwithstanding this disruptive episode, the TC was fully functional again by May 31, 2002, and more productive than ever by the end of the year (TC 2004). It also reached a far wider range of citizens by scheduling special sessions outside of Lima: in 2002–2005, the tribunal held 128 such sessions in 102 different provinces (Alva Orlandini interview 2005).

In 2003 the TC ruled that a number of Fujimori-era judicial practices, such as military tribunals for civilians accused of subversion and life sentences for the crime of terrorism, were unconstitutional. President Toledo sought and received from Congress the authority to create, by legislative decree, new antiterror laws (LAN-RA, Jan. 28, 2003). Under these new rules, over seven hundred cases were promptly reviewed by civilian courts to decide questions of exoneration and retrial (LAN-RA, March 4, 2003). Sendero's maximum leader, Abimael Guzmán, was himself retried twice. The first trial in 2004 fell apart as a result of questions about the judges' impartiality as well as the media circus that surrounded the proceedings, but Guzmán was tried again by a civilian court in 2005 and convicted in 2006 (BBC News, Oct. 14, 2006). At the highest levels of power and in the cases with the greatest visibility, the judiciary was— unlike its role in the 1990s—fostering, rather than threatening, constitutional rule.[43]

Other state agencies crucial to democratic constitutionalism were also markedly improved. Electoral authorities largely continued to play the role of professional, neutral arbiters and administrators that they had reprised with the 2001 elections. In some areas they even extended their roles, such as supervision by the National Office of Electoral Processes (ONPE) in party primaries, as per Peru's new 2003 political party law (see chapter 4). As these agencies properly fulfilled their now expanded missions, there were some conflicts over jurisdiction, particularly between the ONPE and the National Elections Tribunal (JNE). Most of these were straightforward cases of different agencies interpreting the law and their roles differently, such as the confusion over who was responsible for enforcing the membership and organizational requirements of the political party law (Tanaka interview 2005). Other conflicts were more suspicious. In 2004, for example, the ONPE refused to let a pro-Fujimori party register under a new name, but the JNE allowed it (*Caretas,* Nov. 25, 2004). In 2005, the widely respected head of the ONPE, Fernando Tuesta Soldevilla, quit just prior to the end of his first term of appointment, forced out in part by accusations of conflict of interest launched by a *fujimorista* congresswoman (*Caretas,* April 14, 2005). But on the whole, the ONPE, the JNE, and the voter registration agency RENIEC functioned very well, upholding and enforcing the rules for political competition.

As noted above, the Defensoría del Pueblo was one of the few state agencies that had promoted, rather than impeded, constitutionalism in the 1990s. When the first *defensor,* Jorge Santistevan, resigned in November 2000 to take a run at the presidency, Congress appointed Walter Albán as interim *defensor* but left a more permanent appointment up to the legislature to be elected in 2001. The next legislature, however, was divided over what to do with the post, and the interim appointment ended up lasting nearly five years.[44] Uncertainty over its leadership weakened the role that the Defensoría could play in reinforcing the rule of law, but even with this impediment it continued to expand its services to rural and remote areas of Peru and to perform adequately in the face of a rising number of cases to investigate (Pegram 2009).

The decentralization of state services like those offered by the Defensoría and the TC mirrored a much broader process of regionalization in Peru. As noted above, the 1992 self-coup wiped out the rather dysfunctional regional governments designed by President García in the late 1980s. Under President Toledo, Peru went a long way toward rectifying this breach of constitutionalism. In March 2002 Congress ratified changes to the constitution that made it possible to call regional elections that year (*El Comercio,* March 6, 2002). Regional elections held in November 2002 were free and fair contests to choose regional presidents and councils. At one point in the campaign, election authorities warned Toledo not to use public works inaugurations to promote Perú Posible's regional candidates (Ballón 2002b). The attempted tactic was reminiscent of misuses of state resources in the 1990s, but it was a good sign that a state agency admonished the president to change his practices—and, more importantly, that the president complied.

More troubling for constitutionalism was what Toledo did after his party fared poorly in those elections, winning just one regional government. As in the 1980s, regional elections had been held before Congress could agree on a comprehensive set of rules detailing the jurisdictions, policy responsibilities, and fiscal resources of these regions. The Ley

Orgánica de Gobiernos Regionales, passed just before the elections, was deliberately ambiguous (LAN-RA, Dec. 10, 2002). After Perú Posible's disastrous showing, Toledo dithered on devolving power and resources to the regions. How much autonomy and money regions should have, and how to compose the agency charged with advising regional governments, continued to stalemate Congress for months (LAN-RA, Jan. 28, 2003). The National Decentralization Council, which was eventually created to promote regionalization, was not trusted by regional officials, and critics complained that the allocation of funds to the regions was moving too slowly (LAN-RA, Sept. 7, 2004). In 2005 Toledo attempted a compromise, promising an additional 1 percent of all consumer (value-added) and corporate (profitability) taxes to any groups of regions that consolidated into "macro-regions." A referendum to create fewer, larger regions was held in October 2005 but was approved in just one jurisdiction and consequently was not implemented anywhere.

One other problem with the Toledo government's record on decentralization vis-à-vis the rule of law was, in a sense, a product of its success rather than its failings. As regional governments became a genuine arena for politics, some regions began to assert new powers and prerogatives. In June 2005 the Cusco regional government decided to deregulate all coca cultivation in the greater La Convención valley (which could be interpreted as covering nearly the entire region and beyond). Several other regions looked as if they might follow suit. This not only threatened to create a constitutional standoff in Peru, it also jeopardized trade talks, foreign aid, and other aspects of the national government's relations with other national governments. However, Toledo was able to strike a deal narrowly limiting unregulated coca cultivation to the La Convención valley proper (LAN-RA, June 2005).

While the design and implementation of Peru's regional governments were far from perfect, regionalization in the first years of the twenty-first century was more successful than the previous attempt in the late 1980s—and far more faithful to the constitution than the suppression of regional self-government during most of the 1990s. By 2005, regional governments controlled fully 22.5 percent of the national budget. Like never before, Peru's governing elites took major steps toward fulfilling constitutional principles of decentralization long ignored or distorted.

This decentralizing impulse at the nation-state level, in combination with greater civil liberties at street level, meant that Peruvians—not just in Lima but in the *provincias* too—were now free to organize, lobby, strike, protest, and even riot in ways that they had not been during the 1990s. Some of this civil society activity had quite salutary effects on the rule of law. Pro-democracy and human rights groups played an important role in the 2000–2001 transition period, particularly during the OAS-sponsored roundtable talks in the final months of the Fujimori era.[45] Then, networks of Citizen Watch (Vigilancia Ciudadana) groups— grassroots organizations that monitored government activities and denounced corruption—sprang up in the aftermath of the transition (Taylor 2005). The government was publicly supportive of these networks, even when they criticized public officials.

But along with this renewed civic engagement came numerous waves of protests and strikes during 2001–2006, which created a sense of instability. While this too was a manifestation of the political freedoms and civil liberties that Peruvians had regained, some of this direct political action threatened the durability of the newly democratic regime. At the very least, it dramatically exposed the pent-up social demands and persistent institutional fragilities of Peru's national politics.

In June 2002, protests in Arequipa against the privatization of state-owned energy companies turned violent and left two dead (Vargas Gutiérrez 2002). In February 2003, a prominent national leader of coca growers' groups, Nelson Palomino, was arrested; in response, thousands of *cocaleros* protested across Peru, and in April these protesters converged in a march on the capital city. Then, in May 2003, nationwide strikes were launched by teachers, farmers, construction workers, and members of many other sectors, leading the government to declare a state of emergency (LAN-RA, June 24, 2003). The following year, another (slightly smaller) wave of labor protests erupted in July 2004. This time the strikes were also supported by the opposition APRA party and were accompanied by labor unions and some civil society groups—such as the Foro Democrático, led by *aprista* Agustín Haya de la Torre—calling for Toledo's resignation or impeachment, for early elections, or even for a new constitution ("El Foro Democrático busca," *La República,* May 15, 2004). One year later, in August 2005, a wave of protests targeting Peru's economically crucial mineral export sector disrupted production at two of the country's largest mines (LAN-RA, Sept. 2005).

But the episode that most gravely threatened the rule of law occurred on January 1, 2005. The Ethnocacerist Movement or Movimiento

Etnocacerista, ultranationalist army reservists led by Major Antauro Humala—brother of the leader of the October 2000 uprising—staged a rebellion in Andahuaylas. (I analyze the movement in greater detail in chapter 4.) Twenty-one people were taken hostage in a police station; six people would be killed in a three-day standoff that ended with Humala's arrest (BBC News, Jan. 2 and 4, 2005). Social movements and civil society groups, peaceful and violent alike, were revitalized and now operated in a more open political arena.

This coincided with a similar opening in the mass media. A newly freed press gave extensive coverage to these strikes and protests, magnifying their impact. The press also doggedly pursued (and sometimes exaggerated or even fabricated) the personal foibles and political scandals of public figures, especially those at the top: members of Congress, cabinet ministers, even President Toledo and the First Lady. The corruption of the Fujimori years, exposed for all to see in hundreds of hours of *vladivideos,* habituated the public to outrageous scandals and made citizens keenly suspicious of all state institutions and of anyone in power (Sánchez Pinedo interview 2007). So the media served up scandal after scandal, condemnation after condemnation. Some media figures, such as Enrique Zileri, director of the prominent newsweekly *Caretas,* criticized this practice as *denuncialogia,* or obsession with public denunciations. For Zileri this "generates a frenzy of aggression, [and] creates in the population a sense that the country is in chaos, that we can't be governed by a democracy" (Felch 2004, 43). Or as freelance journalist Fernando Yovera put it: "For ten years [under Fujimori] journalists were mute, now they can't shut up: everyone is guilty of everything!" (Felch 2004, 45).

Members of Congress and other politicians I interviewed during the Toledo years uniformly and without fail pointed to a hyperactive press corps as an understandable, if also regrettable, feature of Peru's post-Fujimori era. Congressman Henry Pease noted that "a political opening makes people act crazily" (Pease García interview 2007). Congresswoman Doris Sánchez lamented that the press corps focused on personal issues rather than policy and frequently published baseless rumors (Sánchez Pinedo interview 2007). For Congressman Carlos Ferrero, the media unduly went after Alejandro Toledo in particular: at first because Montesinos's influence on the media was still palpable; then because Toledo was darker skinned, an urbanized highlander (*cholo*) who didn't fit in with the *limeño* elite; and finally, once the culture of *denuncialogía* took hold, the media bashed Toledo just to increase their sales (Ferrero Costa interview 2007).

On a few occasions, the government tried to pressure the media into being less critical, in a faint echo of the bald-faced bribery and blackmail that characterized the SIN's media control operations of the late 1990s. In June 2002, audio recordings were released in which Salomon Lerner Ghitis, a high-level Toledo bureaucrat, seems to be negotiating more favorable media coverage with Moisés and Alex Wolfenson, owners of two notorious Montesinos-controlled tabloid newspapers, in exchange for favorable judicial treatment in corruption and bribery cases. Lerner Ghitis had to resign as head of COFIDE, the state development bank. A year later, in 2003, TV station Panamericana made a similar accusation, claiming that Toledo tried to compel its journalists to pull back on their criticism of his administration (LAN-RA, May 20, 2003). But with the more open political environment and stronger rule of law of the early twenty-first century, these haphazard attempts at media manipulation were uncovered, denounced, and often punished.

The president's confrontations with the media were representative of the role that scandal played more generally in those years. Toledo was buffeted by scandals even before he took office. He had a daughter born out of wedlock who was the object of much media attention on the campaign trail and in the first year of his term.[46] As early as August 2003, fully 55 percent of *limeños* believed that Toledo would not complete his full term of office (DATUM Internacional). By December 2003 political scandals—some real, some contrived—were hitting many of Toledo's top appointees too. Vice President and Foreign Minister Raúl Diez Canseco, caught in a romantic tryst, was accused of improperly using tax laws to favor his girlfriend's father's business. More scurrilous (and unfounded) were 2004 allegations that Prime Minister Beatriz Merino improperly hired a consultant with whom she co-owned property (LAN-RA, Jan. 6, 2004). Some pundits also insinuated that the two women were lovers (Taylor 2007). Merino resigned.

The following years witnessed an even wider range of scandals in the executive branch. Some were relatively prosaic. In 2004, for example, a deputy minister was caught trying to cultivate support from local Perú Posible groups in exchange for the promise of jobs if she were named minister for women's affairs (LAN-RA, Oct. 5, 2004). Also, long-standing

rumors of womanizing, drinking, and drug use continued to dog Toledo. As a capstone to these rumors, in May and June 2005 the Lima
press broke the story of an affair between Toledo and a member of the
presidential palace security detail, Lieutenant Lady Bardales. Allegations
of her "illicit enrichment" were later investigated by Congress, by police,
and by the national comptroller (*La República,* May 10, 2005).

But these scandals were minor compared to several others with more
serious ramifications for the rule of law. One story that emerged in early
2004 was that $2 million in bribes were collected by intelligence chief
César Almeyda in 2002, to facilitate the sale of Peruvian beer manufac-
turer Backus and Johnson to a Colombian company. In July 2004, journalists confirmed that the president and First Lady themselves received a
sizeable cut of the graft (*Caretas,* July 26, 2004). When the special anti-
corruption prosecutor's unit that Toledo had praised for its work investigating Fujimori and Montesinos began turning its attention to his
own government, Toledo vetted the idea of disbanding the unit but was
dissuaded by members of his shrinking Perú Posible legislative bench
(LAN-RA, Oct. 5, 2004; *New York Times,* Sept. 27, 2004).

At one point in late 2004, the president was being battered by multiple scandals, First Lady Eliane Karp de Toledo was accused not only of
taking the brewers' bribe but also of embezzling World Bank funds, the
president's brother Pedro Toledo was being investigated for corruption
and fraud in establishing a new telephone company, and, in a case that
went to the heart of constitutionalism in Peru, the president's sister, Margarita Toledo, stood accused of orchestrating the fraudulent use of hundreds of thousands of voters' names on the 1997–1998 party registration
petition for Perú Posible.

Unlike Fujimori's "signature factory" (*fábrica de firmas*), Toledo's was
never alleged to involve the complicity of electoral authorities or other
public officials at the time. But the idea that the man who stood up to
Fujimori's cheating in the 2000 elections was guilty of using any of the
same fraudulent tactics came as a particularly crushing blow to Toledo's
image. In 2004, Congressman Rafael Rey (leader of the small CODE-
Renovación party) proposed "vacating" Toledo's presidency; he also proposed legislation to allow the president to hold early elections, in the
hope that Toledo might take this escape route instead (Rey Rey interview 2007). In 2005 the legislature took up these allegations of fraudulent party registration.

The ensuing congressional investigation represented an important test of the strengths and limitations of the rule of law among political elites in post-Fujimori Peru. Congress named a special commission led by Edgar Villanueva, a Perú Posible congressman who had left the party, to look into the matter. Toledo was initially not very cooperative, arguing that the accusation did not refer to any of the impeachable crimes listed in Article 117 of the constitution (treason, preventing elections, dissolving Congress, or preventing the operation of Congress or the electoral authorities). Of course, as with Fujimori's ouster in 2000, Toledo could still face a vote to "vacate" the presidency—vague, but also in accordance with the constitution. After much delay, he agreed to give only private, unsworn, oral testimony to the commission (*El Comercio,* July 16, 2006).

The congressional commission ultimately found that Toledo engaged in criminal conspiracy and violations of public trust. Its report suggested that Congress could take whatever action "corresponds constitutionally," though two of its five members did not approve the final draft of this report, and the three who did approve it each recommended a different sanction (RPP Noticias, May 2, 2005).[47] The commission was also hampered by criticism that it downplayed yet another mass signature falsification, this one committed by none other than Rafael Rey's CODE-Renovación party. With the neutrality of this congressional investigation in question, and with less than a year to go before the next presidential elections, on May 19, 2005, the full Congress voted 57–46 against turning the case over to the public prosecutor.[48] As a test of constitutional norms, the state's response to the Perú Posible signature fraud yielded decidedly mixed results.

The executive branch was indeed sullied by scandal, and though not discussed in detail here, additional scandals—some more substantive than others—battered the images of members of Congress. However, few of these scandals rose beyond the level of minor graft or nepotism, and certainly none approached the deeply entrenched government-by-mafia that ruled Peru for most of the Fujimori era. High-level corruption existed under Toledo, but it was qualitatively different in that it did not threaten the very foundations of constitutionalism in Peru. He led the country at a moment in which a confluence of factors now made opinion leaders and elites in government, media, and civil society (and the public at large, too) less willing to tolerate the *mano dura* of the Fujimori years. And perhaps his leadership style and public persona mattered too: Toledo's image, cultivated domestically and internationally, was one of a committed democrat. But whatever the reason, Toledo did not even *attempt* to control politics by extra-constitutional means to the extent that his predecessor did.

The fact that corruption and wrongdoing were so readily uncovered and publicized by the press puts a strangely positive spin on the negative public image that Toledo garnered. While scandal and protest almost brought him down, Toledo nonetheless limped to the finish of his full term of office (see chapter 5). He and his ministers seldom attempted to interfere with the freedom of the press or with opposition politicians and civil society groups. There were exceptions, but these violations were detected and prevented or punished. To a great extent, Toledo played by the rules. And the major achievements of the Toledo era — rebuilding democratic institutions, fulfilling the promise of decentralization, increasing the transparency of government, and holding the state accountable for past wrongs — made those rules even more robust. On the whole, the Toledo presidency, though politically messy, was marked by a revitalized rule of law and a strengthened culture of constitutionalism among political elites.

Conclusions: Constitutionalism in Contemporary Peru

The history of constitutionalism in Peru, from 1985 to 2006, is a story of the death and rebirth of the rule of law as a constraint on powerful political actors. Efforts by President Alan García during his first term of office (1985–1990) to bend the rules of the game or redesign them to his advantage sometimes succeeded, but where his aspirations would have required flagrantly breaking the rules, they were held in check — by politicians' expectations about one another's behavior, by opposition party oversight, and by the professional ambitions of politicians from his own party. By the 1990s, however, economic crisis and political violence had eroded not just formal rules but rule-abiding behavior in politics. Most politicians either accepted, or were unable to deter, the executive opportunistically changing or breaking the rules of the game. In Alberto Fujimori's rhetoric — which rang true for many Peruvians — the procedures of liberal democracy became synonymous with parasitism, impotence, and elitism. After Fujimori's fall, adherence to constitutional norms rebounded during the interim government of Valentín Paniagua, as politicians with otherwise disparate agendas cooperated on forging Peru's regime transition. Under President Alejandro Toledo the rule of law was put to the test, and while the system may have bent under the pressures of scandal and political conflict, it certainly did not break.

In this twenty-one-year period we also see dramatic changes in the power of Peru's executive vis-à-vis the legislature; I explore these shifts in the legislative-executive balance of power in greater detail in chapter 5. But what the present chapter demonstrates is that the dynamics of presidential power cannot be well explained by the formal rules of the game, at least not those at the heart of institutionalist analysis. The constitutional lawmaking powers respectively assigned to the president and the legislature remained surprisingly stable over the entire 1985–2006 period, even with the advent of a new constitution. Other rule changes, such as restructuring the judiciary or altering the rules on presidential reelection in the 1990s, had an impact on executive strength precisely because they institutionalized the state's decreasing propensity to enforce de jure rules on its top leaders and de facto power holders. The rule of law, rather than the specific rules of the game, made an enormous difference among political elites. And as I go on to demonstrate in chapter 5, the legislatures of the 1980s and the early twenty-first century were vastly stronger than the legislatures of the 1990s in their dealings with the executive branch and in their ability to check presidential power, not because of the details of the constitution per se but rather because of the strength of constitutionalism.

Also crucial to this calculus were political parties—not just the formal partisan powers conferred on presidents by electoral rules but the strength and organizational coherence of the parties themselves. If we wish to understand how Fujimori could act alone in ways that García and Toledo could not, we must look beyond these electoral laws and even beyond the size of the president's legislative caucus. We must differentiate political party organizations from more ephemeral electoral movements among both government and opposition groups. Like constitutionalism, party organizational structures—and their absence—have a critical if underappreciated impact on checks and balances in presidential systems of government. Thus it is to political parties that I turn next.

4

Party Organizations and Electoral Movements in Peru, 1985–2006

In Peru, political parties do not exist. . . . I am the [sole] power,

it is true. But it is a power that was granted to me by the people.

—President Alberto Fujimori, June 21, 1993[1]

In this chapter I analyze the precipitous decline and then modest rise of political party organizations in Peru. Notwithstanding their troubled historical legacy, political parties in Peru showed promise in the 1980s.[2] Personalistic, ad hoc electoral movements supplanted parties in the 1990s and continued to be prevalent in the early twenty-first century, even as some of Peru's more traditional parties returned to the political scene.

Electoral movements are personal vehicles for promoting or maintaining an individual candidate or leader. Panebianco described such groups as "parties which pass like a meteor over the political firmament, which spring up and die out without ever institutionalizing" (1988, 53).[3] Though some meteors flash only briefly and others etch longer streaks into the sky, they all share a deliberate lack of organizational development and structural institutionalization. But to understand Peru's "meteor shower" of the 1990s, we first must map out the political firmament in which it took place.

As detailed in chapter 1, the economic crisis and political violence that Peru experienced in the late 1980s was so severe that a decline in party organizational strength seems almost overdetermined, not surprising. The causes for this decline have been thoroughly analyzed elsewhere (Cameron 1994; 1997; Cameron, Blanaru, and Burns 2006; Carrión 1998; Cotler 1995; Dietz and Meyers 2007; Kenney 2003a; 2004; Levitsky and Cameron 2003; Lynch 1999; Tanaka 1998). Less adequately explained are the internal workings of parties and electoral movements and, crucially, the ways in which different party organizational forms affected the legislative-executive balance of power, often regardless of electoral laws or other formal rules. And few works have, as yet, examined the reemergence of some organized parties in the first decade of the twenty-first century and their impact on post-Fujimori politics in Peru.

I begin this chapter by exploring the laws that govern elections and political parties in Peru. I demonstrate that—like the constitutional law-making powers depicted in chapter 3—there was relatively little change in the formal rules of the game that shape the president's "partisan powers" (Mainwaring and Shugart 1997, 5). I then look at the political parties and electoral movements themselves, using the method of process tracing (George and McKeown 1985; George and Bennett 2005). In each of three periods, I analyze party organizational forms and the relationship between leaders and party organizations in Peru. The 1985–1992 period is one of a decline in traditional political parties; the period 1992–2000 was dominated by the executive's own electoral movements; and the years 2000–2006 saw the persistence of the electoral movement model as well as the partial renewal of more traditional party organizations.

This transformation altered the relationship between group leaders and other politicians. In 1985–1990, opposition parties as well as his own APRA party had constraining effects on President García. But the collapse of parties and the rise of electoral movements reduced the extent to which a president could be constrained by opposition groups and, crucially, by his own political group. This was exemplified by the powerful Fujimori presidency, especially in the years following the 1992 *autogolpe*.

In the aftermath of the Fujimori regime, parties were modestly reinvigorated. The APRA party in particular—still and again Peru's best organized and most disciplined—made a surprising comeback, as did its leader, former president Alan García. President Toledo's political group, Perú Posible (PP), was, by design, a personalistic electoral movement not entirely unlike Fujimori's. While a few PP politicians (unlike their *fujimorista* counterparts) did seriously attempt to create an autonomous party organization, they were ultimately unsuccessful. But Toledo was hemmed in by more organized opposition parties and was more compelled to uphold the rule of law too. Consequently, his legislative caucus lacked the authoritarian discipline of Fujimori's and served to constrain, rather than empower, the executive branch.

Electoral Laws and Political Parties in Peru

What is the relationship between political parties and the strength or weakness of the executive in a presidential system? For institutionalist scholars, part of the answer can be found in the electoral laws and other formal rules that shape a president's "partisan powers." Presidential control over her party's legislators is viewed as a by-product of party leaders' control over the nomination and ordering of legislative candidates (Shugart and Carey 1992; Mainwaring and Shugart 1997). Other rules also shape the odds of the president's party enjoying a congressional majority: district magnitude (the number of members elected per legislative district), the timing of elections, and the minimum threshold of votes required to win a seat, to name a few. And a legislative majority is, of course, itself a manifestation of institutional power.

But the same set of formal rules can have one impact on a well-organized political party and a different impact on an ad hoc electoral movement. Future electoral incentives may not be the only motivation for a legislator to act in a loyal or disciplined manner; party discipline can also be achieved through side payments or coercion. Similarly, in a system of weak parties, the balance of forces in the legislature may be as much a consequence of party switching as a product of the design of electoral systems and the results of particular elections. The organizational form of the political party itself has an impact on the power of party leaders and executive office holders. And looking at the case of Peru, the rules of the game indeed tell only part of the story.

Peru's legislative elections use party list proportional representation (PR). Candidate selection—and, in theory, the future loyalty of elected legislators—was highly centralized for most groups during the period I examine. Prior to the 2003 Ley de Partidos Políticos, party leaders were free to choose legislative candidates any way they liked, unfettered by complex selection rules, primary elections, or automatic candidacies (e.g., for sitting legislators). Scores of interviews that I conducted with legislative candidates over twenty years of election cycles indicated that—in electoral movements and even in organized parties—the responsibility for candidate selection frequently fell to the party's presidential candidate (usually the de facto leader) and a handful of advisers.

There were and are limits to the party leader's latitude. For example, since the late 1990s, mandatory gender quotas have shaped the composition of candidate lists for legislative elections.[4] But even more crucial for limiting party leaders' power in Peru is their lack of control over which of their selected candidates are ultimately elected to Congress. This is because of the open-list system—specifically, a double optional preferential vote—which has been in use since the 1985 elections.[5] Rules for preferential voting did not change much in the period under study. Voters indicate the party list they wish to support and, additionally, have the option of specifying up to two particular candidates from their (one) legislative list of choice, identifying the candidate(s) by their number on a party list provided to voters in the polling station. The preferential vote has had a significant impact on the election of legislators, altering outcomes by 26 percent to 45 percent compared to a hypothetical closed-list system in elections from 1985 to 2000 (Tuesta Soldevilla 1996; Transparencia, *Datos* 5, Oct. 18, 2000). And by most accounts, individual candidates from the same list compete with one another much more fiercely than they do with candidates from other lists.[6]

Elections for Peru's president and for all congressional seats are held on the same day, but with the possibility of a presidential runoff election thirty days after the votes are tallied, if no candidate wins a majority in the first round. Compared to truly concurrent elections (held on the same day, no runoff elections, no midterm elections), Peru's reduce the presidential coattails effect and diminish the odds of the president winning a legislative majority of her own. This system, too, was in place for the entire 1985–2006 period.

District magnitude (DM)—the number of seats per district—has changed over time, however. In 1985–1992, average DM in the lower house was 7.01 (Jones 1995b). In 1995–2000 it was a staggering 120, since Peru had a single legislative chamber with 120 seats in a single national district. As noted earlier, rule changes for the 2001 contest included readopting multimember districts, though still within a single 120-seat chamber—so average DM fell to 4.8 (Johnson and Wallack 2006). Consequently, the threshold for winning a congressional seat also changed slightly during the period examined here, since a party must win a high enough percentage of votes within a district to merit at least one seat. When Congress was a single chamber with a single national district, the threshold was effectively lowered to less than 1 percent of the national vote. When Congress (or, previously, the Chamber of Deputies) is divided into departmental electoral districts, district magnitude is lower and the effective threshold higher. (A more explicit vote threshold, or *valla electoral,* took effect in 2006.[7])

Yet knowing about these rules and institutions still tells us relatively little about the party discipline (or lack thereof) that they supposedly fostered. For example, centralized candidate selection can engender loyalty to an individual presidential candidate rather than to an organization. Especially in more "lawless" periods such as 1993–2000 in Peru, the mechanisms for a president's power over a personalistic, ad hoc electoral movement can go far beyond candidate selection and campaign competition—but will last only as long as the leader's grip on the group. In more organized political parties, legislative politicians and candidates have longer time horizons. As Poiré (2000) notes, centralized candidate selection makes for a more disciplined and coherent party only if the party label itself is a valuable asset. In Peru's electoral movements, the party label matters far less than the link to the leader. Group discipline in such movements is based not on legislators' paths to reelection or to another political office, regardless of the rules, but on the leader's popularity, control over material resources, and capacity for coercion. (As we will see, this made Fujimori's electoral movement highly disciplined and Toledo's rather undisciplined.)

One formal rule change that did, belatedly, make a difference was the institution of electronic roll-call voting in 1998. Peru's congressional regulation had long allowed recorded votes when requested by one-third of the members present, and electronic voting equipment had already been installed a year earlier but not used. By early 1999, however, their use had become standard procedure; what is more, vote records were made available online to the public within hours of taking place (Carey 2003b; 2006). This reform increased transparency at a political moment otherwise characterized by opacity. It did not dramatically alter the political tactics of the Fujimori regime, since legislative discipline within his electoral movement was achieved largely through extra-institutional means.[8] But in combination with other government-led transparency initiatives and a newly free press, it may have altered the incentive structures facing legislators in the Toledo era, weakening party discipline in some groups.

Other laws regulating political parties either were ineffectual or had ambiguous consequences. Though traditional political parties might, in retrospect, have benefited from closing off the electoral arena in the 1980s by making party registration more difficult, attempts at reform failed because party leaders did not want to constrain their own range of action with rigid rules or administrative red tape (Rubio Correa 1997; De Valdivia Cano interview 1999; Trujillano interview 1999). So barriers to entry remained low. According to the 1962 Law of Political Elections (Law 14250), all that was required to enroll a political party in Peru was a list of leaders and legal representatives, a petition of adherents' names,[9] a party program and internal statutes, and an unverified confirmation that party committees existed in at least half of all departments. Reforms instituted in 1984 (Law 23903) clarified that a party that won less than 5 percent in a general election would lose official party status and would need to reregister or cease competing.

These minimal requirements were further reduced in the 1993 Constitution, which created the new categories of "groups, movements, or alliances" in electoral law. This allowed groups that were not official political parties to compete in elections with even fewer regulations (no departmental committees or internal statutes required). Campaign financing remained unregulated by design. Budget and expense reporting rules had no sanctions for noncompliance. A 1994 law went so far as to prevent electoral authorities from obtaining and publicizing information from media corporations regarding the amount and cost of campaign ads, or punishing parties even when a declaration of expenditure was demonstrably false (*Caretas,* Jan. 12, 1995). And the 1997 Organic Elections Law (Ley Orgánica de Elecciones, LOE) weakened the organizational structure requirements for parties but increased the required number of adherents' signatures to 4 percent of registered voters—at the time, almost half a million people—and created a mechanism for the electoral authorities to verify the signatures.

The 2003 Political Party Law (Ley de Partidos Políticos, LPP) slightly lowered some entry barriers and slightly raised others. The number of signatures needed to register a party was reduced to just 1 percent of votes cast in the previous national election.[10] Parties winning less than 5 percent of the vote would now be able to stay registered if they won a certain number of seats in Congress.[11] The LPP also increased the regulation of political party organizations, but enforcement of these new rules was uneven. The law raised the bar for local party bases, requiring committees of at least fifty people in at least one-third of provinces across at least two-thirds of all departments. However, electoral authorities have had little capacity to continue to enforce this rule once a party has been initially registered (Tanaka interview 2005).

The LPP also timidly began to address questions of internal democracy and corruption within parties. As of the 2006 elections, four-fifths of all candidates for elected office must first be elected internally; one-fifth can be designated by party leaders or committees. (That four-fifths can be elected in open or closed primaries, and parties can even solicit the help of ONPE in supervising such contests, but the candidates can also be selected by a party committee, as long as that committee is itself elected by a secret ballot of all members.[12]) The Supreme Court, on the recommendation of the ombudsman or the public prosecutor, was authorized to deregister and ban any party that engages in antidemocratic activities, including political violence, terrorism, or drug trafficking.[13] The law also tried to limit legislators' party switching, albeit in modest and easily skirted ways.[14] Financial reporting rules were tightened too, though they still lacked sanctions for noncompliance (Alvarado Dodero interview 2007).[15] Finally, perhaps the most novel change represented in the LPP was also the least popular and most controversial element of the law: public financing, albeit limited, for parties. (Note that many provisions of the LPP, including party financing, were only beginning to take effect at the very end of the 1985–2006 period under study.)

Having briefly summarized the rules governing parties and elections in Peru, I now turn to their organizational reality. Drawing on an ample secondary literature as well as journalistic sources and over a hundred personal interviews with high-level politicians and party leaders, I trace changes over time among political parties and electoral movements across three different periods: 1985–1992, 1992–2000, and 2001–2006.[16]

While the political parties of the 1980s were justly criticized by some contemporaries for having personalistic, caudillo-like leaders, some party organizations indeed enjoyed a measure of autonomy from party leaders and had the capacity to periodically rein in these leaders. Those parties were eclipsed by vastly more personalistic electoral movements in the 1990s. Then, in 2001–2006, Toledo's Perú Posible struggled and failed to move beyond the electoral movement format, but some traditional parties—the APRA party and the Partido Popular Cristiano (PPC)—made a comeback and shared the political arena with electoral movements.

Party Organizations in Peru, 1985–1992

It appeared in 1985 that a new day was dawning for party organizations in Peru. With the victory of the APRA and its presidential candidate Alan García, this party appeared to be fulfilling the promise of its early years, becoming a more national, more mass-based party. In addition, an assortment of smaller leftist parties that had run separately in 1980 unified into the Izquierda Unida (IU). By winning and then successfully presiding over the municipality of metropolitan Lima and half of the city's district-level governments (plus hundreds more nationwide) in the mid-1980s, the left demonstrated that it was capable of governing. While the future of Acción Popular (AP) was unclear after the second Belaúnde presidency, the future for parties in general looked promising in 1985. By 1990, it looked questionable. And by 1992, organized political parties would scarcely exist in Peru.

APRA

Alan García became secretary general of the Partido Aprista Peruano in a bruising leadership convention in 1982 (Solfrini 2001). But fractures within the party healed, and García went on to win internal elections for presidential candidate in February 1984 by a comfortable margin (Taylor 1986). As APRA prepared for the 1985 general elections, departmental committees were responsible for compiling lists of candidates for their district's slate of deputies, and for senators nationwide. In some departments, internal elections were held among party militants. Where APRA

Table 4.1. Legislative Seats Won, 1985 Elections

	Deputies	Senators*
APRA	107	32
IU	48	15
CODE (MBH, PPC)	12	7
AP	10	5(+1)
Independents	2	
Izq. Nac. (FNTC)	1	1
TOTAL	180	60(+1)

*1 ex-president as senator-for-life

Table 4.2. Legislative Seats Won, 1990 Elections

	Deputies	Senators*
FREDEMO	62	20(+1)
APRA	53	16(+1)
C-90	32	14
IU	16	6
IS	4	3
FIM	7	
FNTC	3	1
Other	3	
TOTAL	180	60(+2)

*2 ex-presidents as senators-for-life

did not have a strong infrastructure, a departmental committee made the nominations directly. In either case, the nominations were sent on to the party's Central Political Committee and National Executive Committee, which also reserved the right to drop candidates, reorder the results of internal elections or selection processes, and even add new candidates not considered by the regional-level organizations (Bendezú Carpio interview 1999; Negreiros Criado interview 1999; Pilco Deza interview 1999; Santander Estrada interview 1999; Valle Riestra interview 1999; inter alia). Thus, the process was not quite internally democratic but was characterized by a strong central party organization. The national-level selectorate was influenced in turn by the wishes of the presidential candidate, though it also exercised significant autonomy from him.

The election campaign itself was indeed strongly geared toward the presidential race (Lijphart 1999; Samuels 2002a). The party supplied congressional candidates with printed materials and could arrange for some volunteer labor, but it did not directly fund candidates. In fact, following a practice common in Peruvian politics, successful legislative and municipal candidates and public functionaries for the APRA were required to donate a percentage of their salaries to the party (in this case, 10–15 percent for congresspersons and ministers, 5–10 percent for municipal officials and lower-ranking, national-level bureaucrats).

Although the party worked hard to promote its candidate, Alan García won the presidency of Peru by campaigning not as the leader of a sectarian group but rather as a moderate, reform-minded populist. His slogan was *"mi compromiso es con todos los peruanos"* ("my commitment is to all Peruvians"). At García's insistence, the party's traditional symbols were supplemented with neutral symbols such as the white dove of peace and the Peruvian flag. And after he won the presidency, he tried to put some distance between himself and the party (Stein 1999).

Yet García's executive leadership was not disarticulated from APRA party bases or from civil society. First, as I detailed in chapter 3, other elected politicians had significant sway over political outcomes. APRA senators and deputies had real political clout and served as an effective if inconsistent constraint on executive power. Second, though they complained about being forgotten, the party faithful were indeed rewarded with some patronage positions. They served as administrators in two large national job-creation schemes, the PAIT (Programa de Apoyo al Ingreso Temporal, or Temporary Income Support Program) and its sponsoring agency in the government, COOPOP (Cooperación Popular, or Popular Cooperation), though the temporary jobs created by these programs were themselves used to shore up electoral support among the poor rather than reward loyal partisanship (López García 1986; Graham 1991).[17] Corporaciones Departamentales, or Regional Development Corporations, were a prominent site of patronage appointments as well. Third, party technocrats were involved in day-to-day policymaking. The Comisión Nacional del Plan de Gobierno (the National Commission for the Plan of Government), CONAPLAN, was a group of *apristas* and independent advisers that worked during the presidential transition period (April to

August 1985) to formulate technically detailed plans for governing. Once García assumed power, this group was converted into a government bureaucracy, with a hundred forty offices around the country, ostensibly to gather data, advise legislative commissions, and coordinate the work of government ministries in the implementation of new programs (Graham 1992; Taylor 1986). Though García did go outside the party for some of his high-level advisers, he also brought in figures from within APRA.

At a specially organized national congress in August 1985, García promised militants a role in a party-as-government along the lines of the AD of Venezuela or perhaps even the PRI of Mexico. The party responded by electing an unequivocally "pro-Alan" National Executive Committee (CEN). But as of 1987, according to one APRA deputy, that CEN had held only two meetings in two years, and some militants criticized García for marginalizing the party base. A group of disgruntled *apristas* (the "Federation of the Forgotten Ones") voiced concerns that the party's well-organized cadres were being supplanted by a charismatic leader and "undifferentiated populist masses" (González 1987). The party did not collapse, though. Even as the president himself grew less popular in the late 1980s, most leaders at the district and regional levels stayed in APRA. And when García tried to suspend or expel his critics from the party, other top leaders could often prevent him from doing so (Garrido Lecca interview 2005).

At the next APRA party congress, held in December 1988 after several delays, delegates sharply critiqued García's stewardship. The party elected Luis Alva Castro, García's rival, as secretary general, and informally tapped him to be the 1990 presidential candidate. (His candidacy would be formalized by a vote of acclaim at a 1989 party congress.) Alva Castro had risen to power by cultivating the support of local party bases and affiliated organizations around Peru. While García may have had personal reasons for wanting his successor to fail as a candidate—if he hoped to run again in 1995—Alva and other APRA leaders were nonetheless able to make demands on the president based on the longer-term strategic needs of the party. For example, a 1989 cabinet shuffle removed from office several ministers who were personally allied with García, and replaced them with party stalwarts supportive of Alva. On the other hand, García also quietly offered support to other, rival candidates for president—first Alfonso Barrantes and then Alberto Fujimori (Jochamowitz 1993; Planas 2000; Schmidt 1996).

So the 1990 race was an uphill battle for Alva Castro, and while he stayed in close contention right up until the first round of presidential elections, his party was now showing signs of weakening. As in 1985, APRA congressional candidates were elected or selected at the department level, and lists could later be reordered by the departmental committees and the party's National Executive Committee. But times were changing. First, the party leadership was more interested in inviting independent candidates onto its congressional lists than it had been in 1985. Second, after several years of presiding over severe social and economic crises, the pool of volunteer labor that the party could count on from its rank and file had grown thin. Though the party was still well-organized enough to mount a comprehensive national campaign, in many areas it now had to pay its "volunteers" for campaign activities (Alarcón Bravo interview 1999; Alvarado Contreras interview 1999; Jara Ladrón interview 1999).

By the second round of the 1990 elections, APRA was openly supporting Fujimori over Vargas Llosa. Its initial reasons were ideological: Fujimori seemed vaguely centrist and claimed he would reject neoliberal market reforms, while Vargas Llosa's Libertad movement had been forged precisely out of a critique of García's statist economic policies. But even after Fujimori implemented the neoliberal "shock therapy" he had explicitly campaigned against just months earlier, APRA parliamentarians continued to vote for some of his legislative proposals, though they criticized him publicly.[18] García had resumed his position as de facto leader of the party, and APRA needed Fujimori's support to maintain the ex-president's parliamentary immunity as a senator-for-life (per the 1979 Constitution) and prevent an investigation of corruption in the previous government. By 1991, once the issue of García's prosecution had been voted down in the Chamber of Deputies, APRA did return to a more oppositional role, truer to the wishes of its dwindling party bases. But party politics was being transformed, and electoral movements were overshadowing political parties, even the storied APRA.

The Left

The United Left, or IU, was a coalition of leftist parties that emerged in late 1980 and remained in existence until early 1989. As noted above, the IU ran some highly successful campaigns in the 1983 municipal elections. The coalition's leader, Alfonso Barrantes, won the mayoralty of Lima and in 1984 was polling well for the 1985 presidential elections. But while Barrantes was the figurehead of the coalition, he himself had no particular party affiliation, and his supporters could best be described as "independent leftists." The coalition, on the other hand, brought together small parties with strong left-wing ideologies that were frequently at odds with one another. Coalition-building also papered over critical differences in long-term strategy, particularly on the question of seeking change via electoral competition versus revolutionary violence (Sanborn 1991).

The member parties of the IU in the mid-1980s ran the gamut of left-wing ideologies. The PCP (Partido Comunista Peruano, or Peruvian Communist Party) was Peru's oldest left party, a direct descendant of the group founded by José Carlos Mariátegui in 1928. It remained, until the end of the Cold War, pro-Moscow in orientation and was the dominant political presence in Peru's largest national labor federation, CGTP. But in the 1960s and '70s a new wave of Marxist and neo-Marxist parties emerged: the more nationalist PSR (Partido Socialista Revolucionario, or Revolutionary Socialist Party); the Trotskyite alliance FOCEP (Frente Obrero Campesino Estudiantil y Popular, or Worker, Peasant, Student and Popular Front); the Maoist coalition UNIR (Unión de Izquierda Revolucionaria, or Union of the Revolutionary Left) and its largest member group, PCP–PR (Partido Comunista del Peru–Patria Roja, or Communist Party of Peru–Red Homeland); and various parties that would later form into the neo-Marxist PUM (Partido Unificado Mariateguista, or Unified Mariateguist Party) and the independent leftist APS (Acción Política Socialista, or Socialist Political Action).

These groups varied widely in size, coherence, and civil society linkages. But IU was a coalition, and representation on its national decision-making body (the Comité Directivo Nacional) was "one party, one seat," with a consensus voting rule. The 1989 IU congress would likewise include roughly equal numbers of representatives from each party, regardless of how many members or militants they had. Independent leftists—active in the IU but not members of a party—had no voice but Barrantes' on the Comité and were severely underrepresented by the quota system for IU congress delegates.[19]

The member parties themselves tended to be corporatist (representation via base-level organizations) or Leninist (leadership by a small vanguard group) rather than formally democratic in their internal organization. Some had extensive national organizations and formal mechanisms for consulting their adherents. Others were led by public figureheads who attracted a corps of supporters. For the 1985 general elections, each party was responsible for selecting its candidates internally, and then the parties' representatives within the IU negotiated among themselves—and with Barrantes, who reserved the right to invite independent candidates on an ad hoc basis. The list for the Chamber of Deputies in each department was negotiated at the departmental level but then renegotiated in Lima (Castro Gómez interview 1999). The list for the Senate was negotiated nationally, and Barrantes reserved the right to choose—and place—ten independents on the IU's slate of sixty candidates (Ames Cobián interview 1999).

Like APRA members, IU politicians and bureaucrats on the public payroll were required to contribute to the coalition: normally 10 percent of their monthly salary, then 35 to 50 percent during months leading up to an election campaign. But some IU member parties also had their own resource bases in the unions and peasant organizations they led, and in the nongovernmental organizations (principally funded by European governments) with which they were affiliated.[20] Barrantes also raised money from individual contributors, and the parties did pay into a central coalition fund as well. Unlike APRA or any other contender, some left parties were able to contribute financially to the campaigns of their congressional candidates in 1985. Member parties could also mobilize large numbers of people in demonstrations that would draw media attention to candidates (Pease García interview 1999; Haya de la Torre interview 1999; Tuesta Soldevilla interview 1998).

The coalition managed to maintain some unity while on the 1985 campaign trail, insisting, for example, that every party's leaflets and posters promote the IU and not the individual parties. But aside from election periods there was little incentive for the parties to promote or develop the IU as an organization at the expense of their own individual groups (Breña Pantoja interview 1999). The leaders of small leftist parties had everything to lose by turning control of the coalition over to the larger numbers of left-leaning Peruvians who identified with the IU but were not active in a member party.

Barrantes did not want to formalize the IU as a mass-membership party either. An elected internal party structure might have eliminated

Barrantes' role as the fulcrum for the balance of power among member parties (Degregori interview 1999). In the seven years that he served as its president, Barrantes seldom attended a regularly scheduled meeting of the Comité Directivo, seeing little reason to concern himself with institutional rules or the painstaking work of party building (Ames Cobián interview 1999; Haya de la Torre interview 1999; Murrugara Florián interview 1999).

In 1985 Barrantes came in second in presidential elections, and the IU became the second-largest force in Parliament, with sixty-three of two hundred forty seats. Though Barrantes lost the Lima mayoralty in 1986 to the APRA's Jorge del Castillo (a close ally of Alan García), he was still considered a front-runner for the presidency in 1990, and polls in 1987 and 1988 showed him with a comfortable lead.

Yet precisely at this moment of high aspirations, the IU coalition began to break down. Barrantes worried that some of the more radical left parties were too closely linked with armed revolutionary movements (Letts Colmenares interview 1999; Dammert Egoaguirre interview, 1999). On the other side, both radicals and moderates within the coalition were critical of his absenteeist style of leadership and his inability to mediate conflicts among the member parties (Navarrete Zavaleta interview 1999; Murrugarra Florián interview 1999). In May 1987, Barrantes resigned as president of the Comité Directivo, though he maintained his position as de facto IU presidential candidate for 1990.

The unity of the United Left appeared to rebound a bit in 1988, as a multiparty commission charged with organizing a national IU congress began to resemble something akin to a nationwide IU structure. Independents and member-party stalwarts worked together. For the first time some party leaders even held official positions in both their own party and the IU coalition. Between a hundred fifty thousand and two hundred thousand people were signed up as IU volunteers and activists (Nieto Montesinos 1988; Dammert Egoaguirre interview 1999). But at the same time, fault lines within the coalition were widening. Negotiations over the coalition's program were cleft apart by issues such as the role of the state, cooperation with nonleftist political parties, and the legitimacy of armed struggle in the transition to socialism.

When the six-thousand-delegate congress was held in January 1989, two very different versions of the IU platform were still in play, with

Barrantes' candidacy being used as a bargaining chip. So Barrantes simply decided not to attend the party congress. He was fearful that he would either lose the nomination or be forced to accept an extremist platform that could undermine his political future.[21] But he was also confident that he could run and win on his own (Ames Cobián interview 1999; Dammert Egoaguirre interview 1999; Haya de la Torre interview 1999)

After days of discussion by delegates and backroom negotiations by party leaders at the congress site in Huampaní, the coalition fell apart, and IU split in two. The more moderate PSR, and moderate factions within radical parties like PUM, broke away and formed the ASI (Socialist Accord of the Left) coalition to contest the 1989 municipal elections. For the 1990 elections these moderates formed the IS (Izquierda Socialista, Socialist Left) coalition to run Barrantes as their presidential candidate. The more radical factions remained in the IU but chose former Lima city counselor Henry Pease—a moderate—as their presidential candidate. Several moderate groups, such as the APS and a new group of progressive Catholic lay leaders, MAS (Movimiento de Afirmación Socialista, or Movement of Socialist Affirmation), also decided to stay in IU (Tuesta Soldevilla 2001).

Barrantes' IS had no internal structure for choosing congressional candidates; such decisions were left entirely up to the presidential candidate himself. Independents were recruited at the last minute, as too few candidates had come forward from groups affiliated with the IS. Moreover, with the loss of the IU's best-organized parties and their financial bases, the IS required each candidate to personally donate $20,000—largely for Barrantes' presidential race—in addition to paying for their own individual legislative campaigns (Dammert Egoaguirre interview 1999). In the IU, Pease kept a lower profile, refusing to interfere with parties' internal candidate selection processes or with negotiations among party leaders. Up until the last day for registering presidential candidates, the IU parties—and Pease himself—offered Barrantes the chance to renegotiate his candidacy for a unified left (Pease García interview 1999). But he would not. Barrantes' overestimation of his personal popularity was part of the coalition's undoing.

The infighting severely tarnished the credibility and public image of the left. Financial support dried up, and the pool of militants and volunteers was lost not only by the IS but by the IU as well, as morale among the parties' rank and file sank. And the electoral consequences were devastating: Pease's and Barrantes' vote tallies in the first round of the 1990 elections were 8 percent and 5 percent respectively. The two candidates facing off in the second round were a right-wing independent backed by some traditional parties, Mario Vargas Llosa, and a previously unknown candidate with an ad hoc political movement, Alberto Fujimori.

The Right and the Rise of Electoral Movements

As his 1980–1985 term was winding down, President Fernando Belaúnde and the Acción Popular party that he had led for three decades grew increasingly unpopular. So in the lead-up to the 1985 election, he looked for novel ways to save the party from humiliation at the polls, and he began grooming novelist Mario Vargas Llosa for a future presidential candidacy. Belaúnde's plan was to name Vargas Llosa as Peru's ambassador to the United States, but Vargas Llosa instead asked to be prime minister, and Belaúnde acceded. The parliamentary coalition of the AP and PPC responded with an uproar. The PPC quit the coalition, and even loyal AP senators and deputies rebelled against this unilateral decision by their party leader.[22] Instead of the novelist, Senator Sandro Mariátegui was named prime minister (Vargas Llosa 1994; Cruchaga Belaúnde interview 1999).

After five years in power AP commanded more financial resources than ever.[23] But in the 1985 elections it won just 7 percent of the presidential vote and fifteen of two hundred forty seats in the legislature. AP did not run any candidates in the 1986 municipal elections, even though it had done well in local contests in the past. The party was internally disorganized, and the permanent de facto leadership of Fernando Belaúnde (almost seventy-three years old when he left office) was stifling its organizational development (Zamalloa Loayza interview 1999; Guzmán Romaña interview 1999). The PPC, too, struggled to recreate itself in the late 1980s.

The rejuvenation of the right came from a neoliberal social movement that coalesced around none other than Mario Vargas Llosa. In 1987, the Libertad (Liberty) movement took off as a vitriolic response to President Alan García's bank nationalization scheme (see chapter 3) and other statist economic policies. Vargas Llosa was the public face of the movement and polled well as a presidential candidate. His chief adviser, economist Hernando de Soto of the free-market think tank ILD (Instituto Libertad y Democracia, or Liberty and Democracy Institute), had strongly advised the writer against establishing any formal ties to traditional parties. De Soto believed that the taint of public distrust outweighed any organizational resources that the parties might bring to the table. Vargas Llosa had his own personal financial resources and the backing of many of Lima's wealthiest banking and industrial groups.[24] But in 1988 Miguel Cruchaga (cofounder of the Libertad movement and nephew of ex-president Belaúnde), among others, encouraged Vargas Llosa to ally Libertad with AP and PPC, in a coalition called FREDEMO (Frente Democrático, or Democratic Front) (Cruchaga Belaúnde interview 1999).[25]

The relationships among leaders and party organizations were troubled from the start. The balance of power in the nascent coalition first shifted away from the Libertad movement and toward the parties, particularly AP; ex-president Belaúnde, an experienced pol, was gaining leverage within FREDEMO. And by accord of the three groups, any new groups aspiring to join the Front would be absorbed into the quota allocated to Libertad for purposes of distributing positions on decision-making committees and spots on congressional lists, thus diluting Libertad's influence (Rubio Correa 1988). As late as March 1989, the secretaries general of the two parties, Edmundo del Águila of AP and Ricardo Amiel of PPC, were each still proposing their party's own *líder natural,* their "inherent leader"—Fernando Belaúnde and Luis Bedoya, respectively—as presidential candidates (Vargas Llosa 1994).[26]

But as the elections drew near, the personal popularity and extensive resources of Vargas Llosa then swung the balance of power away from the parties. When AP and PPC were stalemated in choosing FREDEMO candidates for the 1989 municipal elections, Vargas Llosa formally resigned as presidential candidate of the Front and promptly departed on a trip to Europe (Cruchaga Belaúnde interview 1999). He publicly criticized his erstwhile coalition partners, expressing what he would later describe in his memoirs as his "loathing for the political maneuvering in which the Front was submerged" (Vargas Llosa 1994, 93). Remarkably, in response to this resignation, vote intention for Vargas Llosa spiked from its previous level of 36 percent (in Lima and nationally) to 45 percent nationwide and as high as 50 percent in Lima (APOYO 1989; Lynch 1999). The public liked an independent candidate.

FREDEMO eventually agreed on a balance of AP and PPC municipal candidates to run under the Front's banner (Libertad did not field municipal candidates). Vargas Llosa returned to Peru and resumed his role as a pre-candidate for the presidency. But AP and PPC ran the municipal campaign as two entirely separate party operations. And the surprise winner of the Lima mayoralty, independent media mogul Ricardo Belmont, gave the country's political elite a glimpse of the weakly institutionalized, personality-driven electoral movements that would dominate politics throughout the 1990s.

Belmont's campaign was largely a televised affair, based on the top-rated phone-in show *Habla el Pueblo* (The People Speak) and the annual fundraising telethon he hosted. To run for office he launched an electoral movement called Obras (Works), but his real "party organization" was Canal 11/RBC, his media holding company, which owned a television station and numerous radio stations (Planas 2000). With a small campaign team he ran candidates only for mayor and metropolitan council of Lima, not at the district level (Angulo interview 1999).[27] Yet he soundly defeated his competitors, including the mayoral candidate who emerged from the standoff within FREDEMO, Juan Incháustegui of AP—himself an "independent" brought into Belaúnde's cabinet a few years earlier (Vargas Llosa 1994).

FREDEMO remained a loose coalition going into the 1990 elections. Each of the three coalition members selected and ordered its own congressional candidates, who were then alternated sequentially on FREDEMO lists. The organizational structure of AP, never very strong, had significantly declined by 1990. Candidates were required to donate funds to the party as well as fund their own campaigns (del Águila Morote interview 1999). Only a handful of AP departmental committees submitted slates of pre-candidates for the deputies' lists. Decisions on AP candidate selection and placement were made by a small group: current and ex–secretaries general, three at-large representatives, and—the vote with the most weight—Belaúnde (del Águila interview 1999). For districts outside of Lima in particular, Belaúnde himself personally selected the party members and, increasingly, "independents" who would run under the AP label (Trelles interview 1999). Similarly, the PPC had local selection committees in some departments, but, according to the head of the committee for La Libertad, Bedoya himself selected and ordered candidates on all departmental lists (Risco Boada interview 1999).

There were no FREDEMO offices, no FREDEMO staff or organizational structure, just a pact among two center-right political parties and an electoral movement dedicated to electing Vargas Llosa (Mendoza Habersperger interview 1999). In most ads, each group used its own name and logo. There was not one FREDEMO campaign, but three. And because of the preferential vote in congressional elections, they competed fiercely with one another.

In the presidential race, Vargas Llosa shared the funds from his campaign war chest only with an inner circle of Libertad confidantes— not Libertad candidates in particularly strategic races, and certainly not FREDEMO candidates who hailed from the AP or PPC (Cruchaga Belaúnde interview 1999). And this campaign, directed by a New York–based public relations firm, was more expensive and media-intensive than any in Peru's history. It was also mired in contradictions. Vargas Llosa was out on the hustings with Peru's indigenous and mestizo masses, but he was a white, wealthy Europhile, unabashedly elitist and visibly uncomfortable with those masses (Vargas Llosa 1994). What is more, he espoused an antiparty discourse while allying himself with two of Peru's traditional political parties.

After the first round of balloting, when it became clear that the presidential runoff would be between Vargas Llosa and Fujimori, Vargas Llosa offered to withdraw, ostensibly to steer Fujimori away from allying with APRA and the left (Vargas Llosa 1994). This led to outrage within FREDEMO, rumors of a coup d'état if he withdrew, and even intercession by the Cardinal of Peru to convince him to stay in the race.

When Fujimori won, the FREDEMO coalition dissolved almost immediately. Vargas Llosa departed again for Europe several days after the election, decapitating the Libertad movement, which went inactive after the 1990 runoff and officially disbanded with the 1992 *autogolpe* (Merino Lucero interview 1998). In the legislature, each of the three groups caucused separately (Cateriano Bellido interview 1999). Libertad lost four of its fifteen legislators to other parties by late 1991. And instead of consolidating a unified center-right party, the FREDEMO experiment left AP and PPC in turmoil.

The Fujimori Phenomenon

Alberto Fujimori had hoped to become a senator. He had worked with the García government in several capacities and so first tried to get a spot on the APRA list. Then he formed his own political group, to simultaneously run for president and Senate, a dual candidacy that was allowed under electoral law at the time. Even after registering his own presidential candidacy in late 1989, Fujimori still sought to join an existing party: he negotiated with Alfonso Barrantes over a spot on the IS list for Senate (Schmidt 1996). But these negotiations fell through, so he stuck with his own ad hoc group.

Fujimori, of Japanese descent, sought support from Lima's Nisei community; his wife, from a particularly prominent Japanese-Peruvian family, helped develop these ties. He also tapped into several national networks: his colleagues at the Agrarian University and his contacts among other university rectors; a group of evangelical Christian churches, the Iglesia Evangélica Peruana; and the national association of micro-entrepreneurs and small business owners, APEMIPE (Asociación de Pequeños y Medianos Industriales del Perú, or Association of Small and Medium-Sized Industrialists of Peru). These three bases coalesced into a movement called Cambio 90 (Change '90, or C-90).[28]

Leaders of each of the three clusters of support were responsible for legislative candidate selection in C-90, but with Fujimori guiding them (and issuing his own personal invitations to candidates as well). Crucially, the selectorate specifically looked for candidates with no prior background in politics and no record of party affiliation (Arroyo interview 1999). Filling the Senate and Lima deputies' lists was not difficult, but with little time and no party organization to speak of, the deputies' lists for other departments proved to be a challenge. The support networks enlisted operatives to identify potential candidates among local notables in each department, always with Fujimori's final approval (Zegarra Gutiérrez interview 1999). In some departments, candidates from the capital were "parachuted" in—a practice less common, though not unheard of, in more organized parties.

Legislative candidates paid their own campaign expenses and were forbidden from accepting donations from anyone outside of the three core networks of C-90 supporters. Adherents of the evangelical churches mobilized their formidable proselytizing machinery in service of the presidential candidate and the fifty legislative candidates (out of two hundred forty) who were evangelicals (Arroyo interview 1999). Other candidates traveled with Fujimori, following along as he conducted low-budget tours of rural and even urban areas atop a tractor, the movement's symbol. The expenses for Fujimori's own campaign totaled less than $500,000 and were paid largely by the candidate's wife, Susana Higuchi de Fujimori, and her family (Paredes interview 1999).

Fujimori had established something of a public image through an early-morning television program that he hosted. The show, *Concertando,* discussed national issues, particularly agricultural policies and techniques. It was little-known in Lima but more widely watched in rural areas where the state-owned Canal 7 was the only broadcast signal received (Jochamo-witz 1993). Within elite political circles, however, Fujimori was such an unknown that in late 1989 Vargas Llosa had not yet heard of the man who would defeat him just months later (Vivanco Amorín interview 1999). When Fujimori surged in the polls in the last two weeks of the first round, it caught many by surprise.

But becoming a contender did not prompt Fujimori to create a more substantial party organization, during the elections or afterward. This was not merely a problem of scarce time and resources; it was a conscious decision, consistent with Fujimori's antiparty rhetoric and the candidate recruitment techniques used for C-90. Some members of Fujimori's campaign team and representatives of the various sectors that backed him tried to build up a Cambio 90 organization to support him as candidate and, later, as president. However, Fujimori actively discouraged any sort of party-building activities (Arroyo interview 1999; Paredes interview 1999). As a candidate he refused to delegate any significant responsibilities, even to his running mate for first vice president, Máximo San Román, C-90's main link to the micro-entrepreneurs. San Román was not allowed to create a National Campaign Committee, for example (Planas 2000). Immediately after winning office, Fujimori began to dismantle even the scant organizational structures set up for his campaign. He fired Víctor Honma, the honorific secretary general of C-90, a week after the second-round victory (without replacing him); closed the C-90 office soon thereafter; and disavowed any local bases that had formed to support him (Planas 2000).

Fujimori's disdain for institutionalization carried over into his relationship with his own senators and deputies. Those political novices tried to coordinate their legislative activities and policy analysis with one another and with more experienced groups; Fujimori reacted with great displeasure whenever such efforts were made (Paredes interview 1999). The C-90 legislators were themselves divided over support for Fujimori's use of executive decree authority and over his neoliberal reforms in particular, with some of the evangelical parliamentarians quite vocal in their opposition (Arroyo interview 1999).[29] Fujimori instead made common cause with the right, the former FREDEMO member groups whose presidential candidate had, unlike Fujimori, actually campaigned on a neoliberal reform platform.

C-90 was at once too strong and too weak to be of use to the president in 1990–1991. By having their own sectoral interests, some C-90 legislators were too autonomous to always follow Fujimori's orders. But at Fujimori's own behest, there was no party organization to cohere the legislators, lengthen their time horizons, and discipline their legislative behavior by rewarding or punishing them in their career aspirations. They were also too disorganized to constrain the president's decision making. Thus, the group that had ridden Fujimori's coattails to office was rendered irrelevant.

After the *autogolpe* Fujimori founded a new electoral movement, as fluid as C-90 but without the conflicting allegiances. By reinventing his electoral movement in 1992—a tactic he would reprise in 1995, 1998, 2000, and beyond—he reaped many of the benefits of a disciplined political party with none of the constraints of independent party bases, long-term career ambitions, or an organizational counterweight to his leadership.

Looking back, how should we interpret the state of Peru's political parties in their prime? The party system of 1980s Peru presents a study in contradictions. On the one hand, even at its peak it was fragile. Scholars concur that Peru's party system was and is among the most volatile and least institutionalized in Latin America (Mainwaring and Scully 1995; Roberts and Wibbels 1997; Coppedge 1998; 2001a; Sánchez 2009). Prominent Peruvian analysts like Tuesta Soldevilla (1987), Cotler (1995), and Planas (2000) argued that Peru's major parties were personalistic and disorganized even in their 1980s heyday. But this era was nonetheless a watershed for party politics in Peru. There were strong patterns of class-based voting, even among informal-sector workers (Cameron 1994). APRA, IU, AP, and PPC together won 97 percent of the national vote in the 1985 presidential election, 93 percent of the vote in the 1986 municipal elections, and even a majority of votes in the first round of the 1990 election that brought Fujimori to power (Tanaka 1998). These parties were stronger as organizations (and more effective at constraining individual leaders) than the electoral movements that later emerged, as we will see in the sections that follow.

As noted, the reasons that parties failed are myriad. The analysis presented here suggests one additional, previously overlooked factor: the style of leadership within Peru's traditional parties made it especially difficult for them to adapt and recover from crisis and defeat. A party's capacity to adapt depends on a variety of institutional traits (Downs 1957; Mainwaring 1998; Panebianco 1988). Levitsky (2001) finds that a party can be strongly rooted in a society yet poorly routinized in its rules and organization, allowing for both stability and adaptability. So, for example, Argentina's Partido Justicialista was able to change with the times, in part because contestation for its leadership was wide open, yet Peronists still stayed loyal to the party. However, the weak institutionalization of Peru's parties manifested itself differently, closing off competition for top leadership posts rather than opening it. This tied the strategic behaviors of parties too closely to the personal goals of long-time leaders, in ways that were often at odds with the success of the party itself.

Belaúnde's perpetual presence kept AP from growing, as voters continued to punish AP for his performance in government and aspiring young leaders turned elsewhere for opportunities. The demise of the IU stemmed at least in part from Barrantes' belief that he could "go it alone" in 1990 and still maintain voter support. And in the case of APRA, García hobbled the party by only tepidly supporting the 1990 candidacy of fellow *aprista* Alva Castro, in the hope of returning to power; then, in the year that followed, APRA muted its criticism of Fujimori to keep García from being prosecuted for corruption; and finally, for nearly a decade, the immutability of García's leadership while he was in exile virtually paralyzed Peru's best-organized party.

But whatever their organizational weaknesses, parties in 1980s Peru were essential to politics, playing a crucial role in structuring the behavior of political elites. As parties began to decline in the late 1980s and early 1990s, they opened the field to more independent candidates and groups. For the rest of the 1990s they would be crowded out by a new organizational form far less institutionalized than even the most personalistic party: the electoral movement. And the decline of party organizations and the rise of electoral movements helped create an immensely powerful executive branch.

Electoral Movements and Party (Dis)Organization in Peru, 1992–2000

The *autogolpe* of 1992 hit parties and politicians particularly hard. While there was little widespread repression on the scale of the bureaucratic-authoritarian regimes of the Southern Cone in the 1960s and '70s, in the days following the April 5 coup the "political class" in Peru was the target of harassment, arrests, and illegal searches and seizures, including the removal of files from parliamentarians' offices in Congress.

Under international pressure, Fujimori called elections for a Democratic Constituent Congress (CCD) that would draft a "new" constitution for Peru (see chapter 3). In doing so he also made a clean break from his erstwhile congressional caucus. He created a new electoral movement, called Nueva Mayoría (New Majority, NM), incorporating a number of his nonpartisan ministers and other technocrats from the executive branch. In the 1992 CCD elections, NM and C-90 ran a joint list of candidates, with NM candidates outnumbering C-90 candidates almost three to one. They together won forty-four of eighty seats. Recruiting new candidates, creating new party labels, and dropping legislators who would not acquiesce to the executive or who otherwise proved inconvenient: this would be Fujimori's game plan for the rest of the decade.

APRA and AP refused to participate in the CCD because they felt this might legitimize the coup and, what is more, they would have fared poorly at the polls. The left was also largely absent from that race, although several of its most moderate groups joined together to field a list of candidates under the label MDI (Movimiento Democrático de Izquierda, or Democratic Movement of the Left). Of the main traditional parties, only the PPC participated fully. The FIM (Frente Independiente Moralizador, or Independent Moralizing Front), an anti-APRA group that had run only candidates for the Lima district in the Chamber of Deputies in 1990, also participated. Other groups that existed prior to the coup and participated in the CCD were the FNTC (Frente Nacional de Trabajadores y Campesinos, or National Front of Peasants and Workers), a regional party of

Table 4.3. Legislative Seats Won, 1992 Elections

	Democratic Constituent Congress (CCD) Members
C-90/NM	44
PPC	8
FIM	7
Renovación	6
MDI	4
CODE	4
FNTC	3
FREPAP	2
SODE	1
MIA	1
TOTAL	80

the southern highlands, led by the Cáceres Velásquez family, and FREPAP (Frente Popular Agricola–FIA del Perú, or Popular Agricultural Front–FIA of Peru), a party representing the fringe evangelical sect Israelites of the New Universal Pact. A rump group from Libertad joined with right-of-center independents to form Renovación (Renovation), and a similar right-wing splinter group of ex-*apristas* ran as CODE (Convergencia Democrática, or Democratic Convergence). I describe some of these groups in more detail below.

Party organizations were disappearing. Many Peruvians blamed parties and politicians in toto for the dire economic and social crises of the late '80s and early '90s, and now they had an alternative. Politicians' ability to communicate with voters via mass media and to measure voters' preferences via polls rose dramatically in this period, reducing the functional need to create extensive party organizations (Levitsky and Cameron 2003).[30] And the *autogolpe* as well as the president's antiparty rhetoric further marginalized those parties that remained.

Fujimori's Electoral Movements

Cambio 90/Nueva Mayoría developed into a highly successful electoral movement run by just a handful of advisers. Its resources came from the state itself, from corruption, and from the use (and abuse) of television, radio, and the press. As one pro-Fujimori congressman divulged to me, it was the media and, in particular, the army that served the functions of the incumbent's political party (Trelles interview 1999).

Legislative candidates for the 1995 elections were selected by President Fujimori, his brother Santiago Fujimori, and NM leader Jaime Yoshiyama. Most C-90 holdovers from 1990 were removed from the candidates' list by 1995; only three remained. In total, twenty of forty-four sitting *fujimorista* members of the CCD were omitted from the 1995 C-90/NM parliamentary list, after serving just two years (*Caretas,* Jan. 12, 1995). The new candidates from Lima tended to be government technocrats or businesspeople and journalists connected with the Lima news daily *Expreso,* but Yoshiyama and his advisers received approximately one thousand résumés from aspiring candidates (*Caretas,* Nov. 24, 1994). In order to broaden the geographic scope of the group and incorporate more candidates from outside Lima, Yoshiyama sent teams to provincial towns and cities to conduct polls and focus groups on local notables. In some cases, Fujimori or Yoshiyama would put a candidate on the list, and, unless he won, the candidate would have no personal contact with anyone else in C-90/NM (Ibañez interview 1999). Most prospective candidates were, however, interviewed by a psychologist hired by Yoshiyama. One of the traits they were looking for was, tellingly, that candidates be "apolitical" (Conaghan 1996; Torres y Torres Lara interview 1998).

In the 1995 campaign, televised ads and campaign materials for aspiring C-90/NM legislators were tightly controlled. Fujimori and Yoshiyama regulated the content of ads and the degree of media saturation, ensuring that campaigns stayed "on message" and focused on Fujimori as well as the legislative candidate. The most prized campaign resource, one enjoyed by an inner circle of legislators, was traveling with the president as he inaugurated a record number of public works in the months before the elections.

Fujimori won the 1995 presidential elections, and C-90/NM took sixty-seven of a hundred twenty seats in the single-chamber, single-district congress. In government for five more years, the group still did not develop much organizational complexity or stable ties to societal bases. It was, in C-90/NM Congressman Jorge Trelles' words, a "useful machine for elections" (interview 1999). According to C-90/NM Congressman Carlos Ferrero Costa (interview 1999), "It has always worked as a group without statutes, without regulations, with no election of authorities,

Table 4.4. Legislative Seats Won, 1995 Elections

	Members of Congress
C-90/NM	67
UPP	17
APRA	8
FIM	6
CODE–País Posible	5
AP	4
PPC	3
Renovación	3
IU	2
OBRAS	2
FREPAP	1
MIA	1
FNTC	1
TOTAL	120

with no national congress . . . not as a political party." This lack of institutionalization was by design, not due to an absence of power or resources. C-90/NM legislators saw supporting the president as their only role. As one-time president of Congress Ricardo Marcenaro Frers asserted, "We don't want a traditional political group, with political party headquarters, membership cards, discipline, etc. We believe that this is our greatest strength, precisely that we do not have any of that. . . . Fujimori is the project. . . . To be called Cambio 90, Nueva Mayoría, to be called 'Long Live Peru.' . . . The name is meaningless. . . . The logo does not interest us" (interview 1999). These words capture precisely the character of Fujimori's political vehicle. It was an electoral movement, one that was inherently hostile to organizational development and was primarily focused on supporting and maintaining one man in power. Years after the *autogolpe,* Fujimori's supporters in the legislature maintained a strong antiparty discourse. C-90/NM Congressman Trelles (interview 1999) voiced this eloquently: "I do not believe in political parties in Peru. It's like talking about snow at Christmastime [in Peru]: impossible, and foreign. . . . The parties' time has passed."

From 1992 to 2000, Fujimori's organization was highly disciplined and utterly subservient to the president and the executive branch. The project was Fujimori, not C-90/NM. There was no organization to speak of outside of Congress, and among legislators there were no political tactics or organizational linkages except those conducted via President Fujimori and his closest advisors. In V. O. Key's terms (1964), there was no party organization, no party-in-society, and scant party-in-government.

Several months after the 1995 general elections, Peruvians went to the polls to elect municipal authorities. Fujimori had had only limited success in previous municipal elections, as it was much more difficult to field a coherent set of candidates across thousands of municipalities than a hundred twenty congressional candidates in a single national electoral district. Moreover, congressional and first-round presidential balloting take place at the same time, producing a mild "presidential coattails" effect. By contrast, linking a municipal candidate to the president requires more decentralized publicity and a more coordinated organizational effort, particularly given the weakness of party identification and the lack of emphasis on the C-90/NM label in *oficialista* discourse.

The difficulties that Fujimori faced in the 1995 municipal elections were further exacerbated by the crowded and confusing array of groups competing. Nationwide, most of these were local lists whose wider political connections were difficult to ascertain. In the capital city, C-90/NM fielded candidates for mayor of the province of (Metropolitan) Lima and all forty-two districts therein; it was clear to voters who the president's affiliates were. But in other municipalities, there was a multiplicity of "copycat" lists with variations and combinations of the words Cambio, Nueva, and Mayoría, or the numbers 90 or 95.[31] In some cases, more than one group claimed to be Fujimori's official affiliate and made campaign promises based on the material benefits that such ties would supposedly bring. Nationally, 53 percent of valid votes went to independent local lists, versus 20 percent for groups tied to Lima mayor Alberto Andrade (see below) and just 19 percent for Fujimori's actual groups (Tuesta Soldevilla 2007).

The attempted solution to this problem of "brand control" three years later was to create a temporary network of local-level groups. True to form, Fujimori launched a new label for the 1998 elections, a movement called Vamos Vecino (Let's Go, Neighbor). Absalón Vásquez, a former APRA party organizer, created this top-down network utilizing the local apparatuses of the national state: appointed bureaucracies such as prefectures and the CTARs that replaced elected regional governments after

1992. This strategy yielded somewhat better results: in 1998, 33 percent of valid votes were cast for independent lists, while 25 percent voted for Vamos Vecino, though Andrade's Somos Perú won 28 percent (Tuesta Soldevilla 2007).

After the 1998 municipal elections (and 1999 by-elections) Vamos Vecino returned as one of four officially registered groups that supported the presidential candidacy of Alberto Fujimori in 2000. These should not be mistaken for party factions. Though there was some competition between congressional figures, most *fujimoristas* interviewed for this book confirmed that factionalism among them was minimal. The four labels that comprised the Peru 2000 alliance—Cambio 90, Nueva Mayoría, Vamos Vecino, and Peru 2000—were not autonomous organizations. Whatever spoils accrued to politicians were usually doled out by Fujimori (or Montesinos) to individuals directly, not through factional leaders. And in the composition of the hundred-and-twenty-candidate list for the 2000 elections, the most recently fabricated electoral movements, Vamos Vecino and Peru 2000, were only a minor presence, with just eight candidates and one candidate respectively.[32]

When Fujimori announced he was seeking a third term, he did not consult the "party" or his members of Congress. Unlike some of the snap decisions made by García in the late 1980s, this one did not engender any blowback from C-90/NM. Nobody objected; nobody else was waiting in the wings as an aspiring presidential candidate (Hildebrandt interview 2007). These legislators surmised that their political careers, perhaps even their freedom, hinged on Fujimori's continuing in the presidency.

In 2000, the campaigns of pro-Fujimori congressional candidates were de-emphasized in favor of promoting the president, even more than in previous elections. Perhaps Fujimori and Montesinos trusted that they could always purchase a legislative majority after the fact, which they did. And by late 2000, when Fujimori and Montesinos were no longer in power, that manufactured majority abruptly fell apart (Carey 2003b), though the electoral movement itself has proven more resilient.

APRA

In the lead-up to the 1995 elections, the APRA party was wracked by internal conflict over the role of Alan García. Despite being in exile in Bogotá and Paris since 1992, García continued to have the final say on important decisions within the party.[33] The secretary general at the time, Agustín Mantilla, was a loyal *alanista,* but the party's presidential candidate, ex-congresswoman and former education minister Mercedes Cabanillas, was a reformer. Cabanillas was chosen by acclaim at a party congress; presidential candidate selection was not openly competitive. In more competitive internal party elections for its congressional list, reformers largely prevailed over pro-García candidates (*Caretas,* Dec. 22, 1994). But Mantilla reordered the list—and added numerous candidates who had not even competed in the internal elections—without informing Cabanillas. This induced a rift, and Cabanillas's minority group within the party's National Executive Committee (CEN) tried to have some candidates replaced after the list had already been registered (*Caretas,* Jan. 12, 1995).

A divided APRA won just eight seats in Congress and a mere 4 percent of the presidential vote in 1995. Like AP and IU, it had failed to get the 5 percent of the vote required to maintain national party status, and set about collecting signatures to reenroll the party with the National Elections Tribunal (JNE).[34] The party did not field candidates in municipal elections later that year, so a number of *apristas* ran under independent labels. For example, José Murgía was reelected mayor of Trujillo, an APRA stronghold, with an electoral movement of his own in 1995; he then ran again under the APRA label in 1998 municipal elections. By that time, the party had regrouped somewhat and received 7 percent of the vote nationwide at the municipal level. In Lima, APRA also set about renovating its decaying party headquarters, the Casa del Pueblo (House of the People), in an attempt to return it to its once-prominent role as a community center and social service provider. However, the national party structure remained weak, and many ex-*apristas* who ran as independent candidates or formed new electoral movements simply stayed outside the party.

Reformers within the party lost their battle for control of APRA's future. The secretary general elected in 1999 was Congressman Jorge del Castillo, Alan García's legal counsel and close ally. A new public relations campaign to rally the party faithful and regain the support of Peruvian voters was "*Alan Vuelve,*" or "Alan Returns." The plan was for García to return from exile and head the APRA congressional list in the 2000 elections (but not run for president). A poll commissioned by the party supposedly demonstrated that APRA could expect 5–6 percent of the congressional vote with its current batch of candidates, or 18–20 percent of the congressional vote were García to lead the list. García's supporters and even his critics believed that his return would be good for the party (Franco Ballester interview 1999; Cubas Cava interview 1999; Aldave Pajares interview 1999; Santa Maria Calderón interview 1999). So vanguard groups of *"Alan Vuelve"* promoters were set up in cities across Peru, coordinated by former Lima deputy Wilbert Bendezú and former García publicist Hugo Otero. In February 1999, García (live from Belgium) gave his first televised interview since the 1992 *autogolpe*. After resistance from reformers and the suspension of several APRA legislators, what remained of the party hierarchy bent to the logic of the polls and made García's return official party policy.

García, fearing incarceration, ultimately did not return for the 2000 elections. APRA won just 6 percent of the congressional vote and a scant 1.4 percent for presidential candidate Abel Salinas. García's return might have boosted those figures; his second-place finish in presidential elections a year later was impressive, but the circumstances were rather different. In 1999, bringing back the scandal-tainted ex-president had the effect of polarizing the electorate and fragmenting opposition groups, some of whom believed that Fujimori and Montesinos were behind *"Alan Vuelve"* (*Caretas,* Feb. 18 and April 8, 1999).

The Left

The social bases of the IU parties, hit hard by economic crisis and civil war in the late 1980s, were dealt a further blow by neoliberal reforms in the early 1990s. Many former beneficiaries of the neighborhood self-help organizations that were IU strongholds in the 1980s—such as Vaso de Leche (Glass of Milk) and Clubes de Madres (Mothers' Clubs)—became clients of Fujimori's executive-branch welfare programs. Similarly, as market reforms broke peasant communities and cooperatives into private smallholdings, these groups' collective allegiances to leftist parties dissolved as well (Churats interview 1999). Organized labor, already weak, was further debilitated by neoliberal reforms. Labor rights were substantially reduced, and the power of unions was diminished by job instability, the privatization of state enterprises, and new rules that fragmented the way that unions organized at the shop level. By the mid-1990s nine separate and competing "central" labor confederations were operating in Peru. Wage earners made up just 30 percent of the economically active population, and fewer than half of them belonged to unions (Balbi 1997). Crisis had severely weakened Peru's civil society, particularly in the sectors that had gravitated toward left parties in earlier decades (Roberts 1996).

The left's electoral support eroded as well. Most of the IU parties that turned against each other in 1989 had ceased to exist by 1995. In general elections that year, only UNIR and PUM remained in IU, but even those two parties actually ran separate campaigns; each elected just one IU congressman. As a largely symbolic gesture, IU ran former Lima deputy Agustín Haya de la Torre in the presidential race, and he received only 1 percent of the vote. Many of the moderate left's most experienced candidates instead ran with the Union por el Perú (UPP) electoral movement in 1995 and 2000 (see below).

The IU ran no candidates in the 1995 or 1998 municipal elections, but some former IU municipal politicians continued to win office—as independents in 1995, as part of Somos Lima/Somos Perú in 1998 (see below), and, in some instances, as pro-Fujimori candidates. In Lima, for example, the district mayor of San Juan de Miraflores, Adolfo Ocampo Vargas, was twice elected for the IU in the 1980s and then twice elected with pro-Fujimori movements (C-90/NM in 1995 and Vamos Vecino in 1998). In Ocampo's words, his years as an IU mayor during a period of radicalization made him "more pragmatic, learning the difference between theory and practice" (Ocampo Vargas interview 1999). *Oficialista* affiliation brought access to power and resources, powerful temptations for municipal politicians.

Amid the ruins of fragmented labor and peasant movements and co-opted base-level organizations, no party of the left ran in the 2000 general elections.[35]

Acción Popular and the Partido Popular Cristiano

In the 1990s, AP grew even weaker as a national organization but maintained a level of competitiveness in municipal elections. In preparing for the 1995 general elections AP had to cancel primaries it had planned, for lack of resources. A small committee instead drew mainly from among

AP's municipal politicians to fill the list of a hundred twenty congressional candidates. AP had garnered 13 percent of the vote in 1993 municipal elections and won 5 percent in 1995 and 1998. By the July 1999 by-elections, AP had 129 district mayors and 10 provincial mayors. According to the AP secretary general at the time, Valentín Paniagua Corazao (interview 1999), this increased the number of local party organizations to almost a hundred and fifty, mostly outside of Lima. However, at the top rung of the AP party hierarchy, Fernando Belaúnde retained final decision-making authority. On his advice the party took a turn to the right, choosing young entrepreneur Raúl Diez Canseco as its presidential candidate in 1995 (Acurio Velarde interview 1999). He received 1.7 percent of the vote, and the party won four seats in Congress. Five years later, AP presidential candidate Víctor García Belaúnde got a paltry 0.4 percent; the party won just three seats. AP was struggling, though the interim presidency of Valentín Paniagua would later give it a brief reprieve.

The PPC, unlike AP, did hold primaries in 1994 to select candidates for the 1995 elections, although its National Commission could still add to or reorder its congressional list. That year the PPC backed out of the presidential race at the last minute; running only a congressional race, it won a modest three seats. However, the largest threat the PPC faced was that many of its long-time municipal party politicians had great success winning elections as "independents" in 1995 and 1998, particularly in the Lima-Callao area. Both the mayor of metropolitan Lima, Alberto Andrade, and the mayor of Callao, Alex Kouri, were former *pepecistas*. The party had initiated the practice of granting its members "license" to create or join independent electoral movements. However, successful independent candidates took office and never returned to the party; only unsuccessful candidates resumed their PPC affiliation. The best and brightest were being drained from the party (Flores Nano interview 1999). This practice continued in the 2000 elections, as the PPC failed to gather enough signatures to reenroll as an official political party. Though some PPC militants moved to Andrade's Somos Peru movement, the two groups did not form a coalition, nor did the party negotiate spots for its members on other lists. The future of the PPC looked bleak, but it too would recover.

Overall, Peru's traditional political parties were falling apart in the mid-1990s. In the 1995 elections they either launched largely symbolic

presidential campaigns or opted to focus solely on the congressional contest. APRA, AP, and PPC candidates for Congress in 1995 ran their own
campaigns and reaped little benefit from the party. In the cases of AP and
APRA, the ongoing dominance of a de facto leader was an impediment
to internal party reform or adaptation. In the April 1995 elections not one
of these traditional political parties attained the 5 percent of the vote required to maintain official party status (Kay 1995; Palmer 1996). Accu-
mulating the signatures needed to reenroll a party usually entailed collecting 1 to 1.5 million signatures just to net 500,000 registered voters who
had not signed for any other political party or movement since the most
recent general elections. This activity took up all of the organizational
capacity—and money, since most had to pay for professional signature
collectors—that these weakened groups could muster. Fewer elected officials also meant fewer resources, as even at their peak traditional parties
were dependent on the salaries of politicians and bureaucrats to fill their
coffers. The parties of the left, which did have broader bases of material
and human resources within civil society, saw those bases shrink and lose
autonomy.

The Fujimori government co-opted some experienced party organizers and politicians from the remnants of the IU as well as from AP, PPC,
and APRA. But other "independent" lists and new electoral movements
began to emerge in the mid-1990s and likewise incorporated politicians
with roots in traditional parties as well as public figures with their own
media or financial resources. Such movements came to dominate Peru's
national electoral politics in the 1990s, not only on the side of the incumbent President Fujimori but on the opposition side too. And like C-90/
NM, these groups were never designed to be institutionalized party
organizations.

Independent Candidates and Electoral Movements

The most prevalent organizational form for competing in elections in Peru
in 1993–2000 was the ad hoc electoral movement. Though some electoral movements were more successful than others at the polls, what they
had in common was a weak or fluid organizational structure. Because most
of these movements were created for a particular election and thus needed
to be enrolled as new political organizations with the JNE, their principal

activity during their foundational period was simply gathering signatures or, more commonly, paying professional signature gatherers. Once registered, the movements' lack of organization and, for many, their overriding focus on launching a presidential candidate—coupled with the reality of congressional campaigning in a single national electoral district—meant that their campaigns tended to be extremely media-centered.

Obras (Works) provided the model for other would-be outsider politicians. As noted above, it began as a personal campaign vehicle to elect media baron Ricardo Belmont as mayor of Lima in 1989 and then reelect him in 1993. It went national in 1995 with Belmont's run at the presidency but elected only two congressmen, both of whom abandoned the movement and served in Congress as independents. The movement disappeared from both national and municipal politics after 1995.

UPP (Unión por el Perú, Union for Peru) was the most prominent of the electoral movements opposed to President Fujimori in the mid-1990s. It was created in 1994 to launch the presidential candidacy of former United Nations secretary general Javier Pérez de Cuéllar. The UPP was markedly heterogeneous, incorporating a moderate leftist group (MDI), figures from the political center and right, and a small group of evangelical Christian candidates, several of whom were veterans of the original Cambio 90. Pérez de Cuéllar and two advisors (Guido Pennano and Alfredo Barnechea) selected most of the legislative candidates, and the presidential candidate himself reserved the right to assign the first ten spots on the list. Candidates spent their own money on their campaigns and rarely met among themselves, each one seeing his or her allegiance as resting with the leader and not the group (Pease García interview 1999). Though Pérez de Cuéllar lost badly to Fujimori in 1995, seventeen UPP candidates were elected to Congress. However, Pérez de Cuéllar was the only link among these politicians, and though he retained his formal position as head of the party until 1999, he absented himself from Peru right after the 1995 elections. The caucus immediately began to hemorrhage legislators, with some enticed to join the *fujimoristas* and others fleeing to more viable opposition groups (Estrada Choque interview 1999; Cerro Moral interview 1999). There was no party organization at all, and even the UPP's largest headquarters (in Lima and Cusco) stayed open for less than a year after the elections. In 2000 UPP ran former vice president and C-90 senator Máximo San Román for president, winning three seats in Congress and just 0.3 percent of the presidential vote. UPP would return to prominence in the first decade of the twenty-first century, but with a very different message.

FIM (Frente Independiente Moralizador, or Independent Moralizing Front) began as a personal project of former public prosecutor Fernando Olivera in 1990. Like Libertad, it was conceived as a backlash against Alan García and the APRA. FIM won seven seats in the Lima district of the Chamber of Deputies in 1990. The movement went on to win seven seats in the CCD in 1992 and six seats in Congress in 1995. FIM absorbed several politicians from the defunct Libertad movement but was by and large a collection of independents led by Olivera. There was no national party organization. Candidates were chosen in 1990 by Olivera alone and in 1995 by Olivera and a small group of advisers (Cateriano Bellido interview 1999; Falvy Valdivieso interview 1999). Candidates were not financially supported by FIM, and winners were not required to contribute to FIM. FIM held no public rallies and had a temporary office in Lima for campaign periods only. In 2000 FIM again ran only a congressional slate and won nine seats. So while it did not develop any greater degree of organizational complexity, it had a national reputation and attracted an increasing number of voters from across Peru: well-positioned for larger gains in 2001 and a governing role as junior coalition partner.

Renovación (Renovation) was formed by Rafael Rey, a conservative Catholic of the Opus Dei denomination, along with a small group of former Libertad activists, to compete in the 1992 elections for the CCD. In the 1990s it was a "loyal opposition" group that supported most of Fujimori's economic and social program; in fact, two of the three congressmen it elected in 1995 defected to the *oficialista* list by the 2000 elections, leaving only the founder. In the 1995 elections, only Rey appeared in televised ads, and he ran his own campaign with his own funds. There was no party organization outside of its dwindling congressional caucus. A similar group, CODE (Convergencia Democrática, or Democratic Convergence), was formed by right-wing former APRA politician José Barba. It too was launched for the 1992 CCD elections, in which it won four seats. In 1995, CODE entered into an alliance with País Posible (described below); of the five congressmen it elected that year, only two remained affiliated with the group. In 1999, Rafael Rey made an alliance with José Barba to collect signatures and run a slate of candidates for the 2000 elections. The group they registered, Avancemos (Let's Move Forward), was described by their own campaign organizer as a "personal arrangement," not an attempt at party organization (Ruíz interview 1999). Avancemos soon disappeared, its presidential candidate, Federico Salas, co-opted by Fujimori after the 2000 elections, though Rey and Barba would remain prominent in Peru's politics.

Solidaridad Nacional (National Solidarity, SN) was created in 1999 as an electoral movement to promote the presidential candidacy of Luis Castañeda Lossio, a former AP militant who later served as head of Peru's social security health-care administration (Instituto Peruano de Seguridad Social, IPSS) in the 1990s. Castañeda won just 2 percent of the vote in April 2000, and within a few months all five of the legislators elected under the SN label had renounced their affiliations with the movement: two became independents, and three joined the pro-Fujimori caucus. But SN would enjoy more success in the first decade of the twenty-first century.

Somos Lima (We Are Lima) began as an electoral vehicle of Alberto Andrade, once the PPC-affiliated mayor of Miraflores, an affluent Lima suburb. In 1995 Andrade defeated the C-90/NM candidate, Fujimori adviser and former CCD congressman Jaime Yoshiyama, for the mayoralty of metropolitan Lima. Andrade also ran candidates in all forty-two districts of Metropolitan Lima and elected district mayors in twenty of them. In 1998 he won reelection in Lima, defeating the Vamos Vecino candidate, one-time Fujimori prime minister (and former AP party member) Juan Carlos Hurtado Miller. Andrade increased his group's share of Lima district mayors to twenty-two out of forty-two. More importantly, in three years Somos Lima had expanded into a national electoral movement, Somos Perú (We Are Peru, SP). SP fielded candidates (or made alliances with local movements) in all but a handful of provinces and districts in Peru—194 provinces, 1,821 districts, each one with a mayoral candidate and a slate of *regidores* (city counselors)—an organizational feat that only the government-sponsored Vamos Vecino could match. SP won 28 percent of the national vote, which translated into twenty-one provincial mayors and several hundred district mayors and counselors. Unlike most electoral movements, SP actually tried to build an organization; it held local conventions across Peru followed by a six-hundred-delegate national convention in August 1999. Facing this challenge, the Fujimori government pressured municipal authorities elected on the SP ticket to abandon the movement. Between August and December 1999, a total of thirty-two district and provincial mayors cut their ties with SP, either becoming nominally independent or officially allying with Vamos Vecino. And within a few years, the organizational promise shown by SP was undone. Andrade was a presidential candidate in 2000 and faced personal smear campaigns funded and directed by the government. These dirty tricks were effective precisely because electoral movements are organized around an individual leader. Andrade won only 3 percent of the vote, and SP elected just eight legislators, one of whom immediately defected to the *fujimoristas.*

Finally, País Posible (Possible Country)[36] was the creation of 1995 presidential candidate Alejandro Toledo. Unable to collect enough signatures to register, Toledo allied with the parliamentary list of CODE. He came in fourth that year, winning just 3.3 percent of the presidential vote. It was thus a surprise to many analysts when he revived his ad hoc movement as Perú Posible (Possible Peru, PP), holding a party congress in 1999. Even more remarkably, he emerged late in the 2000 election cycle as the chief contender against Fujimori. PP won twenty-nine seats in Congress, though Toledo withdrew from the second round of the presidential race. A year later, PP would be in power.

But in the immediate wake of the 2000 elections, the state of political organization in Peru was grim. Fujimori's electoral movements had maintained their predominance in Congress by less than democratic means. The groups that rose up to challenge Fujimori were themselves electoral movements, built around prominent personalities with varying degrees of political experience. Not all of them were "outsiders," and to the extent that they were "anti-systemic," they were opposed to a decade-long regime that was itself "anti-systemic." What the movements led by Toledo and Castañeda (and, to a lesser extent, Andrade) shared with Fujimori was not a political orientation but a lack of organizational structure. They also shared, even with the "traditional" parties of Peru, a tendency toward personalistic leadership—but without any of the parties' career politicians or intermediate-level leaders as counterweights. And the "traditional" parties looked to be nearly dead, unable to win votes and adherents in a society that was increasingly less organized, more media-centered, and more distrustful of formal institutions. But looks can be deceiving.

Table 4.5. Legislative Seats Won, 2000 Elections

	Members of Congress
C-90/NM/VV/P2000	52
PP	29
FIM	9
SP	8
APRA	6
SN	5
Avancemos (Renovación)	3
AP	3
UPP	3
FREPAP	2
TOTAL	120

Parties or Movements? Electoral Politics in 2001–2006

The results of the 2000 elections did not stand for long. The fall of the Fujimori regime, the return of the rule of law, and the extraordinary elections of 2001 together had the effects of changing the political game and creating opportunities for political organizations—old and new—in Peru. The unequal playing field and the mafia-like tactics used by the incumbent to defeat his political competition were no longer present. The electoral movements created by Fujimori struggled for a time in this new environment, but as we shall see, they ultimately survived, buoyed by Fujimori's unexpected return. Of the opposition electoral movements that emerged in the late 1990s, some, like Andrade's SP, faded away or were relegated to ever-smaller corners of Peru's political arena. Others, like Olivera's FIM, burned bright for a period but ultimately faded too. Castañeda's SN enjoyed electoral success as part of a coalition of movements and small parties, though its future as a stand-alone group seems entirely dependent on its leader's ability to continue to win elections. Pérez de Cuéllar's UPP, as we shall see, became newly relevant for a time by subsuming itself to a new personalistic leader. Even Toledo's PP, in power for five years, floundered as an organization—in part because, unlike Fujimori, Toledo would not or could not use repressive tactics and misuse state resources to build up support for himself and tear down the competition.

Most importantly, old parties thought dead or dormant enjoyed renewed success at the ballot box. With APRA and, to a lesser extent, PPC gaining ground in 2001–2006, the idea that at least some prominent groups competing for votes and making laws in Peru could be party organizations worth the name was revived with surprising alacrity.

The 2001 Presidential and Legislative Elections

In late January 2001 Alan García touched down on Peruvian soil for the first time in nine years and hit the presidential campaign trail running, just ten weeks before election day. He quickly became a contender in a three-way race with Alejandro Toledo and with PPC's Lourdes Flores, now leading the right-of-center Unidad Nacional (National Unity, UN) coalition, which brought together PPC, Rafael Rey's Renovación (RN), Cambio Radical (José Barba's CODE, with a new name), and, eventually, Castañeda's SN.

In the first round of the 2001 presidential elections, Toledo won with 36.5 percent of the vote and faced a runoff against García, who narrowly beat out Flores 25.8 percent to 24.3 percent. Toledo went on to win the second round, 53 percent to 47 percent. Notably, while Toledo's PP electoral movement continued to ride a wave of popularity for his challenge of Fujimori in 2000, its closest contenders were a traditional political party (APRA) and a coalition (UN) that blended a traditional party (PPC) with some of the more enduring electoral movements (RN, SN, and CR). APRA performed wildly better with García than without him: 1.4 percent of the vote in 2000 versus 25.8 percent and a shot at the presidency in 2001. PPC had not fielded a presidential candidate of its own in at least fifteen years, but with Lourdes Flores at the helm, the UN coalition had some appeal beyond its middle- and upper-class Lima core of support.

The short timeframe for the 2001 elections also meant that even organized parties had trouble mounting internal elections or systematic selection processes for their lists of congressional candidates. What is more, the new electoral system required all groups to find candidates in twenty-five different districts of Peru. Traditional parties like APRA mostly fielded their own career politicians. But for electoral movements, the most desirable candidates were those with their own resources: money, fame, access to free media and civil society networks, or experience with another movement or party.[37]

In PP, legislative candidate selection was largely in the hands of Toledo and a group of regional leaders who recruited candidates for departments away from Lima (Taco Llave interview 2007; Waisman Rjavinsthi interview 2007). In APRA, congressional hopefuls were asked to present their résumés to the party's National Executive Committee and National Political Directorate, which selected and ordered candidates (Santa María Calderón interview 2005). AP attempted to hold internal elections, but even after the highly visible success of the Paniagua presidency, the enfeebled party drew few militants to its primaries and instead had to construct a more ad hoc congressional list (Alva Orlandini interview 2005). PPC had lost its party registration but joined an alliance, UN, spearheaded by its own Lourdes Flores. She was not the head of the PPC at the time; that was Ántero Flores-Aráoz, who did not support her negotiating on behalf of the party (interview 2005). But as a highly popular presidential contender, she was in the driver's seat. And in the UN, congressional lists alternated (roughly every third slot) the personal choices of Lourdes Flores, Rafael Rey, and José Barba, the leaders of the PPC, RN, and CR, respectively. Members of Castañeda's SN were also on UN lists, as "invited" candidates.

Congressional campaigns were very focused on presidential candidates and his or her coattails, though in electoral movements polling low in the presidential race, congressional candidates had more autonomy and more individualized publicity strategies (Alvarado Dodero interview 2007; Flores-Aráoz interview 2005; Garrido Lecca interview 2005). APRA ran the most coordinated and integrated campaign. Twenty-five percent of each APRA congressional candidate's campaign materials had to feature Alan García. What is more, every congressional candidate was required to sign a sworn declaration that she would resign her candidacy if she went off message and deviated from the basic five-plank platform adopted by García (Santa María Calderón interview 2005; Zumaeta Flores interview 2007). In UN, campaign activities were likewise focused on Lourdes Flores as presidential candidate.[38] In PP, every candidate ran his or her own campaign, but the images and logos on all PP materials were standardized, and, remarkably, the presidential candidate was required to appear in all print ads produced for congressional candidates. The focus was always on Toledo. As PP leader Luis Solari de la Fuente (interview 2007) put it, in a statement reminiscent of Fujimori's electoral movement, "the [PP] brand *is* the president." Among *fujimorista* candidates themselves, the absence of a viable presidential candidate left them no coattails to ride, but they could count on a small percentage of die-hard voters unperturbed by the scandals that felled their founder. Martha Hildebrandt, pro-Fujimori member of Congress since 1995, said of her 2001 campaign: "I didn't leave my house . . . and still did well!" (interview 2007).[39]

Lima candidates tended to make heavy use of the national media, especially broadcast TV — the same expensive strategy used by candidates under the prior system of a single national district (Flores-Aráoz interview 2005; Zumaeta Flores interview 2007; Santa María Calderón interview 2005). This media-intensive approach focused on increasing personal visibility to win preferential votes; as in previous contests, the harshest competition was within, not between, congressional lists (Ferrero Costa interview 2007; Sánchez Pinedo interview 2007; Alva Orlandini interview 2005). Outside of Lima, it was more feasible to use radio ads and public events or even go door to door. Candidates noted that the free TV spots allocated in 2001, the *franja electoral,* were too scarce and were useful mainly for promoting presidential candidates (Santa María Calderón interview 2005; Zumaeta Flores interview 2007; Sánchez Pinedo interview 2007).

Financing their campaigns was, of course, a pressing issue for candidates and groups. As noted above, elected members of Congress (and other politicians and bureaucrats) had long been asked to pay a percentage of their salaries into some groups' operating accounts. In 2001, groups increasingly asked candidates to also put up money even before running for office. In APRA, each congressional candidate gave money to the CEN for the presidential and general congressional campaigns. UPP asked each legislative candidate to contribute 1,000 soles (roughly $300) for the general campaign, but not everyone could pay (Garrido Lecca interview 2005). The FIM did not ask for money up front, though winning candidates were asked to make purely voluntary donations (Alvarado Dodero interview 2007). And C-90/NM, which in its heyday had never asked candidates or politicians to formally contribute anything, was now doing it too (Hildebrandt interview 2007). Out of power and no longer able to

Table 4.6. Legislative Seats Won, 2001 Elections

	Members of Congress
PP	45
APRA	28
UN	17
FIM	11
UPP	6
SP	4
C-90/NM	3
AP	3
Solución Popular	1
Todos por la Victoria	1
Renacimiento Andino	1
TOTAL	120

misuse state resources, the few remaining *fujimorista* members of Congress were, in 2005, finally asked to kick up a percentage of their salaries. It is telling that the donations were earmarked not for election campaigns or party-building but for the personal legal defense of Alberto Fujimori.

The results of the 2001 elections brought about staggering changes in Congress (see Table 4.6). Of the hundred twenty members elected in 2000, only thirty-five were reelected in 2001—a turnover rate of 71 percent. Congress had more first-time legislators that at any point at least as far back as 1978, and more members from outside the capital city than it had had since 1990 (Pease García 1999, 91; Asociación Civil Transparencia 2001; Tuesta Soldevilla 2002). This can be attributed to a number of factors: the Fujimori-Montesinos scandals, the volatility of regime transition, cleaner elections, and a dramatic redistricting of Congress. The biggest losers in this one-year period were indeed the *fujimoristas.* While C-90/NM/Vamos Vecino/Peru 2000 won 43 percent of seats in 2000 (and then induced another 10 percent or so to switch parties), they won a mere 2.5 percent of seats in 2001. The biggest winner was not PP, which went from 24.1 percent to 39.2 percent of seats in one year; it was APRA, which grew its congressional caucus from 5 percent to 23.3 percent of seats. APRA thus won the second largest block of seats (twenty-eight), behind PP (with a plurality of forty-five).

APRA had positioned itself to the left of Toledo, and after a bruising runoff election (with García already setting his sights on the 2006 race), an alliance between the two was not viable. Toledo instead forged a governing coalition with Fernando Olivera and the FIM: a group that was anti-*aprista* but otherwise more personalistic than ideological. FIM would gain a small number of cabinet appointments in exchange for legislative support. However, this created the most tenuous of parliamentary coalitions, since, as we shall see, neither PP nor FIM wielded strong party discipline among legislators, and Olivera himself was a polarizing figure.

2002 Regional and Municipal Elections

Municipal elections were held in November 2002, and the decentralization process conceived by President Paniagua and executed by President Toledo meant elections for regional officials too. Organized political parties, particularly APRA, performed well. Some of the national-level electoral movements were able to compete in large numbers of local elections across the nation, a difficult feat even for Fujimori's groups while he was in power. The heads of the three largest national political groups—García, Toledo, and Flores—aggressively promoted their respective APRA, PP, and UN local candidates and made scores of appearances across Peru (Ballón Echegaray 2002a; 2002b).

In total, regional and municipal elections drew in seventeen political parties or alliances registered at the national level.[40] APRA competed in 182 of the 194 provincial contests held. PP—without using state resources, as the incumbent Fujimori had—competed in 180. The UN competed in 161, AP in 154, and SP in 125. These national-level groups faced off against each other and against large numbers of groups running candidates only in a specific region (90), province (498), or municipal district (1410) (Ballón Echegaray 2002a). Many of these movements emerged out of protests directed against the central state, and they were popular among young voters (Vargas Gutiérrez 2002). But purely local movements enjoyed less success in 2002 than in the previous two municipal elections. In local district elections, national-level parties and movements garnered 70.3 percent of valid votes, while independent lists won the remaining 29.7 percent. In provincial elections, national-level parties and movements garnered 70.9 percent of valid votes, while independent lists won the remaining 29.1 percent. The percentage of provincial mayoralties won by candidates from groups specific to the province dropped from a peak of 56 percent in 1995, to 33 percent in 1998, to just over 27 percent in 2002.[41] Among national groups, APRA fared best, winning 34 provinces. APRA was followed by SP with 18 and UN with 13. The parties of then-president Toledo (PP) and past interim-president Paniagua (AP) enjoyed a bit less success, with 11 provincial mayors each. But overall, parties competed widely and did well, national-level electoral movements held their own, and truly local groups struggled.

National political groups also performed well in elections for the new regional governments. APRA, Perú Posible, Unidad Nacional, and Somos Peru each competed in twenty or more regions. By far the best results were for APRA: it won twelve of Peru's twenty-five regions. UPP won two regions. Toledo's PP won just a single region, as did SP, FIM, and the New Left Movement (Movimiento Nueva Izquierda). Independent regional movements were less common than at the provincial or district levels, and about as successful; fifty-two organizations competed in just one region each, and seven of them won.

The next municipal and regional elections in 2006 would, by contrast, be an enormous setback for SP, PP, APRA and all other national groups. Vote share of purely local or regional groups sharply increased, and independents won stunning victories in twenty-one of twenty-five regional governments (*El Comercio,* Nov. 20, 2006). But in 2002, national organizations—especially the APRA party—were highly successful.

In the municipal and regional results for APRA and the municipal results for UN, we can see that traditional parties were making a comeback, deepening their institutional development and adapting to a newly decentralized political arena. But those elections were also a referendum on Toledo's performance in his first eighteen months as president as well as a test of PP's organizational capacity. Results on both counts were not positive.

Perú Posible in Power

Typical of an electoral movement, PP was a collection of politicians bound together by support for a presidential candidate, not by shared ideology or programmatic goals (Taylor 2005). Decision making within PP was largely improvised and personalistic rather than bureaucratic or otherwise formally structured (Taylor 2007). The movement did have a small nucleus of candidates and organizers with shared political experience, and a few (e.g., David Waisman, Doris Sánchez) had been working with Toledo since the mid-1990s incarnation of PP. A much larger number joined during the 2000 campaign, especially as it became clear that Toledo would be the last opposition candidate standing in the campaign against Fujimori. Finally, several clusters of more experienced candidates and organizers from other groups joined PP in 2001. These included former AP presidential candidate Raúl Diez Canseco running as Toledo's first vice president and a splinter group from SP led by Anel Townsend (herself also formerly of UPP) that brought in prominent regional leaders like Jorge Chávez Sibina (of the northeastern lowland region Loreto) and Luis Guerrero (of the northern highland region Cajamarca).[42]

Many PP politicians, core members and invited candidates alike, maintain that the group was (re)founded in 1999–2000 with a well-organized, if decentralized, decision-making structure—but that once they won, the executive branch imposed a more personalistic leadership style (Pease García interview 2007; Solari de la Fuente interview 2007). The link between individual members of Congress and the executive became the only one that mattered. This alienated the small but vocal number of militants involved in nascent PP groups around the country.

The naked ambition of these PP militants—real and professed—seeking jobs in the public sector was reminiscent of the first García presidency. In the months after winning the 2001 elections, PP leaders at all levels received thousands of ad hoc requests for employment. Toledo made some efforts to satisfy the group's bases, but his fiscally conservative economic policies did not make for expansive public-sector employment, and he needed the experience that Fujimori-era bureaucratic appointees brought to their jobs (Taco Llave interview 2007). To the extent that PP loyalists were in fact hired, it was done through personal or family networks rather than the organization itself (Tanaka interview 2005). Toledo was criticized in the press for making too many patronage appointments and skewered by his own group for doling out too few. Local PP bases felt they were quickly forgotten and were frustrated by Toledo's neoliberalism and by what they perceived to be an unresponsive Congress (but see chapter 5).

The PP congressional bench was inexperienced and quickly became just as scandal-ridden and unpopular as the executive. What is more, the *bancada* was itself internally divided: political veterans versus newcomers, national versus regional interests, populist versus neoliberal visions of economy and society (Taylor 2005; Ferrero Costa interview 2007). There were also deep fissures between PP and the president over the appointment of independent technocrats versus party politicians as ministers and deputy ministers (Ferrero Costa interview 2007).

The PP members of Congress did caucus together in twice-weekly meetings. President Toledo himself had initially promised to join them twice a month, but in reality the president met with his members of Congress mostly during moments of crisis (Sánchez Pinedo interview 2007; Ferrero Costa interview 2007). At the start of the 2001–2006 period, the forty-five PP legislators tended to bend to the political will of their leader and support the executive. But discipline rapidly declined as Toledo grew less popular and the party more porous. As we will see in chapter 5, PP was plagued by party switching, and even the legislators who stayed could be obstacles as well as assets. Additionally, in the case of coalition partner FIM, professionalism and regular attendance were issues: even before members began abandoning the group, only three or four (out of eleven) could be relied on to show up each and every day Congress was in session (Ferrero Costa interview 2007). Right from the start, the Toledo government had to court congressional votes beyond its own caucus if it wanted to get anything done.

Though it was ultimately fated to remain an electoral movement, PP (like SP in the late 1990s) did make some efforts to develop more of a party organization. But these efforts were fitful and exposed the dysfunctions of the group even as it tried to ameliorate them. A Perú Posible party congress was originally planned for September 2001, then rescheduled for February 2002, then postponed until April 2002. Unlike its previous convention in 1999, PP did set up national structures for membership and representation. In late 2001 it solicited applications from local groups with twenty or more members to be recognized as official party bases. Over six thousand groups applied; these were then verified by party leaders, and over four thousand bases were officially recognized. The bases elected district-level secretaries, who in turn elected provincial-level delegates to the national party convention. Though internal elections were highly contentious processes, they did eventually produce 184 provincial delegates from across Peru and 5 zone delegates for Lima. Also included among the delegates were sixteen members of the national executive committee (Comité Ejecutivo Nacional, CEN), thirty-one members of Congress, and President Toledo himself (Solari de la Fuente interview 2007; *La República,* Feb. 10, 2002).

The April 2002 PP party congress was charged with electing a secretary general, and the process was fraught with tensions. Under heavy pressure from Toledo himself, delegates elected not an individual but a three-member "collegial" secretariat. It consisted of David Waisman, who had been with PP since 1994; Jesús Alvarado, who hailed from the same town as Toledo and joined PP in 2001; and Carlos Bruce, a technocratic adviser and Toledo's preferred candidate. Delegates also ratified Toledo as the life-long, irreplaceable president of PP (*Caretas,* Feb. 14, 2002). Those clauses were later rewritten, in part to comply with the internal democracy requirements of the 2003 Political Party Law (LPP), but even then, Toledo's permanent leadership role was merely tweaked, not eliminated. As political analyst Martín Tanaka commented prior to the 2002 party congress, "Perú Posible is being revealed for what it is: a group that appeared accidentally and then experienced vertiginous growth. . . . So you have a movement in which there are many people united by a general affinity for Toledo but where there are neither ideas nor institutional leadership, apart from Toledo's leadership" (*La República,* Feb. 10, 2002; translation mine).

In order to avoid another chaotic party convention, the three-person PP secretariat extended their terms beyond the two years for which they were elected. When PP delegates finally convened in September 2005 to elect a new secretary general, Toledo and a small group of top PP leaders pushed the candidacy of four-time cabinet minister Javier Reátegui.[43] He won, defeating party cofounder Alberto Cruz by just eleven votes. Cruz was very popular with party bases outside of Lima, and his supporters accused the Lima-based leadership of strong-arming delegates (*La República,* Sept. 12, 2005). (The internal elections were supervised by the ONPE and by the observer group Transparencia, which deemed the balloting process itself free and fair.)

PP's selection of a presidential candidate for 2006 was even messier. The candidate was to be chosen by the CEN and then "ratified," not elected, by delegates at another convention in December 2005. Early speculation centered on David Waisman: long-time PP member, congressman since 2000, former defense minister, and a vice president of Peru. But in early December, Toledo handpicked a complete outsider, businesswoman and naturopath Jeanette Emmanuel. This surprise decision was a product of the group's low approval ratings: other candidates—including, perhaps, Waisman himself (*La República,* Dec. 5, 2005)—may have been unwilling to run in such a bad year, and an outsider could appeal to the antipolitics mood of the electorate.

The press immediately jumped on Emmanuel's lack of experience and on the strife that her selection created within PP. She had never been involved in politics, and even after her nomination she publicly distanced herself from PP (agenciaperu.com, Dec. 4, 2005). Her pro forma ratification by PP delegates looked to be a disaster in the making, so just five days after she was plucked from obscurity, she resigned her candidacy. President Toledo and the CEN met again and made another outside-the-box choice: Rafael Belaúnde, son of former president Fernando Belaúnde and—until that day—a possible vice presidential candidate with the Unidad Nacional coalition (*La República,* Dec. 12 and 14, 2005). PP's national convention ratified Belaúnde in mid-December 2005. However, he was soon feuding with PP leaders on key issues, like the group's policy platform and its congressional candidate lists. Trailing badly in the polls, Belaúnde resigned on January 31, 2006, stunning the remnants of PP and leaving it legally unable to field a presidential candidate (*El Comercio,* Feb. 1, 2006).

Clearly, despite the organizational efforts of some politicians and militants, PP remained, even in power, a rather ad hoc electoral movement. Nobody in PP ever seriously proposed removing Toledo from the presidency of the group, even when he was facing removal as president of the nation (Ferrero Costa interview 2007). The organization was constructed around one man. Without Toledo—or with a highly unpopular Toledo—there was not much to Perú Posible. Secretary General Javier Reátegui admitted in 2006 that Toledo's dual role as president of the republic and of PP had led to the neglect of party-building and to a serious crisis within the group (*El Comercio,* Feb. 5, 2006). Political analyst Carlos Iván Degregori offered a more generous assessment: given the narrow opportunities for party building under Fujimori and the short timeframe for retooling to compete in 2001, it was not surprising that PP remained "an amalgam of individual, group, family and local interests" (Sánchez Leon and Paredes Oporto 2005, 10).

Appreciable numbers of citizens—thirty thousand by one account—did participate in PP before and during Toledo's presidency (Ferrero Costa interview 2007). But by 2005, PP offices in many parts of Peru existed only on paper, to satisfy the regulatory requirements of the new political party laws (Tanaka interview 2005). With no presidential candidate in 2006, PP won just 4 percent of the vote in congressional elections, garnering two seats, both in Lima. Many of the PP bases that had actually continued to function throughout Toledo's presidency, especially in the poorer highland areas of Peru, switched in toto to Ollanta Humala's nationalist movement in 2006 (Ferrero Costa interview 2007). (Toledo himself would launch yet another run at the presidency in 2011 with the support of PP, AP, and SP groups that were by then mere husks.)

APRA Rising

While PP was self-immolating, APRA was, in 2001–2006, rising like a phoenix. Though its revival was due in part to the return of Alan García, the party was also modernizing its organization. At the turn of the twenty-first century, APRA still had remnants of a corporatist structure and statist ideology (Garrido Lecca interview 2005). After the 2001 elections the party began to change. Its "dinosaurs" were still a force but were dying or leaving the party. Instead of corporatist-style sectoral organizations and courses on speech making and rhetoric, APRA developed new forms of outreach: web pages, bulletins, and other publications; forums with municipal officials; conferences on policy issues; and more practical educational opportunities. In 2001, García founded the Institute of Government (Instituto de Gobierno) at the private Universidad de San Martín de Porres to train professionals for political leadership and high-level public administration (Tanaka interview 2005).[44] Local APRA organizations around Peru likewise showed new signs of life and new forms of activism.

Its legislative caucus was also as disciplined as ever. In a 2001–2006 congress rife with ad hoc electoral movements, unprofessional legislators, and party-switching *tránsfugas,* APRA was the only parliamentary group that was always present and always voted as a block (Flores-Aráoz interview 2005). As in its heyday, APRA members of Congress met regularly as a caucus, a *célula parlamentaria* whose leader was elected annually from among the APRA legislators themselves. Once the caucus determined its position on a piece of legislation, all members voted accordingly or faced possible sanctions. The only exceptions were "free votes," those in which legislators were given *libertad de conciencia,* but this only happened three or four times in the first four years of the congressional period (Santa María Calderón interview 2005).

As disciplined as the party was in Congress, the new APRA still had some of its old schisms. Secretary General Jorge del Castillo, a strong supporter of Alan García's ongoing leadership, led one of three distinct factions. Another was led by Mercedes Cabanillas, a reformer since the 1990s. A third was led by Mauricio Mulder, the youngest of the three but perhaps the one most identified with the party's old guard (Garrido Lecca interview 2005).

As the president of the party and its "natural leader," García was able to stay somewhat above the fray. Notwithstanding APRA's development as an organization, it still maintained elements of personalistic leadership (Ballón Echegaray 2005). In 2004, the party's executive committee (CEN) contemplated fusing the positions of party president and secretary general, with García holding both, to maximize his exposure as a presidential candidate in 2006. García declined but pursued a strategy that would both keep the peace and keep any other star in the party from shining too brightly: a collegial secretariat, not unlike the one PP had at the time. At a party congress in mid-2004, delegates representing their party bases debated the matter for more than six hours. When they finally broke their stalemate, they agreed that Del Castillo and Mulder would share the secretary general position, while Cabanillas would become National Political Director (agenciaperu.com, June 7, 2004).[45] This move helped cement party unity and distribute power and visibility among a broader swath of second-tier leaders. As the newspaper *El Comercio* (May 26, 2009) noted, it also had the virtue of preserving the "indisputable and undisputed [party] presidency of the ex-president," Alan García.

In the lead-up to the 2006 elections, García and some of the APRA leaders tried another innovation in party organizing: forming a coalition with a variety of civil society groups, as a broad "social front" (Ballón Echegaray 2005). This was in part a way of rehabilitating the party's image and—at a time of social unrest and deep dissatisfaction with government—presenting the new APRA as a mature, inclusive, consensus-building group, focused above all on governability. To demonstrate this, García organized forums (*encuentros*) with eleven different social sectors, from farmers to teachers to professionals to industrialists. These were news-making events, well attended by a broad range of civil society leaders and citizens. Some *apristas* worried that this strategy—a personalistic leader reaching out directly to voters and supporters—would reverse recent organizational gains and weaken the party structure. But in the first years of the twenty-first century, as in the 1980s, the party organization was a stabilizing force, serving as political ballast to counter its heavyweight leader. Even at its organizational peak, APRA blended bureaucratic and charismatic power, a legacy of founder Haya de la Torre.

And with Haya's successor García back in Peru, the party rebounded in 2001–2006. In 2006 APRA would increase the size of its congressional delegation to thirty-six, and even more remarkably, García would take back the presidential palace, serving a second term in 2006–2011. The party faithful like to say "*el APRA nunca muere*" (APRA never dies). To date they have been right, though internal fragmentation and a poor performance in the 2011 elections again raised serious questions about the future of APRA.

FIM Finished?

From its beginnings as an anti-APRA campaign in the 1980s, FIM developed into an electoral movement that claimed to serve as a watchdog group of sorts, holding those in power accountable. But in the lead-up to the 2001 elections its personalistic leader, Fernando Olivera, began to aim higher. For the first time, FIM put together a comprehensive Plan of Government and even began to organize some local party bases (Alvarado Dodero interview 2007). While Olivera came in a distant fourth in presidential elections, FIM had its best showing yet in legislative elections. With eleven members of Congress, it became the junior partner in Toledo's governing coalition.

After 2001, however, the brief enthusiasm for party building fizzled. FIM voters tended to be skeptical of politics and so had little interest in getting too deeply involved in a party organization. Party bases were reduced to handfuls of notables all vying to get selected as candidates for elected office, with little long-term loyalty or cohesion (Alvarado Dodero interview 2007).

Being in government rather than criticizing it from the outside was also problematic for FIM's watchdog identity. Its members of Congress were bitterly divided over whether to support the Toledo government uncritically or investigate and prosecute the many accusations of corruption that were circulating (*El Comercio,* March 3, 2006). The movement was closely identified with its leader, and he was now the ultimate insider, meeting regularly with the president and even serving in the cabinet as justice minister in 2001 and 2002. Olivera was no longer a credible *moralizador.*

And nobody else in FIM could take on leadership roles in Olivera's stead. The congressional bench was losing members, so there were few potential leaders waiting in the wings; what is more, Olivera would not permit the group to develop much autonomy. In 2002 Toledo appointed him ambassador to Spain, in part to put some distance between Olivera and the presidential palace. Over the next three years Olivera flew back and forth to Lima frequently, sometimes to help Toledo with a political conflagration and keep a divided government from going up in flames and sometimes to put out fires within his own dwindling electoral movement. These constant interventions from afar raised the ire of the public and the press and also denied FIM any chance it may have had to evolve.

In late 2005, Olivera again put himself up as the presidential candidate for FIM. However, in February 2006, facing poor poll numbers, he stepped down to lead FIM's congressional list instead, leaving the movement without a presidential candidate. This self-interested maneuver did not pay off. FIM got just 1.5 percent of the vote, and no one from the party—not even Olivera, a legislator for twenty-one years, since age twenty-seven—won a seat in Congress. FIM lost its official party status and disappeared from the political arena.

Unidad Nacional Grows

As noted above, UN was initially created in 2000 as a coalition of the PPC, RN, and Cambio Radical (José Barba's CODE, with a new name). Castañeda Lossio later brought his SN movement into the coalition; he endorsed coalition leader Lourdes Flores for the 2001 presidential elections when he himself dropped out of the race in January of that year, and SN officially joined UN just after the April elections.

From the start there were tensions between leader (Flores), party (PPC), and electoral movements (RN, CR, and SN). Some PPC leaders resented Flores' role in establishing UN, and they resisted losing the PPC brand and disappearing into the alliance. (These tensions abated a bit when Lourdes Flores regained the PPC presidency in 2001.) Though PPC was strongest in Lima, it now had a network of party bases in other parts of the country and was reluctant to give those up. By contrast, RN and CR—which lacked any organizational structure at all but had leaders popular with conservative sectors of the public—were happy to adopt the UN label. By its founder's own admission, RN had deliberately remained an electoral movement, uninterested in eliciting citizen participation outside of the voting booth (Rey Rey interview 2007).

For the first few years of the 2001–2006 period, the UN alliance strengthened. In Congress, the *bancada* met diligently twice weekly and coordinated their voting bloc fairly well in 2001 and 2002. The alliance got a boost from the electoral successes of Castañeda Lossio, elected mayor of Lima in 2002 (and reelected in 2006) under the UN banner. Castañeda, SN, and UN garnered high approval ratings for their governance of Lima, though Castañeda's success alone could not bind the alliance together durably, and he would later launch his own 2011 presidential run with SN.

The alliance as a whole also made modest inroads into the provinces: it won eleven of its thirteen provincial mayoralties in 2002 outside the department of Lima, though it failed to win a single regional government. In perhaps its greatest victory on the national stage, UN fielded an opposition slate of legislators that wrested control of the governance of Congress from PP in 2004. The PPC's Ántero Flores-Aráoz served as president of Congress in 2004–2005.

The organized party within the alliance, the PPC, attempted to move beyond its traditional support base with new outreach techniques. It echoed many of the strategies adopted by APRA, such as using new media and reaching out to civil society groups. The PPC even created its own think tank, the Peruvian Institute for a Social Market Economy (Instituto Peruano de Economía Social de Mercado). Thus, while UN had traits of an electoral movement—personalistic leadership, fluid structure—its core group, PPC, both broadened and deepened its organization in the early years of the twenty-first century.

These organizational discrepancies contributed to power imbalances within the coalition. What is more, policy disagreements increasingly grated on the coalition's junior members. RN and CR had limited sway, with only three members of Congress between them. RN's Rafael Rey, in particular, found himself at variance with UN on a number of key issues: he opposed censuring Toledo's interior minister in 2004 but also defended *fujimoristas* accused of corruption and was more vicious in his criticism of Toledo than the rest of UN. Conflicts over the composition of congressional lists and differences of opinion with the ascendant Castañeda led both RN and CR to quit the UN alliance right around election day 2006. Schisms and personal ambitions ultimately torpedoed the alliance in 2008. However, from 2001 to 2006 UN (and especially the PPC) should be, on balance, considered a modest success for party organizational development in Peru.

The Disappearing Center: AP, SP, UPP

The traditional AP party and centrist electoral movements such as SP and UPP did not fare as well in 2001–2006. AP had stagnated as a party after governing in 1980–1985 and lost many up-and-coming leaders in the 1990s as they left to found or join electoral movements. *Acciopopulista* Valentín Paniagua became the "accidental" interim president of Peru in 2000 and won great praise for his performance. But he was not eligible to run for reelection, and his successful stint in the presidential palace did not translate into increased voter support for his party; AP won just three seats in Congress in 2001. After leaving executive office, Paniagua resumed his role as secretary general of AP. For the first time in the party's forty-five-year history, someone displaced the aging Fernando Belaúnde as de facto leader. But although AP performed respectably in the 2002 municipal elections with 4.8 percent of the national vote, overall the party was floundering.

SP faced the even more dire prospect of disintegration. Its leader, former Lima mayor Alberto Andrade, had an unsuccessful run at the presidency in 2000 (see above). In 2001, Andrade decided not to run again and instead backed the presidential candidacy of former ombudsman Jorge Santistevan, who dropped out prior to election day. SP did field a congressional slate, though a number of SP's most prominent figures from 2000 ran instead with Unidad Nacional or with Toledo's PP. SP received 5.8 percent of the vote in congressional elections and won just four seats; two of these four members would quit or change groups before 2006. In a more serious blow to his electoral movement, in 2002 Andrade was defeated in his bid for a third term as mayor of Lima by UN's Castañeda Lossio.

For the 2006 elections AP and SP joined together to form the Frente del Centro coalition, with Paniagua as presidential candidate and Andrade running for first vice president and for Congress. The coalition elected just five members of Congress (Andrade and four AP members). The leadership, and perhaps the very existence, of both groups were soon in question. AP founder Belaúnde had passed away in 2002, and then Paniagua died in October 2006, though several other experienced leaders remained involved in the party. For the more personalistic SP, which had already lost its most promising politicians to other groups, Andrade's death in 2009 would leave a gaping hole at the center of the movement.

The Left, UPP, and the New Nationalist Movement(s)

At the turn of the twenty-first century, left parties teetered on the verge of political oblivion in Peru. No left party ran candidates in 2001, though a few veteran politicians of the Peruvian left, like Javier Diez Canseco, did get elected to Congress on the UPP list. The most visible of the remaining left parties was the New Left Movement (Movimiento Nueva Izquierda, MNI), an amalgamation of Patria Roja (PR) and the old pro-Moscow Communist Party. The MNI was led by Alberto Moreno, formerly of UNIR and PR. As noted above, MNI enjoyed modest success in the 2002 municipal and regional elections, winning three provincial mayoralties and one regional government. In 2005 MNI formed a coalition with nine other small political groups, as the Broad Left Front (Frente Amplio de Izquierda). The new Frente Amplio, with MNI's party registration, ran Moreno as its presidential candidate and fielded congressional lists in 2006 but won not a single seat.

The success of Susana Villarán and her center-left coalition, winning the mayoralty of Lima in 2010, would breathe new life into left politics. So, in its way, would the electoral prowess of Ollanta Humala in 2011 (see below). But in 2006, left parties in Peru remained fossilized: the Soviet Union collapsed, and China turned capitalist, but these parties, despite new names and logos, split along the same ideological lines as they had in the 1980s (Tanaka interview 2005).

The UPP, by contrast, was in flux in the early years of the twenty-first century. After 1995, it lost many legislators to party switching, as noted above. It was barely an electoral movement, with scant internal organization and an absentee leader. After the 2000 elections, leaders were split over how firm a position to take vis-à-vis Fujimori's remaining in power and, later, whether or not to attempt another presidential campaign in 2001 (Pease García interview 2007). UPP ultimately ran only a congressional list that year, winning six seats.

The political composition of UPP, and its electoral fortunes, would change dramatically over the next few years, though. Since the early 2000s a new nationalist group known as the *etnocacerista* movement had been growing. Its main leaders were the Humala brothers: Antauro, Ulises, and especially Ollanta Humala. The movement's early core members were disgruntled army veterans and reservists. But it also drew in economic nationalists opposed to neoliberalism, populists with pro-indigenous or anti-European sentiments, and far-right nationalist groups with anti-foreign, especially anti-Chilean, views. The *etnocacerista* ideology was first elaborated by the Humalas' father, Isaac. In his words, it seeks to reclaim the power of the "copper-colored race," blending the "Inca moral code" with a nationalism personified by Marshall Andrés Cáceres, former president and hero of the War of the Pacific. It also had an anti-systemic bent—promoting the death penalty for "traitors" currently in government, for example.[46]

As it evolved, however, *etnocacerismo* became more recognizably a leftist, statist ideology, not unlike those identified with the "Bolivarian" regimes of early-twenty-first-century Latin America (Venezuela, Bolivia, etc.). In 2005, UPP joined forces with its main faction, Ollanta Humala's Peruvian Nationalist Party (Partido Nacionalista Peruana, PNP). The UPP, created to challenge Fujimori, had been vaguely centrist, but its main political stance was simply pro-democracy. Now it was lending its name to a more radical, sometimes violent group that had failed to register with electoral authorities on time. In exchange, UPP hoped to win more congressional seats riding Humala's coattails. This marriage of convenience was not a happy one: the two groups fought bitterly over the composition of their congressional lists (*El País*, Jan. 23, 2006). After the 2006 elections the two groups operated separate legislative caucuses, with the UPP side (again) hemorrhaging members.

Founding UPP leader Pérez de Cuéllar was appalled by the alliance and formally resigned from the party in 2005. Máximo San Román left UPP to run for president with a small electoral movement, Avanza País, then quit that group in late 2005 after his associates invited the even more radical *etnocacerista* brother, Antauro Humala (in prison for leading the Andahuaylas uprising), onto their congressional list (*El Comercio*, Nov. 23, 2005). Even more bizarre, Avanza País replaced San Román with another Humala, engineering professor Ulises Humala, to run for president against his brother Ollanta.

From mid-December 2005 to mid-January 2006, Ollanta Humala led the presidential election polls. His popularity then waned as the nationalist candidate more visibly linked his movement to a foreign patron, Venezuela's Hugo Chávez. A series of scandals hit Humala too: allegations of torture and human rights abuses from his days as a military officer in the 1980s and '90s, and evidence that Humala staged his 2000 uprising not to topple Fujimori but to create a distraction allowing Montesinos to flee the country. But despite these scandals, Humala was back on top of the polls by mid-March.

Ollanta Humala won the first-round presidential election in April 2006, with 31 percent of the vote nationwide and sweeping victories in Peru's central and southern highlands. He lost the June runoff election by 5 percent, but his movement's congressional caucus—though splintered—was the second largest group in the 2006–2011 legislature. (In 2011 Humala would make another run at the presidency, and this time he won.)

Fujimorismo Revived

The downward spiral of Fujimori's political groups seemed almost a foregone conclusion in 2001: revelations of corruption and criminal prosecutions were literally a daily occurrence, and C-90/NM did not run a presidential candidate that year.[47] Three established C-90/NM politicians were elected to Congress in 2001, but two were replaced for having committed crimes that made them ineligible for public office. The three who ended up serving usually voted together but were shunned by most other caucuses and were largely left out of the business of governing. In the words of Congresswoman Martha Hildebrandt (interview 2007), they enjoyed a "proud isolation" ("*orgulloso aislamiento*"). The Fujimori tsunami appeared to be trickling back to sea.

But it did not. For several years after fleeing to Japan, Fujimori had been making statements about returning to Peru and running for office. His supporters, including his daughter Keiko, launched a new incarnation of his electoral movement called Sí Cumple ("He Delivers," roughly translated). Fujimori did a series of broadcasts screened for supporters in Peru and launched a website offering his analysis of current political news. Yet it was hard to believe that Fujimori would gamble on a political comeback. The 2000 congressional resolution that removed Fujimori from power also legally barred him for ten years from holding any public office. Peru's Constitutional Tribunal ruled in February 2005 that this ban also kept him from *running* for office, a view later affirmed by the National Elections Tribunal. But defying expectations yet again, in November 2005 he left a comfortable life in exile and flew, via Mexico, to Chile. Perhaps he thought that recent flare-ups of long-standing diplomatic tensions between Peru and Chile would prevent the authorities from acting on an Interpol warrant for his arrest. He was wrong; he was arrested almost immediately. The hearings and extradition processes lasted nearly two years, but in September 2007 Fujimori indeed returned to Peru—as a prisoner, not a presidential candidate. In the interim, while under house arrest in Santiago and desperate to avoid extradition, Fujimori actually ran in absentia as a candidate for a small conservative party in the upper house of Japan's Diet (legislature) and lost.

Since Fujimori could not run for office in Peru, Sí Cumple no longer had a valid slate of candidates for 2006. So Congresswoman Martha Chávez ran for president under the existing C-90/NM party registration and formed the Alliance for the Future (Alianza por el Futuro, AF—the ex-president's initials). Chávez came in fourth, with 7.8 percent of the vote, but *fujimoristas* did even better in congressional elections, capturing thirteen seats and becoming an important swing voting bloc in the legislature. Keiko Fujimori, the ex-president's daughter, won a seat with the largest number of preferential votes of any candidate: 602,869, more than three times as many as her closest competition. With her father convicted and facing lengthy jail time, Keiko became the public face and the future hope of the movement, though there were tensions between her and Martha Chávez (Hildebrandt interview 2007). *Fujimorismo* was making an unlikely comeback. (And in the 2011 elections, Keiko came within a hair's breadth of winning back her residence in the Palace of Pizarro, this time as president.)

Conclusions

Peru's political arena featured some well-organized if ultimately fragile parties in the 1980s. These parties gave way to fluid, ad hoc personal electoral vehicles in the 1990s. From 2001–2006, electoral movements (especially PP and FIM) persisted, even while some traditional parties (APRA and PPC) were rapidly revived.

APRA's charismatic leader returned to Peru and led the party back from the political wilderness, sparking a process of party reinstitutionalization that went far beyond the role of García himself. AP, by contrast, was hobbled since 1985 by its static leadership and weakened by the loss of party militants to other political forces. Even with Valentín Paniagua's successful interim presidency in 2000–2001, AP's potential for renewed growth was uncertain, though it retained a toehold in municipal and legislative politics in 2001–2006. The parties of the left, held together in the 1980s by a weak coalition, were severely damaged not only by social conflict and economic change in Peru but by the 1989 standoff between leader and parties from which the coalition never recovered. The remnants of those parties continued to play out the ideological scrimmages of the 1980s with little political success, at least not until late in the first decade of the twenty-first century. The party of the democratic right, PPC, was limited by its narrow base among the urban middle and upper classes in the 1980s and '90s. But under the leadership of Lourdes Flores, the Unidad Nacional coalition (anchored by a revived PPC) reached new constituencies and voters in the 2001 elections.

Organized parties' renewal at the turn of the twenty-first century was not a product of voters or citizens more closely identifying with them.[48]

And for the party system overall, renewal was partial at best. To political veteran Henry Pease García—someone who switched parties and movements several times himself—personalistic leadership and the fetishization of political "independence" have taken their toll on Peru's parties. "*Caudillismo* is still strong," he told me in a 2007 interview, and "most parties today are nothing more than political personalities with their entourage." Yet party organizations like APRA and PPC, if still rather personality-driven, were considerably reinvigorated. Voters have shown that, however much they disdain political parties, they will still vote for one if they like the leader at the helm. (As we will see in chapter 5, this, somewhat ironically, helped to rebalance power between legislature and executive in 2001–2006.)

Fujimori's electoral movements dominated other parties and movements in the 1990s, even though his groups were organizationally weak and utterly subservient to him. After the 2000 transition, C-90/NM struggled but then surprisingly regrouped as its personalistic leader returned to Peru, albeit as a captured fugitive, and his daughter took up the mantel of his leadership.

The 2001–2006 Toledo presidency was one in which he, as leader of PP, maintained a fraught relationship with an inexperienced cadre of legislators and militants. Though some in PP sought to develop the organization as a party, such efforts were wracked by internal conflict and lacked any cohering element beyond the persona of the group's leader. Consequently, PP remained an electoral movement, its political fortunes declining as its leader grew more unpopular.

And a new leftist-nationalist group led by Ollanta Humala would emerge in 2006. This electoral movement was highly ideological but also strongly personalistic. It swiftly grew from fringe group to contender for power at the highest level, reflecting the profound distrust and disdain that millions of Peruvians still felt toward their country's political institutions and economic model.

During the entire 1985–2006 period, the formal rules of the game that structure the relationship between leader and party remained, on the whole, stable. Most of the core electoral laws and other rules that shape a president's "partisan powers"—candidate selection, the timing of elections, preferential voting, etc.—did not change dramatically. What did change, for reasons other than the formal rules of the game, was the nature of the political organizations vying for power in Peru.

As party organizations gave way to personalistic, ad hoc electoral movements in the early 1990s, the ability of these political groups to hem in the nation's president—and their own leaders—diminished. In the 1980s, and again in the first decade of the twenty-first century, when "real" party organizations in power or in opposition were stronger, they were more willing and able to constrain the executive branch. In the next chapter I examine the rise and fall of hyper-presidentialism and, more specifically, the concomitant fall and rise in the power of Peru's legislature.

5

Echo Chamber?
The Decline and Rise of Peru's Legislature, 1985–2006

In effect, Parliament became an echo chamber for the proposals
of the [presidential] palace.

—Truth and Reconciliation Commission of Peru,

Final Report, Conclusion 122

In earlier chapters, I traced the decline of constitutionalism and the dis-integration of political parties in Peru from the 1980s to the 1990s. The net result of these two processes was, as I demonstrate in this chapter, a tremendous concentration of power in the executive branch at the expense of other branches of government, especially the legislature. While the performance of Parliament in the 1980s may have left much to be desired in the eyes of scholars and the Peruvian public alike, the legislature's near-total loss of institutional autonomy and capacity during the 1990s was far more pernicious. In 2001–2006, the rule of law improved dramatically, and political party (re)development was evident, if uneven. Consequently, I argue, the importance of the legislature as a site of meaningful political activity—with all of the conflict and discord that entails—increased markedly.

The 1990s decline of parties and constitutionalism strengthened the presidency and weakened the legislature through several interrelated

155

processes. First, the capacity of the legislature for analysis and formulation of legislation, as well as the oversight of government policy, was diminished. The decline of organized parties in the 1990s meant the elimination of sites within (and affiliated with) parties where political analysis had been conducted. In the case of APRA, these were bodies within the party itself; in the parties of the IU these could be nongovernmental organizations with partisan affiliations. Furthermore, as adherence to constitutional norms weakened, the legislature's internal rules and committee structures were ignored or altered, with the effect of cutting off the legislature— particularly the minority opposition groups—from key functions such as grappling with legislation or exercising oversight. In 2001–2006, traditional parties like APRA and PPC (but not the parties of the left) regained their capacities for policy analysis from the opposition benches, even if electoral movements still held a legislative majority. More importantly, the return of the rule of law meant that overall legislative governance, and the functionality of legislative committees in particular, were vastly improved in the early 2000s.

The decline of party organizations and constitutional norms in the 1990s also reduced the incentives for majority legislators, and the opportunity for opposition legislators, to balance the power of the executive. President Fujimori's ephemeral electoral movement structure meant that there was no organizational counterweight to his power. Legislators had no political future without Fujimori himself, and thus the president enjoyed an entirely vertical relationship with his legislators, as we shall see. For opposition legislators, the decline in adherence to constitutional norms meant that many formal and informal checks on executive power were simply no longer available to them, especially after the 1992 *autogolpe*. In 2001–2006 there were some rehabilitated political parties in the opposition and a coalition of electoral movements in government. Opposition parties had not just the capacity but the incentive to check, harass, and almost topple the executive—not unlike the 1990–1992 period of minority government. The disorganized electoral movements in Toledo's legislative coalition offered neither strong support for the president nor a consistent intraparty check on executive power, especially as Toledo himself grew increasingly unpopular and his legislators saw their political futures fading. But having some legitimate parties in opposition once again bolstered the strength of the legislature.

What is more, weak constitutionalism and weak party organizations meant that overcoming the collective action problems of party discipline and harnessing legislators' individual political strategies were problematic for those not in control of state resources. *Transfuguismo*—party switching, be it voluntary or induced—became commonplace in the 1990s, almost always in the direction of the ruling groups. Flouting the rule of law at the highest levels of government gave the executive a powerful array of techniques, licit and illicit, for attracting (or coercing) legislators into actively or tacitly allying with the incumbent regime. But even with stronger elite constitutional norms after 2000, legislators from electoral movements commonly changed their group affiliations. In electoral movements, legislators elected from the same list did not necessarily expect to remain together in a parliamentary caucus after elections were over, let alone coordinate their votes or submit to party discipline. However, instead of being drawn into government, as most *tránsfugas* had in the 1990s, legislators fled from it. By 2006, much of the governing PP-FIM coalition went "independent" or joined other, even more ad hoc groups.

Power was not simply correlated with winning, losing, or keeping a legislative majority. The very size and docility of Fujimori's legislative majority in 1992–2000 were themselves by-products of weak rule of law and weak party organizations. Alan García's APRA majority in 1985–1990 faced similar accusations of rule breaking and submissiveness to the executive, yet that period was nonetheless characterized by a qualitatively different relationship between president and legislators (his own and those of the opposition as well). It was the difference between strong leadership and sheer domination. Similarly, the two periods of minority government—1990–1992, and 2001–2006—differed wildly. This was due in part to the formation of a governing coalition in 2001–2006 versus the absence of such a formal coalition in 1990–1992. But as we shall see, the legislative support and political benefits afforded by Toledo's PP-FIM coalition were rather tenuous. The divergent outcomes of those two periods were also due to differences in elite constitutional norms and internal party dynamics.

In the 1990s, the presidential palace was fortified, and the legislative chamber was emptied of political power. Indeed, one sobriquet used to describe Peru's legislature in those days was "*caja de resonancia*" (sounding-box or echo chamber). The fate of a legislator in the 1990s was to resonate in harmony with the executive or not be heard at all. After 2001, Congress progressively became more of a torture chamber than an echo chamber for the executive branch under President Toledo; the legislature may have been unruly, unprofessional, or treacherous at times, but it was not meek.

Reconsidering Peru's Legislature

Peru's legislatures prior to the 1978 Constituent Assembly are generally characterized as either weak and feckless (most of the time) or obstructionist until quashed by a coup (e.g., 1963–1968). And scholars of the 1980s have often emphasized the weakness of the legislature in that era too. Carol Wise contends that Alan García's 1985–1990 government was "highly insulated" and presidentialist in the extreme (1994, 198–99). Likewise, James Rudolph describes Congress as doomed to "legislate on insignificant matters, such as the declaration of a city as the capital of a typical folk dance" (1992, 79). But as we shall see, for the 1980s this image of an aloof president and an ineffectual legislature is not entirely accurate.

Compared to the 1990s, the Peruvian Congress of the 1980s served as a forum for substantive political debate, and, crucially, it was actively involved in legislation and government oversight. It was only after legislative-executive tensions culminated in the *autogolpe* of 1992 that the legislature became not a servant but a slave to the executive branch. True, the legislature in Peru has always been less proactive than the executive—as is the case in most presidential systems outside the United States (Cox and Morgenstern 2001; Morgenstern 2006). But this should not cause us to ignore the fairly successful reactive role that Peru's Congress played in the 1980s, nor the rapid decline of the legislature in the 1990s, nor its rocky renewal in the first decade of the twenty-first century.

Expert opinion within Peru supports the notion that the power of Congress—and *congresistas*—relative to the executive has indeed changed over time. In an annual survey conducted by the journal *Debate,* the country's leading figures in both the private and the public sectors are asked to name the most powerful people in the country. As Table 5.1 shows, the prominence of individual parliamentarians declined markedly from the 1980s to the 1990s and did not recover much after the turn of the cen-

Table 5.1. Aggregate Number of Top Ten Rankings in Annual Expert Survey *El poder en el Perú* (Power in Peru), 1985–2005

	Legislators	Executive Branch	Other Politicians, Party/ Movement Leaders	Military Officers	Guerilla Leaders	Business Elites	Church Hierarchy	Other
Garcia 1985–1990	3.6	1.6	2.0	0.4	1.0	0.4	0.8	0.0
Fujimori 1990–2000	1.6	4.5	1.5	0.8	0.4	0.5	0.5	0.3
Toledo 2001–2006	1.8	4.8	2.0	0.2	0.0	0.8	0.6	0.0

Source: Debate; Lynch 1999; APOYO S. A.

tury. In 1985, the year of García's election, five legislators were noted among the top ten, compared to just two in 1995 (Fujimori's reelection year) and two in 2001 (Toledo's election year).[1] Fujimori's powerful "intelligence advisor," Vladimiro Montesinos, was permanently ensconced in the number two position from 1992 to 2000.[2] This trend of powerful executive figures also continued into the Toledo years—though I will argue below that Congress as an institution rebounded in the early 2000s, even if few individual legislators stood out as particularly powerful.

The data in Table 5.1 do not prove that a stronger executive and a weaker legislature emerged in Peru, only that expert respondents believed that individual legislators became less notably powerful. Did this indeed correspond with institutional-level power shifts? For the 1990s, I believe that it did. I demonstrate below that the power of the legislature did actually decline in the 1990s, both during the minority government of 1990–1992 and during the majority governments of 1993–1995 and 1995–2000. After the fall of Fujimori the legislature enjoyed a rare moment in the political spotlight during the transition period of 2000–2001. And as governing returned to business as usual, I show that the legislature as a body remained strong and played a much more active role in 2001–2006 than it had in over a decade (even if few individual legislators stood out as high performers).

Legislatures craft and approve legislation, represent the interests of constituents, and engage in oversight of the government of the day (Saiegh 2005).[3] In the 1990s, Peru's legislature was decreasingly able to perform any of these functions. In 2001–2006, it was more empowered to do all three, especially holding the executive accountable.

In the next section I provide a brief overview of the institutional framework of Peru's legislature and show how the rules were used (and abused) for the executive's political gain in the 1990s but then regained some integrity after the turn of the century. I then make the case for the decline and subsequent rise of Peru's legislature based on its capacity for lawmaking, government oversight, and representation.

The Internal Governance of Peru's Congress

Peru's legislature was bicameral until the 1992 *autogolpe,* and the ensuing changes in procedures for approving laws are described in chapter 3.[4] The structure of the current unicameral congress is, with a few exceptions, similar to that of each of the two houses under the previous system.[5] Its governing body is headed by the Mesa Directiva, or Board of Directors, which consists of a president and three vice presidents elected on a single slate by the full congress. Mesa Directiva members in turn sit on and lead all of Congress's most important governing bodies: the Junta Directiva/Consejo Directivo (Counsel of Directors), the Comisión Permanente (Permanent Commission), and—as of 2001—the Junta de Portavoces (Council of Spokespersons).

The Consejo Directivo is composed of members of all official parliamentary groups—those with six or more members—in proportion to their membership. (This same threshold is also used to allocate staff and administrative budgets, so groups of fewer than six *congresistas* have enormous incentives to either band together or join one of the larger caucuses.) The spokesperson of each official parliamentary group is automatically included on the Consejo; groups may have additional representatives on the Consejo, if merited by size. For most of the period under study, the Consejo Directivo controlled the legislative agenda (*orden del día*) and the time allocated to speakers. From 1988 to 1992, as the Junta Directiva, this body also allocated assignments to legislative committees.

The membership of the Comisión Permanente is similarly composed. The 1993 Constitution stipulates that it should "tend to be proportional" to the balance of political forces in the legislature and that its size may not exceed 25 percent of the total Congress, or thirty of a hundred and twenty legislators. Its principal function is to serve as a legislative body when the full congress is not in session. (It also fulfills some of the functions of the pre-1992 senate in impeachment proceedings and, should the executive legally dissolve the legislature, in overseeing executive decrees.)

The Junta de Portavoces was reinstated in 2001, part of a post-Fujimori reform of congressional regulations.[6] This body consists of the Mesa Directiva and one spokesperson from each parliamentary group; the votes of each spokesperson are weighted proportionally according to the size of his or her group. This body is now responsible for setting the initial agenda for congressional debate (though the agenda must then be approved by the Consejo Directivo). It also proposes the annual appointments of members to legislative committees and has the power to fast-track a piece of legislation so that it bypasses the committees.

Peru's legislative committees include special, investigative, and, most important to the legislative process, standing committees (*comisiones ordinarias*). In some older democracies, standing committees developed in order to foster policy expertise and balance the power and sophistication of executive branch bureaucracies. They also came into being because legislators have certain policy areas about which they and their constituents care a great deal. Trading votes on these issues is hard to enforce because the votes do not take place simultaneously, so committees of legislators with specific policy interests emerged as a solution (Shepsle 1978; Weingast and Marshall 1988; Cox and McCubbins 1993). Committees act as legislative gatekeepers, their power based on norms of reciprocity and deference to expertise (Fenno 1973; Shepsle and Weingast 1987).

Prior to the late 1980s, a system of committees did exist in Peru's lower chamber, but their functions were rather informal and underdeveloped, regulated by congressional rules written in 1853. Then the 1988 regulations for the Cámara de Diputados modernized its organizational structure and mandated seventeen specialized standing committees selected by the Junta Directiva (akin to the later Consejo Directivo). Each committee was run by a president, vice president, and secretary and had between seven and nineteen members in total; no deputy could belong to more than two standing committees. New regulations for Peru's unicameral congress, adopted in June 1995, specified fifteen standing committees selected by the president of Congress and then voted on by the full legislature.[7] *Congresistas* could now sit on up to three committees. The total number of standing committees was quickly expanded to twenty-six, then twenty-eight; then in 2003 the number was reduced to twenty-four.[8] After October 2001, the Junta de Portavoces became responsible for proposing committee assignments to be approved by the Consejo Directivo and voted on by the full legislature.

Overall, the formal governance structure of the legislature did not change dramatically during the period under study. However, some internal rules and, crucially, the application of these rules had more majoritarian effects in the 1990s and more pluralistic effects in the 1980s and in 2001–2006. What is more, the Fujimori government and its C-90/NM congressional caucus ignored even rules of their own making when they proved inconvenient, to a much greater degree than what we observed in earlier or later periods. Legislators in general, and minority legislators in particular, were weaker in the 1990s than in the 1985–1990 period. In 2001–2006, Toledo's legislative coalition had to handle a few new rules but, more importantly, had much more respect for the rule of law itself (and faced some well-organized opposition parties too). As a result, the 2001–2006 legislature was far better at performing its functions of legislation, accountability, and representation than its predecessors from the 1990s.

Legislation

Formulating Laws

In the U.S. legislature, standing committees are where the heavy lifting of lawmaking is done. Their role in Latin America's legislatures varies widely, however (Saiegh 2005; Finocchiaro and Johnson 2005).[9] Even within Peru, their role and their effectiveness in lawmaking have fluctuated over time.

Peru's standing committee structure was more functional in 1985–1992—particularly after the 1988 modernization of the Chamber of Deputies—than it was from 1992 to 2000. Interviews with legislators and legislative assistants who served both in the 1980s and in the 1990s confirmed this: committees were indeed sites for analyzing, debating, and crafting laws in the 1980s (Lynch interview 1999; Breña Pantoja interview 1999).[10] In this period, committee assignments generally took into account both the professional expertise and the constituencies of a legislator (Delgado-Guembes 1990). Committees were not well supplied with resources or professional staff, but neither were they the sole locus of legislative analysis: legislators' political parties or affiliated nongovernmental organizations also provided some policy analysis and formulation. Committees also had a more pluralistic power structure in the 1980s. Under the APRA majority, it was not unheard of for an opposition legislator to be named as an officer, or even the president, of a standing committee (*Caretas,* Aug. 10, 1995).

In the 1990s, notwithstanding the dictates of congressional regulations, the assignment of legislators to committees—and even the selection of most committee presidents—did not match expertise with service (Breña Pantoja interview 1999). From 1993 to 2001, the unicameral, single national district of the legislature meant that congresspersons did not have geographically delineated constituencies to serve. While the preferential vote might have motivated legislators to cultivate the support of specific sectors or groups in society, this was not reflected in committee assignments either. Committees simply were not where the important decisions were made in the Fujimori era. Legislators who served as committee presidents did not have much additional work to do but did receive additional resources—the chief impetus for expanding the number of committees to twenty-six in this period. Committee presidencies were also used to reward some party switchers (such as Francisco Pardo Mesones and Dennis Vargas Marín) for defecting to the government bench.

Legislative committees with such limited specialization and expertise did not provide legislators with much capacity to craft or study complex legislation. As party organizations weakened, that capacity diminished even further. What is more, there was no independent source of data gathering or policy analysis. The legislature and its committees thus became even more reliant on the executive branch as a source of information and analysis about proposed legislation, budgets, and government programs.

Committees became a rubber stamp for the will of the majority in the legislature, which was in turn strongly dictated by the executive branch. Under Fujimori, the only committee that ever had an opposition legislator as president was a special committee rather than a standing committee: Beatriz Merino, then of the FIM movement, was named head of the new Women's Issues Committee in 1996 but lost the position when the committee was upgraded to standing status. From 1992 to 2000, only one genuine opposition legislator even served as an officer of a standing committee: Alfonso Grados Bertorini of UPP was named secretary of the Foreign Affairs Committee in 1999. And several standing committees remained largely inactive. The Regulatory Reform Committee, for example, met only six times between August 1998 and May 1999, with several meetings cancelled because of lack of quorum. Other committees met more often, but the meetings frequently consisted of being informed of executive initiatives by ministers, rather than actively formulating or analyzing legislation (*Caretas,* June 3, 1999).

Congressional regulations created in 1993 and formally adopted in 1995 allowed the legislature to approve laws more hastily too. These regulations reduced the requisite number of readings of a bill (and thus the opportunities for parliamentary debate). Prior to the 1993 regulations, bills were to be read either two or three times, depending on the nature of the legislation. The 1993 regulation required just one reading. But what is more, before 1992 the permission to bypass the approval of one or more standing committees required a two-thirds vote of the chamber in question—and there were two chambers, each with their own committees. From 1993 onwards, a simple majority was all that was required under the new regulations to move a bill directly to a floor vote, denying legislators the opportunity to substantively analyze the bill (Planas 1999). According to Pásara (1993), for example, only one-third of all bills considered in the first year of the 1993–1995 Congreso Constituyente Democrático (CCD) passed through the committee structure and received even one committee's approval. In 1993–2000, a number of politically sensitive laws were passed "by surprise": placed on the agenda by the pro-Fujimori majority in the middle of the night, then passed, signed by the president, and published in *El Peruano* by morning (Pease García 2006). Examples include a 1995 amnesty law for past human rights abuses (*Caretas,* June 15, 1995) and a 1997 law on defamation and the press (*Caretas,* April 25, 1997), to name just two.

Every single member of Congress I interviewed in 2005–2007—many of whom also served in the 1980s and 1990s, some in government and some in opposition—noted that committees in 2001–2006 were more likely to actually do the job they were designed to do. Data on the work of committees is sparse and makes it difficult to discern important from unimportant bills. Well into the 1990s, congressional archivists in Peru lacked the capacity to preserve the records of standing committees and so simply burned the paperwork after a period (Delgado-Guembes 1990). But what data we have suggests a sharp downturn in committee activity in the 1990s and an uptick in the next decade. For example, 5,174 bills were reported out of committee (*dictaminados*) in 2001–2006, or 1,035 per year, compared to just 2,859 in 1995–2000, or 572 per year (Pease García 2006). Even as the modern system of standing committees was first being implemented in the Chamber of Deputies, their productivity was higher than in the Fujimori-controlled congress of the late 1990s. In the 1988 and 1989 legislatures, 1,538 bills were reported out of committee, a rate of 769 per year (Delgado-Guembes 1990). And in the 1990 legislature, notwithstanding the paralysis and gridlock that supposedly plagued it, the total was 976 (Delgado-Guembes 1992).

Committee assignments were more systematic in the 1980s and in 2001–2006 too. Multiple electoral districts gave legislators fixed constituencies, providing an additional logic for assignments (though legislators' actual capacity for bringing home "pork" was minimal; see below). The continued prevalence of party switching in 2001–2006 meant that partisan representation and the development of legislators' policy expertise remained problematic, but this was still a better state of affairs than in the 1990s.

Committees were also better staffed with technical advisors and policy analysts in 2001–2006 (Santa María Calderón interview 2005; Waisman Rjavinsthi interview 2007). Their quality did vary: some committees were staffed with bureaucrats, others with trained policy analysts; budgets were such that particularly diligent committee presidents would sometimes pay for committee expenses out of their own operating budgets (Medina interview 2005; Zumaeta Flores interview 2007). Efforts to bolster the quality of research and analysis in Congress similarly improved but in an unsteady way. In November 2002 Congress created the Center for Parliamentary Research (Centro de Investigación Parlamentaria, CIP). However, the CIP was underutilized by members of Congress and was perennially short of resources. From a peak of twenty-two staff members in 2003, it was down to just six staffers by December 2004.[11] The CIP effectively disappeared after 2005 but was replaced in 2008 with another congressional research center, the Centro de Investigación, Análisis Temático y Estadística, CIAE.

Though building a chamberwide institution for policy analysis proved somewhat elusive, the standing committees themselves seemed to have more success wrenching information from the executive branch. In 2001–2006, standing committees requested (and received) the presence of ministers—to report to a committee and help inform its analysis of a bill—a total of 637 times.[12] (We do not have data for earlier periods, but Bernales Ballestros [1990, 171] notes that this practice was a "growing trend" in the late 1980s, while Pease García [2006, 493] states that the figure for 1995–2000 would be "certainly lower" than for 2001–2006.) With this capability, standing committees contributed to the legislature's power to constrain the executive. One high profile example: in 2003 the Economy Committee considered the executive's arguments but ultimately rejected an important bill delegating lawmaking powers for the overhaul of Peru's tax system (LAN-RA, Sept. 9 and Oct. 7, 2003).[13]

The crafting of legislation was also made more transparent. As of October 2001, every project that went to committee had to be published immediately on the legislature's website and stay there at least a week prior to being debated by the full legislature, even if the committee itself was ready sooner (Pease García 2006). This slowed down the legislative process, particularly for complex legislation that required more than one committee to sign off (Santa María Calderón interview 2005). But given the propensity of the *fujimorista* congressional majority of the 1990s to pass laws with no such scrutiny, those delays signified democratic progress.

It was not just that committees functioned more openly and effectively in 2001–2006. Committee structures—indeed, the entire governance structure of Peru's Congress—were also far more pluralistic in 2001–2006 than in 1992–2000 (or even 1985–1990). With fifty-eight votes between them at their peak, the PP-FIM alliance needed just three votes for the qualified majority that would have allowed them to control the Mesa Directiva and all subsidiary governance bodies within the legislature. Out of a combination of necessity and democratic openness, the governing coalition opted instead for multiparty bodies that might maintain the broad alliances and goodwill of the transition period. The Mesa

Directiva elections for the first two legislative years (2001–2002 and 2002–2003) were by consensus vote. PP's Carlos Ferrero held the presidency, but each parliamentary group got one vice president. More importantly, in an unprecedented move, the presidencies and composition of standing committees were distributed by a norm of proportionality. (For example, in 2001–2002, PP held thirteen committee presidencies, APRA seven, UN three, the Unidad de Promoción para la Democracia coalition three, and FIM two.) In 2003–2004, elections for the Mesa Directiva were competitive, but PP won: Henry Pease served as president of Congress and unilaterally kept in place these same norms of proportionality. Even in 2004–2005, when opposition groups led by UN's Ántero Flores-Aráoz took control of the Mesa Directiva, and 2005–2006, when it was recaptured by a diminished PP now led by Marcial Ayaipoma, pluralism continued to guide the selection of committee presidents.

These norms of consensus and multiparty governance were formalized early on in the National Accord (Acuerdo Nacional), signed in March 2002 by President Toledo, the leaders of all major political groups in Parliament, and a number of notable church and civil society leaders. The document put forth thirty-one national goals—focused on democracy and the rule of law, equality and social justice, market competition and social development, transparency and decentralization—that were to be elevated above partisan politics. Though the conciliatory spirit of the Acuerdo would not last long, it did help usher in congressional practices far more pluralistic than those of the previous era.

Legislative Productivity

This broader dispersal of power within the legislature was also visible in the chamber's initiation and approval of laws (*leyes*) and legislative resolutions (*resoluciones legislativas*). However, as suggested above, simply counting laws can be deceiving. Though the quantities initiated and produced might seem to be obvious measures of the relative strength of the legislative and executive branches, on its own this data tells us little about prior agenda setting and bargaining (Tsebelis and Alemán 2005); the rate at which laws proposed by different sources end up becoming law (Saiegh 2004; García Montero 2006; Cheibub 2007); or the relative importance (or frivolity) of the legislation in question. We need only recall the bills recognizing Peruvian folk dances (Rudolph 1992) to remember that simply producing legislation does not in itself indicate legislative power. And the final version of a complex piece of legislation can reconcile and incorporate initiatives from multiple sources, so it is often difficult to ascertain who, exactly, got their way.

Nonetheless, looking at the number of laws passed by the legislature, and the percentage that were first initiated (in whole or in part) by the executive, can be a starting point, a crude measure for assessing the balance of institutional power. Though the 1993 Constitution broadened the range of actors who could propose legislation and opened the process to citizen initiatives, since 1995 only 2.5 percent of all bills came from the judiciary, the *defensor,* or other sources outside the legislative-executive nexus (Pease García 2006, 494). Thus, the percentage of successful legislative projects initiated by the executive sheds light mainly on the role of the legislature throughout the 1985–2006 period under study.

The data presented in Table 5.2 are drawn from several different sources that appear to use different criteria for counting laws.[14] So while we must be careful about making bold statements based on any one source, there are some overall patterns to this data that are incontrovertible.

We see, for example, that the 1985–1990 period was one in which the legislature did play a major role in proposing the bills that eventually became laws. With a majority in both houses, the legislative caucuses of the APRA party appear to have been very adept at passing laws—and the executive relied on this caucus to do the work of crafting legislation too. More than two-thirds of all laws passed in this period originated in one of the legislative chambers. Some of the older *aprista* legislators, especially those who had previously served in the 1963–1968 Parliament or the 1978–1980 Constituent Assembly, felt that Parliament had a diminished role in lawmaking during the 1985–1990 period (Negreiros Criado interview 1999). As I discuss below, President García did make heavy use of decree authority in that era. Moreover, the rate at which executive-introduced bills were ultimately approved in 1985–1990 was a great deal higher than for laws originating in the legislature: a 75 percent success rate for the former versus just 10 percent for the latter (Bernales Ballestros 1990). Nonetheless, the impact of the legislature as the originator of laws passed—what Alcántara Saez et al. (2005) dubbed "legislative participation"—was notably higher (at 69–79 percent) in 1985–1990

Table 5.2. Laws, Legislative Resolutions, and Decrees by Executive, 1985–2006

	1985–1990	1990–1992	1992 (legislature closed)	1993–1995 CCD	1995–2000	2000–2001	2001–2006
# Months	60	20	9	31	60	12	60
# Executive Origin	204[a] 265[c]	13[a]	586[c] 728[f]	319[c]	350[f] 327[g]	104[f] 90[g]	469[f]
# Total Laws Passed	665[a] 980[b,f] 1255[c]	67[a] 140[b,f]	586[c] 728[f]	372[c]	690[d] 823[f]	173[d]	1271[d] 1347[f]
% Executive Origin	31%[a] 21%[c]	19%[a]	100%[c,f]	86%[c]	43%[f]	60%[d,f] 52%[d,g]	35%[f]
# Laws per Month	11.08[a] 16.33[b] 20.92[c]	3.35[a] 7.00[b,f]	65.11[c] 80.89[f]	12.00[c]	11.50[d] 13.72[f]	14.75[d,f]	21.18[d] 22.45[f]
# CDA Decrees	1033[a] 1338[e]	562[a] 575[e]			456[f]		205[f]
# CDA Decrees per Month	17.22[a] 22.30[e]	28.10[a] 28.75[e]			7.60[f]		3.42[f]
# DDA Decrees	263[a] 262[e]	156[a] 158[e]			118[f]		61[f]
# DDA Decrees per Month	4.38[a] 4.37[e]	7.8[a] 7.9[e]			1.97[f]		1.02[f]

a = Delgado-Guembes 1992, 226; b = Delgado-Guembes 1992, 226, 226n4, includes *Resoluciones Legislativas*; c = Pease García 1999, 98, may include decrees; d = Pease García 2006, 71–81, 495, 521; e = Schmidt 1998, 110, 118; f = author's own count using online data archives of Perú's Congreso de la República; g = García Montero 2006, 313.

with an APRA majority government than it would be (at roughly 57 percent) with a C-90/NM majority government in 1995–2000.

Legislators' accounts of their relations with the executive branch in the 1985–1990 period further support the argument that Peru's parliament was more genuinely involved in legislating before Fujimori's 1990 election than it would be in the decade after. Legislators and legislative assistants—majority and opposition—who served in both eras confirmed that the García government had a more fluid and horizontal relationship with the legislature than Fujimori did, before or after the *autogolpe*. Even though some of the most important pieces of legislation in 1985–1990 originated in ministries or with García himself, the executive branch would often informally share advance drafts with Parliament so that legislators could study them and offer comments before the bill was officially introduced (Franco Ballester interview 1999). While this was not the case, for example, with García's 1987 "surprise" banking nationalization, it was the case for other major reforms in sectors such as agriculture and internal security. Moreover, opposition legislators—on the left more so than the right—felt that their opinions were being heard in parliamentary debate and that García was seriously engaged in consensus-building within the legislature (Mariátegui Chiappe interview 1999).[15] Though the executive was in many ways dominant, formal and informal mechanisms enhanced legislators' capacity to influence lawmaking outcomes (Lynch interview 1999; Bernales Ballestros interview 1999).

The 1990–1992 period was decreasingly productive and increasingly conflictive. On average, no more than seven (and perhaps as few as three) laws per month were passed, the lowest productivity rate of any period analyzed here. And at first glance the executive appears to be nearly absent from the lawmaking process, initiating just 19 percent of all bills that became laws. However, as I explain in the next section, the president—lacking a stable working majority in the legislature—made ample use of other mechanisms for making laws, issuing decrees at a record pace. In this way, Fujimori was initially able to implement his reform program relatively unfettered. However, beginning in late 1991 the legislature increasingly attempted to assert its clout by reversing key legislation and passing the highly controversial Law of Parliamentary Control. Moreover, laws that did get passed through the legislative process were vetoed (and those vetoes were overridden) at very high rates in this period, as we shall also see below.

After the dissolution of the legislature in 1992, and before the CCD was elected, the executive produced 100 percent of all legislation—a staggering 586 (or 728) decree-laws (*decretos-leyes*) passed in just nine months, a rate of 65 (or 81) per month.[16] After the CCD assumed legislative functions in 1993, legislative productivity dropped again to 12 laws per month, and what laws it did pass were overwhelmingly (86 percent) proposed by the executive. Legislating became somewhat more balanced in 1995–2000, with the executive proposing 43 percent of all laws passed and the legislature proposing roughly 55 percent. Overall productivity was middling: 823 (or perhaps even just 690) laws passed in five years, a rate of 12–14 per month, regardless of origin. Executive-initiated bills enjoyed a 77–82 percent success rate (327 or 350 laws passed on 427 proposals; see Pease García 2006).

And even the laws originating in the legislature during Fujimori's second term were often dictated directly by the executive branch. C-90/NM legislators' lack of autonomy was notorious. Discipline, though rarely needed, was enforced through both formal and informal means: from withholding resources for legislators' offices to telephone surveillance to outright threats and blackmail. Some *congresistas* even wore beepers that instructed them how to vote (*Caretas,* Oct. 5, 1995). During meetings between the executive and his legislators, it was obvious who had real power, as then–C-90/NM congressman Carlos Ferrero Costa recounted in a 1999 interview:

> Very seldom . . . some topics, the most important topics have been discussed in the *plenito* [caucus], or we will meet with the president. . . . [But even then,] the president has already made an idea on the issue, and he tells you, "The problem is this; now I suggest we do *this.*" It's not like, "OK we have this problem; now what do you think?" and then everyone speaks, and a conclusion arrives by consensus. No, the system is the other way. You go hear what is the opinion of the president, and then you usually back it.

Unlike the late 1980s, informal practices in the late 1990s made the relationship between executive and legislature more, not less, imbalanced and hierarchical.

In 2001–2006, with the Toledo government in the minority and legislating with a shaky coalition, productivity (21–22 laws passed per month) nonetheless rose back to the levels of the 1985–1990 period. This productivity remained constant over most of Toledo's term, even as his political fortunes waned and his legislative coalition fell apart. The 277 laws passed by the 2004 legislature, when Toledo's PP lost control of the Mesa Directiva, were nearly on par with the 294 laws passed by the 2001 legislature, when Toledo's majority coalition was strongest. In the final year of the term legislative productivity fell a bit, to 193 laws— though among these were major pieces of legislation on pension reform, military justice, and the long-delayed selection of a new *defensor del pueblo* (Pease García 2006; Tuesta Soldevilla interview 2007). In sum, over the 2001–2006 period the legislature once again took up the mantel of crafting laws. The executive originated just 35 percent of legislation passed; the legislature, nearly 63 percent. As Morón and Sanborn (2006, 37) put it, "the Executive is no longer leading the legislative process."

For better or worse, in 2001–2006 Peru's legislature also shattered the record for bills proposed, with 13,655 *proyectos* initiated by members of Congress—a 260 percent increase over the 1995–2000 congress. The total number of bills proposed in Peru (14,830) was nine times higher than the number of bills proposed in neighboring Chile or Ecuador in the same period (Reflexión Democrática, n.d.). While most of the laws that ultimately passed in 2001–2006 originated in the legislature, most of the bills originating in the legislature did not end up as laws; their success rate was under 7 percent. Executive-initiated bills, by contrast, had a success rate of roughly 60 percent.

As in every era, some of the bills proposed in 2001–2006 were bound to be trivial or ill conceived. But Peru's legislative agenda was especially overwhelmed as a result of a new fervor for proposing "clone laws": bills that repeat or immaterially tweak other bills or existing legislation, proposed simply to boost the number of *proyectos* that a member of Congress could boast (Pease García interview 2007). Several shifts in legislative politics made such a practice possible and desirable: electronic roll-call voting in Congress left a verifiable record of legislators' votes, and the increased media coverage of Congress (including live feed on cable television and the internet) and other measures to enhance transparency raised public awareness of legislators' activities.[17]

The explosion of *proyectos* and the effort wasted on "credit-taking" exercises that would never become law eventually came to be seen as a problem by legislators themselves. In 2006, as Toledo was leaving office, the formal rules were changed so that, in the future, legislation could only be proposed by a parliamentary caucus, not by an individual legislator. Nonetheless, the abundance of bills in 2001–2006 was indicative of a congress that was once again engaged with the tasks of representation and lawmaking, if not always in the most efficient ways.

Presidential Decrees

One complicating factor in assessing the legislative role of Peru's Congress is the president's use of constitutional decree authority (CDA) and delegated decree authority (DDA), as outlined in chapter 3. Decrees issued under CDA were originally called *decretos supremos* (supreme decrees), or DS's; these were renamed *decretos de urgencia* (DU's) in the 1993 Constitution. Decrees issued under DDA, authority temporarily delegated to the executive by the legislature, are *decretos legislativos* (legislative decrees) or DL's.

DS's were used frequently in the 1985–1990 García government. Delgado-Guembes (1992) claims that 1033 DS's were issued in that period, while Schmidt (1998) has an even higher total, 1,338 — equivalent to 22 decrees per month. To this total may be added 262 (or 263) DL's, 4 per month, issued by García with authority granted by Parliament. This somewhat undercuts the image of legislators taking the lead as lawmakers in 1985–1990. Yet Schmidt's analysis points to the even heavier use of both DS's and DL's in 1990–1992, the first two years of the Fujimori regime. Fujimori issued 562 (or 575) DS's, at a rate of 29 per month, and 156 (or 158) DL's, at a rate of 8 per month. Thus, even though a focus on legislation alone conceals the extent of executive decree authority utilized by García in 1985–1990, the tendency toward executive dominance in lawmaking was clearly exacerbated under Fujimori, even in the early 1990s. As Schmidt (1998, 119) notes, if we compare the ratio of executive decrees with the force of law to legislation proper (regardless of the origin of the bill) we find that García issued 2.4 times as many decrees as laws passed in 1985–1990, while Fujimori issued 10.9 times as many decrees as laws passed between August 1990 and early April 1992. On the other hand, Fujimori's lack of a workable legislative majority was doubtless a mitigating factor: executive decrees were less obviously necessary to García's lawmaking success than to Fujimori's.

In the 1995–2000 period, even with a solid and subservient congressional majority Fujimori issued 456 DU's (under constitutional decree authority) at a rate of 8 per month. Congress also delegated authority to the executive to legislate on a number of issues, resulting in 118 DL's (issued under delegated decree authority) at a rate of 2 per month. The total number of decrees, 574, is still dwarfed by the huge number issued by García, 1,296 or 1,600, depending on the source. However, the most egregious evidence of unilateral executive lawmaking in the 1995–2000 period only came to light after the fall of the Fujimori government: the use of *decretos secretos de urgencia,* secret urgent decrees. As I explain below, some of these decrees created extremely large state expenditures with no transparency or accountability at all to Congress or the public.

In 2001–2006, President Toledo used his CDA to issue some 205 DU's at a rate of 3 decrees per month. More than half of these were issued during the president's first eighteen months in office, the high point of his popularity and political capital. By contrast, the president was granted DDA by Congress only twice, both times after his first eighteen months in office. These generated a total of 61 DL's, roughly 1 per month (if averaged over five years for purposes of comparison). As Toledo's popularity dropped and tensions with Congress increased, the two branches nonetheless maintained a productive working relationship, one that became less, rather than more, unilaterally presidentialist. Peru's legislature, for all its flaws, had grown into a stronger lawmaking role than ever.

Vetoes, Veto Overrides, and Interbranch Conflict

Making laws is of course not the only measure of legislative and executive strength; we also have a record of what happens when the two branches disagree. Looking at twenty years of vetoes and veto overrides, presented in Table 5.3, we see that in the 1985–1990 period a relatively low percentage of laws was vetoed and an even lower percentage of vetoes was overridden by Congress. With the disciplined APRA in the legislative majority, the lead role taken by Congress in drafting legislation, and relatively open lines of communication between executive and legislature (on most issues), this is not surprising. García also avoided Congress—and potential vetoes—by making ample use of presidential decrees.

Table 5.3. Vetoes and Veto Overrides, 1985–2005[18]

	Aug. 1985– July 1990	Aug. 1990– April 1992	Jan. 1993– July 1995	Aug. 1995– Nov. 2000	Nov. 2000– July 2001	Aug. 2001– mid-2005
# of laws vetoed	60	35	46	88	16	249
(as % of laws passed)	(9%)	(52%)	(17%)	(12%)	(14%)	(30%)
# of vetoes overridden	3	8	2	6	2	45
(as % of vetoes)	(5%)	(23%)	(4%)	(7%)	(13%)	(18%)

Sources: Schmidt 1998, 110; Morón and Sanborn 2006.

In 1990–1992, by contrast, both vetoes and veto overrides proliferated. President Fujimori's proclivities for vetoing bills passed by Congress and Congress's proclivities to override these vetoes were more of a symptom than a source of legislative-executive conflict. In 1990 and 1991, the legislature granted the executive decree authority (DDA) on a wide range of political and economic issues—particularly counterinsurgency and economic reform—and renewed this authority several times. But there were early signs of conflict. In September 1990, a dispute occurred over the legality of a presidential decree on prisoner amnesty; a month later, the legislature blocked authorization of supplementary credits to executive ministries; after that, disputes erupted over legislative adjustments to the budget bill and presidential decrees on labor rights (Kenney 1997; Letts Colmenares interview 1999).[19] Congress continued to delegate decree authority to the executive in 1991, but as detailed in chapter 3, in late 1991 and early 1992 the legislature pushed back and attempted to assert greater leverage over the executive branch, particularly with the constitutionally dubious Law of Parliamentary Control. Then, the 1992 budget was again a major source of conflict and was vetoed in a special session of the legislature.

Anecdotal evidence further illustrates the decay of horizontal exchange between the two branches. Some accounts of events immediately prior to the *autogolpe* hold that Vice President (and Senator) Máximo San Román continued to serve as an interlocutor in negotiations between the legislature and Fujimori, via Prime Minister Alfonso de los Heroes (Cameron 1994; Schmidt 1998). However, other sources suggest that, by late 1991,

Fujimori had already signaled his unwillingness to work with Congress (McClintock 1994; Planas 1997; Letts Colmenares interview 1999). According to Senator Alarcón Bravo (interview 1999), by March 1992 Fujimori was refusing to meet with his own vice president, San Román, or with Senate President Felipe Osterling. Then, in a rare meeting he held with C-90 parliamentarians on April 3, Fujimori presented plans for future legislative initiatives and appeared to be trying to bridge the chasm between the two branches (Arroyo interview 1999). He closed Congress later that weekend.

As noted in earlier chapters, there are vigorous debates among scholars regarding the role of legislative-executive conflict in provoking the April 1992 *autogolpe* (Kenney 1997; 2004; see also Delgado-Guembes 1992; Murakami 2007; inter alia). It is likely that these tensions, and the threat of removal by Congress, had some impact on Fujimori's decision to launch the self-coup. Until November or December 1991, the president was able to govern largely by making ample use of *decretos supremos;* then Congress tried to curtail those powers. In his first year in office Congress also granted him DDA, but that route too was being closed off by opposition groups. And as for legislation, Delgado-Guembes (1992) points not only to the frequency of vetoes but to an unusual spike in the number of bills that were stalled in legislative commissions in 1990–1991. This was due at least in part to the political inexperience of the C-90 legislators, but the effect was the same: lawmaking through the bicameral parliament was sluggish at best.

So instead, the executive remade the legislature to suit his needs. After the *autogolpe,* vetoes and veto overrides became a far less contentious issue, though they did not disappear. In the two years of the CCD and five years of the Fujimori-controlled congress, roughly 15 percent of legislation was vetoed—higher than the 9 percent figure from the APRA-controlled congress of the first García presidency. This suggests that some C-90/NM members of Congress were indeed engaged in autonomously crafting laws, though it also suggests that these efforts were not necessarily successful. C-90/NM members of Congress were clear in expressing to me that, on any issue that mattered, the executive always got his way (Trelles interview 1999; Ferrero Costa interview 1999; Marcenaro Frers interview 1999). And looking at the eight veto overrides spread over those seven years, they were not necessarily evidence of Congress flexing its muscle vis-à-vis the executive. One example: in early 1999, Congress passed the General Law of Volunteer Firefighters. President Fujimori approved the bill but vetoed or modified four of the bill's articles. As a result of an error in paperwork between the prime minister's office and the congressional standing Committee on Defense, on March 4 Congress unanimously confirmed the law without accepting the four vetoed and modified clauses (*El Comercio,* March 5, 1999).

In 2001–2006, President Toledo had to contend with a far more unruly congress. They vetoed and overrode each other at rates not seen in Peru since the conflictive 1990–1992 period. Three in ten laws passed by Congress were vetoed by Toledo; nearly two in ten presidential vetoes were overridden by Congress. What is more, conflict over legislation was just the tip of the iceberg. The multiparty governance of the Acuerdo Nacional began to fall apart in the second year of the term, as the Toledo government grew more scandal-ridden and unpopular. Conflicts over ministerial appointments and censures reached a fever pitch at several points, as I describe below. And the specter of removal from office haunted Toledo during the entire second half of his term.

Accountability

The "Void": Impeachment and the Vacating of Political Offices

Recall that Peru's constitution is rather ambiguous on the matter of presidential impeachment. On the one hand, both the 1979 and the 1993 constitutions state that while in office a president can only be charged with the most serious of crimes: treason, blocking electoral processes or the operation of electoral authorities, or illegally dissolving Congress or preventing it from convening.[20] Yet both charters also create an alternate mechanism for removing a president. The office of the president becomes "vacant" not only in the event of his death or resignation (or impeachment for the criminal charges listed above) but also for lesser causes. These include leaving the country without or beyond Congress's permission, or, more ambiguously, being declared "incapacitated" by Congress. In the original Spanish phrasing, the "incapacitation" clause covers both permanent physical disability, *"incapacidad física,"* as well as the vaguer *"incapacidad moral,"* which could be interpreted as either mental disability or moral turpitude. It is this second, more nebulous interpretation that has come into play in recent years.

As noted in chapter 3, Fujimori may have come within striking range of being "vacated" by the Chamber of Deputies in December 1991 after the Senate passed a motion that called him "morally disqualif[ied]" to serve—though the consequences of such a vote were unclear even to the protagonists at the time. This same provision was ultimately used to formally remove Fujimori from office in late 2000 (after his resignation was rejected by Congress). Then, in the 2001–2006 period, when the PP signature falsification scandal first began to break, UN congressman Rafael Rey vetted the idea of declaring Toledo "morally incapacitated" to serve as president, vacating the office and effectively impeaching him. The idea was echoed by some civil society groups, but Congress was divided on the issue and was reluctant to take this drastic step.

In June 2004 the legislature made it more difficult to vacate the presidency, raising the bar to eighty votes. This was done in part, on the recommendation of the Constitutional Tribunal, to harmonize these rules with those covering cabinet censures (*El Comercio,* May 4, 2004). But it also reflects the preferences of the major party caucuses in Congress: most legislators who remained in PP and FIM wanted to protect Toledo, and some (but not all) opposition party figures wanted him to flail and struggle but ultimately hang on until the approaching 2006 elections. Rafael Rey and José Barba actually presented a motion to remove Toledo in February 2005, though the leader of their own UN coalition, Lourdes Flores, did not support them and was disinclined to take the country on a "leap into the void" (*Caretas,* April 28, 2005). At the same time, APRA leaders toyed with the idea of lowering the threshold for vacating back to sixty-one votes but likewise decided that it would be too risky (*Caretas,* April 28, 2005; Zumaeta Flores interview 2007). APRA instead used this threat as leverage to exact concessions on policies and executive appointments.

The ongoing threat of quasi-impeachment took its toll on the Toledo government. Some PP legislators felt that they were expending so much time and effort negotiating Toledo's very survival that it diminished their capacity to legislate (Sánchez Pinedo interview 2007). But as noted above, while the executive branch was weakened, Peru's overall record of legislative productivity remained remarkably consistent from year to year. What is more, legislative-executive conflict did not explode in 2004–2005, when PP lost control of the Mesa Directiva. PP was on the defensive, but the president himself maintained a good working relationship with the main opposition groups, which were better organized than his own electoral movement. This renewed, if informal, commitment to multiparty governance redounded through the final 2005–2006 legislative period too (Tuesta Soldevilla interview 2007). For Toledo, having "real" party caucuses to work with proved as good as, or better than, legislating through his own coalition of ad hoc electoral movements. The president and his ministers met with opposition leaders such as García, Flores, and Paniagua on a regular basis, negotiations that enhanced governability despite interbranch tensions (Taylor 2007).

Unlike 1990–1992, this period of minority government in the legislature did not end with a full-blown crisis of democracy. While Toledo struggled with Congress and was nearly turfed out of office, he took a very different political tack, one that would empower, rather than annihilate, the legislature. And Congress made especially fervent use of these powers to hold the executive accountable, exemplified not only by the near dismissal of the president himself but by the relationship between the legislature and the cabinet too.

Legislatures and Cabinets

Peru's constitution creates mechanisms for horizontal accountability not found in a pure separation-of-powers system. These mechanisms center on the role of the cabinet: the *presidente del Consejo de Ministros* (president of the Council of Ministers—referred to as prime minister or premier) and her ministers. The cabinet is responsible for executing laws and policies and can formulate them too.[21] And although the cabinet is appointed by and can be dismissed by the president, ministers can also be interpellated (questioned) and even censured (forced to resign) by the legislature.

But the weapon of congressional censure has only rarely been deployed. In President Belaúnde's second term (1980–1985) and President García's first term (1985–1990)—both with effective majorities in Congress—not a single minister was censured. Then, in the early 1990s President Fujimori demonstrated the capacity of the president to simply

Table 5.4. Ministerial Accountability to the Legislature

Period	Censure	Interpellation	Question Period	Invited Address
1985–1990	0	n/a	n/a	12(+28)
1990–1992	1	4	n/a	2
1993–1995	0	n/a	n/a	14
1995–2000	0	5	15	12
2001–2006	1	10	55	65

Sources: Bernales Ballestros 1990; Delgado-Guembes 1992; Pease García 1994; 1999; 2006.

ignore a censure if constitutionalism and the rule of law are weak enough. In response to the November 1991 presidential veto of an agrarian reform bill, the legislature censured the minister of agriculture, Enrique Rossl Link. This should have led to his immediate resignation. However, since the 1979 Constitution did not stipulate a time frame for responding to the censure, Fujimori kept the minister on for a month and overtly threatened to dissolve Congress if any more censures were exercised.

After the *autogolpe,* the president enjoyed the support of a friendly legislative majority. The ministerial censure was effectively neutralized in the 1990s. Interpellation—the formal questioning of ministers—required just a one-third majority and would have been within reach of parliamentary groups opposed to Fujimori. (In the 1990–1992 minority government, at least four ministers were formally interpellated in just twenty months.) But in 1995–2000, the *fujimorista* leadership in Congress habitually let motions for interpellation linger indefinitely without putting them to a vote. Consequently, these too slowed to a trickle, with only five during the entire five-year period (Pease García 2006, 495).

The practice of ministers coming to speak at the invitation of the Permanent Commission or the full legislature was also moribund, though this was true even in the 1980s. According to Pease García (1999, 102), only twelve such visits were approved by the APRA majority in the Chamber of Deputies in 1985–1990. Bernales Ballestros (1990, 170) chronicles an additional twenty-eight ministerial visits to the Senate, although these are considered less of an accountability mechanism since only the deputies can follow up with formal interpellation or censure. The practice of ministerial addresses did not improve under Fujimori: in 1990–1992 just two ministers were invited; in 1993–1995 ministers addressed Congress fourteen times; and for 1995–2000 the figure dropped down to twelve.

In the late 1990s ministers also made little use of the *estación de preguntas*. These were vaguely demarcated "question periods," in which one or more ministers were supposed to attend a question-and-answer session in Congress "periodically" (according to Article 129 of the 1993 Constitution). The frequency was further specified in Article 51 of the 1995 Congressional Regulations, which required that "in at least one full session of Congress per month, up to two hours be allotted for the question period." In reality, adherence to this rule was minimal. Only fifteen question periods were conducted in 1995–2000, and twelve of these were in the first two years of the term (Pease García 2006, 495). And even on those rare occasions, legislators' speaking time was limited, with no follow-up questions allowed. The political conversation between legislature and executive in Peru had become increasingly one-sided.

This too changed after 2000. From 2001 to 2006, ministers made sixty-five invited addresses to Congress and were subjected to ten formal interpellations. Question periods were conducted fifty-five times, although none were held in the final two years of the period. Most remarkably, in May 2004 Congress formally censured Interior Minister Fernando Rospigliosi—with some votes from the president's own party. Congress also voted on censuring three other ministers over the course of five years.

In many other widely reported standoffs, legislators wielded their power over ministers less formally but just as effectively. As noted in chapter 3, the press became rapacious in its coverage of government in general and the executive branch in particular. This media pressure, coupled with revitalized congressional oversight, frequently rocked Toledo's ministers back on their heels. For every incident that led to an official motion of censure in Congress, there were numerous other scandals, some ending in resignations.

Toledo's cabinet appointments were more fleeting and chaotic than his predecessors'. This is reflected not so much in the number of prime ministers and cabinets (which was similar across the three presidencies) as in the number of ministerial replacements *within* cabinet periods.[22] García and Fujimori each averaged 1.1 ministers per portfolio per cabinet; 1 in 10 ministers (or 1.5 ministers in a 15-person cabinet) could expect to be replaced. Toledo's cabinets averaged 1.4 ministers per portfolio per cabinet: a staggering 4 in 10 ministers (or 6 ministers in a 15-person cabinet) would not complete any given cabinet period (Tuesta Soldevilla, "Resumen Gabinetes").

What follows is an illustrative, though not exhaustive, synthesis of cabinet instability in 2001–2006. Toledo's first cabinet, led by Prime Minister Roberto Dañino, made three replacements in January 2002: David Waisman (Defense), Luis Solari (Health), and Doris Sánchez (Women and Development), all PP politicians, returned to bolster the group's leadership in Congress and were replaced in the cabinet by independents.[23] Before the year was out, the interior minister (Rospigliosi) would resign in the wake of violent protests in the city of Arequipa, and the prime minister (Dañino) and minister of economy/finance (Pedro Pablo Kuczynski) would leave ahead of the rest of the cabinet. In these last three cases the ministers felt undermined by the president's unsteadiness or by opposition from within the PP caucus in Congress.

Toledo's second cabinet, 2002–2003, was led by Solari, who was returning to the executive branch; midcabinet shuffles included FIM chief Fernando Olivera leaving the Justice Ministry to serve as ambassador to Spain (replaced by another FIM member) and independent Gino Costa resigning from Interior (replaced by a PP member).

A third cabinet was installed in June 2003, and an independent, Beatriz Merino, was brought in as a prime minister. Merino was immensely popular, in stark contrast to the low approval ratings garnered by Toledo and his legislators (Taylor 2007). But in just six months she went through two commerce ministers, two economy/finance ministers, two ministers of energy/mining and two interior ministers (as Rospigliosi returned for a second stint, having served—and been removed—as chief of intelligence in the interim).[24] Then in December 2003 Merino herself was forced by congressional pressure to resign in the face of a somewhat ginned-up scandal (see chapter 3).

This led to another major cabinet reshuffle under a new prime minister, outgoing president of Congress Carlos Ferrero. But this cabinet too faced frequent resignations, starting with the departure of the minister for women and social development, Nidia Puelles, after just four days. Over the nineteen-month period that Ferrero led the cabinet, it oscillated wildly between partisan and independent appointments. At one crisis point in

February 2004, FIM members were completely removed from the cabinet, putting Toledo's legislative coalition in jeopardy. Some opposition leaders even called for Toledo to step aside and let Prime Minister Ferrero run the government, to avoid a deepening crisis of governance.[25] Ferrero had five different ministers of justice; three ministers each in agriculture, energy/mines, interior, production, and labor; and two ministers each in economy/finance, foreign affairs, health, and transportation/communication. His cabinet resigned en masse in two waves of crisis in August 2005.[26]

With this very public chaos in the executive branch and an election year approaching, Toledo actually had trouble filling slots in the final 2005–2006 cabinet. Cabinet veteran Kuczynski was eventually moved into the position of prime minister and enjoyed a year of relative stability with only one midyear replacement, in the Labor Ministry (Tuesta Soldevilla 2008; *NotiSur,* Aug. 26, 2005).

As this dizzying narrative makes clear, Peru's Council of Ministers under President Toledo was a revolving door propelled by scandal, infighting, mismanagement, and, not least, pressure from Congress. As the executive branch was severely weakened, the legislative branch—though unruly—grew manifestly stronger in 2001–2006. Furthermore, its legislators were embedded within the executive branch in ways that had all but disappeared under Fujimori, as we shall now see.

Legislators and Cabinet Recruitment

Beyond oversight and "checks and balances," another point of contact between the legislature and the executive in Peru is the ability (and in some eras, the propensity) of legislators to simultaneously serve as cabinet ministers. Schmidt (1998) argues that members of Congress who serve as ministers, and expect to return to Congress afterwards, have an incentive to maintain good relations with their fellow legislators. For 1985–1990, as noted above, this effect was confirmed by several congressmen who spoke to me of the importance of informal communication between García's ministers and the legislature (Mariátegui Chiappe interview 1999; Lynch interview 1999; Bernales Ballestros interview 1999; Franco Ballester interview 1999). It was common practice in the 1980s for legislators to serve in the cabinet. In fact, legislators held precisely the most important posts of the executive branch: all five of García's prime ministers were also APRA

Table 5.5. Percentage of Ministerial Appointments Held by Members of Congress[27]

	1985–1990 (García)	1995–2000 (Fujimori)	2001–2006 (Toledo)
% of cabinet appointees from legislature	43%	4%	21%
% recalculated without final 6 months of term	49%	4%	22%

Sources: Author's analysis of data in Tuesta Soldevilla 2001 and http://blog.pucp.edu.pe/fernandotuesta/node/603.

legislators, as were four of his six ministers of economy and finance and three of his five ministers of the presidency.

Table 5.5 compares data for three uninterrupted five-year periods. As we can see, the practice of appointing legislators as ministers was extensive in 1985–1990: 43 percent of all appointees to García's cabinet were sitting parliamentarians. Moreover, a number of the nonlegislators who served in the cabinet were named precisely six months prior to the 1990 general elections, in order to legally allow legislator-ministers to run for reelection to Congress. If we omit these end-of-term cabinet shuffles, the proportion rises to 49 percent.

Fujimori's first three cabinets—those prior to the *autogolpe*—included just one C-90 legislator, Deputy Víctor Paredes. The president marginalized his own fledgling electoral movement. He was not able to use cabinet appointments to cobble together a legislative majority either, though his first cabinet was led by former *acciopopulista* Juan Carlos Hurtado Miller and included three left party members who had not been elected to Congress.[28] After that, however, ministers tended to be "independent" appointees with few political loyalties outside of the executive (McClintock 1993). Some of these technocrats then served as the nucleus of the Nueva Mayoría group: several cabinet members from 1992–1993 (including Jaime Yoshiyama, Carlos Torres y Torres Lara, Jaime Freundt-Thurne, and Víctor Joy Way) were elected to the CCD in 1992. When the cabinet was reshuffled in 1993, however, only Freundt-Thurne was retained.

By the 1995–2000 period, just one sitting congressman, Víctor Joy Way, was appointed to the cabinet over the course of five years (though he was appointed twice). Any informal incentives for cooperation and power sharing that the "cabinet connection" once provided were eliminated. Fujimori's preference was to keep legislators—even his own—out of the inner circle of policymakers.

In 2001–2006 we can see a marked increase in the executive's cabinet recruitment among legislators. Though the "cabinet connection" did not fully return to the robust levels of the 1980s, 21–22 percent of all of Toledo's cabinet appointees were sitting members of Congress. Under Toledo the practice was deployed spasmodically and with unstable results. Cabinet shuffles would alternately bring a wave of PP politicians into the executive and then turf them out in favor of independent technocrats, who would in turn clash with the PP congressional caucus. The cabinet was also used to solidify legislative alliances and mollify opposition groups. The PP coalition with FIM brought the latter into the cabinet, but FIM appointees (particularly Olivera) proved so polarizing that the alliance was jeopardized. Toledo also attempted to placate the APRA in 2002–2003 by appointing two ministers with long-standing ties to the party.[29] Though Toledo's record of tailoring his cabinet composition for political ends was not terribly successful, the very relevance of the strategy—using ministerial appointments to keep a legislative coalition together or satisfy opposition groups in Parliament—speaks volumes about the renewed political heft of the legislature.

Oversight and Control Político: *Budgets and Government Spending*

Like other aspects of its institutional strength, the ability of the legislature to effectively oversee the policies and practices of the state were severely curtailed in the 1990s and then partially rebounded in 2001–2006.

In the 1990s, ministers became less accountable to the legislature, and power and resources became ever more concentrated within the executive. One site of executive overreach was the Ministry of the Presidency (MIPRE). This ministry was first created by Alan García in 1985, with the goal of overseeing the execution of presidential policy initiatives. However, MIPRE did not become an important institutional force in the 1980s; major policies and programs were still administered largely by the existing specialized ministries or by stand-alone state agencies. The MIPRE was then eliminated by the outgoing APRA government in 1990 but, tellingly, it was revived by Fujimori less than two weeks after the April 1992 *autogolpe*.

Under Fujimori MIPRE rapidly became a ministerial behemoth. In 1995, MIPRE commanded 23 percent of the total national budget and continued to receive 20–21 percent of annual budgets throughout the remainder of the decade. Within this allocation, just over half of MIPRE's funds in the 1990s went to finance programs housed within the appointed regional governments, the CTARs, run by Fujimori loyalists often drawn from the ranks of the military. Most of the remainder of the MIPRE budget went to two targeted social programs run directly by the president: the National Fund for Compensation and Social Development (FONCODES), a social welfare fund designed to ameliorate the effects of neoliberal economic adjustment, and the National Institute of Education and Health Infrastructure (INFES), a fund specializing in the construction of schools and clinics (Graham and Kane 1998). Other projects funded by MIPRE included water filtration plants and other physical infrastructure. The material products of these expenditures were, in addition to their welfare-improving effects, a sort of state-funded personal publicity program and permanent election campaign for President Fujimori. Commemorative plaques bearing the president's name became ubiquitous in the mostly rural areas served by these programs. And more so than other ministries, MIPRE lacked transparency and defied legislative control. As Wise (2003, 203) described it, "even Fujimori's most polite critics refer to [MIPRE] as the president's own 'mafia.'"

Another oversized ministry was Economy and Finance, or MEF. This ministry consistently accounted for roughly 30 percent of annual budgets, although more than half of this total went directly to paying and servicing Peru's sovereign debt. A major locus of power within the MEF was FONAFE (Fondo Nacional de Financiamiento de la Actividad Empresarial del Estado), a fund that was separate from the rest of the national budget and that managed a variety of "enclave" or autonomous agencies. FONAFE-funded agencies, the MIPRE programs, and other favored initiatives of the Fujimori government, such as PRONAA (Programa Nacional de Asistencia Alimentaria, the food-aid program run through the new Ministry of Women's Affairs and Human Development), all over-

lapped with existing social programs run by the other increasingly neg-
lected ministries. For example it was MIPRE, via the CTARs, that funded
rural health posts and the payroll expenses of all schools outside of the
capital city region—not the Ministries of Health and Education, respectively (Ames et al. 2001). Throughout the 1990s, MIPRE and MEF, plus
the Ministries of Defense and Interior—also bastions of the Fujimori/
Montesinos "mafia"—together accounted for almost 70 percent of annual budgets.

While the legislature has little power to alter the annual budget, it
is, according to the constitution, responsible for holding the state accountable and overseeing the execution of budget expenditures. But Fujimori strategically avoided using "normal" budget channels. His government shielded itself from scrutiny by the legislature and the public at large
through the use of unconstitutional *decretos de urgencia secretos* or secret
urgent decrees. By issuing such decrees using the executive's constitutional
decree authority, but without informing Congress, Fujimori and his inner
circle avoided legislative oversight of some of the proceeds from the privatization of state-owned enterprises in the 1990s. Roughly $2 billion
was redirected toward purchasing military hardware "off the books" and
funding the Fujimori-Montesinos web of corruption. And one of the final
secret urgent decrees issued during the Fujimori regime authorized an increase in the budget of the MEF by 52.5 million soles ($15.5 million),
which was to be paid in cash to intelligence advisor Vladimiro Montesinos
just prior to his fleeing the country (MEF 2001).

Fujimori also took advantage of *créditos suplementarios* (supplementary credits), additions to the annual budget that can be approved by a
three-fifths majority of the Comisión Permanente when Congress is out
of session. Supplementary credits were used to fund a wide range of Fujimori's pet projects, such as the $240 million worth of tractors and agri-
cultural machinery promised during his annual Independence Day address to the nation in 1999 (*Caretas,* Sept. 2, 1999).

Even within the annual budgeting process, parliamentary oversight
of state expenditures was made difficult by a lack of reliable information.
Legislators were entirely dependent on data served up by the executive
branch. And as the 2000 election year approached, official budget data
for that year was deliberately presented in an opaque format that made it
impossible for Congress to compare year-over-year shifts in expenditures

or verify policy changes promised by the government (such as downsizing MIPRE from 20 percent to 7.5 percent of the budget and decentralizing some of its health and education programs to municipal governments; see *Caretas,* Sept. 2, 1999).

Transparency improved significantly in the 2001–2006 period, giving the legislature, along with the media and the public at large, far greater capacity for oversight than in the 1990s. During the interim government of Valentín Paniagua, the structures of ministries and public agencies were retooled so that their accounting ledgers were opened to public scrutiny. The MIPRE was eliminated entirely by Toledo in 2002. Secret decrees were no longer utilized, and supplementary credits were overseen by a more pluralistic Comisión Permanente in Congress. Virtually every member of Congress, government or opposition, interviewed for this book indicated that, under Toledo, the legislature had far more—and far more accurate—information about what government was doing. Legislators still depended on ministers to provide data, and the complexity of annual budgets still overwhelmed the analytical capacity of the legislature at times (Solari de la Fuente interview 2007; Santa María Calderón interview 2005). However, it is clear that information flowed from executive to legislature much more freely than in the 1990s.

If legislators were ever frustrated in their attempts to extract information from Toledo's executive branch, or were deterred by Peru's notoriously slow subpoena processes, they—and all Peruvians—had new tools at their disposal. Building on reforms begun under Paniagua, the Transparency and Access to Public Information laws passed in August 2002 and February 2003 quickly created a mechanism for requesting information about virtually any state entity in a timely and cost-efficient manner. In the first year of this new access-to-information regime, nearly forty thousand requests were received from politicians, NGOs, the media, and the public at large, and more than 95 percent were fulfilled (Article 19, 2006, 55).

If a legislator were to suspect some wrongdoing on the part of the government (or be alerted to it by the public or the press), changes in Peru's public administration made the work of investigating the matter—via standing or special investigative committees—feasible in a way that it had not been since the 1980s. It is to these committees that I turn next.

Table 5.6. Legislative Motions Requesting the Formation of an Investigative Committee and Number of Investigations, 1985–2006[30]

Period	Motions Presented	% Approved	Investigations Launched	Ad Hoc + Standing Committees
1985–1990	206	29.6%	61	n/a
1990–1992	100	10.0%	29	n/a
1993–1995	75	10.7%	8	n/a
1995–2000	263	2.3%	6	5 +1
2001–2006	256	25.8%	66	11 +55 (+179)

Sources: Delgado-Guembes 1992, 298–99; Pease García 1999, 99; 2006, 495.

Investigative Committees and Accountability

Comisiones investigadores, investigative committees, are one more method by which the legislature can exercise its oversight of the ministries and agencies of the executive. Under both the 1979 and the 1993 constitutions, these committees were given many of the same powers that judicial authorities have to investigate individuals and organizations and to compel testimony and the disclosure of documents. As with other facets of accountability, investigative committees were active in the 1980s, then hamstrung by the Fujimori regime (especially after 1992), then revitalized in 2001–2006.

As Table 5.6 demonstrates, the approval of motions requesting the formation of such committees was high in the late 1980s, hit a low in the 1990s, and then rebounded in the early years of the twenty-first century. This is more than just a by-product of Toledo's shaky minority government, as compared to Fujimori's sizeable and disciplined majority. The García government, which also enjoyed a comfortable majority, rarely interfered when legislators—its own or members of the opposition—formed investigative committees, even when the committees' findings were liable to be unflattering or critical of the government. Fully sixty of the sixty-one investigations launched in 1985–1990 were directed at the executive branch (Pease García 1999). In the 1990s, legislators continued to try to use this tool for holding Fujimori accountable. More motions to investigate were presented in 1995–2000 than in 1985–1990, but the motions were voted down or were never even put up for a vote by the *fujimorista* congressional majority.

The oversight capacity of the 1985–1990 era should not, of course, be idealized. Delgado-Guembes (1992) points out that twenty-three of fifty-nine investigative committees in the Chamber of Deputies during the 1985–1990 period ended up producing no report at all, and sixteen others never got the legislature's approval of their final report.[31] Nevertheless, those investigative committees whose reports were not approved (or even written) still had a salutary effect on the transparency and accountability of the executive branch. By holding inquiries into controversial policies or potential corruption, they uncovered information and generated public debate.

Those committees also involved the active participation of opposition legislators. In fact, by many accounts, the three investigative committees that had the greatest impact on political life in Peru in the late 1980s were headed by opposition legislators (Pásara 1993; Planas 1999). The bicameral committee led by IU senator Rolando Ames thoroughly investigated a 1986 massacre of rioting prisoners and concluded, in 1988, that orders given by President García himself and his minister of the interior led unnecessarily to the carnage. In 1989, the Senate committee headed by IU senator Enrique Bernales published what was then regarded as the most comprehensive study of political violence and counterinsurgency strategy in Peru and was highly critical of state policy. Later that same year, an investigative committee led by opposition legislators from the Chamber of Deputies produced a comprehensive report on paramilitary groups in Peru, implicating the APRA party in the operations of the Comando Rodrigo Franco.

In 1990–1992, ten investigative committees were launched by the deputies, and an additional nineteen were created in the Senate. Among these were a few bombshells directed at the executive. For example, on April 2, 1992, the Senate formed a committee to look into accusations that Fujimori and his inner circle were illegally selling donated clothing from Japan. The *autogolpe* followed just three days later.

By contrast, investigative committees were few and far between by the mid-1990s. *Fujimoristas* frequently alleged that congressional investigations would improperly interfere with ongoing legal proceedings—proceedings run by a judiciary that was firmly under executive control (Planas 1999). Pro-Fujimori legislators also argued that Congress's regular standing committees—as well as the Oversight Committee (Comisión de Fiscalización), created by and for Fujimori—served the functions formerly performed by investigative committees. Unlike the investigative committees of the late 1980s, however, the Oversight Committee and other standing committees were invariably controlled by the parliamentary majority. Moreover, on the rare occasion that an investigative committee was formed between 1993 and 2000, it was seldom for the purpose of looking into government activity. For example, only two of the eight committees formed by the 1993–1995 CCD were directed to investigate the executive branch. And if a committee did investigate the Fujimori regime, it never found any fault.

Two examples from 1995–2000 are particularly egregious. A May 1999 committee formed at the request of IU congressman Javier Diez Canseco (but dominated by *fujimorista* legislators) to investigate the April 1992 *autogolpe*—which closed Congress—ended by deciding that this was not a matter relevant to Congress (*El Comercio,* May 14, 1999). And in the aftermath of the 2000 elections, a committee to investigate illegal government actions during the election campaign, presided over by C-90/NM congresswoman Edith Mellado, ended up inculpating the victims and the whistle-blowers rather than the perpetrators. The legislature's propensity to use its powers of investigation to exercise its oversight of government had virtually disappeared.

The contrast with the 2001–2006 period is striking for several reasons. First, in 2001 Congress's internal regulations were changed, lowering from 50 percent to 35 percent the threshold for approving a motion to launch an investigation.[32] The number of congressionally mandated investigative committees in the five years that followed was the highest in Peru's modern history (and the rate at which motions to investigate were approved rivaled the 1985–1990 period). Second, the legislature's standing committee on oversight, the Comisión de Fiscalización, became both more active, investigating even the president and First Lady, and more pluralistic too: the committee was led by legislators from the opposition APRA party for the entire five-year period.[33] The committee was in fact so aggressive that the PP-FIM alliance proposed deactivating the committee in 2005, arguing that other congressional accountability mechanisms were now functioning properly, but the idea did not gain much purchase. Third, unlike the 1995–2000 period, the whole system of standing committees was beginning to fulfill its proper role; they also used their new capacity to conduct investigations on topics relevant to their area of expertise. For 55 of 66 congressionally mandated investigations during this period, the full Congress delegated to a standing committee the responsibility to double as an investigative committee; ad hoc investigative committees were formed for the other eleven investigations. Fourth, standing committees could also launch their own investigations, which they did 179 times in this period. Finally, unlike the similarly active 1985–1990 period, 73 percent of all investigative committees created by a vote of Congress (forty-eight of sixty-six) concluded their work with a report presented to the legislature.[34] Investigations launched autonomously by standing committees had a poorer track record: only 36 percent (64 of 179) concluded with a report to Congress (Pease García 2006, 495). Nonetheless, it is clear that the overall power of the legislature to hold the executive to account rose dramatically in 2001–2006.

Nowhere was this better exemplified than in the Villanueva Commission, which was charged with investigating signature fraud in the registration of Perú Posible. As described in chapter 3, this committee was, after some delay and negotiations over conditions, able to compel testimony by the president himself and very nearly led to his removal. Notwithstanding some problems maintaining its professionalism and neutrality, the committee demonstrated just how much power the legislature had gained over the executive.

Representation

Representation of Constituents' Interests

The Chamber of Deputies—the lower house of what was, prior to 1992, a bicameral legislature—was elected by proportional representation in multiple districts delineated by department (i.e., by geographic subunits). Representation of regional and local interests in Parliament was very uneven, though. In the 1980s, few deputies maintained offices in their home departments (Lynch interview 1999). Moreover, many former deputies interviewed felt that the capital city's deputies dominated the chamber, both de jure in the standing committees and governing bodies of the chamber, and de facto as opinion leaders and liaisons with the president (La Riva Vegazzo interview 1999; Castro Gomez interview 1999; Haya de la Torre interview 1999; Franco Ballester interview 1999).

But whatever their shortcomings and obstacles, deputies' legislative efforts were far more closely oriented toward regional and local issues than any of their post-1992 successors — even after Peru returned to multiple electoral districts in 2001. I analyzed arbitrary samples[35] of legislative proposals from the Chamber of Deputies, the unicameral single-district congress, and the unicameral multiple-district congress. I sampled from the second legislative year in each of four electoral periods, looking for evidence of legislative projects that would affect a particular departmental/local population. In some cases the departmental/local content was clear (places or groups mentioned by name); in other cases, I categorized regional/local content as "likely" if it focused on a group (e.g., mine workers) or geological feature (e.g., the Amazon basin) located in a limited number of departments. While differences in sampling methodologies over time means that these figures are just rough approximations of the total universe of proposals, they illustrate major changes in Peru's legislature.

Table 5.7 demonstrates that regional and local interests were prominent among deputies' lawmaking aspirations. To be sure, these included plenty of merely symbolic bills but also proposals for highway improvements, agricultural subsidies, university construction, and other "pork" projects. Bills with regional or local benefits constituted more than half of all projects proposed in the lower house in 1986 and 1991.

Most of these proposals did not pass, and even pork projects that were passed in the lower chamber were often killed in the Senate (Pilco Deza interview 1999) or, in the case of APRA in 1985–90, by their own party leadership in the executive (Aldave Pajares interview 1999). Several deputies intimated that the best way to get a pork-barrel project for one's department was to negotiate directly with a vice minister or with another bureaucrat and to avoid the legislative arena entirely (Jara Ladrón interview 1999; Aldave Pajares interview 1999; Pilco Deza interview

Table 5.7. Sample Percentages of Bills (*Proyectos*) Proposed with Regional/Local Benefits in the Lower/Single Chamber: Legislative Years 1986, 1991, 1996, 2002

Legislative Year Sampled	Sample Size (n)	% of bills with clear regional/local content	% of bills with likely regional/local content	TOTAL % of bills with regional/local content
1986	169	54.4	3.6	58.0
1991	168	47.6	4.2	51.8
1996	100	9.0	13.0	22.0
2002	768	9.5	10.9	20.4

Source: Author's analysis of data from Congreso de la República del Perú.

1999). There was more attempted credit taking than actual lawmaking going on, and as the majority party in 1985–1990, APRA deputies often tried to block the regionally specific projects of other parties' legislators (Jara Ladrón interview 1999; Castro Gomez interview 1999). But whether promoting or thwarting them, deputies clearly believed that regionally and locally specific projects were a political imperative.

In the minority legislature of 1990–1992, deputies continued to introduce regional/local legislation at a high rate, and successful interparty cooperation on policy issues of common interest to a department was not unusual (Zegarra Gutiérrez interview 1999; Dolmos Vengoa interview 1999). For example, legislation for a multimillion-dollar irrigation project in Chavimochíc, La Libertad, was successfully drafted by a multiparty group of deputies from that department and passed in 1991 (Santa María Calderón interview 1999). However, the low rate at which bills originating in the legislature actually became law in 1990–1992 suggests that deputies were not very successful at pork barreling, even less so than their predecessors in 1985–1990. Nonetheless, this data helps us understand whom they were trying to impress: those they thought they were representing.

With the advent of a unicameral congress with a single electoral district, legislators still had the option of focusing their campaign activities on specific areas of the country. But there is little evidence that these legislators actually provided representation—through pork-barreling, constituent service, or any other mechanism—to the residents of specific areas.

This was confirmed by numerous informants, both pro- and anti-Fujimori (e.g., Torres y Torres interview 1998; Mohme Llona interview 1999). The data in Table 5.6 further underscore how national the focus of legislative proposals became after 1992. In a sample from the 1996 legislative year, just 22 percent of all bills had any regional/local content. A mere 9 percent were clearly oriented toward a specific locale—and the majority of these were targeted at places in and around the capital city, Lima. In the *fujimorista* worldview, decentralized decision making and regional representation were dangerous and detracted from the formulation of coherent national policy. According to C-90/NM congressman and former head of the Constitutional Affairs Committee, Carlos Torres y Torres Lara, it was "a serious mistake" for Peru to have had a political system prior to 1992 in which legislators believed that part of their job was to represent local and regional interests (interview 1998).

Returning to a system of multiple electoral districts in 2001 created new possibilities for regional and local representation of citizens. At the most rudimentary level of descriptive representation, the 2001–2006 congress looked a bit more like the country as a whole. It was the most "provincial" assembly since 1990: 72 percent of all members were born outside of Lima, compared to 63 percent in 1995–2000, 62 percent in 1993–1995, 69 percent (across both chambers) in 1990–1992, and 73 percent (across both chambers) in 1985–1990 (Pease García 1999, 91; Transparencia, *Quién es quién,* 2001). Legislators also attempted to perform the sorts of outreach and constituent service that had never before existed in Peru, even in the pre-1992 Chamber of Deputies (Santa María Calderón interview 2005). They now had local district offices, and most returned to their districts frequently.

But the fall of Fujimori and the return of multiple electoral districts did not lead legislators back to the regionalized and localized legislative proposals that used to flood out of the Chamber of Deputies. The change in the overall percentage of bills with clear or likely regional/local content is totally flat from the 1996 sample to the 2002 sample. The 1990s changed the system of governing itself, and returning to multiple electoral districts could not change it back. First, national budget processes became much more highly centralized from 1992 to 2001. Then, effective regional governments were created in the early 2000s. Congress was no longer where pork was to be won. Voters more than ever *expected* legislators to seek selective benefits for constituents (Santa María Calderón interview 2005; Taco Llave interview 2007). But selective benefits could best be gained by negotiating directly with a national or regional executive (Alvarado Dodero interview 2007; Solari de la Fuente interview 2007; Rey Rey interview 2007). Even with identifiable constituencies to answer to, even with legislators' votes being made more public after electronic roll-call voting was introduced in the late 1990s, and even with the over-all proliferation of bills introduced by legislators in the 2001–2006 period, it appears that their credit-taking efforts focused mainly on broader, national policy issues.

Overall, eliminating the Chamber of Deputies in 1992 seems to have permanently severed a form of connection between legislators and citizens, however unproductive that linkage might have been in the 1980s and early 1990s. Citizens then developed an increasingly direct relationship with the executive, unmediated by other institutions, and it is little wonder that the imbalance of power between legislature and executive became so exaggerated in the 1990s. But even as the legislative-executive balance of power evened out after the turn of the century, and voters once again elected legislators by departmental district, members of Congress did not return to pork-barreling or seeking symbolic recognition for their districts—at least not using legislation as their tool.

Party Unity, Party Switching, and Representation

Even when legislators did not represent a fixed geographic district, they were still elected as part of a group, and as we have seen in previous chapters, these groups can be organized in very different ways. How they are organized, what ideas and policies (if any) they are attached to, and what they do after they are elected are all elements of political representation. Though I examined change over time in party organizations per se in chapter 4, here I turn specifically to the questions of programmatic, partisan representation by legislative caucuses and of party switching among legislators.

A methodical analysis of change over time in party unity in the legislature—the similarities of members' views and their tendency to vote in unison—is hindered by the absence of surveys of parliamentary elites as well as public records of roll-call voting in Peru until the late 1990s. However, journalistic sources and legislators' own opinions and experiences all point to a sharp distinction between the 1980s and 1990s.

APRA legislators were a disciplined force in Parliament in 1985–1990. Dissenting votes or even abstentions were frowned upon and were extremely rare. Conflicts among legislators were resolved within the Célula Parlamentaria Aprista, the APRA legislative caucus. While this body was technically governed by majority rule, it was in fact strongly hierarchical, with party leaders dictating the agenda, the allocation of speaking time, and the votes to be cast in the legislature. President García was certainly at the top of the party hierarchy, but he was not alone (even when he wanted to be). Senior legislators and powerful party insiders still mattered. And the party unity of their caucus gave structure to the legislative process and to the governance of the legislature itself (Aldave Pajares interview 1999; Alvarado Contreras interview 1999; Santa María Calderón interview 1999; Pilco Deza interview 1999).

Opposition parties in 1985–1990 varied in their internal discipline. Within the PPC for example, legislators met each week to coordinate votes, but it was not uncommon for the party leadership to allow legislators to dissent or abstain (Sotomarino Chávez interview 1999). Within the left, even though the IU coalition was divided organizationally along party lines, the legislators were able to vote as a block on a majority of bills and other matters that came before the legislature (Pease García interview 1999). According to former senator Bernales Ballestros (interview 1999), in the 1980s parliamentary debate mattered a great deal to majority and opposition legislators alike precisely because these politicians had party organizations behind them. What is more, party switching was rare.

In the first year after the 1990 elections, the presidencies of both houses of Parliament were held by C-90 legislators, even though this group did not have a majority or even the largest legislative delegation. Yet the president kept his own congressional leadership out of the loop, while counting on PPC and Libertad parliamentarians to support executive initiatives on neoliberal economic reform—a policy that Fujimori had, of course, campaigned against (see Stokes 1999; Kenney 2004). In addition, the discipline of APRA legislators helped Fujimori pass some legislation, as long as the quid pro quo of Alan García's parliamentary immunity was still on the table. C-90 congressman Víctor Paredes, then president of the Chamber of Deputies, claims that he made numerous efforts to coordinate legislative initiatives with members of other parties and movements. However, aside from the continued congressional delegation of decree authority to the executive, Fujimori frowned upon this sort of resourcefulness on the part of his legislators (Paredes interview 1999). This was, perhaps, with good reason, in light of serious doubts about C-90 legislators' lawmaking skills and governance capabilities. Fujimori instead ruled by decree, cutting himself loose from his own ad hoc electoral movement, as outlined in chapter 4.

After the *autogolpe*, pro-Fujimori parliamentary groups were more of an extension of the executive branch than a party per se. Seats held by traditional parties were fewer than they had been in decades. Many opposition legislators found themselves working within an opportunity structure in which forwarding their own careers was not enhanced by maintaining party unity. These opposition legislators increasingly hailed from electoral movements too (e.g., UPP), and acted principally as individuals. As Congressman Henry Pease told me, "once ideological parties disappeared, [there] was absolute personalism" (Pease García interview 1999). In an environment of weak parties and movements, and access to unconstitutional techniques for wielding power, President Fujimori was able to exercise a great deal of control and discipline over his legislators. By contrast, the losing executive candidates who had formed movements specifically to launch their candidacies were unable or unmotivated to control legislators elected under their label.

Analysis of roll-call votes for the final fifteen months of the 1995–2000 period confirms the qualitative assessment of party unity presented here. Carey (2003b) finds that C-90/NM was the most cohesive parliamentary group, followed by APRA, FIM, and UPP, depending on the measure used. The remnants of the traditional left-wing and right-wing parties, scattered and regrouped into heterogeneous caucuses, trailed behind. However, these parliamentary groups were already reconstituted by party switching and defections by this stage of the Fujimori period. One of the reasons that UPP looks disciplined in 1999 is that all of the less-committed members had already left the caucus by then, some of them joining up with Fujimori—even though opposing Fujimori was the UPP's main platform in 1995. As I demonstrate below, party switching had grave consequences for the quality of representation.

What is more, party unity scores beg the question of what (or whom) the parliamentary groups were unified behind. Comparative studies of Latin American legislators using data from the Parliamentary Elites in Latin America (PELA) surveys indicate that, in the mid-1990s, Peru's politicians were moderately cohesive in their views and there were few major policy issues per se on which these groups differed (Hawkins and Morgenstern 2000). The most salient political cleavage in the 1990s was pro- versus anti-Fujimori (Levitsky and Cameron 2003), with very different views about democratic procedure. PELA data from 1995 suggest that what most sharply divided C-90/NM from other groups was the absence of career politicians in its ranks (see Levitt 1998).

In part, this was an effect of the majority's blurring of distinctions between the movement's legislative cohesion and the legislators' personal loyalty to Fujimori. As C-90/NM congressman Jorge Trelles affirmed, there was no functional difference between the government and the party: "There is never a meeting of 'The Party' as such. It's Fujimori with the cabinet, Fujimori with his congresspersons, Fujimori with a small group of advisers" (interview 1999).

This is what was most damaging for representation: the C-90/NM electoral movement was not built around ideas or programs but on personalistic rule. Congressman Ricardo Marcenaro Frers (interview 1999) shared with me his blunt appraisal of the functional role of a C-90/NM legislator: "Whom do I represent? I don't have the faintest idea. . . . I am charged with working for and supporting the work of Alberto Fujimori. That has been my task." Yet by the 1995–2000 period the opposition, too, was mainly comprised of parliamentary groups catapulted into politics by electoral movements lacking any organization outside of Congress itself. Then-congresswoman Beatriz Merino Lucero (interview 1998) noted that, in the absence of party organizations that exist outside the legislature, most legislators opposed to the Fujimori government had neither the incentive nor the capacity to do their jobs as representatives. This led to a certain malaise and drop in professionalism among opposition parliamentarians. Attendance in sessions of Congress and, to a lesser extent, in commissions, dropped precipitously in the late 1990s (*Caretas,* May 6 and June 3, 1999). By 1999, opposition groups did not even bother to field a slate of candidates for the Mesa Directiva. Congresswoman María Ofelia Cerro Moral revealed that, soon after she was elected, the pro-Fujimori caucus tried to lure her away with travel benefits and other perks. When that failed, "They switched to the other game, to start to look to see what they can find out about you. And when they didn't find something to entrap me with, they began to make my political life impossible. Nothing I ever proposed was accepted or moved forward, no matter what, so that one would feel frustrated and give up trying" (interview 1999).

The remnants of traditional political party caucuses were themselves in turmoil. APRA—always noted for its party discipline in Congress—was divided over issues of internal reform and the role of ex-president García, as well as the signing of the Peru-Ecuador peace treaty. At one point in early 1999, all but two of the seven remaining APRA legislators had been suspended by party leaders.

The core of AP combined with CODE and several independents to reach the minimum of six legislators required for a parliamentary group, and the PPC likewise combined forces with Renovación. The Democracy in Action group brought together the two IU congressmen with left-leaning legislators from Obras, FNTC, and UPP. The UPP itself, reduced by numerous incidents of party switching (see below), retained its status as a *grupo parlamentario,* but legislators did little to coordinate votes. Two different parliamentary groups simply called themselves "independent." One incorporated former members of FIM, UPP, and APRA and by 1999 became a proto-legislative group for Alberto Andrade's Somos Perú. The other joined together the remnants of FIM (which fell below the six-member threshold in 1998) and legislators who were elected under the Obras, AP, and UPP labels, and even two C-90/NM members. At least three of the ten congressmen who alighted in this latter "independent" group were actually serving—in their votes and press statements—as a pro-Fujimori fifth column.

Indeed, party switching began to accelerate in the 1995–2000 period. The sixty-seven seats that C-90/NM did win reasonably fairly in 1995 gave Fujimori a comfortable simple majority in the Congress, but it did not ensure a two-thirds majority for parliamentary procedures such as blocking the interpellation of government ministers, even with the support of small "loyal opposition" groups. Defections to C-90/NM began almost immediately after the 1995 elections. Over the course of the 1995–2000 period, thirty legislators—fully one-quarter of the Congress—changed their de facto political affiliation. Of these, six were explicit defections to the government bench. Another four became nominally independent but actively participated in supporting the government and were rewarded with committee presidencies and other perks; several even ran alongside C-90/NM legislators in the Peru 2000 alliance in the following general elections. A number of other *tránsfugas* (defectors) were more guarded in their support for Fujimori but could be counted on to vote with the government at crucial moments.

The Mesa Directiva, dominated by Fujimori supporters, controlled access to resources for legislators and used the most basic infrastructure of the legislative branch—staff, space, benefits—as a carrot-and-stick inducement for discipline among its own legislators and acquiescence among the minority opposition (Carey 2003; *El Comercio,* Sept. 26, 1999). It also made it doubly damaging to small opposition groups when one or more of their legislators would defect to the government bench: loss of organizational resources in addition to losing a voice (however little consideration opposition groups were given) in the governing bodies of the legislature if the size of the parliamentary group fell below six members.[36] This hobbling of opposition groups in Congress made representation a strictly majoritarian affair and contributed to the political neutralization of Peru's legislature.

In Fujimori's Peru, party unity (among his own legislators) and disunity (in the opposition) was also pursued using more nefarious tactics. From the *vladivideos* we now know that organizational perks to loyal members of Congress were complemented, when necessary, with outright bribes. And the means of inducing party switching grew less subtle at the end of the Fujimori era. After the controversial 2000 elections—in which Fujimori did not win even a simple legislative majority, despite conditions that favored the incumbent and handicapped the opposition—the tide of *tránsfugas* was even larger and swifter. Having won fifty-two of a hundred twenty seats in tainted elections, the president and his intelligence adviser began to openly shop around for legislators. These politicians were offered cash payments, real estate, and/or the favorable resolution of judicial proceedings in exchange for switching, openly or tacitly, to the pro-Fujimori bench (McMillan and Zoido 2004). Within weeks of the April 2000 congressional elections, between twelve and seventeen legislators were successfully wooed in this manner before the legislature was even called into session. A comfortable legislative majority had been purchased, with the Peruvian public paying the bill—and paying the price of a further decline in representation.

Of course, there was another way of replacing an inconvenient legislature with a more pliable one, and the self-coup was a tactic that some Fujimori supporters said they were disposed to repeat. In the months leading up to both the 1995 and the 2000 elections, prominent *fujimorista* congresswoman Martha Chávez ominously warned the Peruvian public that another *autogolpe* might follow the elections if President Fujimori were to win without a legislative majority. In 1994, during a televised interview she spoke about the possibility of shutting down the legislature: "I would not rule it out, if there were that [type of] opposition, and neither would I rule out that the Peruvian people, as in 1992, would side with the president and against those politicians who do not understand" (*Caretas,* Nov. 3, 1994). Thinly veiled threats to close Congress were again uttered by Chávez prior to the 2000 elections (*La República,* Aug. 2, 1999). Choosing representatives was apparently all well and good, as long as the "right" ones were chosen.

After Fujimori left office, the potential for meaningful partisan representation in Congress improved markedly. Some of this potential went unrealized, as party unity remained elusive for electoral movements, but the rebirth of one traditional party, APRA, boded particularly well for partisan representation

As Carey's (2003b) analysis demonstrates, once the *vladivideos* were released, party unity plummeted among Fujimori's Peru 2000 legislators, while opposition groups grew more cohesive than ever. But after Fujimori and Montesinos exited the stage and the transition government was completing its work, anti-Fujimori groups reversed some of these gains in party unity, as legislators eyed their chances at reelection (and winning preferential votes).

Surveys indicate that members of the 2001 class of *congresistas* was somewhat more apt (54 percent) than the 1995 class (44 percent) to strongly value party organizations as essential to democracy. Legislators were also much more likely to see their own party as something that existed outside of electoral periods (77 percent, compared to 47 percent in 1995). However, they were only slightly more likely (20 percent, versus 18 percent in 1995) to agree that legislators who vote against their party's positions should be expelled from the group and no more likely (7 percent in both samples) to agree that party leaders should have more power over individual legislators (Universidad de Salamanca n.d.) And as the 2001–2006 period progressed, whatever spirit of interparty and intraparty unity that had emerged during the transition continued to dissipate.

I have suggested here and in earlier chapters that neither the Perú Posible bloc in Congress nor its partners in the FIM were highly disciplined. In the first year of the 2001–2006 period, unity was high in PP and even within the less-organized FIM. But as scandal after scandal broke and President Toledo grew unpopular, this cohesiveness disappeared (Alvarado Dodero interview 2007; Sánchez Pinedo interview 2007). PP attempted to coordinate its legislative votes by majority decision within the caucus. However, even when internal discipline "succeeded," dissident caucus members would vote with PP and then criticize that same vote in the press. As the term wore on, PP's disciplined voting faded, and its self-inflicted wounds grew more severe (Taco Llave interview 2007; Tanaka interview 2005). PP was routinely portrayed in the press as unruly and even cannibalistic.

Opposition groups were not immune to these same problems of unity and discipline. As noted above and in earlier chapters, UN split on some of the most crucial issues of the period (e.g., removing Toledo), and UPP ceased functioning as a caucus almost immediately. Some groups had a core cluster of legislators who *did* behave in a cohesive, disciplined manner; in the case of UN, that core centered on a revitalized traditional political party, the PPC. But outside of this core, parliamentary caucuses were in chaos (Taylor 2007). And over time, only the core remained.

As endemic as party switching was in the late 1990s and in 2000, it grew even worse in 2001–2006. More than a quarter of all members of Congress changed their affiliation over the course of five years. But unlike the Fujimori era (when opposition legislators were bought off and brought into the majority), in this period the hemorrhaging was inflicted on the governing groups, PP and FIM, as well as on the opposition UN. The PP caucus shrank from a high of forty-eight down to thirty-two members; FIM fell from eleven to six; UN dropped from seventeen to eleven. This made cobbling together a coalition to pass legislation difficult and unpredictable.

Most *tránsfugas* left electoral movements or coalitions to join even more ad hoc alliances of "independents" and deserters from other groups, just to be part of a parliamentary caucus with at least six members. One such group (GPDI) was comprised of former PP and FIM members; another (SAUDI) lumped together Somos Perú, AP, UPP, and various independents; yet another (Perú Ahora) was made up entirely of PP dissidents (Taylor 2007). In May 2005 Congress actually debated changing the rules to deter *tránsfugas* more effectively and stabilize parliamentary caucuses. Under the proposed law, legislators who left the groups with which they were elected would simply lose their seats. While the bill was approved by the standing Constitution Committee and even put on the legislative agenda, it never came up for debate. Motions to consider the bill were, unsurprisingly, blocked by the votes of legislators who were themselves *tránsfugas* (*La República,* June 15, 2006; Tanaka interview 2005).

Of all of the parties and movements worth mentioning, only APRA began and ended the 2001–2006 period with the same number of legislators. What is more, the discipline and cohesion that characterized the party's parliamentary caucuses in the 1980s had returned. The twenty-eight-member *bancada aprista* had the best staffers, the most sophisticated policy analysis, and, by the end of Toledo's presidency, the only dependable bloc of votes in Congress (Tanaka interview 2005; Zumaeta Flores interview 2007). Most of all, it had the largest group of politicians who could reasonably expect to stay together whether they won or lost any given parliamentary vote or even a general election. Aside from the still tiny PPC, APRA was the only real party in the party system, but its revival significantly improved the performance of the legislature.

To sum up, much of the potential for partisan representation in the Toledo era went unrealized. PP—a personalistic vehicle to begin with—was too fragmented for legislators to promote any particular platform, or even consistently follow caucus leadership. As one analyst put it, they were "riven with petty jealousies . . . [and] prioritised the pursuit of personal vendettas over group discipline" (Taylor 2007, 13). Party switching, both the reality of it and the constant threat of losing individual legislators, further eroded the coherence of most *bancadas* and made legislative coalition building difficult. The shadow of the future was very short, and consequently cooperation within and across groups was problematic. Outside of APRA and perhaps the PPC, party labels meant little. Party-based representation was one of the more disappointing aspects of Peru's democratic revival in 2001–2006.

Nevertheless, the regeneration of APRA did offer hope for more coherent programmatic, partisan representation. And the presence of this organized party in the opposition bloc mitigated against Toledo exercising the sort of executive-centric power that Fujimori, another electoral movement leader, was able to do with such devastating consequences for political pluralism, the quality of representation, and democracy itself.

Conclusions

Though the constitutional and legal architecture for Peru's legislature changed only modestly from the late 1970s to 2006, there were nonetheless important shifts in power between that branch and the executive. The legislature had greater institutional capacity during the 1985–1990 period than in the decade that followed. Notwithstanding the received wisdom about President García's first term, he and his ministers had a more horizontal relationship with their own majority legislators (because an autonomous APRA party organization existed) and could sometimes be held to account by the opposition minority as well (because of constitutional norms and the presence of organized parties, especially on the left).

The rise of the executive and the decline of the legislature began in 1990, even though 1990–1992 was a period without a legislative majority for the executive. The decline was accelerated by the *autogolpe* and the attendant demonization of political parties and institutions, which resonated strongly with a public fatigued by political and economic crises. Weak constitutional norms decayed the governance structures of the legislature, reduced the role of the opposition in Congress, and enabled Fujimori to manufacture legislative majorities. Weak party organizations reduced opposition legislators' ability, and pro-government legislators' incentive, to autonomously analyze legislation and serve as a counterweight to the executive branch in general and to the president in particular. Thus, neither *fujimorista* nor opposition legislators would or could strike a more balanced legislative-executive relationship from 1993 to 2000.

Comparing the 1985–1990 period with the 1993–2000 era shows us that a disciplined parliamentary majority is, in itself, neither a sign of institutional strength nor a harbinger of institutional weakness. An APRA legislative majority in 1985–1990 may have had to contend with a president whose penchant for unilateral decision making occasionally infuriated them, but they nonetheless played a prominent role in crafting and passing legislation. The C-90/NM majority after 1992 was, by contrast, more of a rubber stamp. And that group's party unity, and the very composition of the legislature itself, were shaped by a deep-rooted corruption that belied the institutional façade of Peruvian politics in the 1990s.

In the measures that tell us about the power of the legislature as an institution—its capacity to make laws, hold government accountable, and represent citizens—we see, overall, a precipitous decline in the 1990s. Peru's parliament was transformed from a locus of lawmaking and genuine political debate to an echo chamber, a *caja de resonancia*. Although, during the 1980s, the legislature was weaker than the executive, it served as a site of meaningful political decision making. After 1992, the C-90/NM majority tried to wall off the effective discussion of legislation, shielding politics from the public eye and blocking the input of opposition legislators. The internal governing bodies of the legislature were dominated by the majority in ways that they were not in the 1980s, and some (e.g., standing committees) were frequently left out of the lawmaking loop entirely. Accountability mechanisms and *control político* waned. Representation of constituents and of party-based interests in the legislature became highly problematic. This new hyper-presidentialism created a relationship of "informal hierarchy," as Moreno, Crisp, and Shugart (2003) phrase it, between the legislature and the executive—a relationship that bodes poorly for the quality of democracy.

After Fujimori and Montesinos fled the country, after an interim government, after new elections in 2001, what changes did we observe in the institutional strength of the legislature? The new legislature was only modestly better at performing its representative functions, although these were difficult to measure. But it was markedly more adept at lawmaking than its predecessors in the 1990s, as its capacity to formulate and analyze legislation was enhanced. And it was infinitely more engaged with holding the executive and his ministers accountable, sometimes to the detriment of political stability and governability. The reasons for this dramatic, if uneven, (re)development of institutional autonomy and capacity in the 2001–2006 legislature mirror the reasons for their earlier decline in the late 1980s and early 1990s: Peru's political class again adhered to the rules of the game, and organized parties, especially APRA (this time in the opposition), made a partial comeback.

Over the course of two decades of institutional politics in Peru, a pattern clearly emerges. Weak political parties and weak elite constitutional norms strengthened presidents and weakened legislatures. Stronger political parties and stronger elite constitutional norms weakened presidents and strengthened legislatures.

These two causal variables are not, of course, wholly deterministic, alone or in tandem. As I have explained here, for example, President Toledo led a personalized electoral movement but could not transform it into the sort of armored vehicle that Fujimori did, in part because some organized political parties reemerged on the opposition benches of Congress and in part because of the more rule-abiding behavior expected and practiced by politicians, including Toledo himself. Looking at other countries in the region, as I do in the next chapter, we will see that several experienced changes in one or both of the "electoral movement" and "constitutional norms" variables without a concomitant change in executive strength vis-à-vis Congress. My point is not that these factors always and exclusively shape presidential power but rather that, on balance, they do.

Statistical models for testing propositions about causal relationships like these are likewise probabilistic, not deterministic. In the next chapter I use regression-style analysis to assess whether the same causal processes that I observed in Peru can be identified elsewhere in Latin America; whether, on the whole, they add up to a more generalized (and generalizable) story; and how such explanations fare compared to institutionalist theories more focused on the details of the formal rules of the game.

6

Institutionalism and Presidential Power
in Latin America

What explains the variations in, and fluctuations of, presidential power in Latin American countries? And how should we study formal organizations and institutions in settings that might be characterized as informally or weakly institutionalized? The preceding chapters' investigation of politics in Peru highlighted both the strengths and the limitations of focusing our attention on the formal rules of the game in the context of a "new" democracy. In this chapter, I test the insights gleaned from that extended case study in a more broadly comparative, cross-national analysis.

Most political scientists agree that formal rules and institutions do matter for political outcomes. However, vast theoretical and empirical lacunae surround the question of precisely *how* formal rules and institutions matter, and whether they matter in distinct ways across different social and political environments (Nohlen 2003; 2006).

In the case of Peru, we saw that the erosion of constitutionalism and the rule of law among politicians had had, by the early 1990s, a pernicious effect on the ability of the legislature to check and balance the power of the executive. After the fall of President Fujimori in 2000, as constitutional norms regained saliency among political elites, Congress regained much of its relevance as a site of lawmaking, representation, and political oversight. Though the key constitutional provisions on legislative-executive relations changed only modestly during the entire 1985–2006 period, actual presidential power fluctuated dramatically. I have argued in this book that constitutionality in general—rather than the specific details of constitutional arrangements—is what limits and curtails the strength of the executive.

While we may have guessed that, on balance, more binding constitutional norms would constrain the executive branch, the politics of Peru also suggested another, more counterintuitive, causal relationship: between party organizational forms and the power of executive office holders. On the face of it, we might assume that a strong, well-institutionalized party organization is a valuable asset to a national political leader, granting that individual access to material resources, human capital, a programmatic brand, and other assets. Yet over the past two decades, across Latin America we have witnessed the resilience, even the resurgence, of a different type of president: the "independent" who, once elected by voters, answers to no organized political group, not even his nominal copartisans. Some of these personalistic electoral vehicles indeed seem to weaken, or add little to, the power of the executives who once created them out of whole cloth (as with Toledo's Perú Posible, which faced better-organized political parties on the opposition benches of the legislature and stronger constitutional norms among political elites). More surprising, though, is that the backing of a fluid, ad hoc party organization—what I have called an electoral movement, as opposed to a political party—*can* be a source of presidential strength, not weakness (as with the various incarnations of Fujimori's groups).

During the twenty-one-year period from 1985 to 2006, the main contours of constitutions and electoral laws—the formal rules of the game that shape presidential strength and legislative-executive relations—remained relatively stable in Peru. Notwithstanding a new constitution in 1993 and the changes it made to the size and shape of Congress, most of the basic institutional features of the legislative-executive relationship did not vary. But the actual power of the executive fluctuated dramatically. Weak constitutional norms and weakly institutionalized political parties contributed to an immense strengthening of presidential power. Then, (much) stronger constitutionalism and (modestly) stronger parties made the executive weaker.

Is this true in Latin America more broadly? And just how well do formal institutional rules predict actual executive power across the region and over time?

Theory and Hypotheses: What Institutionalism Can (and Cannot) Tell Us about Politics in Latin America

As outlined in chapter 2, scholarship on institutions in Latin America has tended to group key variables on legislative-executive relations into two clusters (Mainwaring and Shugart 1997; Carey and Shugart 1998; Shugart 1998).[1] One of these clusters is comprised of the constitutional provisions detailing the lawmaking powers of Congress and the president. These provisions include the rules for vetoes and veto overrides; the authority of the executive to issue decrees with the force of law; and the exclusive right of one branch or another to introduce certain types of legislation, commonly vis-à-vis fiscal matters such as budgets and taxation. Hence the proposition:

> Institutionalist H1: *The more lawmaking power the constitution gives to presidents, the stronger the president will be.*

The second cluster of institutional variables is the electoral rules governing the president's leverage over her legislative copartisans: incentives and disincentives for party unity and discipline as shaped by ballot structures and vote tallying methods. Carey and Shugart (1995) and, later, Wallack, Gaviria, Panizza, and Stein (2003) and Johnson and Wallack (2006) pointed to how legislative candidates get on the ballot, whether voters vote for an individual or a party, and whether vote tallies are pooled across candidates and lists. Combinations of these systemic traits provide incentives for legislative candidates to campaign as loyal partisans or, instead, cultivate a more individualistic voting record and a more personalistic public image. While the interests of executives do not always coincide with those of other party leaders, party unity and discipline make possible a particular form of institutional power for presidents. Thus we might test:

> Institutionalist H2: *The more control over legislators and legislative candidates that electoral rules give to party leaders, the stronger the president will be.*

But these partisan balloting systems are only tools for exerting leverage over legislators; it is of course necessary to also know whether the president's party controls a majority of seats in the legislature. Taken together, the structure of electoral rules and the pattern of electoral outcomes is what Mainwaring and Shugart (1997) refer to as "partisan powers."

A legislative majority can permit presidents to pass their policy goals into law; facilitate the approval of presidential appointees such as judges, ambassadors, or bureaucrats; and perhaps protect against investigations, censures, or impeachments, to name just a few of the benefits. And even if a president falls short of achieving a legislative majority, her leverage in Congress may still vary depending on the size of her caucus and its position vis-à-vis other caucuses on major policy issues (Jones 1995a; Negretto 2006). We might thus expect:

> Institutionalist H3a: *Presidential strength will be greater when the executive's party has a legislative majority than when it does not. In minority situations, presidents will be stronger if her party controls the median legislator than if it does not, and will be weakest if she controls neither the median nor the veto legislator.*

A related issue in institutionalist scholarship is the timing of electoral cycles. The coattails effect of a single-round plurality election for president held concurrently with legislative elections is thought to significantly boost the likelihood of executives' parties garnering a legislative majority. (On Latin America, see Mainwaring and Shugart 1997; see also, inter alia, Cox 1997; Samuels 2002a; Shugart 1995.) Thus:

> Institutionalist H3b: *Presidential strength will be greater in systems with concurrent elections for president and Congress than in other electoral systems.*

Recall that lawmaking and partisan powers tend to be inversely correlated in any given system, so that one set of presidential powers offsets the other (Mainwaring and Shugart 1997). This is purposeful and reflects the process by which formal rules were initially designed and the strategic considerations of the "framers," the individuals and groups that had control over institutional design (Shugart 1998).

But although lawmaking powers, partisan prerogatives, and legislative majorities have a central place in the scholarly literature—including this book—these are not the only institutional factors thought to have an impact on executive power. For example, scholars have also tackled the question of whether, ceteris paribus, pure presidentialism affords an elected executive greater power than he would have under institutional arrangements in which legislatures have some say over the formation and/or survival of cabinets and cabinet members (Duverger 1980; Sartori 1997; Pasquino 1997).[2] Many Latin American systems are indeed fully presidential: the president's cabinet is not subject to a confidence vote by the legislature, nor can ministers be removed by the assembly. However, there are also some weak variations on "president-parliamentarism" (Shugart and Carey 1992) found in the region. In several, a popularly elected president appoints and dismisses cabinet ministers, but ministers can also be censured and/or dismissed by the legislature. These systems further differ among themselves in terms of the strength of, or limitations on, the assembly's censure and dismissal powers. Hence:

Institutionalist H4: *Presidential strength will be greatest in pure presidential systems and will diminish as the powers wielded by the legislature over the cabinet increase.*

Finally, some scholars have focused on the impact of the number of legislative chambers on political outcomes: that is, on bicameral versus unicameral systems (Lijphart 1999; Tsebelis 2002; Tsebelis and Money 1997). Since bicameralism increases the number of veto points in political decision making, it may (ceteris paribus) weaken or limit the power of the executive—particularly where the executive is most often the originator of important legislation, as in Latin America.[3] To find out, we can test:

Institutionalist H5: *Presidential strength will be greater in unicameral systems than in bicameral systems.*

This list of hypotheses is not exhaustive, but it is indicative of the range of theoretical tools that institutionalist scholarship frequently uses to look at presidential power. These propositions have provided us with a great deal of analytical leverage in studying the politics of the "older" democracies and are surely worth exploring in the context of Latin America. Nevertheless, their application to cases in which politics are more informal, less institutionalized, and less stable may be problematic. I demonstrated in previous chapters that politicians' constitutional adherence and the organizational forms of their political parties had an impact on presidential power in Peru. Modeling these two variables rather than assuming their values might serve as a valuable addendum to the institutionalist approach.

This "reality check" begins with two insights, one seemingly obvious, the other counterintuitive. First, a constitution only works to constrain the behavior of elite political actors if those actors obey it. Thus, the details of the rules may matter less than overall norms and expectations about rule-abiding behavior in general. Second, the relationship between electoral laws and the executive's partisan powers over the legislature may change dramatically if parties are largely personalistic.

Pointing out that there is a gap between de jure constitutions and electoral laws and de facto politics on the ground in Latin America is a shopworn argument. As chapter 2 indicated, what made the "new institutionalism" so new for the study of Latin America was that previous generations of scholars—trained in eras of much less widespread formal democracy—felt that they had little reason to take formal institutions seriously or ascribe to them much causal power of their own.[4] The present analysis will allow us to incorporate the important and groundbreaking insights of the institutionalists without discarding earlier scholarship that was skeptical enough of formal institutions to examine them within their broader political contexts—that is, inductively rather than deductively (see Nohlen 2003; 2006). For this reason, as I explained at the end of chapter 2, such an approach could be called "meta-institutionalist."

If there are disparities between constitutionally prescribed rules and actual political practices, as there are in many Latin American countries and other "new democracies," institutional design may not be an accurate representation of the real balance of power between the executive and legislature. O'Donnell (1994a; 1994b; 1999a; 1999b) and others have noted that in some new democracies, elected executive officeholders can wield power relatively free of institutional constraints from within the civilian state apparatus. O'Donnell suggests that weak rule of law, among other factors, makes this possible. The constitutional separation of powers and other institutional features only work to constrain the behavior of elite political actors if "rules are rules"—that is, if the relevant actors more or less follow the precepts of the institutions (or face sanctions if they don't). Thus, the specific details of the rules may matter less than overall norms and expectations about rule-abiding behavior in general.

Where competition over the balance of power between presidents and legislatures can be settled through both constitutional and extra-constitutional means, the result may be that the actor with greater coercive capacity and material resources will be more powerful in practice than on paper. This does not mean that legislatures never prevail over executives in interbranch standoffs. Quite the contrary: as Pérez-Liñán (2007) demonstrates, it is increasingly common in Latin America for an assembly to use impeachment and other techniques to oust a sitting executive in a moment of acute crisis. Nevertheless, on a day-to-day basis, weak rule of law may be more advantageous to the executive than to the legislature—as it was in Peru. Thus:

Meta-Institutional H1: *Presidential strength will be greater when the rule of law is weak than when it is strong.*

In similar fashion, though some institutionalist scholars have thoughtfully engaged with the question of personalism in politics (e.g., Carey and Shugart 1995; Coppedge 1997; Mainwaring and Scully 1995), other scholarship still presumes that politicians competing for national office are organized into political parties or something like them. But many groups competing in Latin America—including some very successful ones—are just loosely affiliated ad hoc movements operated by and for a personalistic leader (Perelli, Picado, and Zovatto 1995). Such "electoral movements" can be distinguished from political parties by the different incentive structures and time horizons they present to politicians. As noted in chapter 2, political parties are organized groups of office-seeking politicians who *stay together even after they lose an election* (Navia 2003). Electoral movements are not organized this way—and what is more, these groups are underinstitutionalized by design.[5] If they lose an election they tend to disperse, perhaps to be reincarnated for the next election, perhaps not. Yet even if they win, they tend to maintain low levels of organizational autonomy and capacity.

When legislators' political affiliation is tied to a particular presidential campaign vehicle rather than to an idea or group that might outlast a given presidency, these legislators may be undisciplined or, alternately, utterly subservient to the executive. But in neither case do they seem likely to make the legislature into an effective arena for autonomous political decision making.[6] Party politicians, by contrast, are more apt to have career aspirations beyond supporting one particular leader. This ambition, and the longer time horizons it fosters, might facilitate bargaining and cooperation with other caucuses and, more importantly, create incentives to build or preserve a legislature with real political clout. As we saw in Peru, organized parties can make a difference both in government and in opposition. For comparative purposes, we will at minimum need to see whether electoral movement leaders who do win executive office have relations with legislatures that differ from those of presidents backed by organized parties. Hence:

Meta-Institutional H2: *Presidential strength will be greater when the president leads an electoral movement rather than an organized political party.*

Assessing institutionalist theory in this way—testing how well institutional versus noninstitutional or extra-institutional factors predict actual presidential strength—represents two major steps forward in our understanding of Latin American politics. First, it tests whether and how well the institutionalist understanding of the legislative-executive relationship correlates with some other existing measurement of this relationship. In other words, do institutionalist measures of executive strength help predict real presidential power—even in settings different from the advanced industrialized democracies from which the approach was derived? How "externally valid" is the institutionalist approach?[7] Second, a meta-institutionalist approach—turning key assumptions about rules and actors into research questions—can broaden the domain of institutionalist theory and help us better understand precisely those political systems where democratic, representative institutions are most fragile.

Data

The data analyzed here cover eighteen Latin American countries from 1985 to 2002 (and up to 2004 in the single-country graphics of the dependent variable).[8] Some country series begin after 1985, since I omit observations that do not have a functioning constitution and at least nominally democratic institutions.[9] While some systems that were democratic in 1985 later veered toward autocracy, even the least democratic systems I include in my analysis could not be considered fully authoritarian. Rather, they are *competitive* authoritarian systems, in which some rules matter while others are routinely violated (see Levitsky and Way 2002). I include such systems precisely in order to assess *which* rules matter and, more broadly, the extent to which constitutionalism—political elites' following the rules—affects the distribution of power. The low democratic quality of these systems is captured in the variables themselves. (No wholly authoritarian country-years are included in the analysis.[10] What is more, my findings are not substantially altered by dropping even debatable or borderline country-years.[11])

Most of the variables described below were drawn or adapted from larger cross-national datasets, though a few are the original work of the author. Readers interested in the details of how variables were operationalized should consult the Data Appendix for a more in-depth overview of sources and coding procedures.

Dependent Variables

The existing literature provides us with several metrics for operationalizing the strength of the president versus the legislature: the bureaucratic capacity of the executive branch relative to the autonomy and capacity of legislatures (Carey, Formanek, and Karpowicz 2002); the number of bills introduced by each, or the rate at which proposals from each branch are codified into law (Bollen 1980; Arat 1991; Beck et al 2001); or evidence of interbranch bargaining (as Cox and Morgenstern 2001 suggest). While each of these approaches has merit, each is also incomplete or problematic.[12]

To enhance reliability, I model two different ways of operationalizing the overall balance of legislative-executive power relations, the dependent variable. Each is based on a different holistic, systematic annual expert assessment of the strength of presidents vis-à-vis assemblies.

One, *Executive Power,* indicates the extent to which presidential power is constrained or unconstrained by other state entities, particularly legislatures. It is derived from the "Executive Constraints" indicator from the *Polity IV* dataset (Marshall and Jaggers 2006). For some models and graphics I present this as ordinal data; the methodological limitations of other (time-series cross-sectional) models required that I transform it into a binary variable, representing constrained versus unconstrained executive power.

To guard against findings that were simply artifacts of the dependent variable's operationalization—specifically, relationships between dependent and independent variables that were conceptual rather than causal—I also model a second dependent variable. *Legislative Ineffectiveness,* derived from the "Legislative Effectiveness" (LEGEFF) variable in Banks's Cross-National Time Series Data (Banks 2007), is an ordinal variable indicating whether or not an effective legislature exists and how much governing autonomy it has.

What does executive power look like across the region, and how has it changed over time? Consider the binary variable described above: distinguishing between times and places in Latin America where executives and legislatures checked and balanced one another as equal or nearly equal branches, versus contexts in which the executive clearly dominated.

Table 6.1 illustrates cross-national variation in the aggregate experience of presidential power over two decades. At one extreme lie Bolivia, Chile, Colombia, Costa Rica, Ecuador, Panama, and Uruguay—all of which had "Executive Constraint" scores indicating parity or near parity between the legislative and executive branches during the entire 1985–2004 period. At the other extreme lie Honduras and El Salvador, which were executive-dominant during the entire period.[13] And in between are countries that shifted on one or more occasion from parity to executive dominance or vice versa.

Figures 6.1–6.4 illustrate some of the more dynamic cases, now using an ordinal version of *Executive Power* covering the years 1985–2004. Mexico experienced a gradual diminishing of its historically high levels of presidential power, culminating in near parity in 1999 (and the hegemonic Partido Revolucionario Institucional losing the presidency in 2000). Guatemala had a sharper decline in the mid-1990s, in the wake of a failed presidential power grab in 1994. Paraguay entered a rocky democratic period in 1989 but kept many executive-dominant features from its authoritarian past for the first several years.

The case study on which this book centers turned out to be the most dynamic of all. In Peru, presidential power fell from near parity in

Table 6.1. Interbranch Parity versus Executive Domination in Latin America, 1985–2004

Country	Years of Interbranch Parity	Years of Dominant Executive	Total # of Years
Argentina (ARG)	11	9	20
Bolivia (BOL)	20	0	20
Brazil (BRA)	18	1	19
Chile (CHL)	15	0	15
Colombia (COL)	20	0	20
Costa Rica (COS)	20	0	20
Dominican Republic (DOM)	9	11	20
Ecuador (ECU)	20	0	20
Guatemala (GUA)	9	11	20
Honduras (HON)	0	19	19
Mexico (MEX)	6	14	20
Nicaragua (NIC)	10	8	18
Panama (PAN)	15	0	15
Paraguay (PAR)	12	4	16
Peru (PER)	10	10	20
El Salvador (SAL)	0	20	20
Uruguay (URU)	20	0	20
Venezuela (VEN)	15	5	20

Adapted from Polity IV data, Marshall and Jaggers 2006.

1985–1988 to parity in 1989–1990, then rose to extreme executive domination through the 1990s, and dropped back down to parity again in 2001. As we can see, this time-series data on Peru corroborates the analyses and the overall narrative of the changing role of the president offered in the preceding chapters.

Independent Variables

Among institutionalist independent variables, *Lawmaking Powers* is an index of constitutional provisions regarding the strength of executive decree authority, the executive's ability to veto legislation, and the president's exclusive right to introduce certain legislation. *Partisan Balloting*

Presidential Power, 1985-2004: Mexico

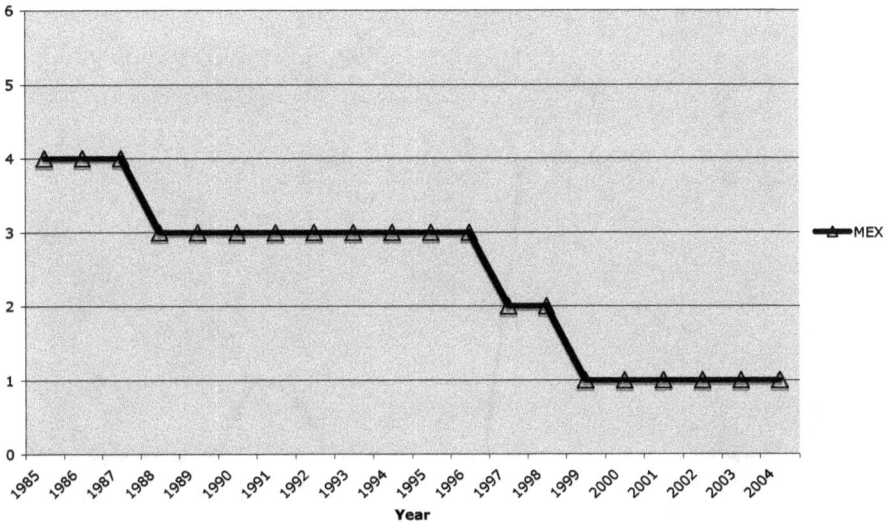

Figure 6.1. Presidential Power in Mexico. Adapted from Polity IV data, Marshall and Jaggers 2006.

Presidential Power, 1985-2004: Guatemala

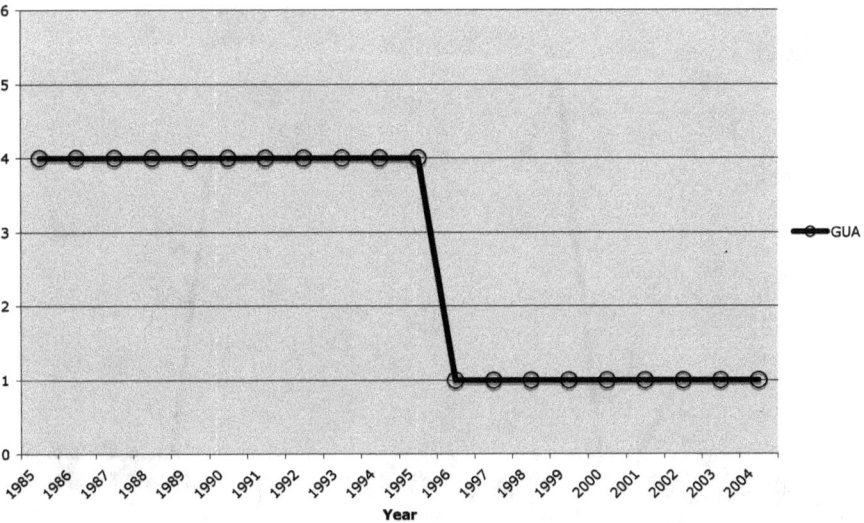

Figure 6.2. Presidential Power in Guatemala. Adapted from Polity IV data, Marshall and Jaggers 2006.

Presidential Power, 1985-2004: Paraguay

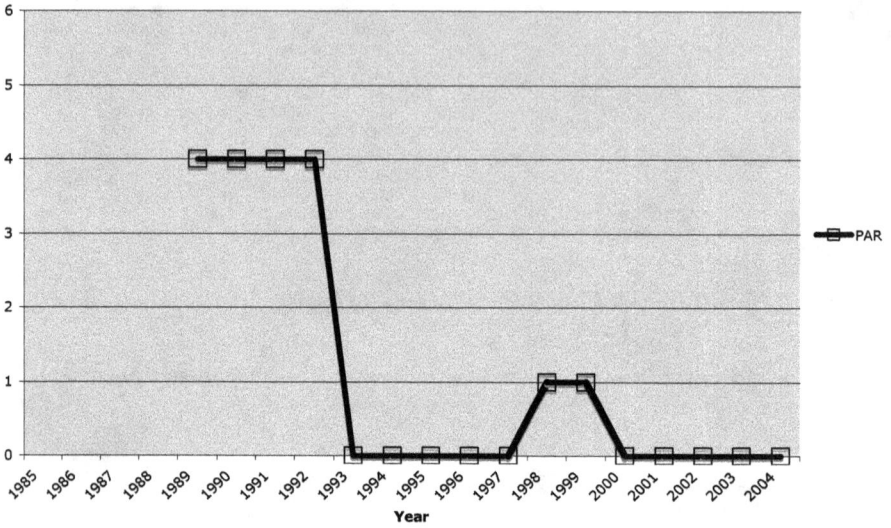

Figure 6.3. Presidential Power in Paraguay. Adapted from Polity IV data, Marshall and Jaggers 2006.

Presidential Power, 1985-2004: Peru

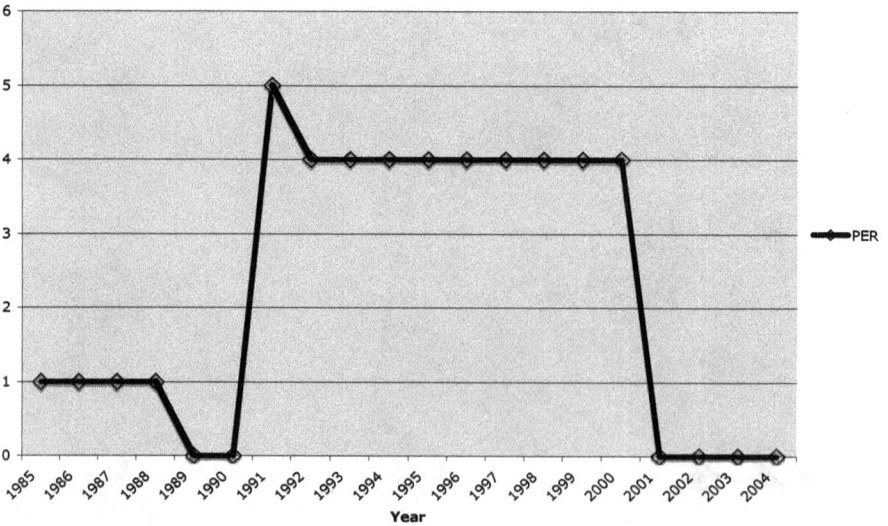

Figure 6.4. Presidential Power in Peru. Adapted from Polity IV data, Marshall and Jaggers 2006.

represents differences in electoral systems: whether voters vote for parties, candidates, or both; whether votes "pool" within party lists; and whether party leaders control ballot access and candidate ordering. *Legislative Majority* indicates whether the president's party commands a legislative majority in the lower (or only) house and, if not, whether it controls the veto legislator and/or the median legislator. *Concurrent Elections* is a dummy variable for systems with legislative elections for the lower house held on the same day as a single-round, first-past-the-post (plurality) vote for the executive. *Cabinet Autonomy* is an index ranging from systems with strong legislative censure power over the cabinet (at the lower end) to pure presidentialism (at the upper end). *Bicameral Legislature* is a dummy variable for systems that feature, by constitutional design, two legislative chambers.

Turning to the meta-institutionalist variables, *Rule of Law* is an index of (a) the strength and impartiality of the legal system and (b) the general level of enforcement of laws. This variable is a reasonable proxy for the more specific concept of elite constitutional adherence, and it correlates fairly solidly (.44, $p < .001$) with another potential proxy variable, one measuring the level of government corruption.[14]

Electoral Movement is a dummy variable indicating that a president's political organization (a) was created for the explicit purpose of launching a particular presidential candidate, (b) is personalistic in its orientation, and (c) has an ad hoc (or nonexistent) organizational structure. This variable includes information about the president's group only, though if party organizational form does make a difference, we should see it there most clearly.

Finally, in order to reduce the threat from the "omitted variable bias," I include two control variables—*National Wealth* and *Economic Growth*—to account for the possibility that leaders of countries that are richer (per capita) or faster-growing are also, ceteris parebus, more powerful executives.

Analysis and Results

I test the hypotheses listed above using data on eighteen Latin American countries over the period 1985–2002. One preliminary question, prior to analysis, is whether the data from these countries can appropriately be pooled into a single equation. Test statistics used to answer this question were cautiously affirmative.[15] A second question might be whether the independent variables—particularly the two meta-institutional variables I propose—are empirically and conceptually distinct enough from the dependent variables they purport to explain. Low bivariate correlation coefficients indicate that they are, though *Rule of Law* and *Legislative Ineffectiveness* were correlated enough to merit caution in interpreting that particular model (Model 5).[16]

Initial tests also indicated both serial correlation[17] and unit-level (i.e., country-level) heteroskedasticity in the data.[18] This is not surprising, as the data is time-series cross-sectional, and institutional variables tend to change especially slowly and infrequently.[19]

There are various ways of addressing these methodological challenges. In Models 1 and 2, I employ a binary dependent variable, and following Beck, Katz, and Tucker (1998) and Beck (2008), I treat this binary time-series cross-sectional (BTSCS) data as grouped duration data. Each observation of the dependent variable is considered part of a "spell" of constrained or unconstrained power, and an additional variable (*Duration*) is used to control for temporal dependence (Tucker 1999). The program also generates natural cubic spline variables—not reported in results—to smooth the hazard rate function and make the time duration variable easier to interpret.

I use a BTSCS logit model to begin my analysis where one would be if one relied on institutionalist theory alone. Model 1 includes only institutional variables and a control for temporal dependence. The first impression here is that some of the factors most commonly cited as shaping executive power—*Lawmaking Powers, Partisan Balloting,* and a *Legislative Majority*—seem not to matter. Institutionalist variables that *are* statistically significant in this model are *Cabinet Autonomy, Concurrent Elections,* and *Bicameral Legislature.*

The meta-institutional and control variables are added in Model 2. In this and all subsequent models, the *Rule of Law* is statistically significant and the organizational form of the president's political group (*Electoral Movement*) is significant in all but Model 5 (where it is nearly so, *p* value = 0.124). As hypothesized in Meta-Institutional H1, weaker rule of law means greater odds of a stronger, less constrained executive. Similarly, there is support for Meta-Institutional H2: having an ad hoc, personalistic electoral movement indeed seems to be a source of strength, not weakness, for the executive. Among institutionalist variables, *Concurrent Elections* drops out of the model, but *Partisan Balloting* becomes significant.

Models 3, 4, and 5 were designed to test the robustness of these results, to see whether they obtain under different model specifications and estimation techniques. The value of *rho* is very small in Model 2, indicating that there would be little difference between a TSCS logit model and an ordinary logit model.[20] This allows me to test Model 3—an ordinary logit model but with cluster-corrected robust standard errors—which confirms that the significance levels of variables in Model 2 were only slightly exaggerated by heteroskedasticity. *Bicameral Legislature* drops out of the model, but all other variables that were significant in Model 2 remain so, at least at the 0.1 level, in Model 3.

With so many slow-changing institutional variables, multicollinearity might also be a concern. However, once the intentionally correlated natural splines (not reported in Table 6.2) and time duration variable are removed from an equation similar to Models 2–3, variance inflation factors (VIFs) indicate no threat from multicollinearity: the highest value is 2.48, and the mean is 1.60.[21]

Model 4 employs an ordinal version of the dependent variable, *Executive Power*, thus recouping the information lost by converting it to binary for use in BTSCS analysis. Here too, the meta-institutional variables (*Rule of Law* and *Electoral Movement*) retain their significance, as does *Cabinet Autonomy*, though *Partisan Balloting* does not.

Based on my case study of Peru, we might also be interested in whether *Rule of Law* and *Electoral Movements* affect executive strength in tandem differently from the way they do independently. So in a model not reported here, I added the interaction term *Rule of Law * Electoral Movement* to Model 4. The interaction term was negative and significant, but the sign and significance of all other variables, including the main effects for those two meta-institutional variables, remained the same. Not surprisingly, the model had collinearity problems; moreover, interpreting interaction effects in an ordered logit model is fraught with complications (Norton, Wang, and Ai 2004; but see Brambor, Clark, and Golder 2006). However, we might guardedly interpret that result to mean that each of the two meta-institutional variables still has a distinct impact (one negative,

Table 6.2. Predicting Presidential Power in Latin America, 1985–2002

	Model 1: BTSCS logit	Model 2: BTSCS logit	Model 3: logit, cluster-robust SE	Model 4: ordered logit, cluster-robust SE	Model 5: ordered logit, cluster-robust SE
	Executive Power (binary)	Executive Power (binary)	Executive Power (binary)	Executive Power (ordinal)	Legislative Ineffectiveness (ordinal)
Lawmaking Powers	−0.309 (0.258)	0.114 (0.252)	0.114 (0.205)	−0.219 (0.238)	0.182 (0.327)
Partisan Balloting	−0.699 (0.444)	1.005*** (0.383)	1.005** (0.428)	0.014 (0.289)	0.377 (0.715)
Legislative Majority	0.369 (0.329)	0.573 (0.380)	0.573 (0.439)	0.446 (0.283)	−0.163 (0.384)
Concurrent Elections	2.102* (1.273)	1.798 (1.185)	1.798 (1.186)	0.478 (0.592)	2.345 (1.580)
Cabinet Autonomy	2.297** (0.956)	1.531*** (0.436)	1.531*** (0.351)	0.501** (0.204)	1.040 (0.635)
Bicameral Legislature	−8.568** (3.679)	−2.130* (1.250)	−2.130 (1.478)	−0.737 (1.005)	−0.715 (1.898)
Rule of Law	—	−1.133*** (0.393)	−1.133* (0.589)	−0.831** (0.376)	−1.3510** (0.630)
Electoral Movement	—	8.905*** (2.942)	8.905** (4.106)	2.838** (1.218)	1.558 (1.012)
National Wealth	—	0.001*** (0.000)	0.001** (0.000)	0.000* (0.000)	−0.001** (0.000)
Economic Growth	—	0.159* (0.085)	0.159* (0.094)	0.032 (0.038)	−0.023 (0.042)
Duration	−3.044*** (0.727)	−3.469*** (0.795)	−3.469*** (0.751)		
Constant	10.838** (4.363)	−3.944 (2.885)	−3.944 (2.641)		
	rho = 0.868	rho = 0.000	pseudo-R^2 = 0.76	pseudo-R^2 = 0.13	pseudo-R^2 = 0.44

*   significant at .1 level
** significant at .05 level
*** significant at .01 level

Table 6.3. Simulated Probabilities of Impact on Executive Power

Independent Variable (IV)	Mean Change in Probability of (Y = 1) Having an "Unconstrained" President, If IV Increases from Minimum to Maximum (with All Other IVs Held to Their Means)
Institutionalist	
Lawmaking Powers	9.3%
Partisan Balloting	*14.1%
Cabinet Autonomy	*20.0%
Legislative Majority	10.3%
Concurrent Elections	12.6%
Bicameral Legislature	−13.7%
Meta-Institutionalist	
Rule of Law	*−25.6%
Electoral Movement	*89.0%

* significant at .1 level or better in Model 3

one positive) on executive strength—even when the value of the other meta-institutional variable is zero—and that the values of one variable intensify the impact of the other.[22]

Finally, Model 5 tests these same hypotheses using a different indicator for the dependent variable: *Legislative Ineffectiveness.* Here, all institutional variables fail significance tests, though *p* values for *Cabinet Autonomy* and *Concurrent Elections* are close to 0.1. By contrast, *Rule of Law* maintains its sign and significance, and, as noted above, *p* values for *Electoral Movement* are also close to 0.1. (However, for reasons I have already indicated, we should interpret Model 5 with caution.)

Even more than the statistical significance of variables, though, we are interested in their explanatory power. How do different variables affect the probability of a given country in a given year having an unconstrained, as opposed to a constrained, chief executive? To assess the relative impact of different institutional traits on presidential power, I used the software program Clarify (Tomz, Wittenberg, and King, 2001) to generate one thousand sets of simulated parameters and run a stochastic simulation of Model 3. I then isolated the impact of specific variables one by one, setting all other parameters to their mean values and determining how the probability of having an unconstrained president changes as any one particular independent variable goes from its minimum to its maximum observed value.

The impact of the institutionalist variables that were statistically significant in Model 3 is appreciable. Thinking about probabilities on a scale from 0 to 100 percent, if a country were to shift from the lowest to the highest observed levels of partisan balloting in the region, then the probability of that country having a powerful, unconstrained president would increase by 14.1 percentage points. Similarly, a shift from minimal to maximal cabinet autonomy would, all else equal, result in a 20-point increase in the probability of having a strong executive.

But the meta-institutional variables have an even greater impact on executive power. Strong rule of law decreases the odds of experiencing an unconstrained presidency by 25.6 percentage points. Even more remarkably, a shift in the organizational form of the executive's group from political party to electoral movement increases the probability of having a powerful, unconstrained executive by 89 percentage points. Thus, electoral movements that propel presidential candidates into office seem to bode particularly poorly for the prospect of effective checks on that executive, while stronger rule of law (and, to an extent, less partisan balloting and weaker presidential cabinet authority) produce a more balanced separation-of-powers system.

To be clear, I do not claim that these meta-institutional variables always and exclusively shape political outcomes this way. There are several examples, in this very dataset, of countries that experienced changes in either the organizational form of the president's party or the strength of constitutional norms (or both) without a concomitant change in executive power—and vice versa. Argentina's executive branch grew more powerful in the 1990s even though President Menem, while something of an "outsider" within the Partido Justicialista, hailed from that well-organized Peronist party, and rule of law, at least according to this data, improved slightly in those years. Ecuador's executive branch remained relatively constrained in the 1990s even though rule of law began to decline and it was led, for a time, by a president backed by a personalistic electoral movement (Sixto Durán and his Unión Republicana, 1992–1996). But my results do strongly suggest that, on balance, constitutionalism and the president's party organization play a crucial role in enhancing or constraining executive power.

Discussion

How well do formal institutions predict actual presidential power in Latin America? The rules of the game for executive-legislative relations, as they are prescribed in laws and constitutions, do indeed have an impact on flesh-and-blood politicians. What is most interesting, however, is which *specific* institutional arrangements "matter."

One of the mainstay hypotheses of institutionalist theory for presidential systems—that the constitutional rules governing executive law-making authority make presidents weak or strong—remarkably found no support at all. The impact of partisan balloting, the electoral rules that affect party leaders' leverage over legislators, was stronger and more reliable. Though party leaders other than the president would, of course, also be empowered by partisanship-enhancing electoral systems, the evidence here suggests that sitting executives can be important (if not exclusive) beneficiaries of such rules. Note, however, that the impact of this variable was sensitive to model specification and disappeared whenever a more information-rich ordinal version of either dependent variable was introduced. What is more, results from models (not reported here) introducing an interaction term between partisan balloting and legislative majorities were nearly identical to main-effects models. Thus, contrary to commonsense institutionalism (see, e.g., Mainwaring and Shugart 1997), the effects of formal electoral rules on presidential power were not contingent on the size or the clout of the legislative caucus backing the president.

These findings also bring to mind O'Donnell's (1994a; 1994b) assertion that many Latin American democracies are characterized by "vertical" accountability but not "horizontal" accountability. In this view, elections are generally free, fair, and competitive, but executives, once elected, tend to be relatively unchecked by other branches or agencies of government. Subsequent scholars such as Moreno, Crisp, and Shugart (2003) have argued that improving the quality of horizontal accountability (they prefer "horizontal exchange") between presidents and assemblies can in fact only be accomplished by improving the quality of vertical account-ability between voters and legislators. (For a dissenting view, see Kenney 2003b.) The fact that electoral rules (i.e., *Partisan Balloting*) proved more important than the constitutional separation of powers (i.e., *Lawmaking Powers*) in my analysis provides some empirical support for that hitherto theoretical argument.

Perhaps most surprisingly, enjoying a legislative majority appears to have no significant impact on a president's overall power vis-à-vis the leg-islature. This was the case regardless of how I measured it: in models not reported here, "dumbing" down this legislative majority variable into a bi-nary, or using an alternative data source with simpler coding rules (e.g., Database of Political Institutions; see Keefer 2007), did not generate sta-tistically significant results either.[23] This echoes findings by Carey and Reynolds (2007): legislative party caucuses may play different roles in old versus new democracies, largely (they argue) as a consequence of program-matic inconsistency and/or weak discipline in the parties of the latter.

Holding legislative and executive elections concurrently was like-wise not significant in any of the fully specified models (though nearly so in Model 5). What is more, the bivariate correlation between concurrent elections and legislative majorities was tiny (coefficient = 0.01). True, other institutional traits also affect the outcomes of legislative elections and the degree of fragmentation in the legislature. But this unexpected finding might call for us to rethink the presumed causal link between the timing and results of elections in the contexts of newer presidential democracies—particularly in light of the electoral movement phenome-non and, more generally, the openness of some systems to "outsider" or nonpartisan candidates.[24]

Institutionalized separation of powers is not entirely absent from the story told by the results I have presented here. Though its statistical significance was weak, bicameralism, as compared to a unicameral system, might modestly constrain executives by adding a veto point and dispers-ing decision-making authority. More compellingly, the single most con-sistently important institutional trait for tipping the legislative-executive balance of power away from the latter turned out to be the capacity of the legislature to censure or dismiss cabinet ministers. No Latin Ameri-can system is truly semi-presidential, and ministerial censures are not common in most of the systems that allow them. Nonetheless, rules that incentivize the executive to even tacitly consider legislators' preferences in cabinet nominations, or that give rise to even the remote threat of censure by the assembly, appear to have a significant constraining effect on executive power.

Overall, however, if we are assessing the analytical usefulness of different approaches, support for many facets of institutionalist theory was rather uneven here. By contrast, the two additional hypotheses that I proposed were quite strongly supported: they were more robust across different estimators, measurements, and model specifications, and they were revealed to have a greater impact on the outcome in question. More broadly, these meta-institutionalist insights add new dimensions to current understandings of institutional politics in less institutionalized democracies.

First, weak de jure constitutionalism indeed appears to empower the executive as the bearer of greater de facto resources and capabilities—financial, material, bureaucratic, informational, military—than the legislature. Respect for the rule of law is more important than, and logically prior to, the separation of powers and the interbranch relations spelled out in formal laws and parchment constitutions.

Note that expert opinion on rule of law was used here as a proxy for constitutionalism, for the more narrow concept of adherence to the rules specifically among politicians and state actors. Future research could attempt to model other proxies—such as expert opinion on elite constitutional norms in particular or, for that matter, surveys of politicians themselves (see Universidad de Salamanca n.d.).

Note as well that this chapter did not examine judiciaries, constitutional tribunals, and other "agencies of restraint" (Collier 1999) such as ombudspersons and regulatory bodies. However, as Moreno, Crisp, and Shugart (2003) note, the abilities of these oversight agents to do their jobs may still depend on the capacity of the legislature for effective horizontal exchange with the executive—which, again, derives from effective vertical accountability to voters, in their view.

So if weak constitutional norms, on balance, strengthen the executive and weaken the legislature, then newer democracies run the risk of getting caught in a vicious cycle of poor representation, feeble oversight, and diminished rule of law. The plight of political institutions in Peru in the 1990s—as depicted in earlier chapters—was characterized by precisely this sort of downward spiral.

My analysis also confirmed that Latin American presidents who were swept into office with fluid, ad hoc electoral movements were less constrained than executives with institutionalized party backing. There is strength in weak parties: an intentionally feeble organization can indeed be a source of executive power, as illustrated by the Fujimori presidency detailed in earlier chapters of this book. Whatever benefits might accrue to a party-affiliated president in terms of resources or institutional capacity can, it seems, be outweighed by the formidable clout wielded by the president who goes it alone and builds his own customized electoral vehicle.

Future research could attempt to model the impact of party organizational forms among opposition groups too. As we saw in the case of Peru in 2001–2006, organized parties in the legislative opposition can make a big difference too. However, we learned from the larger *n* analysis presented here that it is not *only* opposition groups that can serve as a check on the executive in a separation-of-powers system. If the president's political group is an organized political party that performs some function beyond electing a particular president, then its legislators will likely have aspirations for political careers beyond a given presidency. Under these circumstances, the president's copartisans can actually restrain and moderate the executive, even if they also generally support her. This was very much in evidence in 1980s Peru under President García. By contrast, weak personalistic groupings organized around a particular presidential candidate, even when electorally successful, tend to be either a rubber stamp (as under Fujimori) or an empty shell (as under Toledo). Taken together, these findings might provoke scholars to interrogate, even further than I have here, the assumption that formal rules such as electoral laws affect all actors in the same way.

Finally, though I understandably did not put forth any explicit hypotheses about my control variables, there are a few other results here that bear mentioning. It appears that per capita wealth and annual GDP growth correspond with higher presidential power to act in an unconstrained manner (Models 2–4), yet per capita wealth is also linked to greater effectiveness of the legislature (Model 5). Future research might help to unravel this curious result. And the *Duration* variable, which was created to control for serial correlation and which counts the number of years since the initiation of a "spell" of constrained presidential power, is significant and negatively signed in all models in which it appears. Patterns of executive constraint tend to stay consistent from year to year in any given country, changing only periodically if at all. And the longer a country's experience with balanced legislative-executive power lasts, the more likely it is to continue with that balance. As we might have guessed, one of the best ways to ensure horizontal accountability in the future is to foster it in the present.

Conclusions

Institutionalist theory has been invaluable to scholars of new democracies, opening up previously unexplored areas of study and spawning many innovative research programs. Within this approach, however, we would be wise to remain alert to undertheorized differences between old and new democracies and to the unfulfilled assumptions embedded in our theoretical tools.

This chapter demonstrates that some power-allocating rules of the game might indeed operate as expected even in newer democracies, while other institutions have weaker or less predictable effects. Consequently, it may prove difficult to gauge the impact of formal institutions on power relations in new democracies without also grasping crucial cross-national differences in the nature of the players and in the integrity of the rules themselves. Understanding that some political parties are not really political parties, or that constitutional rules are sometimes "made to be broken" by politicians, gets analysts even closer to explaining, and perhaps crafting solutions for, long-standing problems of democratic quality and political power in Latin America and beyond.

So what accounts for the strength or weakness of directly elected executives in Latin America? The results presented here suggest that it would be misleading to portray presidential strength in Latin America as deriving exclusively, or even primarily, from formal institutional powers. Reading the rules of the game tells but an incomplete story about the real foundations of executive power in that region. The rule of law itself and the organizational form of the president's party proved to be crucial in shaping legislative-executive power balances — not only in Peru but throughout the hemisphere.

Future research will, no doubt, more finely hone the data and analysis presented here. It could analyze a longer time series in Latin America or, even better, go beyond the hemisphere and look at a more cross-regional set of data on presidential and semi-presidential systems. Future analysis could also operationalize and test additional proxy variables for elite constitutional norms, model party organizational forms in opposition as well as in the party of the executive, test for interaction effects among an even broader range of variables, and more deeply examine potential endogeneity problems. But adding the commonsense wisdom of meta-institutional insights to the elegance and rigor of institutionalist theory has already helped produce better answers to urgent questions about political power in the sometimes-fragile democracies of Latin America.

There are, to be sure, more deeply institutionalized democracies than ever in the region. Yet the Gordian knot for some Latin American systems continues to be this: weak parties and weak constitutional norms empower strong executives, who then attempt to stay in power by further debilitating political parties and gutting the constitution (see Navia and Walker 2010).[25] And when they fall, they fall at the hands of legislatures that may not be capable of legislating but can, in moments of crisis, push the executive into the void and oust a sitting president. But while it all seems to bode poorly for the future prospects of the region's lowest-quality democracies, analyzing these vicious cycles of institutional weakness might represent a necessary first step toward breaking them.

7

Conclusion
On Balance

In the long sweep of its history as a republic, the cadence of Peru's political "conversation"—the exchanges among elite political actors operating within formal institutions—has not settled into the staid, predictable speech patterns more typical of fully consolidated democracies. The conversation is dynamic; not only its content but its balance—who gets to speak and how loudly—has fluctuated a great deal, even in the relatively recent past.

The 1980s was a period of promise. Electoral democracy with truly universal suffrage emerged for the first time. Constitutional norms increasingly appeared to be infusing and mediating the conversation among key political actors. These interlocutors organized themselves into relatively coherent political parties. And effective, elected assemblies engaged in meaningful political dialogue, both internally and with the executive branch. Crises in the late 1980s and early 1990s muffled debate and rendered the legislative-executive conversation rather one-sided for much of the rest of the decade. Then, the fall of Fujimori in 2000 and the regime transition that followed again raised hopes that the spacious *hemiciclo* of Peru's Congress could be more than the president's cheering section— more than *ayayeros,* as Fujimori once called his overly enthusiastic supporters in and out of government.

What caused a decline in the power of the legislature and a vast increase in the power of the executive in the 1990s? And what led, in the first years of the twenty-first century, to the resuscitation of the assembly's power? Peru's institutional politics were governed by mostly the same rules of the game for the entire duration of the 1985–2006 period, at least according to the letter of the law. The constitutional articles and electoral laws that allocate power between the executive and the legislature did not vary much, even after a new constitution was adopted in 1993. From a strictly formal institutionalist perspective, we should not have seen the drastic increase and then rapid decrease in presidential power that we did in Peru.

But sometimes rules are not effectively binding or are overwhelmed by extra-institutional pressures. In environments where the rules of the political game did not effectively condition the behavior of politicians, we have seen here that the executive is more likely than the legislature to gain power (though this may be changing). In the presidential systems of Latin America, with their legacies of political centralization and authoritarian leadership, adherence to constitutional strictures is, among other things, a mechanism for "taming the prince" (Mansfield 1989)—that is, for constraining executives.

Norms of constitutionalism—politicians' adherence to the rules of the game—played a crucial role in shaping presidential power and legislative-executive relations in Peru, more so than the provisions of specific constitutions. In periods of Peruvian politics (most of them well before the Fujimori years), presidential strength only vaguely mirrored the powers spelled out in formal institutions. A gap between constitutionally prescribed rules and actual political practice was notable. Even during the relatively rule-abiding 1980s, governments sometimes bent, broke, or skirted the rules. Yet in the 1985–1990 presidency of Alan García—a government roundly criticized, at the time, for fostering corruption and displaying a cavalier attitude toward the rules of the game—constitutionalism still served to constrain the executive in ways that were no longer effective by the mid-1990s. In the wake of severe economic crisis and a violent civil conflict, institutions lost their hold on political actors. The gap between rules and practices widened markedly in the 1990s, as political power was routinely wielded extra-legally and extra-constitutionally.

The gap then narrowed again in 2001–2006. The dramatic recovery of the rule of law among Peru's political class in this period once again tamed—some would say hobbled—the president, Alejandro Toledo. The scandal-plagued final days of the Fujimori regime changed the public perception of, and discourse about, government. Just as the economic and security crises had contributed to a decline in constitutional norms in the late 1980s and early 1990s, the increasingly flagrant violations coming to light in 2000 eroded tolerance for the sort of government-by-rule-breaking that had become the norm in the 1990s. This development, coupled with the hands-on reconstruction of democratic institutions and the practice of governing by consensus in the 2000–2001 transition period, changed politicians' expectations about their own, and other political actors', rule-abiding behavior. Nowhere was this more true than in Peru's legislature.

The overall pattern that we see, even in the medium term, is cyclical. A rise in constitutionalism in the late 1970s and early '80s was followed by a decline during the late '80s and early '90s. Then we saw a dramatic resurgence in constitutionalism after the fall of Fujimori, a renewed effectiveness of the rules of the game as a coordination point for the behavior of political elites. Some of this fresh enthusiasm for the rule of law got institutionalized: new access-to-information regimes, new transparency in the lawmaking process, etc. And some of this fervor was instead manifested as scandal-mongering—stoked by media and politicians alike—overloading the public's sense of outrage and putting politicians in a permanent defensive crouch. How this mixed blessing affects politicians over time will be crucial. If everyone believes that everyone in politics is crooked and corrupt, then these new accountability mechanisms—and the rules of the political game itself—may once again lose value among political elites.

Alan García's second presidency, from 2006 (the end of the period of study) to 2011 (when this book was published), represents more continuity than change in terms of adherence to constitutional norms. García and his government had a mixed record. Fewer scandals erupted than during the 2001–2006 Toledo government, though several were enormously damaging. In 2008 García's entire cabinet resigned en masse, ahead of a possible legislative no-confidence vote, when evidence emerged of massive kickbacks to ministers and high-level bureaucrats from oil companies. This *petroaudios* scandal dogged the government for the rest of the term. And without a congressional majority of his own, García needed the support of more conservative groups in Congress not only to legislate but to keep further censures at bay. This sometimes included placating the pro-Fujimori caucus, which diminished the prospects for further prosecutions of corruption and wrongdoing from the previous decade.

APRA also moved to the right on issues such as justice and security, which led the government to try to limit prosecutions of past human rights violations and to clamp down on the present activities of nongovernmental organizations and human rights groups. Notwithstanding these troubling trends, the essential rules of the political game continued to be followed.

Analysts seeking to predict how constitutional norms might fare in the coming years might also look to the success or failure of anti-systemic movements, both inside and outside of electoral politics. In 2006–2011, as in 2001–2006, regional and local protest movements continued to emerge and occasionally turned violent. García's policies on natural resource extraction, in particular, generated periodic waves of dissent, some of which were suppressed with violence. We might also watch for further social unrest and a potential weakening of constitutionalism should Peru's rapid-growth economy begin to slow down, as it eventually must. And the futures of other, more violent actors will be decisive too: the potential revival of insurgencies and, a more likely and immediate danger, the expansion and extension of drug-trafficking rings and other organized crime networks.

In the "high politics" of national elections, Ollanta Humala's nationalist-populist movement regained popularity in 2011 after fading for a few years. Humala pitched himself as more of a moderate leftist and less of an anti-systemic firebrand, and he was rewarded at the polls. His Gana Perú electoral movement, essentially a new label for his Peruvian Nationalist Party (PNP), became a leading force in the 2011 general elections, winning a plurality of seats in the legislature. Then Humala himself won the runoff presidential election.

Essential to the impact of *humalismo* on institutional power in Peru will be the degree to which it respects constitutionalism and the formal rules of the game. As a candidate, Humala first pledged to rewrite Peru's constitution through an elected constituent assembly, though he later claimed that he would instead go through existing legislative channels to reform the 1993 charter (*Gestión,* April 12, 2011). And in an effort to reassure voters and political elites alike, a few weeks before the runoff election, Humala elaborately swore a public oath in the presence of dozens of constitutional scholars and civic leaders in which he pledged to uphold the democratic rules of the game, leaving intact the president's term of office and the ban on immediate reelection (*La República,* May 19, 2011). If and how he tries to change the rules from the presidential palace, and whether he and his legislators abide by norms of constitutionalism, will be crucially important to the future of Peru's institutional politics.

Humala's main competitor in 2011 was none other than Keiko Fujimori, the daughter of the jailed ex-president who led Peru to its nadir of constitutionalism in the 1990s. *Fujimoristas* nearly tripled the size of their congressional caucus to become the second-largest bloc in the assembly, and even more remarkably Keiko very nearly won the runoff presidential election.

Though Keiko Fujimori was a talented campaigner in her own right, and though she took great pains to distance herself from the less salubrious aspects of her father's legacy, the electoral movement she was part of was still organized around the personal appeal of *Alberto* Fujimori. There was even substantial evidence of her father's active involvement—from prison—in the day-to-day logistics of the daughter's campaign (*La República*, May 18, 2011). The new popularity of yet another pro-Fujimori electoral movement raised serious concerns about old threats to constitutionalism and, more specifically, the political resurrection of the ex-president and his confidantes, many of whom were likewise charged and sentenced for their crimes. Despite Keiko's running as a "law and order" candidate, the return of the mafia-like network that ruled Peru in the 1990s—and the chance that Fujimori himself could once again be running things, whether behind bars or, more troubling, freed by his daughter's government—loomed large as threats to constitutionalism. Alberto Fujimori was still trying to get that third term in office, de facto or de jure.

And on that subject: in addition to tracing the cyclical patterns of elite adherence to constitutional norms, this book offers some passing insights on one particular set of rules, those governing presidential reelection. Fujimori forced through the adoption of immediate reelection under the pall of a self-coup. The specious interpretation of the rules that later purported to allow Fujimori to run for office again in 2000 was emblematic of the executive's further descent into lawlessness. Allowing immediate presidential reelection may, under conditions of strong rule of law, produce better political outcomes than banning it and making every president a lame duck. However, in light of the Peruvian experience, immediate reelection as a practice clearly merits some sober second thought. (Peru's Congress thought so too; as noted, it reinstated the 1979 Constitution's restriction on immediate reelection just as Fujimori was exiting the political stage.)

Reelection rules have been controversially altered in other Latin American countries. They have made headlines in Venezuela, Bolivia, and Ecuador and undergirded a regime-shattering political crisis in Honduras. Lest we consider such moves as the domain of populists and left-leaning politicians, it is also worth noting that presidents with a decidedly different ideology, such as Argentina's Carlos Menem and Colombia's Álvaro Uribe, also sought to change reelection laws and bent the rules along the way. (Neither inflicted the devastating damage to institutionality that Fujimori did and that Venezuela's Hugo Chávez, for example, continues to do.)

In fact, thirteen of the eighteen Latin American countries analyzed in chapter 6 loosened their restrictions on presidential reelection during the past twenty-five years. Whatever the intentions with which such reforms are made—be they genuinely democratic, purely Machiavellian, or something in between—constitutions are meant to be long-term frameworks rather than short-term fixes. Gambling over the extent to which not just current but future presidents will resist or be deterred from abusing the power of the state to win reelection may not be worth the risk, as long as we cannot take for granted that Latin America's politicians will have to follow the rules of the game rather than flout or change them.

And if constitutions can be changed, we also need to think about both the content of the rules and the processes of rule making. As Franceschet and Policzer (2010) note, constitutional rules can themselves be undemocratic. For example, some Latin American constitutions assign to the military the role of guarantor of political order. These clauses are more than symbolic statements: in Honduras, the constitutional prerogative of the military was used to justify the ouster of President Manuel Zelaya. And while the trend toward rewriting constitutions in the region may be abating, recent constituent assemblies in Bolivia (2006–2007), Ecuador (2007–2008), and elsewhere proved to be polarizing rather than consensus building, which augurs poorly for the strengthening of constitutional norms.

Just as constitutional clauses turned out to be less important than constitutional adherence itself, I came to similar conclusions about the formal rules for parties and elections. Electoral laws may predict how an organized political party works, but the same rules may not have the same effect on the power dynamic between leader and legislators when they are an ad hoc group of politicians clustered around a personalistic figure.

These sorts of electoral movements increasingly filled Peru's political arena beginning in the late 1980s and early 1990s. The organizational form proved successful at the polls. During the Fujimori regime, however, the winning group's legislators served few purposes beyond their unwavering support for the president in Congress. This does not mean that all *fujimorista* legislators were idle or slavish, just that, by their own admission, they had little leverage—individually or as an organ of democratic lawmaking, representation, and oversight—in their relationship with the president and his inner circle. And they knew their place.

As Peru's Congress was hollowed out, echoing only the voice of the executive, one might have thought that the electoral movement was a weak form of organization. This was true for electoral movements on the legislature's opposition benches; these tended to disintegrate (their members of Congress often co-opted by the incumbent), and they did not exercise any effective constraints on the executive. But under the right circumstances, we have seen, an electoral movement linked to the president himself can in fact offer the executive immense power and leverage over legislators and other political actors.

By the same token, we often think of coherent opposition parties as being crucial for horizontal accountability, and opposition parties did serve this function in the 1985–1990 legislature (where another organized party held a solid majority) and in the 2001–2006 legislature (where a shaky coalition of electoral movements held the majority). Yet organized parties *in* power can promote accountability too. Comparing Peru in the 1980s and the 1990s, we saw that the president with the organized political party was actually more constrained, not more powerful, than the leader of an electoral movement—at least if we conceive of power as the ability to act unilaterally, in an unfettered manner.

After the turn of the century, President Toledo, too, rose to power as the head of an electoral movement—but times had changed. For one thing, as noted above, elite constitutional norms had grown stronger. The 2001 elections were free and fair, and, crucially, Toledo did *not* win a legislative majority. Unlike his predecessor, he could not or would not try to bribe and blackmail his way into a majority, either. And Toledo's leadership style, his political "brand," as it were, emphasized adherence to democratic rules. This turned the electoral movement format into more of a liability and less of an advantage for Toledo; though it sometimes freed him from bargaining and competing with intraparty elites, it seldom afforded him the kind of staunch legislative support that Fujimori could rely on.

For another thing, even though Toledo did not lead an organized political party, organized political parties were back. The revitalization of parties like APRA (and, to a lesser extent, the PPC) in the congressional opposition blocs bolstered the power of the legislature anew and helped keep Toledo in check. These parties, somewhat precarious as they were, allowed Congress to play more of a role in legislation and government oversight, not to mention the linkages (however conflicted) and representation (however imperfect) that they lent to the democratic process.

To be sure, the dichotomy between political parties and electoral movements is not absolute. The capacity of Peru's electoral movements—in power or in opposition—to make laws, represent citizens, and hold government accountable was not zero. It does seem to be the case, however, that these personalistic movements have far fewer structural incentives to nudge legislators toward practices that strengthen, rather than weaken, the functionality of the legislature.

This book also suggests that personalism in party politics is, in many ways, a double-edged sword. Personalistic leadership even within Peru's traditional parties was a key factor in their inability to adapt in the late 1980s and their near disappearance during the 1990s. Yet in the context of weak institutions and unpredictable competition, personalism can sometimes be good short-term strategy for political groups—though it may not be optimal for that group in the long run and though it is surely detrimental for the systemwide development of representative democracy. The persistence of Alan García's leadership of APRA, even after a troubled first presidency and a lengthy period of exile, fueled the party's electoral comeback in the first decade of the twenty-first century, though we have no way of knowing what sort of party might have emerged had García gracefully stepped aside in 1990. Similarly, the near-suicidal determination of Alberto Fujimori to return to the Peruvian political scene—a bloody-mindedness that ultimately landed him in jail—would be risible were it not for the renewed electoral success of his movement in 2006 and, especially, in 2011.

Party politics in 2011 Peru is at something of a crossroads. For those who think that parties are indeed essential to representative democracy, the hope in 2006–2011 was that perhaps the modest revival of organized parties was a longer-term trend, even if the presence of ad hoc electoral movements remains a perennial feature of Peru's politics (as the past two decades suggest it will). In government, APRA was a disciplined force, at least until the 2011 election campaign began. APRA and the *fujimorista* bloc in Congress each displayed a high degree of unity, but other caucuses in Congress remained rather fluid in 2006–2011. What began as five parliamentary groups in 2006 soon became eight parliamentary groups, as both UN and UPP broke into multiple caucuses; party discipline in most of these remained weak (*El Comercio,* July 27, 2009).

Analysts will be keen to observe how APRA fares once it is out of power again. It is telling that, in preparing for the 2011 presidential campaign, APRA chose a candidate who is herself something of an outsider. Mercedes Aráoz, a popular economy and finance minister who had been appointed to cabinet by García as an "independent," was selected in a highly fractious nomination process. However, Aráoz was faring poorly in preelection polls and resigned her candidacy in January 2011 rather than accept longtime party leader Jorge del Castillo—under investigation for corruption related to the *petroaudios* scandal—at the top of the APRA congressional list. In a reprise of the 1990 elections, some suspected that García had his own agenda in promoting the candidacy of an outsider rather than one of the *aprista* stalwarts who had been waiting in the wings for decades: an eye toward running for president yet again in 2016 (infolatam.com, Jan. 17, 2011; *La República,* Jan. 7, 2011). García himself first hinted that he might run in a future election, then recanted and said that he would not (*El Comercio,* May 1, 2011). Though personalistic leadership may have helped APRA regain political momentum in 2001–2006 and then return to the heights of power in 2006–2011, personalistic leadership may now hobble the party as it did in the 1990s. If APRA were to finally collapse, the most durable, stable presence in Peru's already volatile party system would be eliminated.

Indeed, electoral movements could very well continue to crowd out organized parties in the political marketplace. It will be crucial to see if and how the *fujimorista* electoral movement—led by Keiko Fujimori as a proxy for her imprisoned father—will evolve. Though the group continues to resist organizational development, it has also resisted elimination and irrelevance. It has outperformed most other electoral movements in its ability to run candidates and appeal to voters in national elections while out of power for more than a decade at the start of the twenty-first century. The latest incarnation of the movement, Fuerza 2011, brings together many of her father's old supporters as well as "new" candidates that include family insiders like Keiko's brother, Kenji. Thus, it remains highly personalistic, loosely organized, and weakly institutionalized. There was little evidence that the group was becoming more partylike in 2011.

Nor was there much impetus for it to change. In the 2011 general elections, Fuerza 2011 was a huge success: it won thirty-seven seats in Congress, with Kenji Fujimori receiving more preferential votes than any other legislative candidate. Keiko Fujimori made it to the runoff presidential election as the only right-of-center candidate left standing. And then, of course, she very nearly won.

Centrist and center-right votes in the first round were split by three other candidates, all with personalistic electoral movements: Luis Castañeda Lossio, Pedro Pablo Kuczynski, and Alejandro Toledo. The center-right coalition from 2001 to 2006, Unidad Nacional, had disappeared. Rafael Rey's RN remained an enduring if erratic presence in Peruvian politics: RN abandoned the coalition in 2006, then Rey twice served as a cabinet minister under President Alan García, and then he ran for vice president as Keiko Fujimori's running mate. The rest of the UN alliance dissolved in 2008; Lourdes Flores ran for mayor of Lima in 2010 as a PPC candidate (though she kept the UN name as a secondary affiliation). Former UN groups went their separate ways in the 2011 national elections, and the presidential candidates spawned by these groups were not leaders of the PPC (or any other organized party) but rather heads of electoral movements. Kuczynski, who was Toledo's former cabinet chief and economy minister, surged in the final month of the 2011 campaign but ended up finishing third. His alliance (Alianza por el Gran Cambio) was anchored by an electoral movement of his own (Alianza para el Progreso) but also included a weakened PPC and two other small groups. Castañeda Lossio, who finished fifth, was backed by his evaporating SN movement plus the empty shells of UPP and the old C-90. Alejandro Toledo himself returned to politics and again ran for office in 2011, backed by a debilitated Perú Posible and the remnants of SP and AP. As a presidential candidate he led public opinion polls from December 2010 through February 2011, then lost steam and finished fourth. Perú Posible in 2011, out of power for five years, was organizationally weaker and more ad hoc than it had been even back in 2001. This too bodes poorly for organized party politics.

Also uncertain is the future of the democratic left. In 2006, as the period of study for this book ended, well-organized left parties had been nearly absent from Peru's national politics for over twenty years. It was unclear whether reconstructing such parties was even viable and, if so, what sort of organizations they might be and what would be their relationship with an increasingly active but also highly fluid and localized array of civil society groups.

Two events in 2010–2011 shook up the political left in Peru. The first was the 2010 municipal elections. Susana Villarán, a human rights activist and former minister for women and social development, had run for president in 2006, garnering less than 1 percent of the vote. In 2010, however, her Fuerza Social movement built a coalition of civic associations and won the mayoralty of Lima, narrowly defeating the rather heavily favored Lourdes Flores (though Flores' PPC did much better at the district level). The success or failure of this more nimble, flexible form of left-party organization—an ad hoc party organization but one rooted in some organized civil society groups—will be a bellwether for the future of party politics in Peru.

But it was the second event, the success of Ollanta Humala in the 2011 general elections, that might have an even greater impact on Peru's politics. After nearly winning the 2006 presidential election, Humala and his PNP held a large (though undisciplined) bloc of seats in Congress. Then in 2011 his Gana Perú movement won forty-seven seats in Congress, the largest of any party or alliance. And making it into the presidential runoff election as the sole left-of-center candidate, this time Humala won the presidency.

To get there, he and his movement took up many of the left's core economic and social issues (and some prominent figures from the left's heyday in the 1980s backed Humala in 2011), though his ideology, as it were, could still best be described as populist nationalism. More importantly for this study, although his movement had five years of experience in Congress and other public offices, it remained, above all, a personalistic electoral movement. The trajectory of Humala and his electoral movement over the next five years will be another key to understanding the future of party politics in Peru. More crucial than the space that it settles into on the left-right political spectrum will be the extent to which it does or, more likely, does not develop partylike traits.

The case of Peru indeed highlights fundamental questions about the founding and organizational development of new political parties in the contemporary era. Where old parties are destroyed or discredited, where grassroots social movements are fragmented or are disengaged from formal politics, and where politicians can communicate virtually directly with voters and constituents, there may be little impetus today for creating and sustaining new organizations that look like the political parties of yesterday. Can organized parties as we know them reemerge where they are weak or nonexistent, given the accessibility of these mass media and polling technologies, the transformation of social cleavages, and the immediacy of electoral competition? If so, what organizational form should we expect them to take, in light of these incentive structures? If not, and yet elections continue apace, what sorts of regimes will develop? Is it true that democracy is "unthinkable" (Schattschneider 1942, 1) or "unworkable" (Aldrich 1995, 3) without parties—that parties are still "indispensable" to democracy (Lipset 2000)? Could democracy persist but with its institutions taking new shapes, in the absence of stable party organizations as we (used to) know them? By what mechanisms will political actors adhere to and enforce the constitutional rules of the game?

Though I grappled with these questions first for the case of Peru, my findings on that country also led me to investigate how well institutionalist theory, and my own meta-institutional insights, travel in other parts of Latin America. Statistical analysis of the power of Latin American presidencies from 1985 to 2004, presented in chapter 6, confirms that my explanation for change over time in the case of Peru—that weak constitutional norms and weak political party organizations led to a strengthening of the executive branch—is indeed generalizable, at least within this region.

An institutionalist answer to the question of what makes presidents strong—the constitutional rules governing executive authority and the electoral rules that shape leaders' control over the nominations of legislative candidates, as well as the size of the president's legislative caucus— was partially supported. Some formal rules matter, under certain conditions. Electoral laws that feature more partisan balloting did, in some models, strengthen the executive (though winning a legislative majority did not). Constitutions that give legislatures more influence over cabinet composition proved to be more robust constraints on executive power than those that limit the president's lawmaking authority. But strong rule of law and a real political party behind the president matter more, and more consistently, for limiting executive power in Latin America. All of this strongly suggests that knowing the formal rules of the political game and comprehending their implications are necessary but insufficient for analyzing politics in a newer democracy like Peru's. We must look at institutions but also at the actors within them and the contexts that surround them. As generations of social scientists before me long suspected, the rules of the game can only get us so far in understanding Latin American politics.

The findings of this book might encourage us to come back and take a second look at some of the other Latin American case studies touched on in chapter 6. Peru's story—not just its democratic decline but its democratic renewal in the early years of the twenty-first century—could shed light on others in the hemisphere. Analyzing politicians' constitutional adherence and party organizations in other countries in the region might help us gauge the prospects for improving the balance of power between legislature and executive and, with that, the quality of Latin American democracy.

A brief overview of contemporary politics in Venezuela and Colombia—both of which have had strong party systems that later declined and have experienced serious challenges to constitutionalism—provides a poignant paired comparison. According to the Polity IV data, both countries had Executive Constraints scores indicating parity or near-parity between the legislature and the executive in the mid-1980s, and both countries indeed showed a drop in that seven-point score as of 2009. However, while Colombia's score edged slightly downward (from seven to six) in that period, Venezuela's sharply plummeted (from six to three).

The current politics of Venezuela offer a particularly tough road forward toward restoring horizontal accountability, if the framework I have presented here is correct. Adherence to constitutional norms in Venezuela, I would argue, clearly waned in the first decade of the twenty-first century.[1] Whatever one thinks of the rules of the game that used to structure Venezuelan politics, and however one feels about the concrete social and economic goals of President Hugo Chávez, neither the formal rules of the constitution nor the spirit of constitutionalism as a way of doing politics was strong as of mid-2011. In Venezuela's current regime, the goal of building "twenty-first-century socialism" takes precedence over liberal democratic conceptions of political rights, civil liberties, and indeed the rule of law and the role of formal institutions. Though sometimes ignored, the rules of the game have also been rewritten by—and for—the incumbent president. (And as in Peru, some of these modifications were done "by the book" while others were not.) Rules about presidential reelection, of course, have been altered to allow Chávez to stay in office, but similarly self-serving institutional changes have been used to hobble judicial and constitutional oversight, neutralize subnational levels of government, and silence critics in the media (though there has also been some pushback, as when referendum voters rejected the president's proposed constitutional amendments in 2007).

While two attempted military coups in 1992 may have set the stage for the rise of *chavismo,* the 2002 attempted civil-military coup against Chávez was likewise damaging to the constitutional order. It implied that opposition groups in Venezuela had given up on more peaceful, civilian, rule-bound strategies for countering a sitting president. But after 2002, rule of law declined even further, and conditions for competition became even more unfair. By the time the opposition finally regrouped to contest legislative elections in 2010, Chávez gerrymandered districts to diminish the number of seats they could win. And when they nonetheless garnered 65 of 165 seats in Congress, the outgoing pro-Chávez, lame-duck Congress granted the president wide-ranging authority to rule by decree for the following eighteen months.

As for party organizations themselves, the highly stable and highly rigid two-party Punto Fijo system that was initiated in 1958 broke down by the 1990s. The most obvious manifestation of this breakdown was, of course, the 1998 election of Chávez with his Quinta República (MVR) electoral movement. However, it bears remembering that the rise of electoral movements in Venezuela actually began, ironically, with the founder of one of the country's two dominant parties. Rafael Caldera, historic leader of the center-right Comité de Organización Política Electoral Independiente (COPEI) and president of Venezuela from 1969 to 1975, defied his own party and—banking on his personalistic appeal to voters—

ran for office as an independent presidential candidate in 1993. With his ad hoc Convergencia Nacional electoral movement, he won those elections and served a second term from 1994 to 1998. So the *partidocracia* of the Punto Fijo system has actually been gone for nearly two decades, and up to 2011 it showed few signs of return.

The electoral movement with which Chávez first ran, the MVR, was organized in 1997, and its function was to support his 1998 presidential bid. In power, Chávez and the "Bolivarian Revolution" developed mechanisms for linkage with Venezuelan society, though these were mainly through state rather than party apparatuses. And one prominent form of linkage was personalistic in the extreme: Chávez's weekly live television show, *Aló Presidente,* in which he answered phone calls from the public, gave extended speeches on wide-ranging topics, and grilled cabinet ministers and other officials for hours on end. The image fostered was of a president who governed solely as an individual and enjoyed as direct and unmediated a relationship as possible with Venezuela's citizens.

In a similar vein, the main role of MVR in the legislature was simply to support the president's political project. Chavez's legislative caucus did attract the backing of a few small but more autonomously organized leftist groups, though some of these proved to be too autonomous for the president. By the time Chávez reorganized his electoral movement in 2007–2008, the new incarnation—the United Socialist Party of Venezuela—fused together MVR with nearly a dozen Bolivarian or left-revolutionary groups, most of them small and ad hoc, but excluded several of the non-MVR groups that had supported his bloc in the 2005–2010 legislature.

Opposition groups were also organizationally weak, struggling not only with citizens' distrust for parties and politicians associated with the Punto Fijo era but with ongoing state harassment and an extremely unlevel playing field. (Some years they simply gave up and boycotted elections.) However, even with these obstacles and limitations, the opposition—including some new groups as well as some remnants of COPEI and Acción Democrática—returned to perform relatively well in 2010 legislative elections. As of 2011, these groups were loosely organized in the Roundtable for Democratic Unity, channeling a desire for change rather than a particular program or ideology. They have, for now, been marginalized from the exercise of any real legislative power. Though they have made the party system a bit more competitive and pluralistic than it had been in the past decade, the challenges of constructing or reconstructing organized parties—anywhere, but especially in Venezuela—are daunting.

Given these challenges, and the fact that the rules of the game in Chávez's Venezuela were, in 2000–2010, flouted with even more disregard than in Fujimori's Peru in the 1990s, revitalizing checks and balances in what is currently a hyper-presidentialist competitive authoritarian regime will be extremely difficult. (On the other hand, Venezuela's economy performed poorly—by regional standards—in the later years of the decade, and if the global price of oil were to drop, the redistributive policies of the Chávez government would be even harder to sustain.)

The case of Colombia offers a somewhat more solid foundation for balancing legislative-executive relations. In a sense, while rule of law in Colombian society at large is weak, constitutional norms are somewhat more robust. Organized crime and the insurgency that has battled the Colombian state for decades (and the long legacy of civil war before that) have together made citizens highly insecure, fostered rampant human rights violations and violent paramilitary actions, enfeebled legal and judicial systems, and, at times, called into question the ongoing existence—the "stateness" (Linz and Stepan 1996)—of the Colombian state itself.[2] Yet amid all of this violence and corruption, political elites remained surprisingly faithful to the rules of the game governing their behavior within civilian state institutions. The military's counterinsurgency and counternarcotics activities are poorly constrained by the rule of law, but the armed forces are subordinated to civilian authority and are not jeopardizing the continuity of civilian government. Elected legislatures and executives interact more or less as the constitution says they should. Constitutional reforms completed in 1991 were crafted by broad consensus among political groups and were democracy-enhancing in many respects.

Though the 1991 Constitution prohibited presidential reelection, Congress changed this rule in 2004 (and the Constitutional Court approved it in 2005) to facilitate a reelection run by a popular sitting president, Álvaro Uribe. But when Uribe supporters in Congress tried to call a referendum on a law changing the rules again in 2009–2010 so that Uribe could run for a third term, the still-popular leader was then rebuffed by the Constitutional Court (which also found some alleged fraud in the signature collections used to call for the referendum). Unlike Chávez, the president was, in the end, constrained by existing institutions, and Uribe did not run in the 2010 elections.

On the other hand, there were several episodes from the Uribe administration that revealed a *lack* of respect for, and constraint by, the rules of the game. The "parapolitics" scandal that blew open in 2006 exposed deep and troubling ties between pro-Uribe members of Congress and the armed right-wing paramilitary groups that Uribe was supposedly engaged in demobilizing (*Washington Post,* May 17, 2009). In a separate scandal, numerous high-level aides and powerful appointees in Uribe's executive branch—including the Department of Administrative Security, an intelligence service answering directly to the president—were charged with illegally wiretapping judges, journalists, civic leaders, and opposition politicians (*BBC News,* Feb. 21, 2009). And as of mid-2009, nearly twelve hundred members of various security forces were under investigation for extrajudicial killings. Particularly ghoulish was the emerging evidence of "false positives" indicating that the Colombian military had periodically killed civilians and then fabricated evidence of guerilla affiliation (*BBC News,* May 7, 2009). I do not wish to argue here that Colombian political elites are a rule-abiding bunch; my point is merely that the rules do, in large measure, work to constrain them. In each of the episodes of wrongdoing depicted above, investigations were launched, and arrests were made. The executive branch—and even the military—were not as impervious to scrutiny and accountability as in Fujimori's Peru or Chávez's Venezuela.

In terms of party organizations, the Liberals and Conservatives that governed Colombia in the second half of the twentieth century had maintained a power-sharing arrangement, the National Front, not unlike Venezuela's pact. But as a by-product of the electoral system in which they competed, the parties themselves were much more internally fragmented than Venezuela's at the height of *puntofijismo.* Like its neighbor's two-party system, Colombia's began weakening even further in recent years. The Front officially ended in 1974, though elements of it were maintained into the 1990s. In that decade, however, smaller parties and independent candidates began to achieve greater electoral success.

The 2002 victory of a president not running with either major party (or with a proxy for one of the major parties) was an even more transformative moment. Former Liberal Party politician Álvaro Uribe won executive office with the backing of his own personal electoral movement,

Primero Colombia. Both Liberals and Conservatives had their own candidate in the race, though the Conservatives ultimately withdrew and supported Uribe in order to defeat the Liberal, Horacio Serpa. Álvaro Uribe was then reelected with Primero Colombia in 2006, this time running a slate of *uribista* legislative candidates under the label Partido Social de Unidad Nacional, or Partido de la U. The name itself evokes personalistic leadership: the Partido de la U. was formed to coalesce politicians who supported Uribe himself, as the *U* was meant to remind voters. The idea that *uribismo*—with a vague right-wing ideology emphasizing national security—could be a political movement of its own gained traction in the first decade of the new century. While the Liberal and Conservative parties did not disappear, they were seriously weakened. Conservatives endorsed Uribe rather than run a presidential candidate of their own in 2006, though both Liberals and Conservatives continued to win legislative seats: Liberals held on to 18 percent of legislative seats, and Conservatives won 17 percent of seats, in the upper and lower houses combined.

In 2010 Liberals and Conservatives both ran presidential candidates. But many voters and politicians formerly tied to these parties (especially the Conservatives) continued to support *uribismo* via Uribe's protégé, former defense minister Juan Manuel Santos. The Partido de la U. electoral movement won the single largest bloc of legislative seats; with the support of the Conservatives and other *uribista* groups like Cambio Radical, it held an absolute majority in both houses. Despite some analysts' predictions that personalistic support for Uribe would not transfer to Santos, "*uribismo* without Uribe" succeeded in 2010 (*Semana*, Feb. 27 and June 5, 2011).

If the case of Peru is any indication, then the future of horizontal accountability in Colombia will be in large part determined first by the ability of constitutional norms to maintain their hold, however uneven, over political elites and, second, by the capacity of Liberals and Conservatives to replenish their ranks and/or for new party organizations (including, perhaps, an *uribista* party; see below) to develop in their stead. Santos's runoff opponent in 2010, Antanas Mockus, represented Colombia's Green Party, a small but growing party that had won some regional and local elections in 2007. But Mockus's success in 2010 was in large part due to the appropriation of the party label by independents, and in legislative elections the Green Party itself won just 3 percent of seats across both houses. The role of legislative opposition party was thus played primarily by the Liberals, though unlike Venezuela up to 2010—and unlike Peru in the 1990s—there *is* some semblance of effective opposition.

To discern the possibilities for institutional development in these two Andean countries, we can also look to illustrative comparisons from other times and other regions. The Gaullist parties in France began as a personalistic electoral movement but eventually fostered new leadership and grew in organizational complexity once constitutional rule was reconsolidated and de Gaulle himself left the political stage. In our own era, by contrast, Vladimir Putin's United Russia continues (in 2011) to dominate the competitive authoritarian regime that Russia has become. Rule-abiding behavior is not Putin's hallmark, and though he respected term limits and left the presidency in 2008, he became a highly powerful prime minister, overshadowing his protégé, President Dmitry Medvedev. Putin may be eyeing a return to the presidency in 2012 and (taking a page from Fujimori) discarding United Russia to create a new personalistic electoral vehicle for the occasion (Bloomberg.com, May 8, 2011). Under constitutional reforms implemented by his allies, he could serve two six-year terms, staying in power until 2024.

So which way will Colombia and Venezuela go? Santos is a leader backed by a mix of party factions and an electoral movement bequeathed to him by another politician. It seems improbable, but if the *uribista* electoral movement can endure and continue to develop without Uribe, then it may, like de Gaulle's movement, evolve into an organized party. Even now, Santos is not without constraining influences from career politicians with long time horizons. And in a way, President Santos owes his most recent career success to the resilience of constitutional norms: had Uribe run for a third term, Santos simply would not have become president. And unlike Putin, Uribe is actually giving his protégé the leeway to govern on his own. Chávez is a leader less fettered by constitutional norms, and his signature style, like Putin's, is to heap scorn on politics-as-usual and its practitioners. Chávez also has a deep social appeal among some sectors of society and has created numerous state programs to try to reach out to Venezuela's poor, but he has done little in the way of party organizational development. And he has faced, for most of his time in office, opposition from de facto elites but not from well-organized political parties. Neither the rules of the game nor organized parties—the president's or the opposition's—look to be fostering horizontal accountability in Venezuela.

How constrained these leaders are, and how bright the democratic futures of their respective countries look, will be shaped by the same variables I analyzed for the case of Peru. Colombia and Venezuela present interesting contemporary test cases for the evolution of groups that begin as ad hoc personalistic movements, and for the durability of constitutional norms among elite political actors. On both counts, Colombia, even with its ongoing political violence, looks more likely to maintain and enhance checks and balances in the foreseeable future. However, Chávez's brand of antipolitics does appear to be losing some of its popular appeal in the face of economic downturn and high crime rates. And if Peru's 2000–2001 transition taught us anything, it is that these variables can change values rapidly and with regime-altering consequences.

Beyond Latin America, in the spirit of comparative political research, it is my hope that this book will also open new avenues for inquiry about new democracies in other parts of the world: their political organizations and institutions and their legislative-executive relations. Testing the same competing sets of institutional and meta-institutional hypotheses from chapter 6 cross-regionally, for new democracies outside the Americas, would be one logical extension of this research.

For example, the post-Soviet republics of Eastern/Central Europe, like Latin America, display some interesting within-region variations in the strength of elite rule of law and constitutional norms (Roberts 2009). But on the question of political parties, totalitarianism left behind a legacy rather different from the authoritarianism and military rule that dominated Latin America before the Third Wave democratic transitions (Linz and Stepan 1996; Cheibub 2007). Soviet-era regimes were much more ideologically monolithic, tolerating even less political pluralism (Kostadinova and Power 2007). On the one hand, this means that the eventual break with totalitarianism mobilized Eastern/Central European citizens in entirely new ways, with the potential for new forms of party identification. On the other hand, it means that one organized political party—unaccustomed to competition and perhaps highly polarizing, but a party nonetheless—existed in each system prior to democratization (Tavits 2008). This begs comparisons with Latin American cases like Mexico and Paraguay, and former single-party hegemonic systems in other regions (e.g., Taiwan, Turkey). These distinct legacies of partisan politics may have different consequences for citizens' trust in organized parties and, by extension, for the appeal of personalistic groups.[3]

Another axis of comparison could be institutional design itself. As noted in chapter 2, prime ministers in parliamentary systems may not have the same incentives and opportunities to "go it alone," as compared to executives in separation-of-powers systems. They are hired by the legislature and may have to maintain the support of a coalition of groups. Even more so than the increasingly impeachable Latin American president, a prime minister can be readily fired by the legislature with a no-confidence vote. And in some of Eastern/Central Europe's semi-presidential systems, presidents are constitutionally weak, as they too are elected by the assembly and/or are limited in the power they can exercise.[4] Retooling the variables and models analyzed in chapter 6 to cover more parliamentary forms of government would yield new insights about institutionalism and contribute to the ever-evolving dialogue on regime type and the quality of democracy.

My work to date, including this book, has raised some theoretical questions about institutions and institutionalism and, I hope, answered a few as well. It contends that context and extra-institutional factors matter a great deal and that formal laws and institutional designs cannot be examined on paper and then taken at face value.[5] Theories derived from the study of institutions in advanced industrialized democracies have been immensely valuable for scholars of new democracies, leading us to see Latin America through new lenses and to analyze elements of its politics that were previously inaccessible or simply ignored. However, we should also take a cautionary note from historical sociologist Claudio Véliz, who writes: "The extension to Latin America of the universal tenets of various exotic political schemes rests on the absurd assumption that Latin America can be extricated from its historical context and treated as if it were a tabula rasa, its social and historical dimensions regarded either as irrelevant or as sufficiently similar to those of the societies whence the models originate" (1980, 304). This should not deter scholars of institutions in Latin America and other new democracies from applying models and testing theories developed in the old democracies. Instead, it should lead us to problematize and empirically investigate actors, norms, and institutions, rather than make a priori assumptions about them.

Political institutions—the formal rules of the political game—do affect political outcomes. But so do differences among elite political cultures and political actors, especially as these differences can dramatically alter the impact and the effectiveness of the rules themselves. Understanding institutional politics, especially in newer democracies, requires us to illuminate what the formal rules of the game can sometimes obscure: the way the game is really played.

Data Appendix

The dependent variable, the legislative-executive power balance, is operationalized in two different ways. One, *Executive Strength,* is derived from the Polity IV dataset's "Executive Constraints" (XCONST) variable, a 7-point index that gauges "the extent of institutionalized constraints on the decision-making powers of chief executives. . . . In Western democracies these [constraining institutions] are usually legislatures" (Marshall and Jaggers 2008). Coders monitor open-source materials such as newspapers and wire services not for formal rules but for "evidence of effective constraints and independent executive actions" (Marshall 2009). For Models 1 through 3, I converted it into a binary variable representing presidential *power.*[1] I recoded XCONST values 1 through 5 = 1 (i.e., unconstrained presidential power) and values 6 and 7 = 0 (i.e., constrained presidential power), since, in the original indicator, 7 represented parity and 6 was an intermediate category. For Model 4, I returned to the original ordinal scale but inverted it. The second dependent variable— *Legislative Ineffectiveness,* in Model 5—is derived from the "Legislative Effectiveness" (LEGEFF) variable in Banks's Cross-National Time Series Data (Banks 2007). This was an ordinal variable ranging from 0 (no legislature exists) to 3 (effective legislature, with "significant governmental autonomy"), which I inverted.

Lawmaking Powers is an ordinal variable (range: 0–9) adding together three indices each scored 0–3: (a) The size of the legislative majority required to override a presidential veto. 0 = no veto; 1 = simple or absolute majority override; 2 = qualified majority of two-thirds or more required to override, but president cannot veto in some policy areas; 3 = qualified majority of two-thirds or more required to override. (b) The strength of

255

executive authority to issue presidential decrees with the force of law (Carey and Shugart 1998). 0 = no decree authority; 1 = president has delegated decree authority (DDA) only, or both Congress and the president can issue decrees with force of law, or the constitution is ambiguous as to whether decrees are laws or regulations; 2 = president has constitutional decree authority (CDA) with explicit limitations, or decrees are easily reversible by Congress; 3 = president has CDA with few/no limits. (c) The range of policy issues over which only the president has the exclusive right to introduce legislation. 0 = none, or not specified by constitution, or president has exclusive introduction rights only for the annual national budget; 2 = president has exclusive introduction rights for the annual national budget, which Congress cannot increase, *or* president has exclusive introduction rights to budget as well as in other policy areas; 3 = president has exclusive introduction rights for the annual national budget, which Congress cannot increase, *and* president has exclusive introduction rights in other policy areas. Sources: Shugart and Carey 1992; Mainwaring and Shugart 1997; Carey and Shugart 1998; Henisz 2000; Kim 2004; author's interpretation of constitutional texts (Constitution Finder, n.d.; Political Database of the Americas, n.d.).

Partisan Balloting is an ordinal variable (range: 0–6) adding together three electoral system traits, each scored 0–2: (a) The degree to which ballot access and the ordering of candidates is controlled by party leaders. 0 = parties control neither access nor order; 1 = parties control access but not order; 2 = parties control both access and order. (b) Whether voters vote for parties, candidates, or both. 0 = voters vote for one individual candidate; 1 = voters can vote for a party or a candidate (as in open and flexible lists), or a vote for party and candidate are observationally equivalent (as in single-member districts), or voters have multiple votes for multiple candidates; 2 = voters have one vote for a party. (c) Whether votes cast for one candidate on a party list also accrue ("pool") to some/all of the other candidates from the same party within a given electoral tier or district. 0 = no pooling across candidates; 1 = pooling across some but not all members in a district, or across fewer than 5 percent in a tier; 2 = pooling across all members in a district. Sources: Shugart and Carey (1995); Wallack, Gaviria, Panizza, and Stein (2003); Johnson and Wallack (2006); author's own corrections. Ordinal scores for each of the components are sometimes calculated as weighted averages to account for mixed-member electoral systems.

Legislative Majority is an ordinal variable gauging executive control of the lower house. 0 = a party or parties other than the president's controls the median and the veto legislator; 1 = president's party controls the veto legislator but another party has the support of the median legislator; 2 = the president's party lacks a majority itself but has the support of both the veto and the median legislator; 3 = the president's party holds a majority of seats. Source: author's adaptation of Negretto 2006.

Concurrent Elections is a binary variable. Legislative elections held concurrently with a single-round, first-past-the-post (plurality) vote for the executive are considered here to be concurrent (= 1). All other arrangements—majority runoff presidential elections, midterm legislative elections, or any system in which the president and all lower-house legislators are not elected on the same day—are coded nonconcurrent (= 0). Sources: Mainwaring and Shugart 1997; author's own elaboration.

Cabinet Autonomy is an ordinal variable, an index of president-parliamentarism inverted so that higher scores indicate greater executive independence vis-à-vis interbranch survival. In order of increasing presidential power: 0 = allows unrestricted legislative censure of president's ministers, leading to their dismissal; 1 = legislature can censure, leading to ministers' dismissal, but censure also permits president to dissolve the assembly and call for new legislative elections; 2 = legislative censure of ministers is limited, ineffective, or nonbinding; 3 = no constitutional mechanism for censure of ministers by assembly. Sources: author's coding of constitutional texts (Political Database of the Americas n.d.; Constitution Finder, n.d.); also Shugart and Carey 1992.

Bicameral Legislature is a binary variable. A legislature is bicameral (= 1) if it features, by constitutional design, two legislative chambers. Otherwise, coded as unicameral (= 0). It is not necessary that both chambers be elected, or have equal powers and responsibilities granted by the constitution, to be coded as bicameral. Sources: Henisz 2000; author's own elaboration.

Rule of Law is an ordinal variable (range: 0–6), the "Law and Order" index created by PRS, a political risk analysis firm, for its affiliated *International Country Risk Guide*. This additive index has two equally weighted components, each on a 0–3 scale: "The Law sub-component is an assessment of the strength and impartiality of the legal system, while the Order sub-component is an assessment of popular observance of the law" (The PRS Group 2004).

Electoral Movement is a binary variable. A president's political organization is coded as an electoral movement (= 1) if it (a) was created
for the explicit purpose of launching a particular presidential candidate;
(b) is personalistic in its orientation (following the criteria deployed by
Coppedge 1997); and (c) has an ad hoc or nonexistent organizational
structure. All others are considered to be parties (= 0). A president who
formerly belonged to an established party but split off to run for and successfully win the presidency with a personalistic group is coded as an electoral movement president. Presidents elected with an organized party that
they only later split from are coded as party-supported for that term.
Presidents who are personalistic in their leadership style but who have a
stable, autonomous party organization behind them are coded as party-
supported. Electoral movements that develop into organized parties (e.g.,
after the departure of a founding leader) are thereafter coded as parties.
In 1985–2004, 12 percent of all sitting Latin American presidents (by
country-year) hailed from an electoral movement.

National Wealth is GDP per capita, adjusted for Purchasing Power
parity (PPP), in constant 2005 international dollars. *Economic Growth* is
the annualized rate of growth in GDP. Sources for economic variables:
The World Bank Group, World Development Indicators.

Notes

1. Introduction

1. See Hauriou (1916), cited in Gray (2010, 126).

2. See, for example, Linz (1990), Shugart and Carey (1992), Mainwaring and Shugart (1997), Carey and Shugart (1998), Shugart (1998), and many others cited throughout this book.

3. See foundational works by Lijphart (1984; 1999); March and Olsen (1989); and Douglass North (1990).

4. For Moreno, Crisp, and Shugart (2003), "horizontal exchange" is contingent upon the functionality of the legislature's own "vertical accountability"—its responsiveness to voters and citizens. For a dissenting view, and a valuable dissection of the concept of horizontal accountability, see Kenney 2003b.

5. See Huntington (1968), Dahl (1971), Anderson (1974), Linz and Stepan (1996), Zakaria (1997), O'Donnell (1999b). For an excellent overview, see Remmer (1997).

6. Sectors in which the CTP dominated in the 1960s included dockworkers and stevedores, sugarcane workers in the APRA stronghold of the North Coast, white-collar office workers, bus and taxi drivers, textile workers, hotel and restaurant employees, fisheries workers, and miners (Payne 1965).

7. Benavides had earlier served as provisional president in 1914–1915.

8. The main text of the 1933 Constitution does not provide for a presidential veto, partial or package. However, a "Transitory Disposition," a temporary addendum to the charter, states that while the Senate is being reconstituted, the president may exercise a package veto and force Congress to reconsider a bill, with no particular qualified majority in Congress required to override it (Chirinos Soto 1997).

9. Benavides also extra-constitutionally reduced the bicameral legislature to one chamber for several years.

10. Veto override then required a three-fifths vote of Congress.

11. For explanations of the 1968 coup highlighting ideological and professional shifts within the military, see Stepan (1978) and North and Korovkin

(1981). Cotler (1975) and Quijano Obregón (1972) instead emphasize the weakness of Peru's bourgeois class and suggest that the military served as its stand-in, executing the structural reforms required to break the power of Peru's oligarchy.

12. This was the Confederation of Revolutionary Workers of Peru (Confederación de Trabajadores Revolucionarios del Perú, or CTRP).

13. Under Velasco, many sugar plantations had been expropriated and converted from private holdings to government-sponsored cooperatives; see Alexander (2007).

14. For those who subscribe to a class-based analysis (e.g., Cotler 1978; 1983), the explanation for this pattern lies in elite consolidation of power by means of excluding, rather than incorporating, popular demands. As Cotler puts it, "Peru's dominant classes did not succeed in organizing the population around the principles of the state" (1983, 4). Other authors point to fragmented cultures and identities. In this formulation, Peru is a weak state because the nation lacks integration: the dualism of national cultures, and particularly the divide between its small coastal elite and its large indigenous population, was unbridgeable. For historical anthropologist Mark Thurner, postcolonial Peru was little more than a shift "from two republics to one divided" (1997). Finally, for Cecilia Méndez (2005), the story of Peru's weak national state is more a by-product of how history has been written than a reflection of historical reality.

15. See census data (INEI 2007); election data compiled by Tuesta Soldevilla ("Elecciones Presidenciales," n.d.).

16. AP boycotted the 1978 Constituent Assembly elections in protest of this exclusion.

17. Though an economic crisis also hit Peru in the early 1980s, the debacle of the late 1980s was much more severe: multiple years of double-digit drops in GDP per capita and annual inflation rates over 1,000 percent were unique to the latter crisis (see data reproduced in Kenney 2004, 23).

2. Beyond Formal Rules and Institutions:
Theorizing Executive and Legislative Powers

1. O'Donnell (1996) also points to the poor quality of civil and human rights, and the geographic and social heterogeneity of the rule of law, in many new democracies.

2. See O'Donnell (1999b) for a discussion of the distinct liberal, republican, and democratic components of modern representative democracies.

3. Horowitz (1990) disagrees, pointing to the "centripetal" qualities of presidentialism.

4. For Mark Jones (1995a), the problem with presidential regimes is that many of them have electoral laws that tend to produce divided governments,

while presidentialism is most effective when presidents enjoy legislative majorities or near-majorities. Suárez (1982), Diamond, Linz, and Lipset (1989), Lijphart (1990), and Linz (1994) also point to executive-legislative gridlock as a source of policy paralysis and, in some cases, instability and regime breakdown. But for the U.S. case this finding is subject to debate: Cutler (1988), Mann and Ornstein (1993), and Sundquist (1988) see divided government as "obscuring responsibility and reducing effectiveness," while Davidson (1992), Mayhew (1991), and Fiorina (1992) "have begun to challenge these well-established tenets" (Jones 1995a, 22).

5. Shugart and Carey (1992) also point to the president's authority over the cabinet: specifically, the separation or mutual dependency of assembly and cabinet survival. I operationalize this distinction in the cross-national analysis presented in chapter 6.

6. I argue in chapter 4 that organized political parties and party systems are one factor that can "lengthen the shadow of the future" and induce constitutional adherence.

7. A more recent wave of constitutional changes in the "Bolivarian" countries has raised concerns based on the expanded powers they grant to the state and the extended terms of office they offer sitting presidents.

8. The ideological proximity of parties can also be a factor, since, in the absence of an elected majority of legislators, presidents may attempt to form a majority by coalition.

9. Panebianco (1988) conceives of two interrelated (and potentially contradictory) dimensions to party institutionalization: autonomy from other organizations and institutions, and "systemness," or functional interdependence of groups within the party. Janda (1980) equates institutionalization with the acceptance—by other political actors and by the public in general—of a party as a legitimate political presence. On institutionalization more generally, Olsen (2009) highlights clarity and consensus about shared behavioral rules and ways of accessing resources within these rules.

10. For earlier, largely descriptive work on Latin American parties, see Lipset and Solari (1967); McDonald and Ruhl (1989). More recent (and more analytical) work includes Perelli, Picado, and Zovatto (1995); Mercado Gasca (1997); Alcántara Sáez and Freidenberg (2003); Luna and Zechmeister (2005); Kitschelt et al. (2010).

11. In operationalizing this last indicator, organizational strength, Mainwaring and Scully (1995) point to party discipline, loyalty of party elites, the presence of party organizations at the national and local levels, and the ability to command resources as evidence of organizational strength.

12. For an elaboration of the impact of mass media on politics in Latin America, see Coppedge (2001a) and Waisbord (2002), inter alia; on Peru in particular, see Conaghan (2005).

13. Others have employed concepts focused more on a group's orientation vis-à-vis the current political establishment. These include outsider parties (e.g., Sartori 1976; Kenney 1998) and flash parties (Converse and Dupeux 1962), as well as anti-system parties (Sartori 1976; Keren 2000) and anti–political-establishment parties (Schedler 1996).

14. Key (1964) distinguishes among three different functional conceptualizations of political parties: "party as organization," "party in government," and "party in the electorate." Aldrich (1995) prefers "party in elections" for this third conceptualization. See also Beck and Sorauf (1991).

15. Bagehot's study of English politics ([1867] 2001) separates the "dignified" and "efficient" aspects of a political system: the symbolic and ceremonial functions of government, versus selecting and overseeing the executive, representing and informing the public, and actual legislating. Friedrich (1950) divides the functions of legislatures differently, into deliberative versus representative elements. Mill's *Considerations on Representative Government* ([1861] 1905) focuses more on how legislatures express society's opinions and oversee government— and less on their initiation of laws and policies.

16. Though representation is an elusive concept (see Pitkin 1967), a working definition of *legislative* representation would be whether "legislators have the will, ability, and information to make decisions that reflect the interests and needs of society . . . [and citizens have] the will, ability, and information to transmit their needs and interests to the legislature, to evaluate the performance of legislators and their parties, and to reward or sanction their actions" (USAID 2000, 7).

17. For a traditional view, see Friedrich (1950) and Finer (1949). Wheare (1963) argued that the lawmaking power of legislatures did in fact decline in almost all of the "old" democracies of Europe during the twentieth century. Packenham (1970) took issue with assumptions about the "proper" function of a legislative assembly in his analysis of the legitimating role of Brazil's legislature under authoritarian rule.

18. By the 1960s and 70s, the U.S. Congress had arguably lost a great deal of power to federal agencies (i.e., executive bureaucracies) in the civil service reorganization and the "progressive" social reforms of the late nineteenth and early twentieth centuries. For a review of this literature, see Moe and Teel (1970); Robinson (1970).

19. Carey and Shugart (1998) argue that legislatures are more likely to choose to delegate if they are subject to bargaining problems (as a result of low party discipline, lack of information on the effects of policy choices, a bicameral legislative structure that makes decision making more costly, or the urgency and time-sensitivity of the policy issue), or if legislatures do not fear a loss of agency from delegation (as a result of convergence of interests or the ability of legislators or other actors to subsequently check the power of the executive).

Cox (1987) has theorized that legislators ceded power to cabinets in the United Kingdom in order to solve the problem of MPs abusing their control over the legislative agenda and to respond to voters becoming more interested in controlling the eventual outcome of government formation. John Huber (1995) explains why legislators also ceded power to cabinets in other parliamentary systems, based on the same sorts of information-centered models used to explain committee powers and closed rules in the U.S. legislature (see Gilligan and Krehbiel 1987; Krehbiel 1991).

20. Smulovitz and Peruzzotti (2003) posit that agents of accountability can be outside the state as well. Their examples include the media, domestic civil society organizations, and international nongovernmental and intergovernmental organizations (NGOs and IGOs).

3. Constitutions and Constitutionalism in Peru, 1985–2006

1. From Domingo García Belaunde (1996, 28), cited in Miguel Schor (n.d.).

2. Under the 1933 Constitution, any deputy could propose a motion of censure, and only a simple majority was required to approve it. Under the 1979 Constitution, a minimum of forty-five deputies (25 percent of that chamber) was required to introduce a motion of censure, and an absolute majority was needed to pass it (Chirinos Soto 1997).

3. In the 1979 Constitution, the threshold for winning in the first round was a majority of "validly cast votes" (*votos válidamente emitidos*). In 1984 that clause was interpreted by Congress to mean that blank and null votes should be counted. The 1993 Constitution explicitly clarified that spoiled or blank ballots should *not* be counted.

4. As to the question of whether the president could promulgate part of a law while sending other parts back to Congress, the practice is controversial, but the 1993 Constitution has been interpreted as more permissive than the 1979 Constitution (since bills now have the status of law as soon as they are initially approved by the Congress). See Chirinos Soto (1997); Delgado-Guembes (2005).

5. The 1979 Constitution also prohibited Congress from attaching unrelated riders to budget bills. The 1993 Constitution makes no mention of unrelated riders, but kept the 1979 rule that any transfers of credits or expenditures after the budget is approved requires a two-thirds majority in Congress.

6. However, some decrees could be classified as "secret" by the president. In such cases, he is under no obligation to notify Congress, Congress has no chance to amend or nullify the decrees, and the new safeguards on decree authority introduced in the 1993 Constitution are rendered impotent. I touch on this practice again in chapter 5.

7. With Article 118(19) of the 1993 Constitution, the legal status of CDA decrees was elevated to equal standing with actual laws—but Congress was granted the authority to modify or annul them, potentially curtailing the president's prerogative to legislate by decree (Schmidt 1998).

8. In some instances, however, even regular courts could review the constitutionality of such decrees, such as in cases of *amparo,* or "the protection of fundamental rights other than personal liberty" (Schmidt 1998, 126).

9. This was imposed by the 1995 Organic Law of the Constitutional Tribunal.

10. Similar provisions led to a constitutional crisis in Honduras in 2009.

11. For a critical view of reelection in Latin America, see Linz (1994); for a pro-reelection perspective see Naím (1994). Shugart and Mainwaring (1997) and Carey (2003a) have more balanced assessments.

12. These included Senator Jorge Torres Vallejo and deputies Alfredo Barnechea and José Barba.

13. In August 1987 six deputies and two senators from the most radical parties of the United Left coalition launched a hunger strike, trying to link the passage of the bank nationalization bill with an amnesty law allowing the release of suspected terrorists.

14. Immediately after the expropriation announcement, public opinion in Lima was split roughly evenly for and against the proposal, 41 percent to 35 percent, but by November support for the proposal was down to 34 percent and opposition surged to 59 percent (cited in Reyna 2000, 123).

15. It was also rumored that the aggressive move was spurred on by one of the banks leaking incriminating evidence of tax evasion in a real estate transaction by the president.

16. For example, the APRA stronghold of Peru's North Coast was not made into one region. Instead, each coastal department was combined with a highland department.

17. The biggest threat to the integrity of the regional elections held in 1989 and 1990 was that the format of the assemblies—and even the dates of the elections themselves—had been poorly publicized and were misunderstood by many voters.

18. In 1980–1985, Acción Popular had a majority in the Chamber of Deputies but not in the Senate. However, the AP's alliance with the Partido Popular Cristiano was rather durable (1980–1984) and gave this center-right coalition a comfortable majority in both houses.

19. Though it was hatched in anticipation of an APRA or leftist victory in 1990, the military conspiracy known as the "Green Plan" included a program for neoliberal economic reform and quasi-authoritarian government (Rospigliosi 2000).

20. Cabinets can instigate a confidence/no-confidence vote and can even tie policy-oriented legislation to such a vote, but ultimately cannot force the matter.

21. There was massive ballot tampering for preferential votes in legislative elections in the department of Huánuco, and some analysts found the overall number of blank and null votes cast nationwide to be suspicious (McClintock 1999).

22. There were also allegations that social service agencies threatened communities with withdrawal of aid benefits if they did not vote for Fujimori (Churats interview 1999). Note, however, that such accusations were also leveled at APRA in the 1985–1990 period.

23. Cases of presumed foul play in 1996–1997 included the theft of documents from the office of Magistrate Delia Revoredo followed by an aggressive tax audit of the magistrate and her husband and an armed assault against Tribunal president Ricardo Nugent, in which his bodyguard was killed.

24. Suspicious "typographical errors" then distorted the meaning of the Tribunal's ruling on Law 26657 when it was published in the government's official gazette, *El Peruano.*

25. Peruvian law requires that a designated replacement be named to a public position prior to the formal acceptance of a resignation. The two-thirds vote required for this appointment would have been difficult to reach in Congress, even if Fujimori had wished to do so.

26. A less explicit law, passed earlier that year, erected similar barriers to citizen initiatives; see Conaghan (2005).

27. A minimum of 1.2 million signatures was required for the initiative to go forward.

28. According to Article 78 of the American Convention of Human Rights, a signatory state must give one year's advance notice prior to repudiating the treaty and its jurisdiction, and remains responsible for all cases of violations prior to the effective date of withdrawal from the treaty.

29. This section is based largely on my experiences as director of political analysis for a joint National Democratic Institute–Carter Center election observer mission from January through July 2000. The collected findings of this mission have been published; see National Democratic Institute/Carter Center (2000).

30. Eduardo Stein, the head of the OAS observer mission, had the impression that "something very sinister is going on" (cited in Schmidt 2002, 351). Reports from observer groups such as Transparencia and the Carter Center/ NDI were also skeptical.

31. Armed with these parallel vote tabulations, several foreign governments (including the United States) and international organizations applied pressure that may have deterred the use of fraud to win in the first round. While election officials were still counting votes, John Hamilton, the U.S. ambassador to Peru, told reporters: "It is our expectation, based on our high level of confidence in Transparencia and the scientific method of the quick count, that there will be a second-round election" (Rotella 2000).

32. A full catalog of the *vladivideos,* with transcription, is available at http://www2.congreso.gob.pe/sicr/diariodebates/audiovideos.nsf/indice.

33. Resolution 007-2000-CR repealed resolutions 002-1997-CR, 003-1997-CR, and 004-1997-CR. This required only a simple majority, as opposed to the two-thirds majority needed to appoint new magistrates to the Tribunal.

34. Reforms were passed on Oct. 5, during the First Ordinary Legislature of 2000, and then ratified on Nov. 2, the opening session of the Second Ordinary Legislature (which usually begins two or three months later but was rescheduled by congressional resolution).

35. These were based on Peru's twenty-four departments, plus the province of Callao. Votes cast by Peruvians abroad would be counted in the department of Lima.

36. Also, gender quotas for party lists—first introduced in 1997—were increased from 25 percent to 30 percent. See Schmidt (2003).

37. A full draft of the revised constitution under consideration, along with the approval status of each article, is available at http://www.congreso.gob.pe/comisiones/2002/debate_constitucional.htm.

38. One reform affecting legislative-executive relations in particular was that raising the number of votes required to "vacate" the presidency to eighty (*El Comercio,* May 4, 2004). On December 1, 2003, the Constitutional Tribunal ruled that motions to vacate the president should be passed by a qualified, not simple, majority, recommending a two-thirds majority of all active members. In June 2004, Congress indeed approved a resolution requiring a two-thirds majority on such motions. As I explain in chapter 5, by then Toledo was facing the very real possibility of a motion to vacate his presidency.

39. See also data compiled by Proetica, http://www.proetica.org.pe/.

40. The right abhorred the commission's critique of Peru's military, its refusal to refer to armed insurgents only as "terrorists," and its supposed leftist slant (Rey Rey n.d.). But the CVR was also criticized from the left for failing to include even one indigenous Peruvian among its commissioners (see García and Lucero 2008).

41. One intelligence chief (César Almeyda) turned out to be a Montesinos ally; another (Daniel Mora) was caught conspiring to bring down the interior minister; still another (Ricardo Arboccó) resigned after just two days when the public learned that he had long-standing corruption charges pending against him (Serrano Torres 2006).

42. One of the legislature's justifications for taking such extreme action was that the renewal of the three magistrates' terms in December 2001 was unconstitutional—so at least one of those two episodes was indeed against the rules.

43. However, public opinion polls indicated that Peruvians continued to have very low levels of trust in their judiciary. In a June 2005 survey, only 14 per-

cent of Lima residents expressed confidence in their judicial system (Grupo de Opinión Pública de la Universidad de Lima 2005).

44. Congress finally named a permanent *defensora,* former prime minister Beatriz Merino, in 2005.

45. Some NGO leaders then made the leap to prominent positions within the state. For example, Cecilia Blondet of Transparencia and the Instituto de Estudios Peruanos was named minister for women and human development in 2002; Rudecindo Vega, formerly of Transparencia, held high-level positions in ONPE and in several cabinet ministries and then served as housing minister in 2005–2006.

46. Toledo, at long last, legally recognized his daughter in October 2002 (*New York Times,* Dec. 6, 2002).

47. One recommended immediately "vacating" the president; another, suspending Toledo from office while a criminal investigation was launched; and a third suggested letting the president finish his term but banning him from public office for ten years thereafter.

48. Though Congress opted not to sanction the president, the scandal did not fade away. His sister, Margarita Toledo, remained under house arrest almost continuously from January 2005 to February 2006 (agenciaperu.com, Aug. 12, 2005; *El Comercio,* Feb. 25, 2006). And once Toledo left office and lost his presidential immunity, criminal charges were filed against him, his sister, and thirty-four others (*El País,* Dec. 22, 2006).

4. Party Organizations and Electoral Movements in Peru, 1985–2006

1. Originally published in *El Comercio*; cited by Sanborn and Panfichi (1997, 41).

2. On party origins in Peru, see Payne 1965; Klaren 1973; North 1975; Huber Stephens 1983; Rojas Samanez 1987; Sanborn 1991; Graham 1992; Cameron 1994; Tanaka 1998; Planas 2000.

3. Panebianco (1988, 53) called these "pure charismatic parties."

4. For the 2000 elections each list had to have at least 25 percent women; in 2003 this quota was raised to 30 percent for both men and women (Schmidt 2003).

5. A single, mandatory preferential vote was used to elect the 1978 Constituent Assembly but was not used in the 1980 general elections. The double optional preferential vote was instituted with the 1984 revisions to electoral procedures, embodied in Law 23903. In 2005 Congress debated eliminating the preferential vote but ultimately did not.

6. Alvarado Dodero interview 2007; Solari de la Fuente interview 2007, inter alia. An additional effect of the double preferential vote in particular is

that candidates tend to pair up for their campaigns, to save money on ads and events and to defend their votes against intralist fraud at the polls.

7. As per Ley 28617, passed in 2005, to hold any seats won in the 2006 elections a party had to win either five seats across more than one district or 4 percent of the vote nationally. For all subsequent elections the threshold was to be six seats or 5 percent nationally.

8. Carey (2003b) argues that electronic roll-call voting may have helped to unravel the pro-Fujimori legislative coalition in 2000.

9. In 1962, at least twenty thousand signatures were required; by the 1985 elections, it was a hundred thousand.

10. Tougher prior requirements had led many groups to use paid signature collectors and, in some cases, commit forgery.

11. The 2003 LPP initially set this alternate threshold at just one seat. However, a subsequent 2005 law (Ley 28617) raised the seat threshold to six seats across more than one district for all elections after 2006, though it temporarily lowered the vote threshold to maintain party registration to just 4 percent nationally for the 2006 elections. All parties entering into an alliance would get to keep their registration if their cumulative votes topped the threshold, no matter how poorly any individual party had performed.

12. On compliance with these rules, see Transparencia, *Boletín 3,* June 2005.

13. This article has (as of July 2010) never been applied, though in June 2010 President García's cabinet debated using it to exclude pro-Fujimori parties in 2011.

14. The law requires politicians to resign their current position at least five months prior to registering as an official election candidate for another party, but it is unclear whether this even applies to legislative candidates "invited" onto party lists (Sánchez Pinedo interview 2007). A stronger version of the bill, not adopted by Congress, would have immediately stripped any party-switching politician of his or her position (Transparencia, *Datos* 9, April 2003).

15. On financial compliance, see reports of the ONPE's Gerencia de Supervisión de Fondos Partidarios archived at http://www.web.onpe.gob.pe/fondospartidarios.php.

16. In addition to party functionaries and leaders of civil society organizations, I interviewed a sample of top congressional candidates (by ballot position, not vote results) from 1985, 1990, 1995, and 2001. The 1985 and 1990 samples include both upper and lower house candidates. In multidistrict elections, I covered Lima, Cusco, and La Libertad.

17. COOPOP was originally created by Acción Popular but was maintained by García.

18. A few APRA politicians continued, years later, to deny the existence of a deal (Alvarado Contreras interview 1999; Valle Riestra interview 1999). While

the arrangement certainly fell short of a formal pact or coalition, analysts (e.g., Kenney 2004) and many protagonists (Alarcón Bravo interview 1999; Arroyo interview 1999; Jara Ladrón interview 1999; Letts Colmenares interview 1999) agree that APRA cooperated with Fujimori on a range of issues (including keeping Fujimori in office) during his first fifteen months and that this cooperation vanished once García's impeachment was settled. According to one APRA senator from the 1990–1992 period, though, the deal with Fujimori to shield García from prosecution was never formalized or even discussed; it was quietly orchestrated by a small nucleus of the party leadership (Alarcón Bravo interview 1999).

19. At the time of the 1989 IU party congress, independent IU-affiliated leftists constituted approximately one-third of IU membership but only 15 percent of delegates (Ames Cobián interview 1999).

20. A portion of union dues in the CGTP, Peru's largest labor federation, went indirectly to the PCP; PCP militants also made additional voluntary contributions (Del Prado Chávez interview 1999). For SUTEP, the teachers' union, in the mid-80s there was virtually no organizational or financial differentiation between the union and the PCP–Patria Roja party (Tanaka 1998; Grompone interview 1999). PUM parties had strong ties to urban neighborhood groups, mine workers, and peasant movements (Dammert Egoaguirre interview 1999; Mohme Llona interview 1999). Peasant cooperatives also contributed to other parties in the IU coalition, and their leaders sometimes hedged their bets by supporting more than one member party at a time (Churats interview 1999).

21. The fate of Chile's Salvador Allende loomed large for Barrantes (Cameron 1994).

22. There was also a strategic reason for PPC to quit the coalition, namely to distance itself from AP prior to upcoming elections in which they would be running separate candidates.

23. AP politicos and high-level bureaucrats gave the party 10 percent of their salary in 1980–1985.

24. The traditional parties of the right did not have formal ties to organizations of the country's economic elite, which in 1984 formed a nonpartisan business association, CONFIEP (Confederación Nacional de Instituciones Empresariales Privadas, National Confederation of Private Business Institutions) (Tanaka 1998; Amiel Meza interview 1999).

25. They were joined by SODE (Solidaridad y Democracia, or Solidarity and Democracy), a small group of Lima-based technocrats that ran candidates with APRA in 1985.

26. Belaúnde and Bedoya both refused, insisting on Vargas Llosa as the candidate.

27. It was rumored that, in some districts, Belmont's campaign got more spontaneous write-ins (counted as null) than groups actually on the ballot got votes (Mohme Llona interview 1999).

28. By the second-round runoff, others—including APRA and public-sector unions—also threw their support behind Fujimori in an effort to stave off the neoliberal "shock" program that his opponent Vargas Llosa was promising (Baffigo interview 1999).

29. Evangelicals were also disappointed that Fujimori reneged on promises to move toward equalizing the legal standing of Peru's Catholic and Protestant denominations.

30. TV sets were rare in the late 1970s. By 1998, 25 percent of urban households owned a television, and urban and rural Peruvians who did not own sets nonetheless had opportunities to watch TV in social settings or public venues (Webb and Fernandez Baca 1999).

31. "Letterhead" lists (per Planas 1997) and the provinces or districts where they ran include Fuerza 95 (Oroya), Municipio 95 (Puno), Desarrollo 94 (Cusco), Frontera 96 (Tumbes), Romero 95 (Cieneguilla); Cambio y Desarrollo (Piura, Huaraz, Tumbes); Cambio y Mayoría (Pisco and Pucallpa); Cambio Chimbote 95, Juventud Cambio 95 (both in Chimbote); Rumbo al Cambio (Cusco); Movimiento por el Cambio (Lurín).

32. The other hundred and ten candidates were: forty-nine sitting C-90/NM *congresistas,* three other C-90 politicians, six *congresistas* who defected from other groups, twenty-four former state functionaries, ten new candidates recruited by Fujimori and Montesinos, and eleven nominal "independents" (Planas 2000, 360).

33. Though García formally resigned from APRA in August 1994 in the hope of improving the party's image for the 1995 elections, he continued to hold de facto control over the party, with most key positions occupied by García confidantes.

34. The law does not specify which race should be used as the 5 percent benchmark for maintaining official party status. APRA received 7 percent of the vote in legislative elections but only 4 percent in presidential elections and was required to reenroll.

35. The SUTEP teacher's union collected signatures to register Movimiento Nueva Izquierda (New Left Movement)—a new UNIR—but did not make the deadline for 2000.

36. The connotation of the name is "potential," achieving all that is possible for Peru.

37. Henry Pease (PP) had spent decades in politics with a variety of left parties and then with the UPP. Doris Sánchez (PP) was a former vice rector at the Universidad Nacional Mayor de San Marcos, Peru's oldest and largest university. Fausto Alvarado (FIM) was the head of a *fútbol* club in Huaral. David Waisman (PP) was head of the small business section of SNI (the National Association of Industries). José Taco (PP) owned radio stations in Cusco and surrounding areas. Cecilia Tait (PP) was a famous volleyball player. Susana Higuchi (FIM), of course, is a former First Lady, Fujimori's ex-wife.

38. Right-wing figures associated with Fujimori, e.g., RN's Rafael Rey, were so polarizing that they kept low profiles and stayed away from Flores (Rey Rey interview 2007).

39. Hildebrandt did not win her seat in April 2001 but was next in line by vote tally when Luz Salgado was charged with corruption and expelled from Congress in August 2001.

40. ONPE results listed seventeen national-level groups, though JNE registration data listed nineteen.

41. An additional 16.5 percent of provincial mayors elected in 2002 were from movements that ran candidates in some or all provinces within the same department.

42. While this more experienced group of politicians enjoyed great success at the polls, they were not initially given the same voting rights within the embryonic PP party structure as other members of Congress (Solari de la Fuente interview 2007).

43. The next secretary general would oversee the selection of PP's 2006 congressional lists, so there was a lot at stake for legislators and other potential candidates among the delegates.

44. For details see http://www.institutodegobierno.usmp.edu.pe.

45. Mulder was put in charge of internal party organizing, while del Castillo was responsible for APRA's relations with other parties and groups.

46. See interview with both Humala parents, "El Patriarca," Peru.com, Jan. 8, 2005.

47. One of Fujimori's former economy ministers, Carlos Boloña, launched his own electoral movement (Solución Popular) that year, but it was not formally tied to Fujimori.

48. A 1995 *Imasen* poll in Lima showed that 65 percent of voters had no affinity for any political party or movement; a 2003 *Datum* poll in Lima had a nearly identical figure, 66 percent.

5. Echo Chamber? The Decline and Rise of Peru's Legislature, 1985–2006

1. Legislators who were also vice presidents or served for a time as ministers are counted here as legislators.

2. Because he had been cashiered from the military and worked directly with Fujimori on military and nonmilitary issues, Montesinos is categorized as executive, not military.

3. This last function is described by the Spanish terms *fiscalización,* or *control político,* both of which are constitutionally ascribed to Peru's legislature.

4. On whether a bicameral legislature is stronger or weaker vis-à-vis the executive than a unicameral legislature, see chapter 6.

5. One difference is that under the 1979 system, there were additional layers of interchamber commissions and governing bodies as well.

6. Prior to 1992 the Senate also had a body called the Junta de Portavoces.

7. The fifteen *comisiones ordinarias* specified in the 1995 congressional regulations are Constitution and Regulation of Congress; Labor and Social Security; Health, Population, and Family; Education, Culture, and Sport; Justice; Human Rights and Pacification; Economy; Budget and General Accounts; Foreign and Interparliamentary Relations; Political and Economic Decentralization; National Defense and Internal Order; Tourism, Telecommunications, and Infrastructure; Agriculture, Environment, and the Amazon Region; Supervision/Accountability; Energy, Mines, Fisheries, Industry, and Commerce.

8. Some of the original fifteen were split into more focused committees: e.g., Industry and Commerce was separated from Energy, Mines, and Fisheries. Wholly new committees included Constitutional Accusations, Indigenous Affairs, Science and Technology, Prevention of Abuses of Authority, Women's Affairs and Human Development, Small and Micro-Enterprise, Legislative Simplification, and Regulatory Reform.

9. Epstein and O'Halloran (1999) doubt that legislatures in new presidential democracies will ever have the capacity for sophisticated policy analysis; lawmaking will continue to be dominated by the executive. Others now see legislative committees in Latin America as gaining strength and worthy of scholarly attention (Finocchiaro and Johnson 2005).

10. Delgado-Guembes (1992) presents a dissenting opinion, emphasizing that in the 1980s and early 1990s committees would spend a lot of time putting together *dictamenes* (resolutions regarding legislative projects), the majority of which were never put on the legislative agenda and were automatically shelved at the end of the legislative period.

11. Note that fifteen of the twenty-two CIP staff in 2003 were hired with aid money from the U.S. Agency for International Development; see CIP 2005.

12. Standing committees also launched 179 congressional investigations and were charged by the legislature to undertake 55 more, as I discuss below.

13. The *comisión* later agreed to limited decree authority in specific areas of tax policy.

14. In most cases, the count is of laws (*leyes*) and legislative resolutions (*resoluciones legislativas*) but not decrees or congressional resolutions (*resoluciones legislativas del congreso*). In Table 5.2, the two different tallies from Delgado-Guembes (1992) are, respectively, without (*a*) and with (*b*) legislative resolutions. Pease García (1999) likely mixes executive decrees in with some tallies but not others, so this particular source (*c*) should be used with caution; his totals for the 1990–1992 period were so far off of other sources that I exclude them here, but Pease García (2006) data on 1995–2006 appear to be much more accurate. Likewise, García Montero has a total of 1,468 laws passed in 1995–2000 and 440

passed in 2000–2001; this either includes decrees and/or congressional resolutions or is an error. Where possible, only data from the same source in any given period are used to calculate percentages. For 1995–2006, the laws initiated by the executive were calculated from Congress's online archives, counting all executive bills leading to laws with a final status of "passed" and "published" (*promulgado ley, publicado ley*). Finally, note that the 2000–2001 data includes legislation passed under both Presidents Fujimori (34 laws) and Paniagua (139 laws).

15. This is consistent with other accounts of García's rapprochement with the left as public opinion, too, trended leftward in the mid-1980s (Graham 1992; Planas 2000).

16. *Decretos-leyes,* the laws issued in 1992 while there was no legislature, should not be confused with *decretos legislativos,* which result from congressionally delegated decree authority (DDA).

17. One might also argue that multiple electoral districts tied legislators' future electoral success to generating bills for their constituents, but as I demonstrate in this chapter, *proyectos* in 2001–2006 were seldom regionally focused.

18. Note that the periodization and numbers of laws in this table differ slightly from Table 5.2 and that data do not include the final six months of the Toledo presidency.

19. See below for further analysis of budgets and the use of supplementary credits.

20. See Article 210 of the 1979 Constitution and Article 117 of the 1993 Constitution.

21. Ministers and their staff are often the intellectual authors of legislation introduced by the executive. Also, all laws introduced by Peru's president must be countersigned by one or more ministers, and all decrees with the status of law (whether constitutionally delineated or delegated by the legislature) must be approved by the full cabinet.

22. There are no fixed cabinet periods in Peru. Each president since 1980 has, on average, appointed roughly one cabinet per year, though specific cabinets have lasted anywhere from three to twenty-eight months.

23. There were several reasons for the move, including clashes with Prime Minister Dañino and breaking scandals (e.g., Sánchez had hired family members and PP cronies). But Toledo also did it because he felt vulnerable in Congress and wanted to send three key leaders out of the executive and back into the legislature. This speaks volumes about the legislature's newfound importance as a political arena. Ironically, these three ministers turned the PP parliamentary caucus against the newly composed cabinet, insisting that they stick to the previous *plan de gobierno* (strategic plan) and keep all the PP partisans they hired on staff (Vargas León n.d., 37–38).

24. In this same period Toledo's chief of staff (*secretario general del palacio de gobierno*), Guillermo Gonzáles Arica, was forced by PP legislators to resign.

25. This would essentially have converted Peru from a largely presidential (or weakly president-parliamentary) system to a premier-presidential system, in Shugart and Carey's terms (1992). Among the most prominent proponents of the idea were UN's Lourdes Flores and the political editor of major news daily *El Comercio,* Juan Paredes Castro.

26. Ministers objected first to Toledo's acquiescence to regional coca legalization in Cusco and then to the appointment of FIM chief Olivera as minister of foreign relations.

27. The count is of discrete individuals per ministry per cabinet period. If the same person stays in the same ministry after a cabinet shuffle or is renamed to the same ministry after a hiatus, he is counted once; if a minister moves to head a different ministry, she is counted twice. Positions included in the analysis are prime minister and ministers of agriculture, economy/finance, education, energy/mines, industry/trade/tourism, justice, fisheries/production, presidency, foreign relations, health, labor/social promotion, transportation, and women/development. The Defense Ministry (not headed by civilians in the 1980s and 1990s) and some ministries that were created, split up, or closed within the period under analysis have been omitted. President Toledo broke with tradition and began appointing civilian defense ministers in 2001. Two of Toledo's defense ministers were members of Congress, so including this ministry in the table would further accentuate the increased linkages between cabinet and legislature in 2001–2006.

28. They were Gloria Helfer Palacios (IU) at the Ministry of Education, Carlos Amat y Leon (IS) at Agriculture, and Fernando Sánchez Albavera (IS) at Energy/Mines.

29. Javier Silva Ruete was named minister of economy and finance, and Allan Wagner was named minister of foreign relations.

30. Two caveats are in order. First, Pease García (1999) organizes data by calendar year, while Pease García (2006) does so by legislative year, so up to eight of the investigations attributed to 1990–1992 may be from the 1985–1990 period, and one attributed to 1993–1995 may in fact be from 1995–2000. Second, investigations done by the standing committees can be requested verbally without a formal motion, so the number of investigations as a proportion of motions is not a precise accounting of how active the legislature was in investigating the executive but does offer a close approximation.

31. Delgado-Guembes (1992) has total figures that differ slightly from Table 5.6 but nonetheless point to a large number of investigations in 1985–1990.

32. Pease García (2006, 95) notes a loophole. A 50 percent majority is still required to introduce a motion; a determined majority can still keep a minority from launching an investigation.

33. Javier Velásquez Quesquén served as committee president for four years, Mauricio Mulder for one year.

34. In 1995–2000, all six investigations did conclude with a report.

35. The 1986 and 1991 samples were taken by randomly selecting alphabetical sections of the (handwritten) parliamentary log of the Chamber of Deputies for both the first and the second *legislaturas ordinarias* (i.e., all of the regularly scheduled legislative sessions) for the years indicated above. The 1996 and 2002 samples were taken by randomly selecting a month during each legislative session (April 1997 and October 2002 were picked) and analyzing project summaries on Congress's website, http://www.congreso.gob.pe/. Data for the 1996 legislative year is less reliable than for 2002, as the summaries of bills are shorter and less informative.

36. Individual backbench legislators in 1995–2000 normally had four staff members paid for by the Congress: two assistants, a secretary or technician, and a driver/security guard. Officers of standing committees got additional staffers and other material resources.

6. Institutionalism and Presidential Power in Latin America

1. The Parliamentary Powers Index developed by Fish (2006; Fish and Kroenig 2009) includes a mix of formal legislative powers, bureaucratic resources, and interbranch investiture/dissolution powers.

2. On semi-presidentialism and democratic crisis/performance, see Linz 1994; Elgie 2004; Skach 2005; Kirschke 2007; Elgie and McMenamin 2008; Cheibub and Chernykh 2008. On semi-presidentialism generally, see Siaroff 2003; Elgie and Moestrup 2007. Scholarship combining lawmaking, partisan, and interbranch powers into a single analysis includes Frye 1997, Metcalf 2000, and Hartlyn and Luna 2007.

3. On the other hand, bicameralism makes more difficult the process of bargaining with the executive branch. This could decrease the credibility of promises offered by the leadership of either chamber and might lead presidents to avoid the legislative arena altogether, if possible. And where legislatures are first movers, adding a veto player would actually weaken that side.

4. For this more traditional view, see Mezey 1979; Needler 1995. For a more inclusive approach covering both high- and low-quality democracies, see Johnson and Crisp 2003; Crisp, Escobar-Lemmon, et al. 2004. For work that also includes informal institutions in Latin American politics, see Levitsky and Helmke 2006.

5. For Levitsky (2001), party institutionalization occurs along two dimensions: value infusion and behavioral routinization. Electoral movements score low on both.

6. On governing party weakness in new democracies, see Carey and Reynolds 2007.

7. For more skeptical scholarship on institutionalist theory in new democracies, see Weyland 2002; Carroll and Shugart 2005; Clark and Golder 2006.

On constitutionalism see Weingast 1997, inter alia; for Latin America, see also Monsalve and Sottoli 1998; Alberts 2009. On party organizations, see Randall and Svåsand 2001; for Latin America, see Levitsky 2001; Alcántara and Freidenberg 2003; Jones and Mainwaring 2003; Freidenberg and Levitsky 2006.

8. Too many variables were irrelevant for too many countries in the late 1970s and early 1980s, while others were not available more recently than 2002–2004. Thus, to avoid truncating the data too unevenly or having too many "empty cells," I analyzed a time period somewhat shorter than the entire post–Third Wave era.

9. Thus, the Honduras series begins in 1986, Nicaragua in 1987, Paraguay in 1989, and Panama and Chile in 1990.

10. For example, Peru did experience a democratic interruption with the April 1992 *autogolpe* but began and ended that calendar year (the time unit of the observation) with an elected legislature of sorts.

11. Borderline country-years would include Nicaragua 1987–1990, Mexico 1985–1997, and Peru itself for several years in the 1990s.

12. First, organizational capacity does not tell us what a branch of government actually does with this capacity. Second, it is challenging to distinguish trivial from nontrivial legislation in aggregate data—and as Jones (1995a) notes, systems of producing laws are too varied across countries, even within Latin America, to simply compare legislative outputs. Third, evidence of interbranch bargaining requires costly case-by-case data gathering that would make large-*n* analysis like this one rather impractical. One laudable effort to hedge against these shortcomings is the Index of Legislative Institutional Power (see García Montero 2006).

13. In Polity IV country reports, Honduras's "executive branch has traditionally dominated the legislative and judicial branches of government . . . despite recent efforts to modernize the political system," and in El Salvador "the presidentialist nature of Central American politics, along with the endemic class warfare found in these countries, have worked together to restrict the preeminence of parliaments" (see Marshall and Jaggers 2008).

14. Correlation is with Transparency International's (TI) "Corruption Perceptions Index," for the country-years in which that data is available (too few to include this variable in time-series cross-sectional analysis). See Transparency International n.d.

15. Chow tests conducted for each of three subregions indicated that Central America and the Caribbean have coefficients similar to the Andean region, but that the Southern Cone is different. However, the values of the test statistic for the Southern Cone suggested that the problem was not that it had too different an equation but rather too little variation on some of the independent variables within this region. A better test is the jackknife (or "cross-validation") procedure in which models are repeatedly reestimated, dropping one country at a time. If

one jackknifes by country, all variables that are statistically significant in a full time-series logit model maintain the sign of their coefficient, and even significance levels remain unchanged in all but two reestimations.

16. Correlation coefficients were as follows, using ordinal versions of variables: Electoral Movement and Executive Power = 0.23; Electoral Movement and Legislative Ineffectiveness = −0.06; Rule of Law and Executive Power = −0.29; Rule of Law and Legislative Ineffectiveness = −0.39.

17. With an ordinal DV, within-unit, first-order serial correlation of errors was > 0.3 for every unit and > 0.9 for several. Wooldridge tests for autocorrelation confirmed (p value = 0.000) serial correlation for both binary and ordinal DV models.

18. Breusch/Pagan Lagrangian multiplier tests for heteroskedasticity (p value = 0.000).

19. An additional decision was whether to estimate fixed effects (FE) or random effects (RE) logit models. An FE model is generally called for when there is unit-to-unit heterogeneity. However, the FE approach greatly narrows the analysis, eliminating cross-sectional effects (akin to modeling a dummy variable for each country). It also cannot estimate variables that do not change over time and has difficulty with slow- or seldom-changing variables (Beck 2008). Consequently, institutional variables—the focus of this study—present particular problems for FE models. A Hausman test comparing the coefficients from fixed and random effects models indicated that fixed effects were not necessary (p value = 1.000). Because institutional variables do not change frequently, the FE model that generated the coefficients for this test was itself problematic: groups and variables were dropped from the model because of a lack of variation. Thus, for reasons both methodological and pragmatic, I use only RE models here.

20. *Rho* is the proportion of total variance in the model contributed by unit-level variance. Though rounded to zero, the actual value of *rho* in Model 2 is 2.53e-07.

21. Most statisticians hold that any VIF under 4 or 5 is not a problem. Chatterjee, Hadi, and Price (2000) use an individual threshold of 10 and a mean VIF of "substantially larger than 1" as a combined rule-of-thumb test.

22. The negative interaction term means that negative impact of Rule of Law on Executive Strength is even stronger when that executive leads an Electoral Movement rather than an organized party and that the positive impact of Electoral Movement on Executive Strength is even stronger when Rule of Law is low.

23. Under very particular model specifications, having a legislative majority (or even a minority caucus with policy leverage) could have the predicted impact—not on either of the DVs analyzed here but on other political outcomes, such as legislative success rates or participation in legislative production. This confirms the findings of García Montero (2006). However, the mismatch

between those outcomes and the results reported here underscores the notion that legislative productivity is just one of a number of different manifestations of legislative-executive relations. What is more, in the least constrained presidentialist regimes, executives may seek to avoid the legislative nexus altogether and rely instead on executive decrees or informal political tactics.

24. Given the evidence, presented in earlier chapters, of party-switching in Peru—and its prevalence in other Latin American countries, most notably Brazil—we might also problematize the distinction between winning a legislative majority at the polls and gaining or losing one afterwards.

25. This observation also raises the methodological problem of endogeneity: the causal arrow between dependent and independent variables may also be reversed. However, "process tracing" the case of Peru as I did in earlier chapters revealed a clear direction of causality, at least in that country, from weakened parties and constitutions to a strengthened executive.

7. Conclusion: On Balance

1. The country's score in the PRS Group's 6-point "Law and Order" index, used in chapter 6 as a close proxy for constitutionalism, has declined notably. Comparing (more or less) the first and second halves of President Hugo Chávez's initial decade in power, this index averaged 3.9 out of 6 for the years 1997–2001 and just 2.2 out of 6 for the years 2002–2006.

2. Colombia's score in the PRS Group's 6-point "Law and Order" index, used in chapter 6 as a close proxy for constitutionalism, has been consistently low, averaging just 1.3 out of 6 in 1985–2004.

3. The observations in this section inform a joint research program I am undertaking with my colleague Tatiana Kostadinova, and I draw heavily on her insights here.

4. Russia's strong presidency is an exception.

5. See also Nohlen (2003; 2006).

Data Appendix

1. In the original data, for 1985–2004, 36 percent of all country-year observations scored a 7, 31 percent scored a 6, 21 percent scored a 5, and the remaining 12 percent scored in the 1–4 range ($n = 360$; mean = 5.63; standard deviation = 1.47; variance = 2.16; skewness = −1.23; kurtosis = 3.99).

References

Abad Yupanqui, Samuel, and Carolina Garcés Peralta. 1993. "El gobierno de Fujimori: Antes y después del golpe." In *Del golpe de estado a la nueva constitutión,* ed. Enrique Bernales et al. Lima: Comisión Andina de Juristas.

Abente, Diego. 1995. "A Party System in Transition: The Case of Paraguay." In *Building Democratic Institutions: Party Systems in Latin America,* ed. Scott Mainwaring and Timothy R. Scully. Stanford, CA: Stanford University Press.

Alberts, Susan. 2009. "How Constitutions Constrain." *Comparative Politics* 41 (2): 5–29.

Alcántara Sáez, Manuel, and Flavia Freidenberg, eds. 2003. *Los partidos políticos de América Latina,* 3 vols. México, DF: FCE-IFE.

Alcántara Sáez, Manuel, Mercedes García Montero, and Francisco Sánchez López. 2005. *Funciones, procedimientos y escenarios: Un análisis del Poder Legislativo en América Latina.* Salamanca: Ediciones Universidad de Salamanca.

Aldrich, John. 1995. *Why Parties? The Origin and Transformation of Party Politics in America.* Chicago: University of Chicago Press.

Alemán, Eduardo. 2004. "Presidential Success in the Legislative Arena." Paper prepared for the annual meeting of the Southern Political Science Association, New Orleans, January.

Alemán, Eduardo, and Thomas Schwartz. 2006. "Presidential Vetoes in Latin American Constitutions." *Journal of Theoretical Politics* 18 (1): 98–120.

Alemán, Eduardo, and George Tsebelis. 2005. "The Origins of Presidential Agenda-Setting Power in Latin America." *Latin American Research Review* 40 (2): 3–26.

Alexander, Gerard. 2001. "Institutions, Path Dependence, and Democratic Consolidation." *Journal of Theoretical Politics* 13 (3): 249–70.

Alexander, Robert J. 2007. *A History of Organized Labor in Peru and Ecuador.* Westport, CT: Praeger.

Ames, Rolando, et al. 2001. *Situación de la Democracia en el Perú (2000–2001).* Lima: International IDEA/Pontificia Universidad Católica del Perú.

Anderson, Perry. 1974. *Lineages of the Absolutist State.* New York: Verso.

APOYO S. A. Opinion y Mercado. Various dates. *Opinión Data* (previously *Informe de Opinión*).

Arat, Zehra F. 1991. *Democracy and Human Rights in Developing Countries.* Boulder: Lynne Rienner.

Article 19. 2006. *Time for Change: Promoting and Protecting Access to Information and Reproductive and Sexual Health Rights in Peru.* January. Archived at http://www.article19.org/pdfs/publications/peru-time-for-change.pdf.

Asociación Civil Transparencia. 2001. *¿Quién es Quién? Congreso de la República 2001–2006.* Lima: Transparencia.

Astiz, Carlos A. 1969. *Pressure Groups and Power Elites in Peruvian Politics.* Ithaca, NY: Cornell University Press.

Ausland, Aaron, and Alfonso Tolmos. 2005. *Focus on Corruption: How to Secure the Aims of Decentralization in Peru by Improving Good Governance at the Regional Level.* A Joint Policy Analysis Paper for the National Council of Decentralization and the Office of the Public Defender, Peru.

Bagehot, Walter. [1867] 2001. *The English Constitution.* New York: Cambridge University Press.

Balbi, Carmen Rosa. 1996. "El fujimorismo: Delegación vigilada y ciudadanía." *Pretextos* 9:187–223.

———. 1997. "Politics and Trade Unions in Peru." In *The Peruvian Labyrinth: Polity, Economy, Society,* ed. Maxwell Cameron and Phillip Mauceri. University Park, PA: Pennsylvania State University Press.

Ballón Echegaray, Eduardo. 2002a. "¿Habrá nuevo mapa electoral en el país?" *QueHacer* 137:8–15.

———. 2002b. "Sobre Héroes y Tumbas: El Apra en la Encrucijada." *QueHacer* 139:10–13.

———. 2005. "Cuando Caen las Sombras: El APRA en el Escenario Electoral." *QueHacer* 156:30–37.

Banks, Arthur S. 2007. Banks's Cross-National Time Series Data Archive: 1815–2005. Computer file.

Barr, Robert. 2003. "The Persistence of Neopopulism in Peru? From Fujimori to Toledo." *Third World Quarterly* 24 (6): 1161–78.

Bartolini, Stefano, and Peter Mair. 1990. *Identity, Competition, and Electoral Availability: The Stabilisation of European Electorates, 1885–1995.* Cambridge, UK: Cambridge University Press.

Beck, Nathaniel. 2008. "Time-Series—Cross-Section Methods." In *Oxford Handbook of Political Methodology,* ed. Janet Box-Steffensmeier, Henry Brady, and David Collier. New York: Oxford University Press.

Beck, Nathaniel, and Jonathan Katz. 1995. "What to Do (and Not to Do) with Time-Series Cross-Section Data." *American Political Science Review* 89 (3): 634–47.

Beck, Nathaniel, Jonathan N. Katz, and Richard Tucker. 1998. "Taking Time Seriously: Time-Series Cross-Section Analysis with a Binary Dependent Variable." *American Journal of Political Science* 42 (4): 1260–88.

Beck, Paul Allen, and Frank J. Sorauf. 1991. *Party Politics in America.* 7th ed. New York: HarperCollins.

Beck, Thorsten, et al. 2001. "New Tools in Comparative Political Economy: The Database of Political Institutions." *World Bank Economic Review* 15 (1): 165–76.

Benton, Allyson. 2005. "Dissatisfied Democrats or Retrospective Voters? Economic Hardship, Political Institutions, and Voting Behavior in Latin America." *Comparative Political Studies* 38 (4): 417–42.

Bernales Ballestros, Enrique. 1990. *Parlamento y democracia.* Lima: Constitución y Sociedada.

Blaustein, Albert, and Jay Sigler. 1988. *Constitutions That Made History.* New York: Paragon House.

Blondel, Jean, and Waldino Suárez. 1981. "Las Limitaciones Institucionales del Sistema Presidencialista." *Criterio* (Buenos Aires) (Feb.): 57–71.

Bollen, Kenneth A. 1980. "Issues in the Comparative Measurement of Political Democracy." *American Sociological Review* 45 (2): 370–90.

Brambor, Thomas, William Roberts Clark, and Matt Golder. 2006. "Understanding Interaction Models: Improving Empirical Analyses." *Political Analysis* 14 (1): 63–82.

Cameron, Maxwell. 1994. *Democracy and Authoritarianism in Peru.* New York: St. Martin's Press.

———. 1997. "Political and Economic Origins of Regime Change in Peru: The Eighteenth Brumaire of Alberto Fujimori." In *The Peruvian Labyrinth: Polity, Economy, Society,* ed. Maxwell A. Cameron and Phillip Mauceri. University Park: Pennsylvania State University Press.

Cameron, Maxwell A., Ana-Maria Blanaru, and Lesley M. Burns. 2006. "The Separation of Powers Reconsidered: Presidentialism and the Rule of Law." Paper presented at the 2006 meeting of the American Political Science Association, Philadelphia.

Campbell, Angus, et al. 1960. *The American Voter.* New York: Wiley.

Carey, John M. 1997a. "Institutional Design and Party Systems." In *Consolidating the Third Wave Democracies,* ed. Larry Diamond et al. Baltimore: Johns Hopkins University Press.

———. 1997b. "Strong Candidates for a Limited Office: Presidentialism and Political Parties in Costa Rica." In *Presidentialism and Democracy in Latin America,* ed. Scott Mainwaring and Matthew Soberg Shugart. New York: Cambridge University Press.

———. 2000. "Parchment, Equilibria, and Institutions." *Comparative Political Studies* 33 (6/7): 735–61.

———. 2003a. "The Reelection Debate in Latin America." *Latin American Politics and Society* 45 (1): 119–33.

———. 2003b. "Transparency Versus Collective Action: Fujimori's Legacy and the Peruvian Congress." *Comparative Political Studies* 36 (9): 983–1006.

———. 2006. "Recorded Voting and Accountability in the United States and Latin American Legislatures." In *Exporting Congress? The Influence of the U.S. Congress on World Legislatures,* ed. Timothy J. Power and Nicol C. Rae. Pittsburgh: University of Pittsburgh Press.

———. 2007. "Competing Principals, Political Institutions, and Party Unity in Legislative Voting." *American Journal of Political Science* 51 (1): 92–107.

Carey, John M., Frantisek Formanek, and Ewa Karpowicz. 2002. "Legislative Autonomy in New Regimes: The Czech and Polish Cases." In *Legislatures: Comparative Perspectives on Representative Assemblies,* ed. D. Roderick Kiewiet, Gerhard Loewenberg, and Peverill Squire. Ann Arbor: University of Michigan Press.

Carey, John M., and Andrew Reynolds. 2007. "Parties and Accountable Government in New Democracies." *Party Politics* 13 (2): 255–74.

Carey, John M., and Matthew Shugart. 1995. "Incentives to Cultivate a Personal Vote." *Electoral Studies* 14 (4): 417–39.

———. 1998. "Calling Out the Tanks or Filling Out the Forms?" In *Executive Decree Authority,* ed. John M. Carey and Matthew Soberg Shugart. New York: Cambridge University Press.

Carrión, Julio. 1998. "Partisan Decline and Presidential Popularity: The Politics and Economics of Representation in Peru." In *Deepening Democracy in Latin America,* ed. Kurt von Mettenheim and James Malloy. Pittsburgh: University of Pittsburgh Press.

———. 2006. "Conclusion: The Rise of Electoral Authoritarianism in Peru." In *The Fujimori Legacy: The Rise of Electoral Authoritarianism in Peru,* ed. Julio Carrión. University Park: Pennsylvania State University Press.

Carroll, Royce, and Matthew Shugart. 2005. "Neo-Madisonian Theories of Latin American Institutions." Working Paper 05'01. Center for the Study of Democracy, University of California–Irvine.

Carter, David, and Curtis Signorino. 2007. "Back to the Future: Modeling Time Dependence in Binary Data." Dept. of Political Science, University of Rochester. Unpublished ms.

Centellas, Miguel. 2008. "From 'Parliamentarized' to 'Pure' Presidentialism: Bolivia after October 2003." *Latin Americanist* 52 (3): 5–30.

Chatterjee, Samprit, Ali S. Hadi, and Bertram Price. 2000. *Regression Analysis by Example.* New York: Wiley.

Cheibub, José Antonio. 2002a. "Minority Governments, Deadlock Situations, and the Survival of Presidential Democracies." *Comparative Political Studies* 35 (3): 284–312.

————. 2002b. "Presidentialism and Democratic Performance." In *Constitutional Design: Institutional Design, Conflict Management, and Democracy in the Late Twentieth Century,* ed. Andrew Reynolds. Oxford: Oxford University Press.

————. 2007. *Presidentialism, Parliamentarism, and Democracy.* New York: Cambridge University Press.

Cheibub, José Antonio, and Svitlana Chernykh. 2008. "Constitutions and Democratic Performance in Semi-Presidential Democracies." *Japanese Journal of Political Science* 9 (3): 269–303.

Cheibub, José Antonio, Adam Przeworski, and Sebastian Saiegh. 2004. "Government Coalitions and Legislative Success under Presidentialism and Parliamentarism." *British Journal of Political Science* 34:565–87.

Chirinos Soto, Enrique. 1986. *Historia de la República.* Lima: Editores Importadores.

————. 1997. *Constitución de 1993: Lectura y Comentario.* 4th ed. Lima: Antonella Chirinos Montalbetti.

CIP (Centro de Investigación Parlamentaria). 2005. *Plan de Trabajo.* Archived at http://www.congreso.gob.pe/historico/cip/plan/Plan_Trabajo_2005.pdf.

Clark, William Roberts, and Matt Golder. 2006. "Rehabilitating Duverger's Theory: Testing the Mechanical and Strategic Modifying Effects of Electoral Laws." *Comparative Political Studies* 39 (6): 679–708.

Clarke, Kevin A. 2005. "The Phantom Menace: Omitted Variable Bias in Econometric Research." *Conflict Management and Peace Science* 22 (4): 341–52.

Close, David. 1995. *Legislatures and the New Democracies in Latin America.* Boulder: Lynne Rienner.

Collier, David, Fernando Daniel Hidalgo, and Andra Olivia Maciuceanu. 2006. "Essentially Contested Concepts: Debates and Applications." *Journal of Political Ideologies* 11 (3): 211–46.

Collier, David, and Steven Levitsky. 1997. "Democracy with Adjectives: Conceptual Innovation in Comparative Research." *World Politics* 49 (3): 430–51.

Collier, Paul. 1999. "Learning from Failure: The International Financial Institutions as Agencies of Restraint in Africa." In *The Self-Restraining State: Power and Accountability in New Democracies,* ed. Andreas Schedler, Larry Diamond, and Marc F. Plattner. Boulder: Lynne Rienner.

Collier, Ruth Berins, and David Collier. 1991. *Shaping the Political Arena: Critical Junctures, The Labor Movement, and Regime Dynamics in Latin America.* Princeton, NJ: Princeton University Press.

Colton, Timothy, and Cindy Skach. 2005. "A Fresh Look at Semipresidentialism: The Russian Predicament." *Journal of Democracy,* 16 (3): 113–26.

Conaghan, Catherine. 1995. "Polls, Political Discourse, and the Public Sphere: The Spin on Peru's Fuji-golpe." In *Latin America in Comparative Perspective: New Approaches to Methods and Analysis,* ed. Peter H. Smith. Boulder: Westview Press.

———. 1996. "The Irrelevant Right: Alberto Fujimori and the New Politics of Pragmatic Peru." Paper prepared for conference on Conservative Parties, Democratization, and Neoliberalism in Latin America, University of California–San Diego, May 31– June 1.

———. 1998. "The Permanent Coup: Peru's Road to Presidential Reelection." *LASA Forum,* Spring.

———. 2005. *Fujimori's Peru: Deception in the Public Sphere.* Pittsburgh: University of Pittsburgh Press.

Conaghan, Catherine, and James Malloy. 1994. *Unsettling Statecraft: Democracy and Neoliberalism in the Central Andes.* Pittsburgh: University of Pittsburgh Press.

Constitution Finder. n.d. Archived at http://confinder.richmond.edu.

Converse, Philip E., and Georges Dupeux. 1962. "Politicalization of the Electorate in France and the United States." *Public Opinion Quarterly* 26 (1): 1–23.

Coppedge, Michael. 1997. "A Classification of Latin American Parties." Kellogg Institute Working Paper Series, No. 24. Notre Dame, IN: University of Notre Dame.

———. 1998. "The Dynamic Diversity of Latin American Party Systems." *Party Politics* 4 (4): 547–68.

———. 2001a. "Latin American Political Parties: Political Darwinism in the Lost Decade." In *Political Parties and Democracy,* ed. Larry Diamond and Richard Gunther. Baltimore: Johns Hopkins University Press.

———. 2001b. "Party Systems, Governability, and the Quality of Democracy in Latin America." Paper prepared for presentation at the Representation and Democratic Politics in Latin America conference, Department of Humanities of the Universidad de San Andrés and the Department of Political Science of the University of Pittsburgh, Buenos Aires, Argentina, June 7–8.

———. n.d. "Electoral Reform Processes." In *Administration and Cost of Elections (ACE) Project.* Online encyclopedia. http://www.aceproject.org.

Cotler, Julio. 1975. "The New Model of Political Domination in Peru." In *The Peruvian Experiment: Continuity and Change Under Military Rule,* ed. Abraham Lowenthal. Princeton, NJ: Princeton University Press.

———. 1978. *Clases, estado, y nacion en el Peru.* Lima: Instituto de Estudios Peruanos.

———. 1983. "Democracy and National Integration in Peru." In *The Peruvian Experiment Reconsidered,* ed. Cynthia McClintock and Abraham F. Lowenthal. Princeton, NJ: Princeton University Press.

———. 1986. "Military Interventions and 'Transfer of Power to Civilians' in Perú." In *Transitions from Authoritarian Rule: Latin America,* ed. Guillermo O'Donnell, Philippe Schmitter, and Laurence Whitehead. Baltimore: Johns Hopkins University Press.

————. 1995. "Political Parties and the Problems of Democratic Consolidation in Peru." In *Building Democratic Institutions: Party Systems in Latin America,* ed. Scott Mainwaring and Timothy Scully. Stanford, CA: Stanford University Press.

Cox, Gary W. 1987. *The Efficient Secret: The Cabinet and the Development of Political Parties in Victorian England.* Cambridge, UK: Cambridge University Press.

————. 1997. *Making Votes Count: Strategic Coordination in the World's Electoral Systems.* New York: Cambridge University Press.

Cox, Gary W., and Matthew McCubbins. 1993. *Legislative Leviathan: Party Government in the House.* Berkeley: University of California Press.

Cox, Gary W., and Scott Morgenstern. 2001. "Latin America's Reactive Assemblies and Proactive Presidents." *Comparative Politics* 33 (2): 171–90.

————. 2002. "Epilogue: Latin America's Reactive Assemblies and Proactive Presidents." In *Legislative Politics in Latin America,* ed. Scott Morgenstern and Benito Nacif. Cambridge, UK: Cambridge University Press.

Crabtree, John. 1992. *Peru Under García: An Opportunity Lost.* Pittsburgh: University of Pittsburgh Press.

Crisp, Brian F., Maria C. Escobar-Lemmon, Bradford S. Jones, Mark P. Jones, and Michelle M. Taylor-Robinson. 2004. "Vote-Seeking Incentives and Legislative Representation in Six Presidential Democracies." *Journal of Politics* 66 (3): 823–46.

Cutler, Lloyd. 1988. "Some Reflections about Divided Government." *Presidential Studies Quarterly* 18:485–92.

CVR (Comisión de la Verdad y Reconciliación). 2003. "Informe Final." Archived at http://www.cverdad.org.pe/ingles/ifinal/conclusiones.php.

Dahl, Robert. 1971. *Polyarchy: Participation and Opposition.* New Haven, CT: Yale University Press.

————. 1989. *Democracy and Its Critics.* New Haven, CT: Yale University Press.

Dalton, Russell J., Scott C. Flanagan, and Paul Allen Beck, eds. 1984. *Electoral Change in Advanced Industrial Democracies: Realignment or Dealignment?* Princeton, NJ: Princeton University Press.

DATUM Internacional. Various dates. Public opinion poll data.

Davidson, Roger H., ed. 1992. *The Postreform Congress.* New York: St. Martin's Press.

Degregori, Carlos Iván. 1987. "Sendero Luminoso: El Desafío Autoritario." *Nueva Sociedad* 90:25–34.

————. 1989. *Que Difícil es Ser Dios: Ideología y Violencia Política en Sendero Luminoso.* Lima, Perú: El Zorro de Abajo Ediciones.

Delgado-Guembes, César. 1990. "El Régimen de las Comisiones Ordinarias en la Cámara de Diputados." *Revista del Foro (Colegio de Abogados de Lima)* 77 (1): 267–317.

———. 1992. *Qué Parlamento Queremos.* Lima: Cultural Cuzco.

———. 2005. "Promulgación y observación de leyes." In *La constitución comentada,* vol. 2, ed. Walter Gutiérrez. Lima: Gaceta Juridica.

Diamond, Larry. 1998. "Political Culture and Democratic Consolidation." Estudio/Working Paper 118. Madrid: Instituto Juan March.

———. 1999. *Developing Democracy: Toward Consolidation.* Baltimore: Johns Hopkins University Press.

Diamond, Larry, Jonathan Hartlyn, and Juan J. Linz. 1999. "Introduction: Politics, Society and Democracy in Latin America." In *Democracy in Developing Countries: Latin America,* ed. Larry Diamond, Jonathan Hartlyn, Juan J. Linz, and Seymour Martin Lipset. 2nd ed. Boulder: Lynne Rienner.

Diamond, Larry, Juan J. Linz, and Seymour Martin Lipset, eds. 1989. *Democracy in Developing Countries: Latin America.* Boulder: Lynne Rienner.

Diaz Cayeros, Alberto. 2006. *Federalism, Fiscal Authority, and Centralization in Latin America.* New York: Cambridge University Press.

Dietz, Henry A. 1992. "Elites in an Unconsolidated Democracy: Peru during the 1980s." In *Elites and Democratic Consolidation in Latin America and Southern Europe,* ed. John Higley and Richard Gunther. New York: Cambridge University Press.

Dietz, Henry A., and David J. Myers. 2007. "From Thaw to Deluge: Party System Collapse in Venezuela and Peru." *Latin American Politics & Society* 49 (2): 59–86.

Dix, Robert. 1989. "Cleavage Structures and Party Systems in Latin America." *Comparative Politics* 22 (1): 23–37.

———. 1992. "Democratization and the Institutionalization of Latin American Political Parties." *Comparative Political Studies* 24 (4): 488–511.

Downs, Anthony. 1957. *An Economic Theory of Democracy.* New York: Harper.

Duff, Ernest. 1985. *Leader and Party in Latin America.* Boulder: Westview Press.

Durand, Francisco. 1996. "El fenómeno Fujimori y la crisis de los partidos." *Revista Mexicana de Sociología* 58 (1): 97–120.

Duverger, Maurice. 1954. *Political Parties: Their Organization and Activity in the Modern State.* Trans. Barbara and Robert North. London: Methuen; New York: Wiley.

———. 1980. "A New Political System Model: Semi-Presidential Government." *European Journal of Political Research* 8 (2): 165–87.

Easton, David. 1965. *A Systems Analysis of Political Life.* New York: John Wiley.

Elgie, Robert. 2004. "Semi-Presidentialism: Concepts, Consequences and Contesting Explanations." *Political Studies Review* 2 (3): 314–30.

Elgie, Robert, and Iain McMenamin. 2008. "Semi-presidentialism and Democratic Performance." *Japanese Journal of Political Science* 9 (3): 323–40.

Elgie, Robert, and Sophie Moestrup, eds. 2007. *Semi-Presidentialism Outside Europe.* New York: Routledge.

Ellner, Steve, and Daniel Hellinger, eds. 2003. *Venezuelan Politics in the Chávez Era: Class, Polarization, and Conflict.* Boulder: Lynne Rienner.

Elster, Jon. 1988. Introduction to *Constitutionalism and Democracy,* ed. Jon Elster and Rune Slagstad. Cambridge, UK: Cambridge University Press.

Epstein, David, and Sharyn O'Halloran. 1999. *Delegating Powers: A Transaction Cost Politics Approach to Policy Making under Separate Powers.* New York: Cambridge University Press.

Eulau, Heinz, and Moshe Czudnowski, eds. 1976. *Elite Recruitment in Democratic Polities.* New York: Sage.

Eulau, Heinz, and Michael Lewis-Beck, eds. 1985. *Economic Conditions and Electoral Outcomes: The United States and Western Europe.* New York: Agathon Press.

Felch, Jason. 2004. "Have Peru's Press Heroes Gone Too Far?" *Columbia Journalism Review* 43 (2): 43–47.

Fenno, Richard F., Jr. 1973. *Congressmen in Committees.* Boston: Little, Brown.

Ferrero Costa, Raúl. 1993. *La democracia: En riesgo? Una respuesta constitucional.* Lima: Luis Alfredo.

Finer, Herman. 1949. *Theory and Practice of Modern Government.* New York: H. Holt.

Finocchiaro, Charles, and Gregg Johnson. 2005. "Presidential Leadership and Legislative Committees: An Exploration of Gatekeeping in Latin America." Paper presented at the Annual Meeting of the Midwest Political Science Association, Chicago.

Fiorina, Morris. 1992. "An Era of Divided Government." *Political Research Quarterly* 107:387–410.

Fish, M. Steven. 2006. "Stronger Legislatures, Stronger Democracies." *Journal of Democracy* 17 (1): 5–19.

Fish, M. Steven, and Matthew Kroenig. 2009. *The Handbook of National Legislatures: A Global Survey.* New York: Cambridge University Press.

Forment, Carlos A. 2003. *Civic Selfhood and Public Life in Mexico and Peru.* Vol. 1 of *Democracy in Latin America, 1760–1900.* Chicago: University of Chicago Press.

Foweraker, Joe. 1998. "Institutional Design, Party Systems, and Governability: Differentiating the Presidential Regimes of Latin America." *British Journal of Political Science* 28:651–76.

Franceschet, Antonio, and Pablo Policzer. 2010. "After Honduras: Constitutions and the International Promotion of Democracy." Presented at the Canadian Political Science Association conference, Montreal, June 1–3.

Freidenberg, Flavia, and Steven Levitsky. 2006. "Informal Institutions and Party Organization in Latin America." In *Informal Institutions and Democracy: Lessons from Latin America,* ed. Steven Levitsky and Gretchen Helmke. Baltimore: Johns Hopkins University Press.

Friedrich, Carl J. 1950. *Constitutional Government and Democracy: Theory and Practice in Europe and America.* Boston: Ginn.

Frye, Timothy. 1997. "A Politics of Institutional Choice: Post-Communist Presidencies." *Comparative Political Studies* 30 (5): 523–52.

Fuentes, Carlos. 1991. *The Campaign.* Trans. Alfred Mac Adam. New York: Farrar, Straus, Giroux.

Fujimori, Alberto. 1992. "Mensaje a la nación del Presidente del Perú, Ingeniero Alberto Fujimori." Unpublished speech, April 5.

Gallie, Walter Bryce. 1956. "Essentially Contested Concepts." *Proceedings of the Aristotelian Society* 56:167–98.

García, María Elena. 2005. *Making Indigenous Citizens: Identities, Education, and Multicultural Development in Peru.* Stanford, CA: Stanford University Press.

García, María Elena, and José Antonio Lucero. 2008. "Exceptional Others: Politicians, Rottweilers, and Alterity in the 2006 Peruvian Elections." *Latin American and Caribbean Ethnic Studies* 3 (3): 253–70.

García Belaunde, Domingo. 1996. "Constitutional Processes in Latin America." In *Contemporary Constitutional Challenges,* ed. César Landa and Julio Fáundez. Lima: Pontificia Universidad Católica del Perú, Fondo Editorial.

García Montero, Mercedes. 2006. "Presidentes y Parlamentos: Un análisis sobre el control de la actividad legislativa en América Latina." Ph.D. diss., Ciencia política y de la Administración, Universidad de Salamanca.

Gates, Scott, et al. 2006. "Institutional Inconsistency and Political Instability: Polity Duration, 1800–2000." *American Journal of Political Science* 50 (4): 893–908.

George, Alexander, and Andrew Bennett. 2005. *Case Studies and Theory Development in the Social Sciences.* Cambridge, MA: MIT Press.

George, Alexander, and Timothy McKeown. 1985. "Case Studies and Theories of Organizational Decision Making." *Advances in Information Processing in Organizations,* vol. 2. Greenwich: JAI Press.

Gibson, Edward L., ed. 2004. *Federalism and Democracy in Latin America.* Baltimore: Johns Hopkins University Press.

Gilligan, Thomas, and Keith Krehbiel. 1987. "Collective Decision-Making and Standing Committees." *Journal of Law, Economics, and Organization* 3:287–335.

González, Raúl. 1987. "Los olvidados." *QueHacer* 47 (June–July): 18–22.

Graham, Carol. 1991. "The APRA Government and the Urban Poor: The PAIT Programme in Lima's *Pueblos Jóvenes.*" *Journal of Latin American Studies* 23 (1): 91–130.

———. 1992. *Peru's APRA: Parties, Politics, and the Elusive Quest for Democracy.* Boulder: Lynne Rienner.

Graham, Carol, and Cheikh Kane. 1998. "Opportunistic Government or Sustaining Reform? Electoral Trends and Public Expenditure Patterns in Peru, 1990–1995." *Latin American Research Review* 33 (1): 67–104.

Gray, Christopher Berry. 2010. *The Methodology of Maurice Hauriou: Legal, Sociological, Philosophical.* New York: Rodopi.

Grupo de Opinión Pública de la Universidad de Lima. 2005. "Barometro Social: III Encuesta Anual sobre confianza en las instituciones, Lima Metropolitana y el Callao, 5–6 de noviembre del 2005." Archived at http://weblogs .elearning.ubc.ca/peru/archives/021144.php.

Gunther, Richard, and Larry Diamond. 2001. "Types and Functions of Parties." In *Political Parties and Democracy,* ed. Larry Diamond and Richard Gunther. Baltimore: Johns Hopkins University Press.

Gurr, Ted. 1990. *Polity II: Political Structures and Regime Change, 1800–1986.* Ann Arbor: Inter-University Consortium for Political and Social Research.

Hagopian, Frances. 1998. "Democracy and Representation in Latin America in the 1990s: Pause, Reorganization or Decline?" In *Fault Lines of Democracy in Post-Transition Latin America,* ed. Felipe Agüero and Jeffrey Stark. Coral Gables, FL: North-South Center Press, University of Miami.

Haines, Charles Grove. 1930. *The Revival of Natural Law Concepts: A Study of the Establishment and of the Interpretation of Limits on Legislatures with Special Reference to the Development of Certain Phases of American Constitutional Law.* Cambridge, MA: Harvard University Press.

Hardin, Russell. 1989. "Why a Constitution?" In *The Federalist Papers and the New Institutionalism,* ed. Bernard Grofman and Donald Wittman. New York: Agathon Press.

———. 1999. *Liberalism, Constitutionalism, and Democracy.* New York: Oxford University Press.

Hartlyn, Jonathan. 1998. "Latin America's Parties." *Journal of Democracy* 7 (4): 174–77.

Hartlyn, Jonathan, and Juan Pablo Luna. 2007. "Constitutional Reform in Latin America: Intentions and Outcomes." Paper presented at the Congress of the Latin American Studies Association, Montreal.

Hartlyn, Jonathan, and Arturo Valenzuela. 1998. "Democracy in Latin America since 1930." In *Latin America: Politics and Society since 1930,* ed. Leslie Bethel. New York: Cambridge University Press.

Hauriou, Maurice. 1916. "Le fondement de l'autorité publique." *Revue du droit public* 33:20–25.

Hawkins, Kirk, and Scott Morgenstern. 2000. "Cohesion of Legislators in Latin America: Patterns and Explanations." Paper presented at the 2000 Annual Meeting of the American Political Science Association, Aug. 30–Sept. 3, Washington, DC.

Henisz, Witold. 2000. "The Institutional Environment for Economic Growth." *Economics and Politics* 12 (1): 1–31.

Higley, John, and Richard Gunther, eds. 1992. *Elites and Democratic Consolidation in Latin America and Southern Europe.* New York: Cambridge University Press.

Hilliker, Grant. 1971. *The Politics of Reform in Peru: The Aprista and Other Mass Parties of Latin America.* Baltimore: Johns Hopkins Press.

Holmes, Stephen. 1999. Foreword to *Limiting Government: An Introduction to Constitutionalism,* by András Sajó. New York: Central European University Press.

Horowitz, Donald L. 1990. "Comparing Democratic Systems." *Journal of Democracy* 1 (4): 73–79.

Huber, Evelyne. 1995. "Assessments of State Strength." In *Latin America in Comparative Perspective: New Approaches to Methods and Analysis,* ed. Peter H. Smith. Boulder: Westview Press.

Huber, John. 1995. *Rationalizing Parliament: Legislative Institutions and Party Politics in France.* New York: Cambridge University Press.

Huber Stephens, Evelyne. 1983. "The Peruvian Military Government, Labor Mobilization, and the Political Strength of the Left." *Latin American Research Review* 18 (2): 57–93.

Huntington, Samuel. 1968. *Political Order in Changing Societies.* New Haven, CT: Yale University Press.

IMASEN S. A. Various dates. Public opinion poll data.

INEI (Instituto Nacional de Estadística e Informática). 2007. *Historia De Los Censos En El Perú.* http://www.inei.gob.pe/Censos2007/Documentos/Historia_Censos.pdf (accessed Sept. 30, 2009).

Inter-American Court of Human Rights. 1999. Constitutional Court Case, Competence, Judgment of September 24, 1999, (Ser. C) No. 55.

Janda, Kenneth. 1980. *Political Parties: A Cross-National Survey.* London: Macmillan.

Jochamowitz, Luis. 1993. *Ciudadano Fujimori.* Lima: Peisa.

Johnson, Gregg, and Brian Crisp. 2003. "Mandates, Powers and Policies." *American Journal of Political Science* 47 (1): 128–42.

Johnson, Joel W., and Jessica S. Wallack. 2006. "Electoral Systems and the Personal Vote." Dataset and documentation. Archived at http://dss.ucsd.edu/~jwjohnso/espv.html.

Jones, Mark. 1995a. *Electoral Laws and the Survival of Presidential Democracies.* Notre Dame, IN: University of Notre Dame Press.

———. 1995b. "A Guide to the Electoral Systems of the Americas." *Electoral Studies* 14 (1): 5–21.

Jones, Mark, and Wonjae Hwang. 2005. "Party Government in Presidential Democracies: Extending Cartel Theory Beyond the U.S. Congress." *American Journal of Political Science* 49 (2): 267–82.

Jones, Mark P., and Scott Mainwaring. 2003. "The Nationalization of Parties and Party Systems: An Empirical Measure and an Application to the Americas." *Party Politics* 9 (2): 139–66.

Karl, Terry Lynn. 1995. "The Hybrid Regimes of Central America." *Journal of Democracy* 6 (3): 72–86.

Katz, Richard S., and Peter Mair, eds. 1994. *How Parties Organize: Change and Adaptation in Party Organizations in Western Democracies.* Thousand Oaks, CA: Sage.

———. 1995. "Changing Models of Party Organization and Party Democracy: The Emergence of the Cartel Party." *Party Politics* 1 (1): 5–28.

———. 2002. "The Ascendancy of the Party in Public Office." In *Political Parties: Old Concepts and New Challenges,* ed. Richard Gunther, José Ramón Montéro, and Juan J. Linz. New York: Oxford University Press.

Kaufmann, Daniel, Aart Kraay, and Pablo Zoido-Lobatón. 2002. *Governance Matters II: Updated Indicators for 2000–01.* Washington, DC: World Bank.

Kay, Bruce H. 1995. "'Fujipopulism' and the Liberal State in Peru, 1990–1995." Duke-UNC Program in Latin American Studies Working Paper #19, December.

Keefer, Philip. 2007. DPI2006: Database of Political Institutions: Changes and Variable Definitions. Development Research Group, World Bank.

Keefer, Philip, and Stephen Knack. 1997. "Why Don't Poor Countries Catch Up? A Cross-National Test of an Institutional Explanation." *Economic Inquiry* 35:590–602.

Kenney, Charles. 1997. "¿Por qué el autogolpe?" In *Los enigmas del poder: Fujimori 1990–1996,* ed. Fernando Tuesta Soldevilla. 2nd ed. Lima: Fundación Friedrich Ebert.

———. 1998. "Outsider and Anti-Party Politicians in Power: New Conceptual Strategies and Empirical Evidence from Peru." *Party Politics* 4 (1): 57–75.

———. 2003a. "The Death and Rebirth of a Party System, Peru 1978–2001." *Comparative Political Studies* 36 (10):1210–39.

———. 2003b. "Horizontal Accountability: Concepts and Conflicts." In *Democratic Accountability in Latin America,* ed. Scott Mainwaring and Christopher Welna. New York: Oxford University Press.

———. 2004. *Fujimori's Coup and the Breakdown of Democracy in Latin America.* Notre Dame, IN: University of Notre Dame Press.

Keren, Michael. 2000. "Political Perfectionism and the 'Anti System' Party." *Party Politics* 6 (1): 107–16.

Key, V. O. 1964. *Politics, Parties, and Pressure Groups.* New York: Crowell.

Kim, James. 2004. "Revisiting Delegation of Decree Authority." Paper presented at the annual meeting of the American Political Science Association, Chicago.

Kirchheimer, Otto. 1966. "The Transformation of Western European Party Systems." In *Political Parties and Political Development,* ed. Joseph LaPalombara and Myron Weiner. Studies in Political Development 6. Princeton, NJ: Princeton University Press.

Kirschke, Linda. 2007. "Semipresidentialism and the Perils of Power-Sharing in Neopatrimonial States." *Comparative Political Studies* 40:1372–794.

Kitschelt, Herbert. 2001. "Party and Party System Dynamics in Latin America: An Inductive Comparative Exploration Prompted by the Salamanca 1997–98 Politicians' Survey." Dept. of Political Science, Duke University. Unpublished manuscript.

Kitschelt, Herbert, et al. 2010. *Latin American Party Systems*. New York: Cambridge University Press.

Klaren, Peter. 1973. *Modernization, Dislocation, and Aprismo: The Origins of the Aprista Party*. Austin: University of Texas Press.

———. 2000. *Peru: Society and Nationhood in the Andes*. New York: Oxford University Press.

Koelbe, Thomas. 1995. "The New Institutionalism in Political Science and Sociology." *Comparative Politics* 27 (1): 231–43.

Koole, Ruud. 1996. "Cadre, Catch-All or Cartel? A Comment on the Notion of the Cartel Party." *Party Politics* 2 (4): 507–23.

Kostadinova, Tatiana, and Timothy J. Power. 2007. "Does Democratization Depress Participation? Voter Turnout in the Latin American and Eastern European Democratic Transitions." *Political Research Quarterly* 60 (3): 363–77.

Krehbiel, Keith. 1991. *Information and Legislative Organization*. Ann Arbor: University of Michigan Press.

Lagos, Marta. 1997. "Latin America's Smiling Mask." *Journal of Democracy* 8 (3): 125–38.

LAN-RA. Various dates. *Latinnews,* Latin American Newsletters/Latin American Regional Reports–Región Andina.

Landa, César. 2001. "The Scales of Justice in Peru: Judicial Reform and Fundamental Rights." University of London Institute of Latin American Studies Occasional Papers, No. 24. University of London.

Lasswell, Harold D., Daniel Lerner, and C. Easton Rothwell. 1952. *The Comparative Study of Elites: An Introduction and Bibliography*. Stanford, CA: Stanford University Press.

Lawson, Kay, ed. 1980. *Political Parties and Linkage: A Comparative Perspective*. New Haven, CT: Yale University Press.

Lawson, Kay, and Peter Merkl, eds. 1988. *When Parties Fail: Emerging Alternative Organizations*. Princeton, NJ: Princeton University Press.

Leithner, Chris. 1997. "Of Time and Partisan Stability Revisited: Australia and New Zealand, 1905–90." *American Journal of Political Science* 41 (4): 1104–27.

Levitsky, Steven. 1998. "Institutionalism and Peronism: The Concept, the Case, and the Case for Unpacking the Concept." *Party Politics* 4 (1): 77–92.

———. 2001. "Organization and Labor-Based Party Adaptation." *World Politics* 54 (1): 27–56.

Levitsky, Steven, and Maxwell A. Cameron. 2003. "Democracy Without Parties? Political Parties and Regime Change in Fujimori's Peru." *Latin American Politics and Society* 45 (3): 1–33.

Levitsky, Steven, and Gretchen Helmke, eds. 2006. *Informal Institutions and Democracy: Lessons from Latin America*. Baltimore: Johns Hopkins University Press.

Levitsky, Steven, and Lucan A. Way. 2002. "Elections Without Democracy: The Rise of Competitive Authoritarianism." *Journal of Democracy* 13 (2): 51–65.

Levitt, Barry. 1998. "Parties and Politicians in Contemporary Peru: Exploring New Forms of Electoral Representation." Paper presented at the Twenty-First Congress of the Latin American Studies Association, Chicago, IL, September.

Lijphart, Arend. 1984. *Democracies: Patterns of Majoritarian and Consensus Government in Twenty-one Countries*. New Haven, CT: Yale University Press.

———. 1990. "The Political Consequences of Electoral Laws, 1945–85." *American Political Science Review* 84:481–96.

———. 1999. *Patterns of Democracy: Government Forms and Performance in Thirty-Six Countries*. New Haven, CT: Yale University Press.

Linz, Juan J. 1990. "The Perils of Presidentialism." *Journal of Democracy* 1 (1): 51–69.

———. 1994. "Presidential or Parliamentary Democracy: Does It Make a Difference?" In *The Failure of Presidential Democracy*, ed. Juan J. Linz and Arturo Valenzuela. Baltimore: Johns Hopkins University Press.

Linz, Juan J., and Alfred Stepan, eds. 1978. *The Breakdown of Democratic Regimes*. Baltimore: Johns Hopkins University Press.

———. 1996. *Problems of Democratic Transition and Consolidation*. Baltimore: Johns Hopkins University Press.

Linz, Juan J., and Arturo Valenzuela. 1994. *The Failure of Presidential Democracy*. Baltimore: Johns Hopkins University Press.

Lipset, Seymour Martin. 2000. "The Indispensability of Political Parties." *Journal of Democracy* 11 (1): 48–55.

Lipset, Seymour Martin, and Stein Rokkan. 1967. *Party Systems and Voter Alignments*. New York: Free Press.

Lipset, Seymour Martin, and Aldo Solari, eds. 1967. *Elites in Latin America*. New York: Oxford University Press.

López García, Víctor. 1986. *PAIT: Los Pobres Trabajan Para Los Pobres*. Lima: Centro de Documentación e Información Andina.

Luna, Juan Pablo, and Elizabeth Zechmeister. 2005. "Representation in Latin America: A Study of Elite-Mass Congruence in Nine Countries." *Comparative Political Studies* 38 (4): 388–416.

Lynch, Nicolás. 1998. "Crisis y perspectivas de los Partidos Políticos en el Perú." *Revista de Sociología UNMSM* 10 (11): 7–24.

———. 1999. *Una tragedia sin héroes: La derrota de los partidos y el origen de los independientes, Perú, 1980–1992*. Lima: Fondo Editorial UNMSM.

Lyne, Mona. 1997. "The Voter's Dilemma, Factions, and Strange Bedfellows, or: Why Latin American Political Parties Historically Weakened Democracy and How We Can Tell." Paper presented at the Twentieth International Congress of the Latin American Studies Association, Guadalajara, Mexico, April.

Magaloni, Beatriz. 2001. "Transition Games from Single-Party Authoritarianism: The Case of Mexico." Paper presented at conference on Advances and Setbacks in the Third Wave of Democratization in Latin America, University of Notre Dame, Notre Dame, IN, April.

Mainwaring, Scott. 1998. "Party Systems in the Third Wave." *Journal of Democracy* 9 (3): 67–81.

Mainwaring, Scott, and Timothy Scully. 1995. *Building Democratic Institutions: Party Systems in Latin America.* Stanford, CA: Stanford University Press.

Mainwaring, Scott, and Matthew Soberg Shugart. 1997. "Conclusion." In *Presidentialism and Democracy in Latin America,* ed. Scott Mainwaring and Matthew Soberg Shugart. New York: Cambridge University Press.

Mair, Peter, ed. 1990. *The West European Party System.* New York: Oxford University Press.

———. 1997. *Party System Change: Approaches and Interpretations.* Oxford: Clarendon Press.

Mallon, Florencia. 1995. *Peasant and Nation: The Making of Postcolonial Mexico and Peru.* Berkeley: University of California Press.

Mann, Michael. 1984. "The Autonomous Power of the State: Its Origins, Mechanisms, and Results." *European Journal of Sociology* 25:185–213.

Mann, Thomas, and Norman Ornstein. 1993. *Renewing Congress: A Second Report.* Washington, DC: Brookings Institution Press.

Mansfield, Harvey. 1989. *Taming the Prince: The Ambivalence of Modern Executive Power.* New York: Free Press.

March, James G., and Johan P. Olsen. 1984. "The New Institutionalism: Organizational Factors in Political Life." *American Political Science Review* 78 (3): 734–48.

———. 1989. *Rediscovering Institutions: The Organizational Basis of Politics.* New York: Free Press.

Marshall, Monty G. 2009. Personal email communication with author. January 29.

Marshall, Monty G., and Keith Jaggers. 2006. *Polity IV Project: Dataset Users' Manual.* Arlington: Polity IV Project.

———. 2008. *Polity IV Project: Political Regime Characteristics and Transitions, 1800–2007.* Version p4v2007. Computer file. Center for Systemic Peace, George Mason University, Williamsburg, VA. Archived at http://www.systemicpeace.org/polity/polity4.htm.

Mayhew, David R. 1991. *Divided We Govern: Party Control, Lawmaking, and Investigations, 1946–1990.* New Haven, CT: Yale University Press.

McCarty, Nolan. 2000. "Proposal Rights, Veto Rights, and Political Bargaining." *American Journal of Political Science* 44 (3): 506–522.

McClintock, Cynthia. 1989. "Peru's Sendero Luminoso Rebellion: Origins and Trajectory." In *Power and Popular Protest: Latin American Social Movements,* ed. Susan Eckstein. Berkeley: University of California Press.

———. 1993. "Peru's Fujimori: A Caudillo Derails Democracy." *Current History* 92 (572): 112–119.

———. 1994. "Presidents, Messiahs, and Constitutional Breakdowns in Peru." In *The Failure of Presidential Democracy,* ed. Juan J. Linz and Arturo Valenzuela. Baltimore: Johns Hopkins University Press.

———. 1998. *Revolutionary Movements in Latin America: El Salvador's FMLN and Peru's Shining Path.* Washington, DC: U.S. Institute of Peace Press.

———. 1999. "¿Es autoritario el gobierno de Fujimori?" In *El juego político: Fujimori, la oposición y las reglas,* ed. Fernando Tuesta Soldevilla. Lima: Fundación Friedrich Ebert.

———. 2006. "Electoral Authoritarian Versus Partially Democratic Regimes: The Case of the Fujimori Government and the 2000 Elections." In *The Fujimori Legacy: The Rise of Electoral Authoritarianism in Peru,* ed. Julio Carrión. University Park: Pennsylvania State University Press.

McDonald, Ronald H., and J. Mark Ruhl. 1989. *Party Politics and Elections in Latin America.* Boulder: Westview Press.

McFarland Sánchez Moreno, Maria. 2001. "When a 'Constitution' Is a Constitution: Focus on Peru." *Journal of International Law and Politics* 33:561–616.

McIlwain, Charles Howard. 1947. *Constitutionalism: Ancient and Modern.* Ithaca, NY: Cornell University Press.

McMillan, John, and Pablo Zoido. 2004. "How to Subvert Democracy: Montesinos in Peru." *Journal of Economic Perspectives* 18 (4): 69–92.

MEF (Ministerio de Economía y Finanzas del Perú). 2001. *Transparencia Económica y Fiscal: Estado de avance y tareas pendientes.* June.

Méndez, Cecilia. 2005. *The Plebeian Republic: The Huanta Rebellion and the Making of the Peruvian State, 1820–1850.* Durham, NC: Duke University Press.

Mercado Gasca, Lauro. 1997. "Visiting Party Loyalties in Latin America." Paper presented at the Twentieth International Congress of the Latin American Studies Association, Guadalajara, Mexico, April.

Metcalf, Lee Kendall. 2000. "Measuring Presidential Power." *Comparative Political Studies* 33 (5): 660–685.

Mezey, Michael L. 1979. *Comparative Legislatures.* Durham, NC: Duke University Press.

Michels, Robert. [1911] 1959. *Political Parties.* New York: Dover Publications.

Migdal, Joel. 1994. "The State in Society: An Approach to Struggles for Domination." In *State Powers and Social Forces: Domination and Transformation in the Third World,* ed. Joel Migdal, Atul Kohli, and Vivienne Shue. New York: Cambridge University Press.

Mill, John Stuart. [1861] 1905. *Considerations on Representative Government.* New York: Dutton.

Moe, R. C., and S. Teel. 1970. "Congress as Policy Makers." *Political Science Quarterly* 85:443–470.

Monsalve, Sofía, and Susana Sottoli. 1998. "Ingeniería constitucional versus institucionalismo histórico-empírico: Enfoques sobre la génesis y la reforma de las instituciones políticas." In *El Presidencialismo renovado: Instituciones y cambio político en América Latina,* ed. Dieter Nohlen and Mario Fernández B. Caracas: Editorial Nueva Socieded.

Moreno, Erika, Brian F. Crisp, and Matthew Soberg Shugart. 2003. "The Accountability Deficit in Latin America." In *Democratic Accountability in Latin America,* ed. Scott Mainwaring and Christopher Welna. New York: Oxford University Press.

Morgenstern, Scott. 2002. "Explaining Legislative Politics in Latin America." In *Legislative Politics in Latin America,* ed. Scott Morgenstern and Benito Nacif. Cambridge, UK: Cambridge University Press.

———. 2004. *Patterns of Legislative Politics: Roll-Call Voting in Latin America and the United States.* Cambridge, UK: Cambridge University Press.

———. 2006. "Limits on Exporting the U.S. Congress Model to Latin America." In *Exporting Congress? The Influence of the U.S. Congress on World Legislatures,* ed. Timothy J. Power and Nicol C. Rae. Pittsburgh: University of Pittsburgh Press.

Morgenstern, Scott, and Benito Nacif. 2002. *Legislative Politics in Latin America.* New York: Cambridge University Press.

Morón, Eduardo, and Cynthia Sanborn. 2006. *The Pitfalls of Policymaking in Peru: Actors, Institutions and Rules of the Game.* Inter-American Development Bank, Latin American Research Network, Working paper #R-511 (April).

Mueller, Dennis C. 1996. *Constitutional Democracy.* New York: Oxford University Press.

Muller, Edward, T. O. Jukam, and Mitchell Seligson. 1982. "Diffuse Support and Antisystem Political Behavior: A Comparative Analysis." *American Journal of Political Science* 26 (2): 240–64.

Muller-Rommel, Ferdinand, and Geoffrey Pridham, eds. 1991. *Small Parties in Western Europe: Comparative and National Perspectives.* Newbury Park, CA: Sage.

Munck, Gerardo, and Jay Verkuilen. 2002. "Conceptualizing and Measuring Democracy: Comparing Alternative Indices." *Comparative Political Studies* 35 (1): 5–34.

Murakami, Yusuke. 2007. *Perú en la era del chino: La política no institucionalizada y el pueblo en busca de un salvador.* Lima: Instituto de Estudios Peruanos.

Naím, Moisés. 1994. "The Second Stage of Reform." *Journal of Democracy* 5 (4): 322–48.

National Democratic Institute/Carter Center. 2000. *Peru Elections 2000: Final Report of the National Democratic Institute/Carter Center Joint Election Monitoring Project*. Washington, DC: NDI.

Navia, Patricio. 2003. "Partidos políticos como antídoto contra el populismo en América Latina." *Revista de Ciencia Política* 23 (1): 19–30.

Navia, Patricio, and Sebastián Saiegh. 2001. "Political Parties as Insurance Mechanisms for Office Seeking Politicians." Paper presented at the annual meeting of the Midwest Political Science Association, Palmer House Hilton, Chicago, April.

Navia, Patricio, and Ignacio Walker. 2010. "Political Institutions, Populism, and Democracy in Latin America." In *Democratic Governance in Latin America*, ed. Scott Mainwaring and Timothy R. Scully. Stanford, CA: Stanford University Press.

Needler, Martin. 1995. "Conclusion: The Legislature in a Democratic Latin America." In *Legislatures and the New Democracies in Latin America*, ed. David Close. Boulder: Lynne Rienner.

Negretto, Gabriel. 2006. "Minority Presidents and Democratic Performance in Latin America." *Latin American Politics & Society* 48 (3): 63–92.

Nieto Montesinos, Jorge. 1988. "¡Y el congreso de I. U. . . . va!" *QueHacer* 54 (August–September): 32–38.

Nohlen, Dieter. 2003. *El contexto hace la diferencia*. Mexico City: UNAM.

———, ed. 2006. *El institucionalismo contextualizado: La relevancia del contexto en el análisis y diseño institucionales*. Mexico City: Editorial Porrua/UNAM.

Norris, Pippa, ed. 1997. *Passages to Power: Legislative Recruitment in Advanced Democracies*. New York: Cambridge University Press.

North, Douglass. 1990. *Institutions, Institutional Change, and Economic Performance*. New York: Cambridge University Press.

North, Liisa. 1975. *Orígenes y crecimiento del Partido Aprista: El cambio socio-económico en el Perú*. Lima: Universidad Católica.

North, Liisa, and Tanya Korovkin. 1981. *The Peruvian Revolution and the Officers in Power, 1967–1976*. Montreal: Centre for Developing-Area Studies, McGill University.

Norton, Edward C., Hua Wang, and Chunrong Ai. 2004. "Computing Interaction Effects and Standard Errors in Logit and Probit Models." *Stata Journal* 4 (2): 154–67.

O'Donnell, Guillermo. 1994a. "Delegative Democracy." *Journal of Democracy* (5) 1: 55–69.

———. 1994b. "The State, Democratization, and Some Conceptual Problems." In *Latin American Political Economy in the Age of Neoliberal Reform: Theoretical and Comparative Perspectives for the 1990s*, ed. William C. Smith, Carlos H. Acuña, and Eduardo A. Gamarra. Coral Gables, FL: North-South Center, University of Miami; New Brunswick, NJ: Transaction Publishers.

———. 1996. "Illusions about Consolidation." *Journal of Democracy* 7 (2): 34–51.

———. 1999a. "Horizontal Accountability in New Democracies." In *The Self-Restraining State,* ed. Andreas Schedler, Larry Diamond, and Marc F. Plattner. Boulder: Lynne Rienner.

———. 1999b. "Polyarchies and the (Un)Rule of Law in Latin America." In *The (Un)Rule of Law and the Underprivileged in Latin America,* ed. Juan Méndez, Guillermo O'Donnell, and Paulo Sérgio Pinheiro. Notre Dame, IN: University of Notre Dame Press.

Olsen, Johan P. 2009. "Change and Continuity: An Institutional Approach to Institutions of Democratic Government." *European Political Science Review* 1 (1): 3–32.

Oppenheimer, Andres. 2000. "Slow-Motion Coup May Hit Peru." *Miami Herald,* March 5.

Ostrom, Elinor. 1995. "New Horizons in Institutional Analysis." *American Political Science Review* 89 (1): 174–78.

Packenham, Robert. 1970. "Legislatures and Political Development." In *Legislatures in Developmental Perspective,* ed. Allan Kornberg and Lloyd D. Musolf. Durham, NC: Duke University Press.

Paéz, Angel. 2009. "Fujimori oculta origen de US$15 millones que devolvió al fisco." *La República,* July 15. http://www.larepublica.pe/politica/15/07/2009/fujimori-oculta-origen-de-us-15-millones-que-devolvio-al-fisco-0 (accessed June 29, 2010).

Palmer, David Scott, ed. 1994. *The Shining Path of Peru.* 2nd ed. New York: St. Martin's Press.

———. 1996. "'Fujipopulism' and Peru's Progress." *Current History* 95 (598): 70–75.

———. 2000. "Democracy and Its Discontents in Fujimori's Peru." *Current History* 99 (634): 60–65.

Panebianco, Angelo. 1988. *Political Parties: Organization and Power.* New York: Cambridge University Press.

Pásara, Luis. 1993. "El rol del Parlamento: Argentina y Perú." *Desarrollo Económico* 32 (128): 603–24.

Pasquino, Gianfranco. 1997. "Semi-Presidentialism: A Political Model at Work." *European Journal of Political Research* 31 (1): 128–37.

Payne, James. 1965. *Labor and Politics in Peru: The System of Political Bargaining.* New Haven, CT: Yale University Press.

Payne, J. Mark, Daniel Zovatto, Fernando Carrillo Flórez, and Andrés Allamand Zavala. 2002. *Democracies in Development: Politics and Reform in Latin America.* Washington, DC: Inter-American Development Bank and the International Institute for Democracy and Electoral Assistance.

Pease García, Henry. 1994. *Los Años de Langosta: La escena política del fujimorismo.* Lima: La Voz Ediciones/IPADEL.

————. 1999. *Electores, Partidos y Representantes: Sistema electoral, sistema de partidos y sistema de gobierno en el Perú*. Lima: Pontificia Universidad Católica del Perú, Departamento de Ciencias Sociales.

————. 2006. *Por Los Pasos Perdidos: El Parlamento peruano entre el 2000 y el 2006*. Lima: Fondo Editorial del Congreso del Perú.

Pederson, Morgens N. 1983. "Changing Patterns of Electoral Volatility in European Party Systems, 1948–1977: Explorations in Explanation." In *Western European Party Systems: Trends and Prospects,* ed. Peter Merkl. New York: Free Press.

Pegram, Thomas. 2009. "Weak Institutions, Rights Claims and Pathways to Compliance: The Transformative Role of the Peruvian Human Rights Ombudsman." Paper presented at CRISE Workshop, How Can the Law Help Reduce Group-Based Inequalities? Oxford, May 14–15.

Penfold-Becerra, Michael. 2004. "Federalism and Institutional Change in Venezuela." In *Federalism and Democracy in Latin America,* ed. Edward L. Gibson. Baltimore: Johns Hopkins University Press.

Pereira, Anthony. 2000. "An Ugly Democracy? State Violence and the Rule of Law in Post-Authoritarian Brazil." In *Democratic Brazil: Actors, Institutions, and Processes,* ed. Peter R. Kingstone and Timothy J. Power. Pittsburgh: University of Pittsburgh Press.

Perelli, Carina, Sonia Picado S., and Daniel Zovatto, eds. 1995. *Partidos y Clase Politica en America Latina en los 90*. San José: IIDH.

Pérez-Liñán, Aníbal. 2005. "Democratization and Constitutional Crises in Presidential Regimes: Towards Congressional Supremacy?" *Comparative Political Studies* 38 (1): 51–74.

————. 2007. *Presidential Impeachment and the New Political Instability in Latin America*. Cambridge, UK: Cambridge University Press.

Perkins, Doug. 1996. "Structure and Choice: The Role of Organizations, Patronage and the Media in Party Formation." *Party Politics* 2 (3): 355–75.

Peters, B. Guy. 1999. *Institutional Theory in Political Science: The New Institutionalism*. New York: Pinter.

Pitkin, Hanna Fenichel. 1967. *The Concept of Representation*. Berkeley: University of California Press.

Planas, Pedro. 1997. "¿Existe un sistema de partidos en el Perú?" In *Los enigmas del poder: Fujimori 1990–1996,* ed. Fernando Tuesta Soldevilla. 2nd ed. Lima: Fundación Friedrich Ebert.

————. 1999. *El Fujimorato: Estudio político-constitucional*. Lima: Kelly.

————. 2000. *La democracia volátil: Movimientos, partidos, líderes políticos y conductas electorales en el Perú contemporaneo*. Lima: Friedrich Ebert Siftung.

Poiré, Alejandro. 2000. "Do Electoral Institutions Affect Party Discipline?" Paper prepared for the Twenty-Second Congress of the Latin American Studies Association, Miami.

Political Database of the Americas (PDBA). n.d. Archived at http://pdba .georgetown.edu.

Poole, Keith, and Howard Rosenthal. "The Polarization of American Politics." *Journal of Politics* 46:1061–79.

Power, Timothy J., and Mark J. Gasiorowski. 1997. "Institutional Design and Democratic Consolidation in the Third World." *Comparative Political Studies* 30 (2): 123–55.

Powers, Nancy. 1997. "Re-electing Neoliberals: Competing Explanations for the Electoral Success of Fujimori and Menem." Paper presented at the Twentieth Congress of the Latin American Studies Association, Guadalajara, Mexico.

Protsyk, Oleh. 2003. "Troubled Semi-presidentialism: Stability of the Constitutional System and Cabinet in Ukraine." *Europe-Asia Studies* 55 (7): 1077–95.

The PRS Group. 2004. *A Business Guide to Political Risk for International Decisions.* Syracuse: The PRS Group.

Przeworski, Adam. 2004. "Institutions Matter?" *Government and Opposition* 39 (4): 527–40.

Putnam, Robert D. 1976. *The Comparative Study of Political Elites.* Englewood Cliffs, NJ: Prentice-Hall.

Quijano Obregón, Aníbal. 1972. *Nacionalismo, neoimperialismo, y militarismo en el Perú.* Buenos Aires: Ediciones Periferia.

Quiroz, Alfonso W. 2008. *Corrupt Circles: A History of Unbound Graft in Peru.* Baltimore: Johns Hopkins University Press.

Randall, Vicky, and Lars Svåsand. 2001. "Party Institutionalisation and the New Democracies." In *Democracy and Political Change in the "Third World"*, ed. Jeff Haynes. New York: Routledge.

Rawls, John. 1971. *A Theory of Justice.* Cambridge, MA: Harvard University Press.

Reflexión Democrática. n.d. *La Legislación en Números.* http://www.reflexion democratica.org.pe/pdfs/legisnum.pdf.

Reiter, Dan, and Erik Tillman. 2002. "Public, Legislative, and Executive Constraints on the Democratic Initiation of Conflict." *Journal of Politics* 64 (August): 810–26.

Remington, Thomas F., and Steven S. Smith. 1996. "Political Goals, Institutional Context, and the Choice of an Electoral System: The Russian Parliamentary Election Law." *American Journal of Political Science* 40 (4):1253–79.

Remmer, Karen. 1991. "The Political Impact of Economic Crisis in Latin America in the 1980s." *American Political Science Review* 85 (33): 778–800.

———. 1993. "The Political Economy of Elections in Latin America, 1980–1991." *American Political Science Review* 87 (2): 393–408.

———. 1997. "Theoretical Decay and Theoretical Development: The Resurgence of Institutional Analysis." *World Politics* 50 (1): 34–61.

Rey Rey, Rafael. n.d. "La CVR." Unpublished manuscript.

Reyna, Carlos. 2000. *La anunciación de Fujimori: Alan García 1985–1990.* Lima: DESCO.

Riker, William. 1964. *Federalism: Origins, Operation, Significance.* Boston: Little, Brown.

Roberts, Andrew Lawrence. 2009. *The Quality of Democracy in Eastern Europe: Public Preferences and Policy Reforms.* New York: Cambridge University Press.

Roberts, Kenneth. 1995. "Neoliberalism and the Transformation of Populism in Latin America: The Peruvian Case." *World Politics* 48 (1): 82–116.

———. 1996. "Economic Crisis and the Demise of the Legal Left in Peru." *Comparative Politics* 29 (1): 69–92.

———. 1999. *Deepening Democracy? The Modern Left and Social Movements in Chile and Peru.* Stanford, CA: Stanford University Press.

Roberts, Kenneth, and Moisés Arce. 1998. "Neoliberalism and Lower-Class Voting Behavior in Peru." *Comparative Political Studies* 31 (2): 217–46.

Roberts, Kenneth, and Erik Wibbels. 1999. "Party Systems and Electoral Volatility in Latin America: A Test of Economic, Institutional, and Structural Explanations." *American Political Science Review* 93 (3): 575–90.

Robinson, James. 1970. "Staffing the Legislature." In *Legislatures in Developmental Perspective,* ed. Allan Kornberg and Lloyd D. Musolf. Durham, NC: Duke University Press.

Rojas Samanez, Alvaro. 1987. *Los partidos políticos en el Perú.* 6th ed. Lima: Editorial F & A.

———. 1994. *Los partidos políticos en el Perú: Nuevos retos, otro rol.* Lima: Salgado Editores.

Rospigliosi, Fernando. 2000. *Montesinos y la fuerzas armadas: Cómo controló durante una década las instituciones militares.* Lima: Instituto de Estudios Peruanos.

Rotella, Sebastian. 2000. "A Delay in Vote Count Raises Tensions in Peru." *Los Angeles Times,* April 11. http://articles.latimes.com/2000/apr/11/news/mn-18381 (accessed July 23, 2009).

Rubio Correa, Marcial. 1988. "El FREDEMO y el tercio de Vargas Llosa." *QueHacer* 51(March–April): 7–8.

———. 1997. *Ley de partidos políticos: Las reglas que nadie quiso aprobar.* Lima: Pontificia Universidad Católica del Perú, Fondo Editorial.

Rudolph, James. 1992. *Peru: The Evolution of a Crisis.* Westport, CT: Praeger.

Rueschemeyer, Dietrich, Evelyne Huber Stephens, and John D. Stephens. 1992. *Capitalist Development and Democracy.* Chicago: University of Chicago Press.

Saiegh, Sebastián. 2004. "Win Some, Lose Some: Explaining the Variation in Latin American Chief Executives' Legislative Success Rates." Presented at the Congress of the Latin American Studies Association, Las Vegas, NV, October 7–9.

———. 2005. "The Role of Legislatures in the Policymaking Process." Presented at the IDB Workshop on State Reform, Public Policies and Policy

Making Processes, Inter-American Development Bank, Washington, DC, February 28–March 2.

Sajó, András. 1999. *Limiting Government: An Introduction to Constitutionalism.* New York: Central European University Press.

Samuels, David. 2002a. "Presidentialized Parties: The Separation of Powers and Party Organization and Behavior." *Comparative Political Studies* 35 (4): 461–83.

———. 2002b. "Progressive Ambition, Federalism, and Pork-Barreling in Brazil." In *Legislative Politics in Latin America,* ed. Scott Morgenstern and Benito Nacif. Cambridge, UK: Cambridge University Press.

Samuels, David, and Matthew Shugart. 2003. "Presidentialism, Elections and Representation." *Journal of Theoretical Politics* 15 (1): 33–60.

Sanborn, Cynthia. 1991. "The Democratic Left and the Persistence of Populism in Peru: 1975–1990." Ph.D. diss., Harvard University.

Sanborn, Cynthia, and Aldo Panfichi. 1997. "Fujimori y las raíces del neopopulismo." In *Los enigmas del poder: Fujimori 1990–1996,* ed. Fernando Tuesta Soldevilla. 2nd ed. Lima: Fundación Friedrich Ebert.

Sánchez, Omar. 2009. "Party Non-Systems: A Conceptual Innovation." *Party Politics* 15 (4): 487–520.

Sánchez León, Abelardo, and Martín Paredes Oporto. 2005. Interview with Carlos Iván Degregori. *QueHacer* 156:8–18.

Sartori, Giovanni. 1976. *Parties and Party Systems: A Framework for Analysis.* New York: Cambridge University Press.

———. 1997. *Comparative Constitutional Engineering: An Inquiry into Structures, Incentives, and Outcomes.* 2nd ed. New York: New York University Press.

Schattschneider, Elmer Eric. 1942. *Party Government.* New York: Farrar and Rinehart.

Schedler, Andreas. 1996. "Anti-Political-Establishment Parties." *Party Politics* 2 (3): 291–312.

Schedler, Andreas, Larry Diamond, and Marc F. Plattner. 1999. *The Self-Restraining State: Power and Accountability in New Democracies.* Boulder: Lynne Rienner.

Schlesinger, Joseph. 1966. *Ambition and Politics: Political Careers in the United States.* Chicago: Rand McNally.

———. 1994. *Political Parties and the Winning of Office.* Ann Arbor: University of Michigan Press.

Schmidt, Gregory. 1996. "Fujimori's 1990 Upset Victory in Peru: Electoral Rules, Contingencies, and Adaptive Strategies." *Comparative Politics* 28 (3): 321–55.

———. 1998. "Presidential Usurpation or Congressional Preference? The Evolution of Executive Decree Authority in Peru." In *Executive Decree Authority,* ed. John M. Carey and Matthew Soberg Shugart. New York: Cambridge University Press.

———. 2002. "The Presidential Election in Peru, April 2000." *Electoral Studies* 21 (2): 339–63.

———. 2003. "The Implementation of Gender Quotas in Peru: Legal Reform, Discourses and Impacts." Paper presented at International IDEA workshop, The Implementation of Quotas: Latin American Experiences, Lima, Peru, February 23–24.

———. 2005. "¿'Crimen perfecto'? Personeros, observadores y fraude en el escrutinio de la elección presidencial del año 2000 en el Perú." *Elecciones* 4 (5): 141–71.

Schmitter, Philippe. 2001. "Parties Are Not What They Once Were." In *Political Parties and Democracy,* ed. Larry Diamond and Richard Gunther. Baltimore: Johns Hopkins University Press.

Schor, Miguel. n.d. "The Rule of Law and Democratic Consolidation in Latin America." Unpublished paper. Archived at the Latin American Studies Association Section on Law and Society in Latin America, http://darkwing.uoregon.edu/~caguirre/schorpr.html.

Scott, Robert. 1966. "Political Parties and Policy-Making in Latin America." In *Political Parties and Political Development,* ed. Joseph LaPalombara and Myron Weiner. Princeton, NJ: Princeton University Press.

Seligson, Mitchell, and Julio F. Carrión. 2002. "Political Support, Political Skepticism, and Political Stability in New Democracies." *Comparative Political Studies* 35 (1): 58–82.

Serrano Torres, Jorge. 2006. "La reconstrucción del sistema de inteligencia peruano." *Agencia IPI,* July 17. Archived at http://www.voltairenet.org/article142053.html (accessed Aug. 10, 2009).

Shamir, Michael. 1984. "Are Western Party Systems Frozen?" *Comparative Political Studies* 17 (1): 35–79.

Shepsle, Kenneth. 1978. *The Giant Jigsaw Puzzle: Democratic Committee Assignments in the Modern House.* Chicago: University of Chicago Press.

Shepsle, Kenneth, and Barry Weingast. 1987. "The Institutional Foundations of Committee Power." *American Political Science Review* 81 (1): 85–104.

Shively, W. Phillips. 1972. "Voting Stability and the Nature of Party Attachments in the Weimar Republic." *American Political Science Review* 66:1203–25.

Shugart, Matthew Soberg. 1995. "The Electoral Cycle and Institutional Sources of Divided Presidential Government." *American Political Science Review* 89 (2): 327–43.

———. 1998. "The Inverse Relationship Between Party Strength and Executive Strength: A Theory of Politician's Constitutional Choices." *British Journal of Political Science* 28:1–29.

Shugart, Matthew Soberg, and John Carey. 1992. *Presidents and Assemblies: Constitutional Design and Electoral Dynamics.* New York: Cambridge University Press.

Shugart, Matthew Soberg, and Scott Mainwaring. 1997. "Presidentialism and Democracy in Latin America: Rethinking the Terms of the Debate." In *Presidentialism and Democracy in Latin America,* ed. Scott Mainwaring and Matthew Soberg Shugart. New York: Cambridge University Press.

Siaroff, Alan. 2003. "Comparative Presidencies: The Inadequacy of the Presidential, Semi-Presidential and Parliamentary Distinction." *European Journal of Political Research* 42 (3): 287–312.

Skach, Cindy. 2005. *Borrowing Constitutional Designs: Constitutional Law in Weimar Germany and the French Fifth Republic.* Princeton, NJ: Princeton University Press.

Smulovitz, Catalina, and Enrique Peruzzotti. 2003. "Societal and Horizontal Control: Two Cases of a Fruitful Relationship." In *Democratic Accountability in Latin America,* ed. Scott Mainwaring and Christopher Welna. Oxford: Oxford University Press.

Snyder, James M., and Michael M. Ting. 2002. "An Informational Rationale for Political Parties." *American Journal of Political Science* 46 (1): 90–110.

Solfrini, Giuseppe. 2001. "Populism and Authoritarianism in Peru: An Old Vice in the Neoliberal Era." In *Miraculous Metamorphoses: The Neoliberalization of Latin American Populism,* ed. Jolle Demmers, Alex E. Fernández Jilberto, and Barbara Hogenboom. New York: Zed Books.

Stein, Steve. 1999. "The Paths to Populism in Peru." In *Populism in Latin America,* ed. Michael L. Conniff. Tuscaloosa: University of Alabama Press.

Stepan, Alfred. 1978. *The State and Society: Peru in Comparative Perspective.* Princeton, NJ: Princeton University Press.

———. 2004. "Toward a New Comparative Politics of Federalism, Multinationalism, and Democracy: Beyond Rikerian Federalism." In *Federalism and Democracy in Latin America,* ed. Edward L. Gibson. Baltimore: Johns Hopkins University Press.

Stepan, Alfred, and Cindy Skach. 1993. "Constitutional Frameworks and Democratic Consolidation: Parliamentarianism Versus Presidentialism." *World Politics* 46 (1): 1–22.

———. 1994. "Presidentialism and Parliamentarism in Comparative Perspective." In *The Failure of Presidential Democracy,* ed. Juan J. Linz and Arturo Valenzuela. Baltimore: Johns Hopkins University Press.

Stimson, James A. 1985. "Regression in Time and Space: A Statistical Essay." *American Journal of Political Science* 29 (4): 914–47.

Stokes, Susan. 1995. *Cultures in Conflict: Social Movements and the State in Peru.* Berkeley: University of California Press, 1995.

———. 1996. "Public Opinion and Market Reforms: The Limits of Economic Voting." *Comparative Political Studies* 29 (5): 499–530.

————. 1997. "Are Parties What's Wrong with Democracy in Latin America?" Paper presented at the Twentieth Congress of the Latin American Studies Association, Guadalajara, Mexico.

————. 1999. "What Do Policy Switches Tell Us about Democracy?" In *Democracy, Accountability and Representation,* ed. Adam Przeworski, Susan Stokes, and Bernard Manin. New York: Cambridge University Press.

Strom, Kaare. 1990. *Minority Government and Majority Rule.* New York: Cambridge University Press.

Suárez, Waldino. 1982. "El poder ejecutivo en América Latina: Su capacidad operativa bajo regímenes presidencialistas de gobierno." *Revista de Estudios Políticos* 29:109–44.

Sundquist, James. 1988. "Needed: A Political Theory for a New Era of Coalition Government in the United States." *Political Science Quarterly* 103 (4):613–35.

Tanaka, Martín. 1998. *Los espejismos de la democracia: El colapso del sistema de partidos en el Perú, 1980–1995, en perspectiva comparada.* Lima: Instituto de Estudios Peruanos.

————. 2006. "From Crisis to Collapse of the Party Systems and Dilemmas of Democratic Representation: Peru and Venezuela." In *The Crisis of Democratic Representation in the Andes,* ed. Scott Mainwaring, Ana María Bejarano, and Eduardo Pizarro Leongómez. Stanford, CA: Stanford University Press.

Tavits, Margit. 2008. "Party Systems in the Making: The Emergence and Success of New Parties in New Democracies." *British Journal of Political Science* 38 (1) (January): 113–33.

Taylor, Lewis. 1986. "Peru's Alan García: Supplanting the Old Order." *Third World Quarterly* 8 (1): 100–136.

————. 2005. "From Fujimori to Toledo: The 2001 Elections and the Vicissitudes of Democratic Government in Peru." *Government and Opposition* 40 (4): 565–96.

————. 2007. "Politicians Without Parties and Parties Without Politicians: The Foibles of the Peruvian Political Class, 2000–2006." *Bulletin of Latin American Research* 26 (1): 1–23.

TC (Tribunal Constitucional del Perú). 2004. "Memoria."

Teivainen, Teivo. 2000. *Enter Economy, Exit Politics: Transnational Politics of Economism and Limits to Democracy in Peru.* Helsinki: The Finnish Political Science Association/Helsinki University Printing House.

Thelen, Kathleen, and Sven Steinmo. 1992. "Historical Institutionalism in Comparative Politics." In *Structuring Politics: Historical Institutionalism in Comparative Analysis,* ed. Sven Steinmo, Kathleen Thelen, and Frank Longstreth. New York: Cambridge University Press.

Thurner, Mark. 1997. *From Two Republics to One Divided: Contradictions of Postcolonial Nationmaking in Andean Peru.* Durham, NC: Duke University Press.

Tomz, Michael, Jason Wittenberg, and Gary King. 2001. Clarify: Software for Interpreting and Presenting Statistical Results. Cambridge, MA: Harvard University. Archived at http://gking.harvard.edu/clarify.

Transparency International (TI). n.d. "Corruption Perceptions Index." Archived at http://www.transparency.org/policy_research/surveys_indices/cpi.

Tsebelis, George. 1995. "Decision Making in Political Systems: Veto Players in Presidentialism, Parliamentarism, Multicameralism, and Multipartyism." *British Journal of Political Science* 25 (3): 289–326.

———. 2002. *Veto Players: How Political Institutions Work.* Princeton, NJ: Princeton University Press.

Tsebelis, George, and Eduardo Alemán. 2005. "Presidential Conditional Agenda Setting in Latin America." *World Politics* 57 (3): 396–420.

Tsebelis, George, and Jeannette Money. 1997. *Bicameralism.* New York: Cambridge University Press.

Tucker, Richard. 1999. BTSCS: A Binary Time-Series Cross-Section Data Analysis Utility. Version 4.0.4. Cambridge, MA: Harvard University. Archived at http://www.fas.harvard.edu/~rtucker/programs/btscs/btscs.html.

Tuesta Soldevilla, Fernando. 1987. "Presidencia, secretarias generales y otros cargos: Una propuesta." *La República,* May 7.

———. 1994. *Perú político en cifras.* 2nd ed. Lima: Fundación Friedrich Ebert.

———. 1997. "El impacto del sistema electoral sobre el sistema político peruano." In *Los enigmas del poder: Fujimori 1990–1996,* ed. Fernando Tuesta Soldevilla. 2nd ed. Lima: Fundación Friedrich Ebert.

———. 2001. *Perú político en cifras.* 3rd ed. Lima: Fundación Friedrich Ebert.

———. 2002. *La Circunscripción Electoral: Perú y la Región Andina.* Lima: ONPE.

———. 2007. "Elecciones Municipales," http://blog.pucp.edu.pe/fernando tuesta/node/603?q=node/478 (November 27).

———. 2008. "Ministros—Gabinetes," http://blog.pucp.edu.pe/fernando tuesta/node/603?q=node/632 (November 25).

———. n.d. "Elecciones Presidenciales," http://blog.pucp.edu.pe/fernando tuesta/node/603?q=node/488.

———. n.d. "Resumen Gabinetes por Gobierno," http://blog.pucp.edu.pe/ fernandotuesta/files/Resumen%20Gabinetes%20por%20Gobierno.pdf.

United Nations Economic Commission for Africa (UNECA). 2002. *Harnessing Sustainable Technologies for Development.* Addis Ababa, Ethiopia: UNECA.

Universidad de Salamanca. n.d. Encuesta a Diputados Peruanos: Series de Indicadores. Instituto de Estudios de Iberoamérica y Portugal, Equipo de Investigación sobre Élites Parlamentarias.

USAID (U.S. Agency for International Development). 2000. *USAID Handbook on Legislative Strengthening.* USAID Center for Democracy and Governance, Technical Publication Series (February).

Van Biezen, Ingrid. 2000. "On the Internal Balance of Party Power: Party Organizations in New Democracies." *Party Politics* 6 (4): 395–417.

Vargas Gutiérrez, José Luis. 2002. "¡Erupcionó Arequipa!" *QueHacer* 136:72–77.

Vargas León, Carlos. n.d. "Liderazgos en transición: Trayectorias de liderazgo político en el Perú." Instituto de Estudios Peruano. Unpublished manuscript.

Vargas Llosa, Mario. 1994. *A Fish in the Water: A Memoir.* Trans. Helen Lane. New York: Farrar, Straus, Giroux.

Vega Centeno, Imelda. 1986. *Aprismo popular: Mito, cultura, e historia.* Lima: Tarea.

Velarde, Julio. 1994. "Macroeconomic Stability and the Prospects for Growth, 1990–93." In *Peru in Crisis: Dictatorship or Democracy?* ed. Joseph S. Tulchin and Gary Bland. Boulder: Lynne Rienner/The Woodrow Wilson International Center for Scholars.

Véliz, Claudio. 1980. *The Centralist Tradition in Latin America.* Princeton, NJ: Princeton University Press.

Waisbord, Silvio. 2002. "Media Populism: Neopopulism in Latin America." In *Supporting and Undermining Populism: The Media and Neo-Populist Movements,* ed. Gianpietro Mazzoleni, Bruce Horsfield, and Julianne Stewart. Westport, CT: Praeger.

Wallack, Jessica Seddon, Alejandro Gaviria, Ugo Panizza, and Ernesto Stein. 2003. "Particularism Around the World." *World Bank Economic Review* 17 (1): 133–43.

Wattenberg, Martin. 1990. *The Decline of American Political Parties, 1952–1984.* Cambridge, MA: Harvard University Press.

Webb, Paul, and Stephen White, eds. 2007. *Party Politics in New Democracies.* Oxford: Oxford University Press.

Webb, Richard, and Graciela Fernandez Baca. 1994. *Perú en Números: Anuario Estadístico.* Lima: Instituto Cuánto.

———. 1999. *Perú en Números: Anuario Estadístico.* Lima: Instituto Cuánto.

Weber, Max. 1947. *The Theory of Social and Economic Organization.* Ed. Talcott Parsons. New York: Free Press.

Weingast, Barry. 1997. "The Political Foundations of Democracy and the Rule of Law." *American Political Science Review* 91 (2): 245–63.

Weingast, Barry, and William Marshall. 1988. "The Industrial Organization of Congress." *Journal of Political Economy* 96 (1): 132–63.

Welch, David A. 2005. *Painful Choices: A Theory of Foreign Policy Change.* Princeton, NJ: Princeton University Press.

Weldon, Jeffrey. 1997. "Political Sources of *Presidencialismo* in Mexico." In *Presidentialism and Democracy in Latin America,* ed. Scott Mainwaring and Matthew Soberg Shugart. New York: Cambridge University Press.

Werlich, David P. 1978. *Peru: A Short History.* Carbondale: Southern Illinois University Press.

Weyland, Kurt. 1996a. "Neoliberalism and Neopopulism in Latin America: Unexpected Affinities." *Studies in Comparative International Development* 31 (3): 3–31.

———. 1996b. "Risk Taking in Latin American Economic Restructuring." *International Studies Quarterly* 40 (2): 185–207.

———. 1998. "A Paradox of Success? Determinants of Political Support for President Fujimori." Presented at the Fifty-Sixth Annual Meeting of the Midwest Political Science Association, Chicago.

———. 2002. "Limitations of Rational-Choice Institutionalism for the Study of Latin American Politics." *Studies in Comparative International Development* 37 (1): 57–85.

Wheare, K. C. 1963. *Legislatures.* New York: Oxford University Press.

Wise, Carol. 1994. "Commentary." In *Peru in Crisis: Dictatorship or Democracy?* ed. Joseph S. Tulchin and Gary Bland. Boulder: Lynne Rienner/The Woodrow Wilson International Center for Scholars.

———. 2003. *Reinventing the State: Economic Strategy and Institutional Change in Peru.* Ann Arbor: University of Michigan Press.

World Bank Group. World Development Indicators. WDI Online, http://www.worldbank.org/data/onlinedatabases/onlinedatabases.html.

Wormuth, Francis D. 1949. *The Origins of Modern Constitutionalism.* New York: Harper.

Zakaria, Fareed. 1997. "The Rise of Illiberal Democracy." *Foreign Affairs* 76 (6): 22–43.

Interviews Conducted by the Author

All interviews were conducted in person unless otherwise indicated.

Members of Congress/Congressional Candidates

Partido Aprista Peruano (PAP, or APRA)

Alarcón Bravo, Absalón. 1999. Lima, Peru, March 22.
Aldave Pajares, Augusto. 1999. Trujillo, Peru, Sept. 14.
Alvarado Contreras, Luis. 1999. Lima, Peru, March 11.
Avendaño García, Nestor. 1999. Cusco, Peru, July 9.
Bendezú Carpio, Wilbert. 1999. Lima, Peru, Sept. 4.
Del Castillo Gálvez, Jorge. 1999. Lima, Peru, April 27.
Franco Ballester, Alberto. 1999. Lima, Peru, March 8.
Jara Ladrón, Julio. 1999. Cusco, Peru, July 12.
Negreiros Criado, Luis. 1999. Lima, Peru, Sept. 11.
Pilco Deza, Luis Fernando. 1999. Telephone, Trujillo, Peru, Sept. 19.
Santa María Calderón, Luis. 1999. Trujillo, Peru, Sept. 15.
———. 2005. Lima, Peru, Dec. 14.
Santa María Silva, Alejandro. 1999. Lima, Peru, Aug. 26.
Santander Estrada, Carlos. 1999. Lima, Peru, July 22.
Valle Riestra, Javier. 1999. Lima, Peru, May 6.
Zumaeta Flores, César. 1999. Lima, Peru, March 18.
———. 2007. Miami, FL, Oct 5.

Cambio-90/Nueva Mayoría

Arroyo, Victor. 1999. Lima, Peru, March 4.
Baffigo, José. 1999. Lima, Peru, March 13.
Ferrero Costa, Carlos. 1999. Lima, Peru, Aug. 9.

309

Hildebrandt, Martha. 2007. Lima, Peru, Oct. 16.
Ibañez, Gaston. 1999. Lima, Peru, March 6.
Marcenaro Frers, Ricardo. 1999. Lima, Peru, Aug. 12.
Paredes, Victor. 1999. Lima, Peru, March 9.
Torres y Torres Lara, Carlos. 1998. Lima, Peru, Dec. 29.
Trelles, Jorge. 1999. Lima, Peru, Feb. 3.
Vivanco Amorín, Luis Efraín. 1999. Lima, Peru, Feb. 19.
Zegarra Gutiérrez, Vladimiro. 1999. Cusco, Peru, July 13.

Left-Wing and Center-Left Parties: Izquierda Unida and Izquierda Socialista Coalitions, Unión por el Perú (UPP)

Ames Cobián, Rolando. 1999. Lima, Peru, March 17.
Bartra Germany, Jorge. 1999. Trujillo, Peru, Sept. 13.
Bernales Ballestros, Enrique. 1999. Lima, Peru, April 19.
Breña Pantoja, Rolando. 1999. Lima, Peru, May 18.
Castro Gómez, Julio. 1999. Lima, Peru, July 30.
Cerro Moral, María Ofelia. 1999. Lima, Peru, July 23.
Dammert Egoaguirre, Manuel. 1999. Lima, Peru, March 11, April 15.
Del Prado Chávez, Jorge. 1999. Lima, Peru, May 14.
Dolmos Vengoa, Bernardo. 1999. Cusco, Peru, July 13.
Estrada Choque, Aldo. 1999. Lima, Peru, Aug. 3.
Garrido Lecca, Hernán. 2005. Lima, Peru, Dec. 16.
Guerra García, Francisco. 1999. Lima, Peru, Feb. 19.
Haya de la Torre, Agustín. 1999. Lima, Peru, April 30.
Letts Colmenares, Ricardo. 1999. Lima, Peru, May 3, 5.
Mohme Llona, Gustavo. 1999. Lima, Peru, May 7.
Muña Márquez, Victorino. 1999. Cusco, Peru, July 10.
Murrugarra Florián, Edmundo. 1999. Lima, Peru, March 23.
Navarrete Zavaleta, Manuel. 1999. Trujillo, Peru, Sept. 15.
Pease García, Henry. 1999. Lima, Peru, May 19.
Villanueva Sánchez, Francisco. 1999. Trujillo, Peru, Sept. 13.

Center-Right and Right-Wing Parties: Acción Popular, Libertad, Partido Popular Cristiano, Frente Democrático Coalition, Frente Independiente Moralizador, Renovación, Solidaridad Nacional, Unidad Nacional

Acurio Velarde, Gastón. 1999. Lima, Peru, Feb. 16.
Alva Orlandini, Javier. 1999. Lima, Peru, April 13.
————. 2005. Lima, Peru, Dec. 13.
Alvarado Dodero, Fausto. 2007. Lima, Peru, Oct. 19.
Cateriano Bellido, Pedro. 1999. Lima, Peru, March 22.
Chirinos Soto, Enrique. 1999. Lima, Peru, April 21.

Cruchaga Belaúnde, Miguel. 1999. Lima, Peru, Feb. 16.
Del Águila Morote, Edmundo. 1999. Lima, Peru, April 27.
Falvy Valdivieso, Dennis. 1999. Lima, Peru, May 5.
Flores-Aráoz, Ántero. 2005. Lima, Peru, Dec. 13.
Flores Nano, Lourdes. 1999. Lima, Peru, April 28.
Gonzales Muñiz, Edwin. 1999. Cusco, Peru, July 12.
Grau Umlauff, Fernando. 1999. Lima, Peru, Feb. 22.
Guzmán Romaña, Juan. 1999. Cusco, Peru, July 10.
La Riva Vegazzo, Iván. 1999. Trujillo, Peru, Sept. 13.
Mariátegui Chiappe, Sandro. 1999. Lima, Peru, March 24.
Mendoza Habersperger, Elías. 1999. Lima, Peru, March 18.
Merino Lucero, Beatriz. 1998. Lima, Peru, Dec. 17.
Paniagua Corazao, Valentín. 1999. Lima, Peru, April 13.
Rey Rey, Rafael. 2007. Lima, Peru, Oct. 18.
Risco Boada, Rafael. 1999. Trujillo, Peru, Sept. 17.
Sotomarino Chávez, Celso. 1999. Lima, Peru, March 9.
Velarde Aspíllaga, Javier. 1999. Lima, Peru, March 9.
Zamalloa Loayza, Rodolfo. 1999. Cusco, Peru, July 13.

Perú Posible/País Posible

Ferrero Costa, Carlos. 2007. Lima, Peru, Oct. 17.
Pease García, Henry. 2007. Lima, Peru, Oct. 16.
Sánchez Pinedo, Doris. 2007. Lima, Peru, Oct. 15.
Solari de la Fuente, Luis. 2007. Lima, Peru, Oct. 16.
Taco Llave, José. 2007. Lima, Peru, Oct. 16.
Waisman Rjavinsthi, David. 2007. Lima, Peru, Oct. 16.

Other Parties: Frente Nacional de Campesinos y Trabajadores, Convergencia Democrática, Frente Popular Agrícola-FIA del Perú

Cáceres Velásquez, Roger. 1999. Lima, Peru, March 22.
Guevara Cáceres, Benicio. 1999. Cusco, Peru, July 11.
Noriega Febres, Javier. 1999. Lima, Peru, March 18.
Vargas Marín, Dennis. 1999. Lima, Peru, May 9.

Other Political Party Leaders/Public Officials

Amiel Meza, Ricardo. 1999. Lima, Peru, Feb. 19 (PPC leader).
Angulo, Ricardo. 1999. Lima, Peru, Aug. 23 (Lima Municipal Council, 1989–1993).

Belaúnde Terry, Fernando. 1999. Lima, Peru, April 16 (AP party; president of Peru, 1963–1968, 1980–1985).
Cubas Cava, Juan de Dios. 1999. Trujillo, Peru, Sept. 16 (APRA party; president of La Libertad–San Martin region, 1990–1992).
Murgía, José. 1999. Trujillo, Peru, Sept. 16 (APRA party; mayor of Trujillo, 1998–2002).
Ocampo Vargas, Adolfo. 1999. Lima, Peru, Feb. 19 (district mayor of San Juan de Miraflores, Lima; with IU in 1984–1989 and with C-90/NM/VV in 1995–2002).
Otero, Hugo. 1999. Lima, Peru, Aug. 13 (APRA publicist and adviser to Alan García).
Pércovich Roca, Luis. 1999. Lima, Peru, April 14 (AP party; former deputy for Ancash, 1963–1968, 1980–1985; during 1980–1985 period also served at times as prime minister, minister of fisheries, minister of interior, and minister of foreign relations).
Ruíz, Wilder. 1999. Lima, Peru, April 23 (Libertad organizer, 1987–1990; adviser to Congressman Rafael Rey, 1995–2000).
Vílchez Cruza, Simon. 1999. Trujillo, Peru, Sept. 14 (APRA party, Confederación de Trabajadores Peruanos union leader).

Academic Experts/Political Consultants and Analysts

Cameron, Maxwell. 1998. Lima, Peru, Dec. 28 (professor of political science, University of British Colombia).
Churats, Juan V. 1999. Cusco, Peru, July 13 (researcher, Centro Bartolomé de las Casa; consultant to Cusco peasant federations).
Conaghan, Catherine. 1999. Lima, Peru, July 26 (professor of political science, Queen's University).
Degregori, Carlos Iván. 1999. Lima, Peru, Sept. 10 (senior fellow, Instituto de Estudios Peruanos).
De Valdivia Cano, Ramiro. 1999. Lima, Peru, Jan. 18 (magistrate, National Elections Tribunal, 1995–2001).
Grompone, Romeo. 1999. Lima, Peru, Aug. 10 (senior fellow, Instituto de Estudios Peruanos).
Huaroc, Vladimiro. 1999. Lima, Peru, Sept. 1 (*defensoría del pueblo,* Assistant Defender for Electoral Affairs).
Lynch, Nicolas. 1999. Lima, Peru, May 17 (professor of political science, Universidad Nacional San Marcos).
Medina, Percy. 2005. Lima, Peru, Dec. 15 (secretary general, Transparencia).
Monge, Carlos. 1999. Lima, Peru, Aug. 31 (senior fellow, DESCO).
Panfichi, Aldo. 1999. Lima, Peru, Aug. 14 (director of the Faculty of Social Sciences, Pontificia Universidad Católica del Perú).

Planas Silva, Pedro. 1999. Lima, Peru, Jan. 8 (political journalist; constitutional scholar, Universidad de Lima).

Power Manchego, Jorge. 2000. Lima, Peru, Feb. (lawyer and constitutional scholar).

Sanborn, Cynthia. 1998. Lima, Peru, Dec. 16 (professor of political science, Universidad del Pacífico).

Tanaka, Martín. 1999a. Lima, Peru, Feb. 4 (fellow, Instituto de Estudios Peruanos).

———. 1999b. Lima, Peru, Sept. 27.

———. 2005. Lima, Peru, Dec. 16.

Trujillano, Jesus. 1999. Lima, Peru, Jan. 19 (secretary, Jurado Nacional de Elecciones).

Tuesta Soldevilla, Fernando. 1998. Lima, Peru, Nov. 31 (professor of political science, Universidad de Lima; former head of ONPE electoral authority).

———. 1999. Lima, Peru, June 3.

———. 2007. Lima, Peru, Oct. 19.

Index

All locations and institutions are in Peru unless otherwise indicated. Page references followed by t *indicate tables and those in italics indicate figures.*

314

Barry S. Levitt

is assistant professor of politics and international relations
at Florida International University.

www.ingramcontent.com/pod-product-compliance
Lightning Source LLC
Chambersburg PA
CBHW071833270326
41929CB00013B/1977